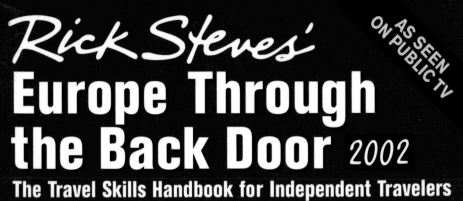

Rick Steves'
Europe Through
the Back Door 2002

The Travel Skills Handbook for Independent Travelers

Rick Steves'
EUROPE THROUGH THE BACK DOOR
2002

AVALON
TRAVEL

Other ATP travel guidebooks by Rick Steves
Rick Steves' Best of Europe
Rick Steves' Europe 101: History and Art for the Traveler (with Gene Openshaw)
Rick Steves' Mona Winks: Self-Guided Tours of Europe's Top Museums
    (with Gene Openshaw)
Rick Steves' Postcards from Europe
Rick Steves' France, Belgium & the Netherlands (with Steve Smith)
Rick Steves' Germany, Austria & Switzerland
Rick Steves' Great Britain
Rick Steves' Ireland (with Pat O'Connor)
Rick Steves' Italy
Rick Steves' Scandinavia
Rick Steves' Spain & Portugal
Rick Steves' Florence (with Gene Openshaw)
Rick Steves' London (with Gene Openshaw)
Rick Steves' Paris (with Steve Smith and Gene Openshaw)
Rick Steves' Rome (with Gene Openshaw)
Rick Steves' Venice (with Gene Openshaw)
Rick Steves' Phrase Books: German, Italian, French, Spanish/Portuguese, and
    French/Italian/German

Avalon Travel Publishing, 5855 Beaudry Street, Emeryville, CA 94608

Text copyright © 2002, 2001, 2000, 1999, 1998, 1997, 1996, 1995, 1994, 1993, 1992,
    1990, 1988, 1987, 1986, 1985, 1984, 1982, 1981, 1980 by Rick Steves
Cover copyright © 2002, 2001, by Avalon Travel Publishing, Inc. All rights reserved.
Maps copyright © 2001 Europe Through the Back Door

Printed in the United States of America by R. R. Donnelley.
Twentieth edition. First printing October 2001.

For the latest on Rick's lectures, guidebooks, tours, and public television series, contact
Europe Through the Back Door, Box 2009, Edmonds, WA 98020, tel. 425/771-8303,
fax 425/771-0833, www.ricksteves.com, or e-mail: rick@ricksteves.com.

ISSN 1096-794X
ISBN 1-56691-353-5

Europe Through the Back Door Editors: Risa Laib, Jacquie Maupin
Avalon Travel Publishing Editor: Kate Willis
Research Assistance: Jacquie Maupin
Copy Editor: Donna Leverenz
Production & Typesetting: Kathleen Sparkes, White Hart Design, Albuquerque, NM
Interior Design: Kathleen Sparkes
Cover Design: Janine Lehmann
Maps: David C. Hoerlein
Cover Photo: Rothenburg, Germany; Leo de Wys Inc./Steve Vidler
Photography: Rick Steves (unless otherwise credited)

Distributed to the book trade by Publishers Group West, Berkeley, California

To the People of Europe

Rich Sorensen

Acknowledgments

Danke to Risa Laib for her travel savvy and editing. *Dank u wel* to Gene Openshaw, Dave Hoerlein, Steve Smith, Rich Sorensen, and Brian Carr Smith for research assistance. And *grazie* to the following for help in their fields of travel expertise: Dave Hoerlein (artful maps); Matthew Brumley (tours); Kevin Christian (travel insurance); Elizabeth Holmes and Dale Torgrimson (travel agents, travel insurance, flights); Craig Stoltz and Michael Shapiro (booking flights online); Katherine Widing and Wide World Books (guidebooks, biking); Book Passage; Laura Terrenzio and the staff at RailEurope (train travel); Dave Fox (flights within Europe); Richard Walters (biking); Brooke Burdick (cyberskills); Ruth "where are you" Kasarda, Gail Morse, and Pam Negri (women traveling); Alan Spira, M.D., and Craig Karpilow, M.D. (health for travelers); Arlan Blodgett (photography); Anthony Blikre (digital cameras); Brad McEwen (bus tours); Anne Steves (travel with kids); and Brian Carr Smith (traveling as a student). *Merci* for support from my entire well-traveled staff at ETBD and in particular to Anne Kirchner for keeping things in order while I'm both in and out. *Spasiba* also to Pat Larson, Sandie Nisbet, and John Givens at Small World Productions for introducing so many travelers to this book through our public television series, *Travels in Europe with Rick Steves*. Finally, *tusen takk* to my parents for dragging me to Europe when I didn't want to go and to my wife, Anne, for making home my favorite place to travel.

Contents

Preface

The average American traveler enters Europe through the front door. This Europe greets you with cash registers cocked, $5 cups of coffee, and service with a purchased smile.

To give your trip an extra, more real dimension, come with me through the back door. Through the back door a warm, relaxed, personable Europe welcomes us as friends. We're part of the party—not part of the economy.

Traveling this way, we become temporary Europeans, part of the family—approaching Europe on its level, accepting and enjoying its unique ways of life. We'll demand nothing, except that no fuss be made over us.

This "Back Door–style" travel is better because of—not in spite of— your budget. Spending money has little to do with enjoying your trip. In fact, spending less money brings you closer to Europe. A lot of money forces you through Europe's grand front entrance, where people in uniforms greet you with formal smiles. But the back door is what keeps me in my wonderful European rut.

Since 1973 I've spent a hundred days a year exploring Europe. For the first five trips I traveled purely for kicks. Then it became clear: Each trip was going smoother ... I must be learning from my mistakes. And I saw people making the same mistakes I had made: mistakes costly in time, money, and experience. It occurred to me that if I could package the lessons I've learned into a class or book, others could learn from my mistakes rather than their own. I could help others enjoy a better, smoother trip. (And I'd have a good excuse to go back to Europe every summer to update my material.) Since 1978 I've been doing just that—traveling with my teaching in mind, making mistakes, taking careful notes, losing my traveler's checks just to see what will happen, ordering a margarita and getting pizza. This book, which has evolved over 20 editions, is my report to you.

My readers (many of whose grandkids warned, "You shouldn't be doing this") are having great trips and coming home with money in the bank for next summer. I'm careful not to send people to Europe with too much confidence and not enough money, reservations, or skills. If I did, trips would suffer, and I'd hear about it. But judging from the happy *gelato*-stained postcards my road scholars send me, it's clear that those who equip themselves with good information and expect themselves to travel smart, do.

The first half of this book covers the skills of Back Door European travel—packing, planning an itinerary, finding good hotels, getting around, and so on. The second half gives you keys to my favorite discoveries, places I call "Back Doors," where you can dirty your fingers in pure Europe—feeling its fjords and caressing its castles. So raise your travel dreams to their upright and locked positions and let this book fly you away. Happy travels!

Rick Steves' Back Door Travel Philosophy

Travel is intensified living—maximum thrills per minute and one of the last great sources of legal adventure. Travel is freedom. It's recess, and we need it.

Experiencing the real Europe requires catching it by surprise; going casual... "Through the Back Door."

Affording travel is a matter of priorities. (Make do with the old car.) You can travel—simply, safely, and comfortably—anywhere in Europe for $80 a day plus transportation costs. In many ways, spending more money only builds a thicker wall between you and what you came to see. Europe is a cultural carnival, and, time after time, you'll find that its best acts are free and the best seats are the cheap ones.

A tight budget forces you to travel close to the ground, meeting and communicating with the people. Never sacrifice sleep, nutrition, safety, or cleanliness in the name of budget. Simply enjoy the local-style alternatives to expensive hotels and restaurants.

Extroverts have more fun. If your trip is low on magic moments, kick yourself and make things happen. If you don't enjoy a place, maybe you don't know enough about it. Seek the truth. Recognize tourist traps. Give a culture the benefit of your open mind. See things as different, but not better or worse. Any culture has much to share.

Of course, travel, like the world, is a series of hills and valleys. Be fanatically positive and militantly optimistic. If something's not to your liking, change your liking.

Travel is addicting. It can make you a happier American, as well as a citizen of the world. Our Earth is home to 6 billion equally important people. It's humbling to travel and find that people don't envy Americans. Europeans like us, but, with all due respect, they wouldn't trade passports.

Globe-trotting destroys ethnocentricity. It helps you understand and appreciate different cultures. Travel changes people. It broadens perspectives and teaches new ways to measure quality of life. Many travelers toss aside their hometown blinders. Their prized souvenirs are the strands of different cultures they decide to knit into their own character. The world is a cultural yarn shop, and Back Door Travelers are weaving the ultimate tapestry. Join in!

PART ONE
Travel Skills

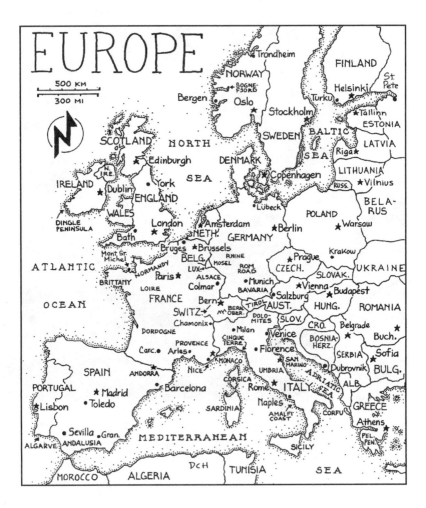

GETTING STARTED

1. Take a Tour or Be Your Own Guide?

A European adventure is a major investment of time and money. A well-planned trip is more fun, less expensive, and not necessarily more structured. Planning means understanding your alternatives and choosing what best fits your travel dreams. From the start, you need to decide if you're taking a tour or going on your own.

Do you want the security of knowing that all your rooms are reserved and that a guide will take you smoothly from one hotel to the next? Do you require comfortable American-style hotels? Will you forgo adventure, independence, and the challenge of doing it on your own in order to take the worry and bother out of traveling? If you don't mind sitting on a bus with the same group of tourists and observing rather than experiencing, a tour may be just the right way for you to scratch your travel bug bites. There's a tour for just about every travel dream. Your travel agent can help you.

For many people with limited time and money, tours are the most efficient way to see Europe. Without a tour, restaurant meals and big, modern hotel rooms can be very expensive. Large tour companies book thou-

Eight and forty tourists baked in a bus

sands of rooms and meals year-round and can, with their tremendous economic clout, get prices that no individual tourist can match. For instance, on a tour with Cosmos (one of the largest and cheapest tour companies in Europe), you'll get fine rooms (with private baths), some restaurant meals, bus transportation, and the services of a European guide—all for under $100 a day. Considering that many of the hotel rooms alone cost $100, that all-inclusive tour price is great.

Efficient and "economical" as tours may be, the tour groups that unload on Europe's quaintest towns experience things differently. They are treated as an entity: a mob to be fed, shown around, profited from, and moved out. If money is saved, it's at the cost of real experience. For

Not all tours are as exciting as their brochures make them sound.

me, the best travel values in Europe are enjoyed not gazing through the tinted windows of a tour bus but by traveling independently.

This book focuses on the skills necessary for do-it-yourself European travel. If you're destined for a tour, read on anyway (especially Chapter 27: Bus Tour Self-Defense). Even on a bus with 50 other tourists, you can and should be in control, equipped with a guidebook, and thinking as an independent traveler. Your trip is too important for you to blindly trust an overworked, underpaid tour guide.

BEING YOUR OWN GUIDE

As this book has evolved with my experience as a tour guide, I find myself simply encouraging readers to travel with the same thoughtfulness and foresight. As a tour guide, I call ahead to reconfirm reservations, ask at hotel check-in if there's any folk entertainment tonight, and call restaurants to confirm that they're open before I cross town. A good guide reads ahead. Equip yourself with good information, use local entertainment periodicals, and talk to other travelers. Ask questions or miss the festival.

Putting together a dream trip requires skills. Consider this book a do-it-yourself manual.

TRAVELING ALONE

One of your first big decisions is whether to travel alone or with a friend. Consider the pros and cons of solo travel.

You have complete freedom and independence. You never have to wait for your partner to pack up; you never need to consider a partner's wishes when you decide what to see, where to go, how far to travel, how much to spend, or even when the day has been long enough. You go where you want when you want, and you can get the heck out of that stuffy museum when all the Monets start to blur together.

You meet more people when you travel alone because you're more approachable in the eyes of a European, and loneliness will drive you to reach out and make friends. When you travel with someone, it's easy to focus on your partner and forget about meeting Europeans.

Solo travel is intensely personal. Without the comfortable crutch of a friend, you're more likely to know the joys of self-discovery and the pleasures found in the kindness of strangers. You'll be exploring yourself as well as a new city or country.

But loneliness can turn hotel rooms into lifeless cells. And meals for one are often served in a puddle of silence. Big cities can be cold and ugly when the only person to talk to is yourself. Being sick and alone in a country where no one knows you is, even in retrospect, a miserable experience.

Combating loneliness in Europe is easy. The continent is full of lonely travelers and natural meeting places. You're likely to find vaga-buddies in hostels, in museums (offer to share your *Mona Winks* chapter), on one-day bus tours, and on trains. Eurailers buddy up on the trains. If you're carrying a Cook Train Timetable, leave it lying around, and you'll become the most popular kid on the train. Travel as a student, whatever your age: Students have more fun, make more friends, and spend less money than most travelers. Board the train with a little too much of a picnic—and share it with others. Be bold; if you're lonely, others are, too.

TRAVELING WITH A PARTNER

Having a buddy overcomes the disadvantages of solo travel. Shared experiences are more fun, and for the rest of your life there will be a special bond between you and your partner. The confident, uninhibited extrovert is better at making things happen and is more likely to run into exciting and memorable events. When I travel with a partner, it's easier for me to be that kind of "wild-and-crazy guy."

Traveling with a partner is cheaper. Rarely does a double room cost as much as two singles. If a single room costs $50, a double room will generally be around $60, a savings of $20 per night per person. Virtually everything is cheaper and easier when you share costs: picnicking, guidebooks, banking, maps, magazines, taxis, storage lockers, and much more. Besides expenses, partners can share the burden of time-consuming hassles, such as standing in lines at train stations and post offices.

Traveling without a tour, you'll have the locals dancing with you—not for you.

You can get real close to traditional Europe—sometimes too close.

Remember, traveling together greatly accelerates a relationship—especially a romantic one. You see each other constantly and make endless decisions. The niceties go out the window. Everything becomes very real; you're in an adventure, a struggle, a hot-air balloon for two. The experiences of years are jammed into one summer.

Try a trial weekend together before merging dream trips. A mutual travel experience is a good test of a relationship—often revealing its ultimate course. I'd highly recommend a little premarital travel.

Your choice of a travel partner is critical. It can make or break a trip. Traveling with the wrong partner can be like a two-month computer date. I'd rather do it alone. Analyze your travel styles and goals for compatibility. One summer I went to Europe to dive into as many cultures and adventures as possible. I planned to rest when I got home. My partner wanted to slow life down, to get away from it all, relax, and escape the pressures of the business world. Our ideas of acceptable hotels and the purpose of eating were quite different. The trip was a near disaster.

Many people already have their partner—for better or for worse. In the case of married couples, minimize the stress of traveling together by recognizing each other's needs for independence. Too many people do Europe as a three-legged race, tied together from start to finish. Have an explicit understanding that there's absolutely nothing selfish, dangerous, insulting, or wrong about splitting up occasionally. This is a freedom too few travel partners allow themselves. Doing your own thing for a few hours or days breathes fresh air into your togetherness.

TRAVELING WITH THREE OR MORE COMPANIONS

Traveling in a threesome or foursome is usually troublesome. With all the exciting choices Europe has to offer, it's often hard for even a twosome to reach a consensus. Unless there's a clear group leader, the "split and be independent" strategy is particularly valuable.

To minimize travel partnership stress, go communal with your money. Separate checks and long lists of petty IOUs are a pain. Pool your resources, noting how much each person contributes, and just assume everything equals out in the long run. Keep track of major individual expenses but don't worry who got an extra postcard or cappuccino. Enjoy treating each other to taxis and dinner out of your "kitty," and after the trip, divvy up the remains. If one person consumed $25 or $30 more, that's a small price to pay for the convenience and economy of communal money.

IF YOU'VE READ THIS FAR . . .

. . . you've got what it takes intellectually to handle Europe on your own. If you're inclined to figure things out, you'll find Europe well-organized and explained, usually in English. But some people are not inclined to figure things out. They figure things out to earn a living 50 weeks a year, and that's not their idea of a good vacation. These people should travel with a tour . . . or a spouse. But if you enjoy the challenge of tackling a great new continent, you can do it.

2. Gathering Information

Those who enjoy the planning stage as part of the experience invest wisely and enjoy tremendous returns. Study ahead. This kind of homework is fun. Take advantage of the wealth of material available: guidebooks, classes, videos, libraries, the Internet, and tourist information offices.

GUIDEBOOKS

Guidebooks are $20 tools for $3,000 experiences. Many otherwise smart people base the trip of a lifetime on a borrowed copy of a three-year-old guidebook. The money they saved in the bookstore was wasted the first day of their trip, searching for hotels and restaurants long since closed. As a writer of guidebooks, I am a big fan of their worth. When I visit someplace as a rank beginner—a place like Belize or Sri Lanka—I equip myself with a good guidebook and expect myself to travel smart. I travel like an old pro, not because I'm a super traveler, but because I have good information and I use it. I'm a connoisseur of guidebooks. My trip is my child. I love her. And I give her the best tutors money can buy.

Too many people are penny-wise and pound-foolish when it comes to information. I see them every year, stranded on street corners in Paris— hemorrhaging money. It's flipping off of them in 100-euro notes. Con artists smell a helpless victim and close in. These vacations are disasters. Tourists with no information run out of money, fly home early, and hate the French.

With a good guidebook, you can come into Paris for your first time, go anywhere in town for a dollar on the subway, enjoy a memorable bistro lunch
for $10, and pay just $60 for a double room in a friendly hotel (with a singing
maid) on a pedestrian-only street a few blocks from the Eiffel Tower. All
you need is a good guidebook covering your destination.

Before buying a book, study it. How old is the information? The
cheapest books are often the oldest—no bargain. Who wrote it? What's
the author's experience? Does the book work for you—or the tourist industry? Does it specialize in hard opinions—or superlatives? For whom is it
written? Is it readable? It should have personality without chattiness and
information without fluff.

Don't believe everything you read. The power of the printed word is
scary. Most books are peppered with information that is flat-out wrong.
Incredibly enough, even this book may have an error. Many "writers" succumb to the temptation to write guidebooks based on hearsay, travel
brochures, other books, and wishful thinking. A writer met at the airport
by an official from the national tourist board learns tips handy only for
others met at the airport by an official from the national tourist board.

Bookstores that specialize in travel books have knowledgeable salespeople and the best selection. Visit the Independent Travel Stores Association at www.travelstores.org/ to find the store nearest you. If you have
a focus, there's a book written just for you. There are books written for
those traveling with toddlers, pets, grandparents, and wine snobs. There
are books for vegetarians, galloping gluttons, hedonists, cranky teens, nud-
ists, pilgrims, gays, bird-watchers, music lovers, campers, hikers, bikers,
and motorcyclists. Some are for the rich and sophisticated, others are for
the cheap and earthy.

While travel information is what keeps you afloat, too much information can sink the ship. I buy several guidebooks for each country I visit,
rip them up, and staple the chapters together into my own personalized
hybrid guidebook. To rip a book neatly, bend it over to break the spine,
visualize your destination, and pull chapters out with the gummy edge
intact (or just butcher and staple). Bring only the applicable pages. There's
no point in carrying 120 pages of information on Scandinavia to dinner
in Barcelona. When I finish seeing a country, I give my stapled-together
chapter on that area to another traveler or leave it in my last hotel's lounge.

Here's a rundown of my favorite guidebooks:

Let's Go: Written for young train travelers on tight budgets, Let's
Go guidebooks include the huge *Let's Go: Europe*, a Western Europe book,
and individual country guides. Covering big cities, small towns, and the
countryside, Let's Go guides offer listings of budget accommodations and

Never underestimate the value of an up-to-date guidebook.

restaurants; information on public transportation; capsule social, political, and historical rundowns; and a refreshingly opinionated look at sights and tourist activities. Let's Go doesn't teach "Ugly Americanism," as do many prominent guidebooks.

Let's Go guides are updated annually, hit the bookstores in December, and are sold in Europe for 50 percent more than U.S. prices. Always use the current edition. If you've got more money, stick to its higher-priced accommodations listings (although in many cities it lists only hostels and student hotels). With its hip student focus, Let's Go offers the best coverage on hosteling and the alternative nightlife scene.

Because of its wide scope, *Let's Go: Europe* is good only for the speedy, whirlwind–type itinerary. The book's drawback is that nearly every young North American traveler has it, and the flood of backpacker business it generates can overwhelm a formerly cozy village, hotel, or restaurant and give it a whopping Daytona Beach hangover.

Individual country guides in the series cover Britain, Ireland, France, Germany, Switzerland/Austria, Italy, Spain/Portugal, Eastern Europe, Greece, Turkey, Israel, Egypt, and the Middle East. With 10 times the information and one-tenth the readership of *Let's Go: Europe*, they don't have the negative impact that the big Europe book has on the featured destinations.

Lonely Planet guidebooks: Published in Australia, these are the top independent budget travel guidebooks for most countries in Asia, Africa, and South America. Lonely Planet has successfully invaded Europe with bricklike Western Europe, Central Europe, Scandinavian, Mediterranean, Eastern Europe, and all-Europe editions. They also publish guidebooks on individual countries and many cities. The Lonely Planet guides offer no-nonsense facts and opinions without the narrow student focus of Let's Go. They are widely available in English editions throughout Europe. Their drawback is they are not updated annually; check the publication date before you buy.

Rough Guides: This fast-growing British series (formerly the Real Guides) includes books about every part of Europe as well as a fat all-Europe edition. They are a great source of hard-core, go-local-on-a-vagabond's-budget information. While the hotel listings are skimpy and uninspired, these books are written by Europeans who understand the contemporary and social scene better than American writers. Rough Guides are particularly strong on Eastern European countries.

Frommer Guides: Arthur Frommer's classic guide, *Europe on $5 a Day*, is now *Europe from $70 a Day*. It's great for the 26 most important big cities but ignores everything else—and there's so much more! It's full of reliable and handy listings of budget hotels, restaurants, and sightseeing ideas compiled by the father of budget independent travel himself.

Frommer books on specific countries cover regions, towns, and villages as well as cities but are not as good as Frommer's Europe book. Arthur sold his name, and that's the only thing "Frommer" about these guides. Frommer guidebooks give good advice on which sites are essential when time is short. They are especially well-attuned to the needs of older travelers, but handle many with unnecessary kid gloves.

Karen Brown's Country Inn series: These are great for people with extra bucks and an appetite for doilies under thatch. Her recommended routes are good, and her listings are excellent if you plan on spending $150 to $300 a night for your double rooms. My splurges are Karen's slums.

Michelin Green Guides: These famous tall green books, available in dryly translated English all over Europe, have minimal information on hotels and restaurants but are a gold mine of solid, practical information on what to see. A French publisher, Michelin has English editions covering some regions of France and most countries of Europe. (The English editions are available in Europe—especially in France—for lower prices than in the U.S.) French speakers will find more editions available. Each book includes small but encyclopedic chapters on history, lifestyles, art, culture, customs, and economy. (Only the most recent editions contain information on hotels and restaurants.) These practical books are a tour guide's best friend. All over Europe tour leaders are wowing their busloads by reading from their Green Guides. ("And these are fields of sugar beets. Three-quarters of Austria's beet production lies along the banks of the Danube, which flows through 12 countries draining an area the size of the Sudan.") A wonderful and unique feature of the Green Guides is their handy "worth a journey/worth a detour" maps. The prominence of a listed place is determined by its importance to you, the traveler, rather than its population. This means that a cute visit-worthy village (like Rothenburg) appears bolder than a big, dull city (like Dortmund). These books are filled with fine city maps and are designed for drivers, ideally on Michelin tires.

The Michelin Red Guides are the hotel and restaurant connoisseur's bibles. But I don't travel with a poodle, and my taste buds weren't designed to appreciate $100 meals.

Blue Guides: The Blue Guides (which have nothing to do with European brothels) take a dry and scholarly approach to the countries of Europe. They're ideal if you want to learn as much about history, art, architecture, and culture as you possibly can. With the *Blue Guide to Greece*, I had all the information I needed about any sight in Greece and never needed to hire a guide. In addition to its many country guides, the series offers theme books on Britain: churches and chapels, English gardens, Victorian architecture, and so on. Scholarly types actually find a faint but endearing personality hiding between the sheets of their Blue Guides.

City guides: Specializing in information overload, these guides can be great for travelers staying put for a week in a city. Let's Go, Lonely Planet, and Rough Guides all publish straightforward guides to Europe's grandest cities. The creatively crafted **Access Guides** offer the ultimate in-depth source of sightseeing information for London, Paris, Rome, and Florence/Venice/Tuscany/Veneto. Two pricey series that also cover the biggies are **Eyewitness** and **Knopf** ($25 each, widely available in Europe; guides on Amsterdam, Paris, London, Rome, Venice, Florence/Tuscany, Prague, and more, plus some regions and countries). These heavy guides feature futuristic, high-tech, visually super, friendly layouts with appealing color illustrations and tiny bullets of background text. Travelers love the Eyewitness format. Knopf is the more highbrow of the two. I don't travel with these, but if I ever need to locate, say, a Caravaggio painting in a church, I seek out a tourist with a copy and ask for a quick peek. **Fodor's City Packs,** which are more portable and contain fold-out maps, are also worth considering (covering London, Dublin, Amsterdam, Paris, Berlin, Prague, Rome, Venice, Florence, and more).

Cadogan guidebooks: Cadogan (rhymes with toboggan) guides are readable and thought-provoking, giving the curious traveler a cultural insight into many regions. The series, distributed by Globe Pequot Press, includes Scotland, regions of France, Ireland, Italy, Italian islands, Tuscany, Umbria, Spain, Portugal, Morocco, Greek islands, Turkey, and more. They're good pre-trip reading. If you're traveling alone and want to understand tomorrow's sightseeing, Cadogan gives you something productive to do in bed.

Overseas Work and Study: *Transitions Abroad* publishes the excellent, annual *Alternative Travel Directory: The Complete Guide to Travel, Study & Living Overseas* ($24.95 postpaid) and *Work Abroad: The Complete Guide to Finding a Job Overseas* ($19.95 postpaid, tel. 800/293-0373, www.transitionsabroad.com). Vacation Work publishes Susan Griffith's

Work Your Way Around the World, Alex Lipinski's *Directory of Jobs & Careers Abroad*, and David Woodworth's *Overseas Summer Jobs*. Council Exchanges offers a work-abroad program (not for credit) for full-time students, a worldwide volunteer program for students over age 18, and opportunities for B.A. grads to teach English in China. Call for their free *Student Travels* magazine (tel. 888/COUNCIL, www.councilexchanges.org). Council-International Study Programs offers undergrads nearly 20 study-abroad programs (for credit) in 10 European countries (tel. 800/40-STUDY, www.ciee.org/isp).

RICK STEVES' GUIDEBOOKS

Country Guides: While *Europe Through the Back Door* covers travel skills, my country guides are blueprints for your actual trip. Annually updated, they weave my favorite sights, accommodations, and restaurants into trip strategies designed to give you the most value out of every day and every dollar. These books (which come out in December) cut through the superlatives. Yes, I know "you can spend a lifetime in Florence." But you've got a day and a half, and I've got a great plan.

These are the most up-to-date books on the market. In order to experience the same Europe that most of my readers do, I insist on doing my research in the peak tourist season. Also, my country guides are selective, covering fewer destinations in each country but covering each destination in more depth. While it's generally accepted in the travel publishing world that no one personally updates "annual" guidebooks annually, with fewer sights to visit, my research partners and I actually do.

My guidebooks will help you explore (and enjoy) Europe's big cities, small towns, and regions, mixing must-see sights with intimate Back Door nooks and offbeat crannies. *Rick Steves' Best of Europe*,

Rick Steves' Guidebooks

Country Guides
Rick Steves' Best of Europe
Rick Steves' France, Belgium & the Netherlands
Rick Steves' Germany, Austria & Switzerland (with Prague)
Rick Steves' Great Britain
Rick Steves' Ireland
Rick Steves' Italy
Rick Steves' Scandinavia
Rick Steves' Spain & Portugal

City Guides
*Rick Steves' Florence**
Rick Steves' London
Rick Steves' Paris
Rick Steves' Rome
*Rick Steves' Venice**

*Available March 2002
(*Avalon Travel Publishing*)

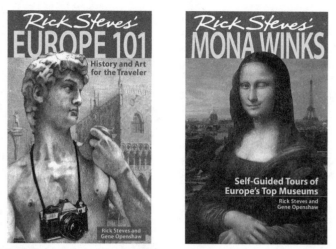

Rick Steves' art guides make your sightseeing more meaningful.

twice the size of the others, covers Europe's top destinations—including many of the Back Doors described in the last half of this book. If the table of contents lists all your destinations, this book will serve your trip as well—and cheaper—than several individual country guides.

City Guides: My city guides cover London, Paris, Rome, and—new for 2002—Venice and Florence (all co-authored with Gene Openshaw, Paris also co-authored with Steve Smith). If you're staying a few days in any of these grand cities, you'll find this reliable, in-depth information invaluable. These annually updated guides also include fun, "Mona Winks" self-guided tours of the top sights, emphasizing the great art with photos and commentary. (London, Paris, and Rome are available in January; Venice and Florence in March.)

Rick Steves' Europe 101: History and Art for the Traveler is the only fun travelers' guide to Europe's history and art (co-authored with Gene Openshaw, 2000). This easy-to-read manual is full of boiled-down, practical information to carbonate your sightseeing. Written for smart people who were sleeping in their art history classes before they knew they were going to Europe, *101* is the perfect companion to all the country guides... and your passport to goose bumps. After reading *Europe 101*, you can step into a Gothic cathedral, excitedly nudge your partner, and marvel, "Isn't this a great improvement over Romanesque!"

Rick Steves' Mona Winks: Self-Guided Tours of Europe's Top Museums gives you a breezy, step-by-step, painting-by-sculpture walk through the best two hours or so of Europe's 20 most overwhelming and exhausting

museums and cultural obligations
(co-authored with Gene Openshaw,
2001). It covers the great museums
of London, Paris, Venice, Florence,
Rome, Amsterdam, and Madrid.
Museums can ruin a good vacation...unless you are traveling with
Mona. Don't assume you can buy
good English guidebooks on the
spot for Europe's sights and museums. Museum guidebooks available
in Europe are too big, too expensive, and so dry that if you read
them out loud your lips would chap.
If you're interested in art, you need
Mona Winks.

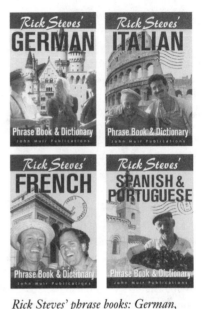

*Rick Steves' phrase books: German,
Italian, French, Spanish/Portuguese,
French/Italian/German (not shown)*

Rick Steves' Phrase Books
for French, Italian, German, Span-
ish/Portuguese, and French/Ital-
ian/German (1999) are the only
phrase books on the market designed by a guy who speaks only
English. That's why they're so good. They're based on 25 years of experience struggling with other phrase books. These are both fun and practical, with a meet-the-people and stretch-the-budget focus. Mr. Berlitz
knew the languages, but he never stayed in a hotel where you need to ask,
"When is the water hot?"

In my autobiographical book, ***Rick Steves' Postcards from Europe***, I
take you on a private tour of my favorite 3,000-mile loop through Europe:
from Amsterdam through Germany, Italy, and Switzerland, with a grand
finale in Paris. Along the way, my European friends offer a wry, contemporary look at Europe and America. My Italian friend Roberto says, "My
wife was born in Florida...I know, strange because most people die there."
Postcards also captures tourists' odd, sometimes unexpected reactions to
Europe. Bumping into nurses at Michelangelo's *David*, I'm told that David
is a "great IV start." Shuffled among my *Postcards* are stories from my past,
including my first trip to Europe—my parents forced me to go. Twenty-
five years later, I can't stop. The reasons are in *Postcards*. I hope you'll
distill from it a knack for enjoying Europe as I do.

My books are published by Avalon Travel Publishing go to (www
.travelmatters.com).

TRAVEL LITERATURE

Consider some trip-related recreational reading. A book on the court of Louis XIV brings Versailles to life. Books such as Michener's *Iberia* for Spain and Portugal, Stone's *The Greek Treasure* for Greece and Turkey, Wordsworth's poems for England's Lake District, and Uris' *Trinity* for Ireland are real trip bonuses. After reading Irving Stone's *The Agony and the Ecstasy*, you'll visit friends in Florence—who lived there 500 years ago. Personal accounts are fun, such as *Notes from a Small Island* by Bill Bryson (on Britain), Peter Mayle's Provence books, and the Travelers Tales series (available for Ireland, France, Italy, and Spain). Your hometown library has a lifetime of valuable reading on European culture. Dewey gave Europe the number 914. Take your travel partner on a date to the library and start your trip early.

Paging through coffee-table books on places you'll be visiting (e.g., *Hill Towns of Tuscany*, *Castles of North Wales*) can give you some great, often untouristy, sightseeing ideas. If travel partners divide up their studying, they can take turns being "guide" and do a better job. Your local travel bookstore stocks good travel literature as well as guidebooks.

MAPS

Drivers need first-class maps. Excellent, up-to-date maps with the European place names spelled as you'll see them in your travels are on sale throughout Europe. My unique Europe Planning Map—designed specifically to highlight the off-beat and obscure places I've discovered over the last 25 years—makes it easy to find these special places. Giving this map to a trucker trying to locate Stuttgart would be a cruel stunt. But if you're planning a Back Door European vacation, this is a great tool ($5; for our free newsletter/catalog, contact 425/771-8303 or www.ricksteves.com). The Michelin 970 Europe map is also good. Both Let's Go and Lonely Planet sell maps of major cities.

Drivers should consider picking up regional Michelin maps (scale 1:200,000, $7–9 each, cheaper in Europe) or the popular and inexpensive Michelin road atlases for each country (1:200,000 with city maps and indexes; maps and atlases sold at European gas stations, bookshops, newsstands, and tourist shops). Spend half a traffic jam learning the key. Handy sightseeing information, such as scenic roads and towns, ruined castles, hostels, mountain huts, viewpoints, and costs and opening schedules of remote roads can be found on good maps by good map readers.

By train, you can wing it with the map that comes free with your Eurailpass and the free (or cheap) little maps of each town that you can pick up at the local tourist offices as you go.

Maps can double as handy excuses to communicate with new friends. You can haul out the map and show them where you've been and where you're going.

TALK WITH OTHER TRAVELERS

Both in Europe and here at home, travelers love to share the lessons they've learned. Learn from other tourists. Firsthand, fresh information can be good stuff. Keep in mind, however, that all assessments of a place's touristic merit are a product of that person's personality and time there. It could have rained on her parade, he could have shared an elevator with the town jerk, or she may have been sick in "that lousy, overrated city." Or he might have fallen in love in that "wonderful" village. Every year, I find travelers hell-bent on following miserable travel advice from friends at home. Except for those found in this book, treat opinions as opinions.

Take advantage of every opportunity (such as train or bus rides) to swap information with travelers you meet from other parts of the English-speaking world. This is particularly important when traveling beyond Western Europe.

CYBERSPACE

Cyberspace is filled with free online travel talk. Various Web sites offer global weather reports, news, travel advice, visa information, and flight and hotel reservation services. Vagabonds between trips hang out in travel forums.

Google Groups and **Topica** are directories of newsgroups and e-mail lists with directions on how to jump into the fray. If you have a particular concern, you can get a world of advice through your computer modem. Use the many discussion lists to contact a European living in the area you want to visit, or a traveler who has just returned. Often travelers find a place to stay with European residents through these forums.

Easy-to-use search tools will help you find what you need. **Hotbot, Google**, and **Yahoo! Travel** can zero in on key travel resources. (Follow the search tips provided.)

Several Web sites pull up information according to destination and interest. **About.com, The Independent Traveler,** and **Maporama** feature travel tips, city maps, and information on cultural sites for most European destinations. **Unmissable.com, whatsonwhen.com,** and **Events Worldwide** make it easy to track down live concerts, sporting events, and cultural happenings. To keep up with local news, read **www.europeantimes.com**.

The **Tourism Offices Worldwide Directory** is a searchable directory of Tourist Information (TI) locations, phone numbers, and Web site addresses. The books *The Practical Nomad Guide to the Online Travel*

Good Sources for Travel Information Online

About.com: http://goeurope.about.com
Amazon: www.amazon.com
Bed and Breakfast: www.bedandbreakfast.com
Council Travel: www.counciltravel.com
Cybercafes: www.cybercafes.com
Dan Youra's Ferry Guide: www.youra.com/ferry/intlferries.html
Deutsche Bahn: www.reiseauskunft.bahn.de/bin/query.exe/en
Europe Through the Back Door: www.ricksteves.com
European Railway Server: http://mercurio.iet.unipi.it
Eurotrip: www.eurotrip.com
Events Worldwide: www.eventsworldwide.com
Google: www.google.com
Google Groups: http://groups.google.com/
Graffiti Wall: www.ricksteves.com/graffiti
Hostelling International: www.hiayh.org
Hotbot: www.hotbot.com
The Hotel Guide: www.hotelguide.com
Hotmail: www.hotmail.com
The Independent Traveler: www.independenttraveler.com
Internet Guide to Hostelling: www.hostels.com
Maporama: www.maporama.com
Michelin: www.viamichelin.com
Motoeuropa: www.ideamerge.com/motoeuropa
Ocean24: www.ocean24.com/ferry
OANDA: www.oanda.com/channels/traveler/
RoadNews: www.roadnews.com
STA Travel: www.statravel.com
Subway Navigator: www.subwaynavigator.com
TeleAdapt: www.teleadapt.com
Topica: www.topica.com
Tourism Offices Worldwide Directory: www.towd.com
Unmissable.com: www.unmissable.com
Universal Currency Converter: www.xe.net/currency/
Whatsonwhen.com: www.whatsonwhen.com
Yahoo! Travel: http://travel.yahoo.com/
Yahoo! Mail: http://mail.yahoo.com

For more travel tips and links, visit www.ricksteves.com/links

Ricksteves.com

With my Web site, www
.ricksteves.com, this book
becomes just the tip of
an informational iceberg
sharing the collective travel experience of my
50-person staff (logging
well over 2,000 days of
European travel each
year) and legions of Back
Door travelers we call our
Road Scholars.

www.ricksteves.com

  Ricksteves.com is completely free, fast, and user-friendly. You'll find my latest guidebook updates (www.ricksteves.com/update), European country information, a monthly travel e-newsletter (easy and free sign up), dispatches I send directly from Europe, and scripts for all 68 of our PBS-TV programs. Look for the very latest version of our rail-pass guide (included in the appendix of this book). The Media Kit includes a sampling of newspaper articles on our work, and our Marketplace covers all the travel gear, guidebooks, videos, railpasses, and tours we offer.

  Our Graffiti Wall (www.ricksteves.com/graffiti) is one of the most

Marketplace by Edward Hasbrouk and *Internet Travel Planner* by Michael Shapiro include information on how to book a flight, stay online while on the road, and find online travel planning tips and resources. If you're looking for a good guidebook, check out the wide selection at **Amazon.com.**

  Get the latest exchange rates with the **Universal Currency Converter or OANDA.**

  Find out about the International Student Identity Card and other student travel opportunities through **Council Travel** or **STA Travel.**

  The **Hotel Guide** and **BedandBreakfast.com** list hotels, inns, and B&Bs in Europe. You can search a destination, choose a hotel, and book your reservation online. For the traveler on a shoestring budget, **Eurotrip**, the **Internet Guide to Hostelling**, and **Hostelling International** offer cheap accommodations and transportation resources on the Internet.

  Plan your European train travel with the help of **Deutsche Bahn's** online timetable search service. The **European Railway Server, Dan** popular corners of our site. It is an immense (yet well-groomed) collection of message boards where our Road Scholars share their experience on the most important or perplexing travel issues of the day. As you read this book, remember that nearly every chapter has a corresponding thread growing on our Graffiti Wall with hundreds of postings on the topic.

Scrawl on our Graffiti Wall

With more than a hundred topics, there's something for everyone: Room Finding Tricks, Are Hotel Reservations Necessary?, Best European Hostels, Tipping Tips, Drinking the Water, Vegetarian Tips, Shopping Finds, Jet-Lag Cures, Tourist Scam Alert, Staying Healthy, Travel with Disabilities, Leaping the Language Barrier, Phoning and Mailing Home, Flying to and within Europe, Driving in Europe, Sleeping on Trains, Off-Season Travel Tips, Packing Light, Photography in Europe, Non–Rick Steves Guidebooks, Travel with Kids, Women Travel, Solo Travel, Savvy Seniors, Minority Travel Forum, Travel Partners Wanted, and much more.

Youra's Ferry Guide, and **Ocean24** lead you to the Web sites of the European railway and ferry systems. Find your way around underground with **Subway Navigator.** Drivers like **Motoeuropa** and **Michelin's site, Viamichelin.** For information on booking flights online, see Chapter 9.

Stay in touch with home through cybercafés—coffeehouses that offer Internet access and e-mail services. Check **Cybercafes.com** for a listing of these plugged-in places. Many universities, schools, libraries, and hotels offer e-mail services at little or no cost.

Travelers without laptops can use **Hotmail.com** or **Yahoo! Mail** to pick up and send e-mail at any place with Web access. These sites offer this free service in order to show you a few advertisements. Simply find the sites on the Web, follow their prompts for five minutes, and you'll have your own address with plenty of handy tools for free. Now tell your friends and you're connected.

If you're traveling with a laptop, see if your Internet service offers global roaming services in Europe to get online with a local phone call. **RoadNews** offers tips on necessary hardware and software and where to find an Internet connection. **TeleAdapt** provides similar know-how as well as information on the adapters you'll need to connect your modem to the various telephone plugs throughout Europe.

TRAVEL MAGAZINES AND NEWSLETTERS

Transitions Abroad is the best travel periodical on overseas work and study, as well as thoughtful, responsible travel (6 issues a year, $28 subscription, tel. 800/293-0373, www.transitionsabroad.com). *International Travel News*, printed on newsprint in black and white, is packed with down-and-dirty travel news, industry announcements, reports from traveling readers, globetrotting personals, and advertisements from creative small-time travel operators (monthly, $18 subscription, tel. 800/486-4968). The intellectual *Consumer Reports Travel Letter* is a little too focused on the industry rather than independent travel, but it does tedious, necessary studies and reports on the most confusing and expensive aspects of international travel (monthly, $39 subscription, tel. 800/234-1970).

At Europe Through the Back Door (ETBD), we publish a free, 64-page quarterly newsletter filled with travel articles, book updates, letters from our "road scholars," and a complete rundown on how the 50 of us working together at ETBD keep busy (free copy, tel. 425/771-8303, www.ricksteves.com).

CLASSES

The more you understand a subject, the longer it stays interesting. Those with no background in medieval architecture are the first to get "cathedraled out." Whether you like it or not, you'll be spending lots of time browsing through historic buildings and museums. Those who read or take trip-related classes beforehand have more fun sightseeing in Europe.

There are plenty of worthwhile classes on many aspects of Europe. Although you can get by with English, a foreign language—even a few survival phrases—can only make Europe more fun. A basic modern European history course brings Europe and its "dull" museums to life. A class in Eastern European studies shines some light on that murky demographic chaos.

Art history is probably the most valuable course for the prospective tourist. Don't go to Europe—especially Italy or Greece—without at least having read something on art and architecture.

Europe Through the Back Door's Travel Center, located in Edmonds,

Washington (30 minutes north of Seattle), is a library for people planning their trips. Spend the day (and not a penny) watching videos, perusing books and reader feedback, taking one of our many free travel classes, checking out our latest research, and making sure you've got the best itinerary (tel. 425/771-8303).

TRAVEL VIDEOS

The world is anxiously waiting for good travel videos. So far, most are uninspired destination picture books or cheesy promos sponsored by tourist boards or hotel groups. Most local TV travel shows shamelessly sell segments and are little more than disguised ads.

I'm doing my best to change this. My latest series, *Rick Steves' Europe*, with 16 new shows, is airing on more than 250 public TV stations throughout the United States. The new shows take a fresh look at well-loved destinations, introduce new favorites, and include a three-episode class on essential travel skills. The 52 episodes of my earlier series, *Travels in Europe with Rick Steves*, also air on public television. All of the shows are sold as videos (55–80 minutes each). For more information, see page 467.

I give classes around the U.S. All 24 hours of these slide show/lectures are available on 12 simple but clean, information-packed two-hour videos. These include classes on each region of Europe, budget travel skills, and "European Art for Travelers" (for our free newsletter/catalog, contact us at 425/771-8303 or www.ricksteves.com).

TOURIST INFORMATION OFFICES

Tourism is an important part of Europe's economy. Virtually every European city has a tourist information office located downtown and loaded with maps and advice. This is my essential first stop upon arrival in a town. But you don't need to wait until you get to Europe. Each European country has a national tourist office in the United States with a healthy promotional budget. Switzerland, for instance, figures you'll be doing the Alps, but you've yet to decide if they'll be French, Swiss, or Austrian Alps. They are happy to send you a free package of promotional information to put you in a Swiss Alps frame of mind. Just call or send a postcard to the office of each country you plan to visit. Ask for specific information to get more than the general packet. If you want to sleep in a castle on the Rhine, river-raft in France, or hut-hop across Austria, there's a free brochure for you. Ask for an English-language schedule of upcoming events and for maps of the country and various cities you'll be visiting. I find it's best to get answers to specific questions by telephone.

EUROPEAN NATIONAL TOURIST OFFICES IN THE U.S.

Austrian National Tourist Office: Box 1142, New York, NY 10108-1142, tel. 212/944-6880, fax 212/730-4568, www.austria-tourism.at/us, e-mail: info@oewnyc.com. Ask for their "Vacation Kit" with map. Fine hikes and city information.

Belgian National Tourist Office: 780 Third Ave. #1501, New York, NY 10017, tel. 212/758-8130, fax 212/355-7675, www.visitbelgium.com, e-mail: info@visitbelgium.com. Hotel and city guides; brochures for ABC lovers—antiques, beer, and chocolates; maps of Brussels; and a list of Jewish sights.

British Tourist Authority: 551 Fifth Ave., 7th floor, New York, NY 10176, tel. 800/462-2748, fax 212/986-1188, www.travelbritain.org, e-mail: travelinfo@bta.org.uk. Request the Britain Vacation Planner. Free maps of London and Britain. Regional information, garden tour map, and urban cultural activities brochure.

Czech Tourist Authority: 1109 Madison Ave., New York, NY 10028, tel. 212/288-0830, fax 212/288-0971, www.czechcenter.com, e-mail: travelczech@pop.net. To get a weighty information package (1–2 lbs, no advertising), send a check for $4 to cover postage and specify places of interest. Basic information and map are free.

Denmark (see Scandinavia)

Finland (see Scandinavia)

French Government Tourist Office: For questions and brochures (on regions, barging, and the wine country), call 410/286-8310. Ask for the Discovery Guide. Materials delivered in 4 to 6 weeks are free; there's a $4 shipping fee for information delivered in 5 to 10 days.
Their Web site is www.franceguide.com and their offices are ...

   In New York: 444 Madison Ave., 16th floor, New York, NY 10022, fax 212/838-7855, e-mail: info@francetourism.com.

   In Illinois: 676 N. Michigan Ave. #3360, Chicago, IL 60611-2819, fax 312/337-6339, e-mail: fgto@mcs.net.

   In California: 9454 Wilshire Blvd. #715, Beverly Hills, CA 90212, fax 310/276-2835, e-mail: fgto@gte.net.

German National Tourist Office: 122 E. 42nd Street, 52nd floor, New York, NY 10168, tel. 212/661-7200, fax 212/661-7174, www.visits-to-germany.com, e-mail: gntony@aol.com. Maps, Rhine schedules, events calendar, castles, winery tours, and city and regional information.

Greek National Tourist Organization: 645 Fifth Ave., New York, NY 10022, tel. 212/421-5777, fax 212/826-6940, www.gnto.gr, e-mail: gnto@greektourism.com. General how-to booklet, maps of Athens and Greece, plenty on the islands.

Hungarian National Tourist Office: 150 E. 58th Street, New York, NY 10155, tel. 212/355-0240, fax 212/207-4103, www.gotohungary.com, e-mail: info@gotohungary.com. Substantial annual "Travel Planner." "Routes to your Roots" booklet for Hungarian descendants. Spas, castles, horseback riding, free maps.

Irish Tourist Board: 345 Park Ave., 17th floor, New York, NY 10154, tel. 800/223-6470 or 212/418-0800, fax 212/371-9052, www.irelandvacations .com. Useful "Ireland Magazine." Ireland map, events calendar, golfing, outdoor activities, historic sights. The Irish Tourist Board now also provides information to travelers who wish to visit Northern Ireland. Learn more about sightseeing opportunities and ask about a vacation planner packet, maps, walking routes, and horseback riding.

Italian Government Tourist Board: Check www.italiantourism.com and contact the nearest office...

    In New York: 630 Fifth Ave. #1565, New York, NY 10111, brochure hotline tel. 212/245-4822, tel. 212/245-5618, fax 212/586-9249, e-mail: enitny@italiantourism.com.

    In Illinois: 500 N. Michigan Ave. #2240, Chicago, IL 60611, brochure hotline tel. 312/644-0990, tel. 312/644-0996, fax 312/644-3019, e-mail: enitch@italiantourism.com.

    In California: 12400 Wilshire Blvd. #550, Los Angeles, CA 90025, brochure hotline tel. 310/820-0098, tel. 310/820-1898, fax 310/820-6357, e-mail: enitla@earthlink.net.

Luxembourg National Tourist Office: 17 Beekman Place, New York, NY 10022, tel. 212/935-8888, fax 212/935-5896, www.visitluxembourg.com, e-mail: luxnto@aol.com. Maps, events calendar, biking, hiking, B&Bs.

Netherlands Board of Tourism: 355 Lexington Ave., 19th floor, New York, NY 10017, tel. 888/GO-HOLLAND, fax 212/370-9507, www .goholland.com, e-mail: info@goholland.com. Great country map, events calendar, seasonal brochures, $3 donation requested for mailing.

Norway (see Scandinavia)

Polish National Tourist Office: 275 Madison Ave. #1711, New York, NY 10016, tel. 212/338-9412, fax 212/338-9283, www.polandtour.org, e-mail: pntonyc@polandtour.org. Warsaw and Krakow information, regional brochures, maps.

Portuguese National Tourist Office: 590 Fifth Ave., 4th floor, New York, NY 10036, tel. 800/PORTUGAL or 212/354-4403, fax 212/764-6137, www.portugalinsite.com, e-mail: tourism@portugal.org. Videotapes, maps, information on regions, castles, and beach resorts. Very helpful.

Scandinavian Tourism: P.O. Box 4649, Grand Central Station, New York, NY 10163, tel. 212/885-9700, fax 212/885-9710, www.goscandinavia.com,

e-mail: info@goscandinavia.com. Good general booklets on all the Scandinavian countries. Be sure to also ask for specific country info and city maps.
Tourist Office of Spain: Check their Web sites (www.okspain.org and www.tourspain.es) and contact their nearest office...
   In New York: 666 Fifth Ave., 35th floor, New York, NY 10103, tel. 212/265-8822, fax 212/265-8864, e-mail: oetny@tourspain.es.
   In Illinois: 845 N. Michigan Ave. #915E, Chicago, IL 60611, tel. 312/642-1992, fax 312/642-9817, e-mail: chicago@tourspain.es.
   In Florida: 1221 Brickell Ave. #1850, Miami, FL 33131, tel. 305/358-1992, fax 305/358-8223, e-mail: oetmiami@tourspain.es.
   In California: 8383 Wilshire Blvd. #960, Beverly Hills, CA 90211, tel. 323/658-7188, fax 323/658-1061, e-mail: espanalax@aol.com.
Sweden (see Scandinavia)
Switzerland Tourism: For questions and brochures call 877/794-8037. Comprehensive "Welcome to the Best of Switzerland" brochure, great maps and hiking material. Or contact 608 Fifth Ave., New York, NY 10020, fax 914/682-9093, www.myswitzerland.com, e-mail: info.usa @switzerlandtourism.ch.
Turkish Tourist Office: 821 United Nations Plaza, New York, NY 10017, tel. 212/687-2194, fax 212/599-7568, www.tourismturkey.org, e-mail: ny@tourismturkey.org. Numerous maps, hotel guides, and brochures on regions, spas, and outdoor activities.

MIDDLE EASTERN AND NORTH AFRICAN TOURIST OFFICES IN THE U.S.
Egyptian Tourist Authority: 630 Fifth Ave. #1706, New York, NY 10111, tel. 877/77-EGYPT or 212/332-2570, fax 212/956-6439, www.egypttourism.org, e-mail: egyptourst@aol.com.
Israel Government Tourist Office: 800 Second Ave., 16th floor, New York, NY 10017, tel. 888/77-ISRAEL or 212/499-5660, fax 212/499-5665, www.goisrael.com, e-mail: info@goisrael.com. Request the "All You Ever Wanted to Know About Israel" packet. Interest brochures for Catholic, Protestant, and Jewish faiths.
Moroccan National Tourist Office: 20 E. 46th Street #1201, New York, NY 10017, tel. 212/557-2520, fax 212/949-8148, www.tourism-in -morocco.com. Good country map. Information on cities and regions.

3. Paper Chase
While going to Europe isn't all that complex, your trip will be smoother if you consider these documents and details well before your departure date.

PASSPORTS

In Western Europe, the only document a U.S. citizen needs is a passport. For most travelers, the only time any customs official will look at you seriously is at the airport as you reenter the United States. Most European border crossings are a wave-through for U.S. citizens.

Passports, good for 10 years, cost $60 ($40 to renew). Minors under 16 pay $40 for a passport good for five years. You can apply at some courthouses or some post offices. For details and the location of the nearest passport application office, call 800/688-9889 (http://travel.state.gov /passport_services.html). Although they say applications take six weeks (and you should be prepared for delays), most passports are processed more quickly. If you want to fly to Europe within two weeks and can prove you're in an emergency situation (by showing a purchased plane ticket or a letter from work requiring you to travel overseas on short notice), go in person to the nearest U.S. Passport Agency and pay an additional $35 speed fee. They'll issue your new passport the same day or within one day.

As you travel, take good care of your passport. But Americans, notorious passport-grippers, need to relax when it comes to temporarily giving it up. As you cross some Eastern European borders by train, a usually unofficial-looking character will come down the aisle picking up all the passports. Relax, you'll get it back later. When you sleep in a *couchette* (night train sleeping car) that crosses a border, the car attendant will take your passport so you won't be disturbed when the train crosses the border at 3 a.m. And hotels routinely take your passport "for the night" so they can register you with the police. This book work must be done for foreign guests throughout Europe. Receptionists like to gather passports and register them all at the same time when things are quiet. Although it's unreasonable to expect them to drop whatever they're doing to register me immediately, I politely ask if I can pick up my passport in two hours. I just don't like my passport in the top drawer all night long.

A passport works well for collateral in cases when you don't have the cash right now (hefty deposits on bike rentals, hotels that don't trust you, etc.).

Losing your passport while traveling is a major headache. If you do, contact the police and the nearest U.S. consulate or embassy right away. You can get a short-term replacement, but you'll earn it. A photocopy of your passport (and a couple of passport-type photos) can speed the replacement process.

VISAS

A visa is a stamp placed in your passport by a foreign government, allowing you to enter their country. Visas are not required for Americans traveling in Western Europe and most of the East. Currently Canadians need visas to visit the Czech Republic.

Turkey requires Americans and Canadians to purchase a visa ($45 for Americans, $50 in Canadian cash for Canadians), which is easy to get upon arrival at the border or airport. For more information, see www.turkey.org. Americans can get a visa in advance by money order through the Turkish embassy (2525 Massachusetts Ave. N.W., Washington, D.C., 20008, tel. 202/612-6740) or the Turkish consulates in New York (821 United Nations Plaza, New York, NY 10017, tel. 212/949-0160), Chicago (360 N. Michigan Ave. #1405, Chicago, IL 60601, tel. 312/263-0644 ext. 28), Houston (1990 Post Oak Blvd., #1300, Houston, TX 77056, tel. 713/622-5849), or Los Angeles (4801 Wilshire Blvd. #310, Los Angeles, CA 90010, tel. 323/937-0118). Canadians can contact the Turkish embassy at 197 Wurtemburg Street, Ottawa, Ontario K1N 8L9 (tel. 613/789-4044).

Travelers to **Russia** also need visas, which are best applied for in advance. You'll pay $70 for processing within two weeks (pricier for a quicker turnaround). For more details, visit www.russianembassy.org or contact the Russian consulate nearest you: in Washington D.C. (2641 Tunlaw Road, Washington, D.C. 20007, tel. 202/939-8907), in New York (9 East 91st St., New York, NY 10128, tel. 212/348-0926), in San Francisco (2790 Green St., San Francisco, CA 94123, tel. 415/928-6878), and Seattle (2323 Westin Building, 2001 6th Ave., Seattle, WA 98121, tel. 206/728-1910).

For **travel beyond Europe**, get up-to-date information on visa requirements from your travel agent or the United States Department of State (http://travel.state.gov/foreignentryreqs.html).

If you do need a visa, it's usually best to get it at home before you leave. If you forget, virtually every country has an embassy or consulate (which can issue visas) in the capital of every other European country.

SHOTS

At this time, shots are not required for travel in Europe. But this can change, so check the inoculation requirements with your doctor or a travel medicine clinic before you leave home. Countries "require" shots in order to protect their citizens from you and "recommend" shots to protect you from them. If any shots are recommended, take that advice seriously. (For more information, see Chapter 21: Staying Healthy.)

STUDENT CARDS AND HOSTEL MEMBERSHIPS

The International Student Identity Card (ISIC), the only internationally recognized student ID card, gets you discounts on transportation, entertainment, and sightseeing throughout Europe and includes some medical insurance. If you are a full-time student or have been one in the last year (and can prove it), get one. The cost is $22 from Council Travel, STA Travel, or from your university foreign study office (turn your ISIC card into a phone card for an extra $20—see Chapter 20: Phones). Teachers of any age can sometimes get similar student-type discounts with an ITIC (International Teacher Identification Card), but this is often not honored. Nonstudent travelers under age 26 can obtain an International Youth Travel Card for similar discounts. Council Travel and STA Travel offices sell all of these cards for $22 apiece; for their nearest offices, call 800/2-COUN-CIL (www.counciltravel.com) or 800/777-0112 (www.statravel.com).

If you plan to stay four or more nights at a hostel, a hostel membership will pay for itself. Before you leave, get a hostel membership card from your local hostel or Hostelling International at 202/783-6161 and www.hiayh.org (for more information, see Chapter 15: Sleeping). Your hostel membership card can also double as a phone card (see Chapter 20: Phones).

RAILPASSES AND CAR RENTAL

Most railpasses are not sold in Europe and must be purchased before you leave home. Car rental is usually cheaper when arranged before your trip through your hometown travel agent. For most, an international driver's permit is not necessary (but if you're getting one, do it at AAA before your departure—for $10 and 2 passport photos). For specifics on driving and train passes, see Chapters 9 through 12 on transportation and the "European Railpasses" guide in the appendix.

TRAVEL INSURANCE—TO INSURE OR NOT TO INSURE?

Travel insurance is a way to buy off the considerable financial risks of traveling. These risks include accidents, illness, missed flights, canceled tours, lost baggage, emergency evacuation, and getting your body home if you die. Each traveler's risk and potential loss varies, depending on how much of the trip is prepaid, the kind of air ticket purchased, your state of health, value of your luggage, where you're traveling, what health coverage you already have, and the financial health of the tour company or airline. For some, insurance is a good deal; for others, it's not.

Travel agents recommend travel insurance because they make a commission on it, they can be held liable for your losses if they don't explain insurance options to you, and sometimes because it's right for you. But the final decision is yours. What are the chances of needing it, how able are you to take the risks, and what's peace of mind worth to you?

You can design your own coverage with à la carte policies from Travel Insured International (tel. 800/243-3174, www.travelinsured.com) or Access

America (tel. 800/284-8300, www.accessamerica.com). The insurance menu includes four courses: medical, baggage, trip cancellation, and flight insurance. Tailor it to your needs, then compare to the comprehensive travel insurance that's explained below.

Medical insurance generally covers only medical and dental emergencies. Check with your medical insurer—you might already be covered by your existing health plan. Find out about deductibles, if any, and the procedure for reimbursement of emergency expenses. Generally, your expenses are out-of-pocket, and you bring home documentation to be reimbursed. While many policies cover you overseas, Medicare and some HMOs do not.

Emergency evacuation (e.g., nine one-way, first-class seats on a plane) can be extremely expensive and is usually not covered by your regular medical insurance. If you're considering this type of insurance, ask the insurance company if it covers your flight home or simply to the nearest hospital.

Pre-existing conditions are now generally covered in medical and trip cancellation coverage, but check with your agent or insurer before you commit. The $22 ISIC student identity card includes basic travelers' health coverage (see page 26).

Baggage insurance costs about $4 or $5 per day per $1,000 coverage (and doesn't cover items such as cash, eyewear, and photographic equipment). Homeowners' insurance (with the "floater" supplement, if necessary, to cover you out of the country) is cheaper, and you'll have coverage even after your trip. Travelers' baggage insurance will cover the deductibles and items excluded from your homeowners' policy. Double-check the particulars with your agent. If your policy doesn't cover rail-passes, consider buying the $10–12 insurance deal sold with the pass.

Trip cancellation or interruption insurance covers the financial penalties or losses you incur when you cancel a prepaid tour or flight for an acceptable reason. These include if:

(1) you, your travel partner, or a family member cannot travel due to sickness or a list of other acceptable reasons;

(2) your tour company or airline goes out of business or can't perform as promised;

(3) a family member at home gets sick, causing you to cancel;

(4) for a good reason, you miss a flight or need an emergency flight.

In other words, if, on the day before your trip, you or your travel partner breaks a leg, you can both bail out (if you both have travel insurance), and neither of you will lose a penny. And if, one day into your tour, you have an accident, both of you will be flown home, and you'll be reimbursed for the emergency one-way return flight (which usually costs far more than your economy round-trip fare) and whatever portion of the tour you haven't used.

People who aren't on a tour get coverage for their prepaid expenses (such as their flight and any nonrefundable hotel reservations). This insurance costs about 6.5 percent of the amount you want covered. For example, a $1,500 tour and $500 airfare can be insured for $130. (There are worst-case, fly-home-in-a-hurry scenarios where you could need more coverage.) This is a good deal if you figure there's a better than 1-in-20 chance you'll need it. The rugged, healthy, unattached, and gung-ho traveler will probably skip this coverage. I have for more than 25 trips, and my number has yet to come up. If you're paying out a lot of up-front money for an organized tour (which is expensive to cancel), if you have questionable health, or if you have a loved one at home in frail health, you should probably get this coverage.

Flight insurance (crash coverage) is a statistical rip-off that heirs love. More than 60,000 airplanes take off and land safely every day. In 1998 there was not a single passenger fatality on any commercial American airline. The chances of being in an airplane crash are minuscule.

Comprehensive travel insurance, such as Travel Guard's or Access America's, gives you everything but the kitchen sink for about 6 to 9 percent of your prepaid trip cost (airfare, car rental, tour, etc.) depending on your age. This can be a better deal for travelers with less of the trip prepaid (those without tours) because coverage is the same regardless of the premium you pay. This covers any deductible expense your existing medical insurance plan doesn't cover. For $6 extra per day you can get a supplemental collision damage waiver (CDW) on rental cars rather than pay $10 to $25 a day at a rental office in Europe (see below and Chapter 11). As a bonus, many major insurance companies are accessible by phone 24 hours a day, handy if you have problems in Europe.

Collision Damage Waiver (CDW) Insurance is a point of much confusion. When you rent a car, you are usually liable for the entire value of that car. Car rental agencies charge a rip-off $10 to $25 a day to buy this risk away. Travel Guard sells the same thing for $6 a day; it's accepted throughout Europe *except* in the Republic of Ireland and Italy (tel. 800/826-1300, www.travelguard.com). With some credit cards you are covered automatically when you rent the car using that card. (For details, see Chapter 11.)

Go with a big-name company. Avoid buying insurance from a no-name company on the Web. Not all insurance companies are licensed in every state. If you have to make a claim and encounter problems with a company that isn't licensed in your state, you don't have a case.

Your travel agent has insurance brochures. Ask your agent which insurance he or she recommends for your travels and why. Study the brochures. Consider how insurance fits your travel and personal needs, compare its cost to the likelihood of your using it and your potential loss—and then decide.

4. Pack Light Pack Light Pack Light

The importance of packing light cannot be overemphasized, but, for your own good, I'll try. You'll never meet a traveler who, after five trips, brags, "Every year I pack heavier." The measure of a good traveler is how light she travels. You can't travel heavy, happy, and cheap. Pick two.

Limit yourself to 20 pounds in a carry-on-size bag. A 9" x 22" x 14" bag fits under most airplane seats. That's my self-imposed limit. At ETBD we've taken thousands of people of all ages and styles on tours through Europe. We allow only one carry-on bag. For many, this is a radical concept. "9 x 22 x 14 inches? That's my cosmetics kit!" But they manage and they're glad they did. And after you enjoy that sweet mobility and freedom, you'll never go any other way.

You'll walk with your luggage more than you think you will. Before leaving home, give yourself a test. Pack up completely, go into your hometown, and practice being a tourist for an hour. Fully loaded, you should enjoy window shopping. If you can't, stagger home and thin things out.

When you carry your own luggage, it's less likely to get lost, broken, or stolen. (Many travelers claim that airline employees rifle through checked luggage.) A small bag sits on your lap or under your seat on the bus, taxi, and airplane. You don't have to worry about it, and, when you arrive, you can leave immediately. It's a good feeling. When I land in London, I'm on my way downtown while everyone else stares anxiously at the luggage carousel. When I fly home, I'm the first guy the dog sniffs.

Keep in mind that more and more airlines are limiting your carry-on luggage weight as well as size. Call your airline (or read the fine print on your ticket) to find out their policy. For example, British Air and SAS have a maximum of 13 and 18 pounds respectively. It's only worth fighting to carry on your bag if you have a tight connection. If you do check your bag, mark it inside and out with your name, address, and emergency phone number. While many travelers lock their bags, I never have.

Too much luggage marks

Older travelers traveling like college kids—light, mobile, footloose and fancy-free, wearing their convertible suitcase rucksacks—have nothing to be ashamed of.

you as a typical tourist. It slams the back door shut. Serendipity suffers. Changing locations becomes a major operation. Con artists figure you're helpless. Porters are a problem only to those who need them. With one bag hanging on your back, you're mobile and in control. Take this advice seriously.

BACKPACKADEMIA—WHAT TO BRING?

How do you fit a whole trip's worth of luggage into a small suitcase or rucksack? The answer is simple: Bring very little.

Spread out everything you think you might need on the living room floor. Pick up each item one at a time and scrutinize it. Ask yourself, "Will I really use this snorkel and these fins enough to justify carrying them around all summer?" Not "Will I use them?" but "Will I use them enough to feel good about carrying them over the Swiss Alps?" Regardless of my budget, I would buy them in Greece and give them away before I would carry that extra weight over the Alps.

Don't pack for the worst scenario. Risk shivering for a day rather than taking a heavy coat. Think in terms of what you can do without—not what will be handy on your trip. When in doubt, leave it out. I've seen people pack a whole summer's supply of deodorant, tampons, or razors, thinking they can't get them there. The world's getting really small; you can buy Dial soap, Colgate toothpaste, Tampax, Nivea cream, and Bic razors in Sicily. Tourist shops in major international hotels are a sure bet whenever you have difficulty finding some personal item. And if you can't find one of your "essentials," ask yourself how 300 million Europeans can live without it.

Whether you're traveling for three weeks or three months, you pack exactly the same. Rather than take a whole trip's supply of toiletries, take enough to get started and look forward to running out of toothpaste in Bulgaria. Then you have the perfect excuse to go into a Bulgarian department store, shop around, and pick up something you think might be toothpaste....

RUCKSACK OR SUITCASE?

Whether you take a rucksack or a small soft-sided suitcase with a shoulder strap is up to you. Packing light applies equally to rucksack or suitcase travelers. Hard-sided suitcases with one-inch wheels are impractical. Bobbling down Europe's cobblestones, you'll know what I mean. (Those physically unable to lug a bag can manage best with the popular soft-sided bags with bigger wheels.)

Most young-at-heart travelers go the rucksack route. If you are a suitcase person who would like the ease of a rucksack without forgoing the "respectability" of a suitcase, try a convertible suitcase/rucksack with zip-

away shoulder straps. These carry-
on-size bags give you the best of both
worlds. I live out of one of these for
three months at a time (for our news-
letter/catalog, contact us at 425/771-
8303 or visit www.ricksteves.com).

Unless you plan to camp or
sleep out a lot, a sleeping bag is a
bulky security blanket. Even on a
low budget, bedding will be provided. (Hostels provide all bedding
free or for a small fee and often
don't allow sleeping bags.) Don't
pack to camp unless you're going to

*The same carry-on-the-plane-sized
bag works as a suitcase or a rucksack.*

camp. Without a sleeping bag, a medium-size rucksack is plenty big.

Pack your rucksack only two-thirds full to leave room for picnic food
and souvenirs. Sturdy stitching, front and side pouches, padded shoulder
straps, and a low-profile color are rucksack virtues. Many travelers figure
an internal frame is worth the extra money and get a high-tech bag for
$150 to $200. Packing very light, I manage fine without the extra weight
and expense of these fancier bags. I'm not wild about the bags with a zip-
off day bag. I travel with the convertible rucksack pictured here and supplement it with a separate day bag.

Entire books have been written on how to pack. It's really quite simple: Use stuff bags (one each for toiletries, underwear and socks, bigger
clothing items, camera gear and film, and miscellaneous stuff such as a
first-aid kit, stationery, and sewing kit). Roll and rubber band clothes, or
zip-lock them in airless baggies to minimize wrinkles.

CLOTHING

The bulk of your luggage is clothing. Minimize by bringing less and washing more often. Every few nights you'll spend 10 minutes doing a little
wash. This doesn't mean more washing, it just means doing it little by
little as you go.

Be careful to choose dark clothes that dry quickly and either don't
wrinkle or look good wrinkled. To see how wrinkled shirts will get, give
everything a wet rehearsal by hand-washing and drying once at home.
You should have no trouble drying clothing overnight in your hotel room.
I know this sounds barbaric, but my body dries out a damp pair of socks
or shirt in a jiffy. It's fun to buy clothes as you travel—another reason to
start with less.

For winter travel, you can pack just about as light. Add a down or pile coat, long johns (quick-drying Capilene or superlight silk), scarf, mittens, hat, and an extra pair of socks and underwear since things dry more slowly. Pack with the help of a climate chart (see the appendix). Layer your clothing for warmth, and assume you'll be outside in the cold for hours at a time.

During the tourist season (April through September), the concert halls go casual. I have never felt out of place at symphonies, operas, or plays wearing a decent pair of slacks and a good-looking sweater. Pack with color coordination in mind. Some cultural events require more formal attire, particularly outside of the tourist season, but the casual tourist rarely encounters these.

Many travelers are concerned about appropriate dress. European women wear dresses or skirts more often than pants. American women generally feel fine in pants, but in certain rural and traditional areas, they'll fit in better and may feel more comfortable in a skirt or dress. Women who prefer to wear slacks don't pack a dress and have no regrets.

Your clothes will probably mark you as an American. Frankly, so what? Europeans will know anyway. I fit in and am culturally sensitive by watching my manners, not the cut of my clothes.

Some sacred places, mostly in southern Europe, have modest dress requirements for men and women: no shorts or bare shoulders. Except at the strict St. Peter's in Rome, the dress code is often loosely enforced. If necessary, it's usually easy to improvise some modesty (a hairy-legged man can borrow a nearby tablecloth to wear as a kilt, a woman in a sleeveless blouse can wear maps on her shoulders). In southern cities—no matter how hot it is—grown men look goofy in shorts.

Go casual, simple, and very light. Remember, in your travels you'll meet two kinds of tourists—those who pack light and those who wish they had. Say it once out loud: "PACK LIGHT."

WHAT TO PACK

Indicates items available through our Back Door Catalog (call 425/771-8303 or visit www.ricksteves.com).

Shirts. Bring up to five short-sleeved or long-sleeved shirts in a cotton/polyester blend. Arrange mix according to season.

Sweater. Warm and dark is best—for layering and dressing up. It never looks wrinkled and is always dark, no matter how dirty it is.

Pants. Bring two pairs: one lightweight cotton and another superlightweight for hot and muggy big cities, and churches with modest dress codes. Jeans can be too hot for summer travel. Linen is great. Many like lightweight pants/shorts with zip-off legs. Button-down wallet pockets are safest.

Shorts. Take a pair with pockets—doubles as a swimsuit for men.

Swimsuit. Especially for women.

Underwear and socks. Bring five sets (lighter dries quicker).

One pair of shoes. Take a well-used, light, and cool pair, with Vibram-type soles and good traction. I like Rockports or Easy Spirits. Sturdy, low-profile-colored tennis shoes with a good tread are fine, too.

Jacket. Bring a light and water-resistant windbreaker with a hood. Gore-Tex is good if you expect rain. For summer travel, I wing it without rain gear but always pack for rain in Britain.

A tie or scarf. For instant respectability, bring anything lightweight that can break the monotony and make you look snazzy.

*****Money belt.** It's essential for the peace of mind it brings. You could lose everything except your money belt, and the trip could still go on. Lightweight and low-profile beige is best.

Money. Bring your preferred mix of a credit or debit card, an ATM cash card, traveler's checks, a few personal checks, and some hard cash. Bring American dollars (Europeans get a kick out of seeing George Washington fold up into a mushroom) for situations when you want to change only a few bucks. I rely on an ATM card with a credit card and $400 in cash as a backup. (For details, see Chapter 13: Money.)

Documents and photocopies. Bring your passport, airline ticket, railpass or car rental voucher, driver's license, student ID, hostel card, and so on. Photocopies and a couple of passport-type photos can help you get replacements if the originals are lost or stolen. Carry photocopies separately in your luggage and keep the originals in your money belt.

You'll want a careful record of all reservations (bring the hotels' written confirmations) along with a trip calendar page to keep things up-to-date as your trip evolves.

*****Small daypack.** A small nylon daypack is great for carrying your sweater, camera, literature, and picnic goodies while you leave your large bag at the hotel or train station. Fanny packs (small bags with thief-friendly zippers on a belt) are a popular alternative but should not be used as money belts.

Camera. Put a new battery in your camera before you go. Bring a protective and polarizing lens, midrange zoom lens, cleaning tissue, and a trip's worth of film. Store everything in a low-profile nylon stuff bag, not an expensive-looking camera bag.

Picnic supplies. Bring a small tablecloth to give your meal some extra class (and to wipe the knife on), salt and pepper, a cup, a damp washcloth in a baggie for cleaning up, and a Swiss Army–type knife with a corkscrew and can opener. A plastic plate is handy for picnic dinners in your hotel room.

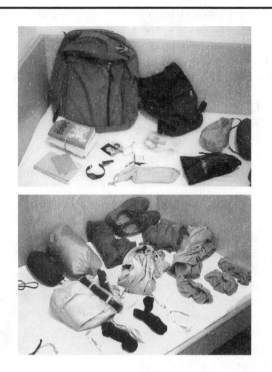

One carry-on-size bag?? Here's everything I traveled with for two months (photos taken naked in a Copenhagen hotel room): convertible 9" x 22" x 14" suitcase/rucksack; lightweight nylon day bag; ripped-up sections of three guidebooks, notes, maps, journal, tiny pocket notepad; wristwatch; tiny Swiss Army knife; pocket-sized radio with earplugs; money belt (with ATM card, credit card, driver's license, passport, plane ticket, train pass, cash, sheet of phone numbers and addresses); second money belt tied inside my bag for "semi-precious" documents; toiletries stuff bag (with squeeze bottle of shampoo, soap in a plastic container, shaver, toothbrush and paste, comb, nail clippers, travel alarm clock, squeeze bottle of liquid soap for clothes); camera gear stuff bag (with camera, polarizer lens, cleaning tissues, film); miscellaneous bag with family photos, tiny odds and ends; light rain jacket; long khaki cotton pants (button pockets, no wallet), superlight long pants, shorts, five pairs of socks and underwear, long-sleeved shirt, two short-sleeved shirts, T-shirt; stuff bag with sweater, plastic laundry bag; and a light pair of shoes (Rockports).

Zip-lock baggies. Get a variety of sizes. They're great for packing left-over picnic food, containing wetness, and bagging potential leaks before they happen. The two-gallon jumbo size is handy for packing clothing.
Water bottle. The plastic half-liter mineral water bottles sold throughout Europe are reusable and work great.
Wristwatch. A built-in alarm is handy. Otherwise, pack a small *travel alarm clock. Cheap-hotel wake-up calls are particularly unreliable.
Earplugs. If night noises bother you, you'll love a good set of plugs such as those made by Sleep-well.
First-aid kit. See Chapter 21: Staying Healthy.
Medicine and vitamins. Keep medicine in original containers, if possible, with legible prescriptions.
Extra eyeglasses, contact lenses, and prescriptions. Many travelers find their otherwise-comfortable contacts don't work in Europe. Bring your glasses just in case. Contact solutions are widely available in Europe.
Sunglasses, depending on the season and your destination.

*Toiletries kit. Sinks in cheap hotels come with meager countertop space and anonymous hairs. If you have a nylon toiletries kit that can hang on a hook or a towel bar, this is no problem. Put all squeeze bottles in zip-lock baggies, since pressure changes in flight cause even good bottles to leak. Consider a vacation from cosmetics. Bring a little toilet paper or tissue packets (sold at all newsstands in Europe). Fingernail clippers and tweezers (for retrieving lost bank cards)

With a hangable toiletries kit, you know the hairs on the toothbrush are yours.

are also handy. My Sonicare electric toothbrush holds a charge from home for 30 one-minute brushes.
Soap. Not all hotels provide soap. A plastic squeeze bottle of concentrated, multipurpose, biodegradable liquid soap is handy for laundry and more.
*Clothesline. Hang it up in your hotel room to dry your clothes. The handy twist kind needs no clothespins.
Small towel. You'll find bath towels at all fancy and moderately priced hotels, and most cheap ones. Although $30-a-day travelers will often need to bring their own towel, $60-a-day folks won't. I bring a thin hand towel

Checklist of Essentials

- ❏ 5 shirts
- ❏ 1 sweater
- ❏ 2 pairs pants
- ❏ 1 pair shorts
- ❏ 1 swimsuit (women only)
- ❏ 5 pair underwear and socks
- ❏ 1 pair shoes
- ❏ 1 jacket
- ❏ Tie or scarf
- ❏ Money belt
- ❏ Money—your mix of:
  - ❏ ATM cash card
  - ❏ Credit card or debit card
  - ❏ Hard cash
  - ❏ Traveler's checks
  - ❏ A few personal checks
- ❏ Documents plus photocopies
  - ❏ Passport
  - ❏ Airline ticket
  - ❏ Driver's license
  - ❏ Student ID and hostel card
  - ❏ Railpass/car rental voucher
  - ❏ Insurance details
- ❏ Daypack
- ❏ Picnic supplies
- ❏ Zip-lock baggies
- ❏ Camera, battery, film, lenses, stuff bag
- ❏ Water bottle
- ❏ Wristwatch and alarm clock
- ❏ Earplugs
- ❏ First-aid kit
- ❏ Medicine
- ❏ Extra glasses/contacts and prescriptions
- ❏ Sunglasses
- ❏ Toiletries kit
- ❏ Soap
- ❏ Laundry soap
- ❏ Clothesline
- ❏ Small towel
- ❏ Sewing kit
- ❏ Travel information
- ❏ European map
- ❏ Address list (e-mail, mailing addresses
- ❏ Postcards or photos from home
- ❏ Journal
- ❏ Notepad and pen

for the occasional need. Washcloths are rare in Europe. While I don't use them, many recommend the quick-drying "Sport Sponge"—a chamois in a plastic box.

Sewing kit. Clothes age rapidly while traveling. Your flight attendant may have a freebie for you. Add a few safety pins.

Travel information (minimal). Rip out appropriate chapters from guidebooks, staple them together, and store in a zip-lock baggie. When you're done, give them away.

Packing Tips for Women

Thanks to ETBD tour guides Kendra Roth, Margaret Berger Cassady, and Joan Weigant for the following tips:
If you're not going to wear it more than three times, don't pack it! Every piece of clothing you bring should match or complement each item or have at least two uses (e.g., sandals double as slippers, a scarf as a shoulder wrap).

Tops: Bring two or three T-shirts, one or two short-sleeved blouses, and one or two long-sleeved shirts. Long-sleeved shirts with sleeves that roll up can double as short-sleeved shirts. Look for a wrinkle-camouflaging pattern or blended fabrics that show a minimum of wrinkles. Silk dries quickly and is lightweight.

Pants and Shorts: Try the pants with the zip-off legs that convert to shorts. These are especially good in Italy, allowing you to cover up inside churches and stay cool outside. Comfortable, dark-colored pants don't show dirt or wrinkles, and some have loose-fitting waistbands that accommodate money belts and big Italian meals. Lightweight pajamas or an oversized shirt will get you modestly to the bathroom down the hall. You might feel more comfortable wearing a skirt or pants (not shorts) in Amsterdam, Paris, or Italian cities where the local women really dress up.

For durable, pricey travel clothes, consider Ex Officio (tel. 800/644-7303, www.exofficio.com) and TravelSmith (tel. 800/950-1600, www.travelsmith.com). Also see Tilley's, below.

Skirts: Some women bring one or two skirts because they're as cool and breathable as shorts, but dressier. And skirts make life easier than pants when you're faced with a squat toilet! A lightweight skirt made with a blended fabric will pack compactly. Make sure it has a comfy elastic waistband or drawstring. Tilley's makes expensive but great skirts (and other items) from blended fabric that feels like cotton (tel. 800/884-3797, www.tilley.com). You can wash them, wring them out, hang them to dry, and even wear them, and they still won't wrinkle. Denim or twill trouser skirts go with everything, and can easily be dressed up or down.

Shoes: Bring one pair of good, comfortable walking shoes. Mephisto, Timberland, and Rykers look dressier and more European than sneakers but are still comfortable. For a second pair, consider sandals or Tevas in summer, or dark leather flats in winter (can be worn with opaque hose and a skirt to dress up).

Socks, Underwear, and Swimsuit: Cotton/nylon–blend socks dry

faster than 100 percent cotton, which loses its softness when air dried. Sport socks nicely cushion your feet. It's impossible to look stylish when wearing walking shoes and these little white socks, but comfort's more important. Try silk or stretch lace undies, which dry faster than all cotton, but breathe more than nylon. Bring at least two bras (what if you leave one hanging over your shower rail by accident?). A sports bra doubles as a hiking/sunning top. You don't need a bikini to try sunbathing topless on European beaches. Local women with one-piece bathing suits just roll down the top.

Jacket: Neutral colors (black, beige, loden green) look more European than bright colors if you want to fit in. If your waterproof jacket doesn't have a hood, take a mini-umbrella or buy one in Europe. These are easy to find—vendors often appear with the rain.

Shoulder and Off-season Variations: Silk long johns are great for layering, weigh next to nothing, and dry out quickly. Bring gloves and some kind of hat. Wear shoes that are water-resistant or waterproof.

Toiletries: All feminine products (even many of the same brands) are sold all over Europe, but it's easier to figure out how many tampons, pads, or panty shields you'll need and bring them with you rather than having to buy a too-small or too-large box in Europe. If you bring birth control pills (or any timed-dosage prescription), take the time difference into account. If you usually take a pill with breakfast, take it with lunch or dinner in Europe. Remember to bring the pills on the plane each way to take at your home-dosage time, too.

Accessorize, accessorize: Scarves give your limited wardrobe just the color it needs. They dress up your outfit, are lightweight and easy to pack, and, if purchased in Europe, make a great souvenir. Sleeveless vests and button-up cardigans can be worn alone or mixed-and-matched with other clothes to give you several different looks. A crushable hat is handy for sunny or cold days. Most women feel safe wearing engagement/wedding rings while traveling, but leave other valuable or flashy jewelry at home. A few pairs of inexpensive earrings are fun to bring.

European map. Get a map best suited to your trip's overall needs and pick up maps for specific local areas as you go.

Address list. A list of e-mail addresses and mailing addresses will help keep you in touch. Taking a whole address book is not packing light. Consider typing your mail list onto a sheet of gummed address labels before you leave. You'll know exactly who you've written to, and the labels will be perfectly legible.

Postcards or small picture book from your hometown, and family pictures. A zip-lock baggie of show-and-tell things is always a great conversation piece with Europeans you meet.

Journal. An empty book to be filled with the experiences of your trip will be your most treasured souvenir. Use a hardbound type designed to last a lifetime, rather than a spiral notebook. Attach a photocopied calendar page of your itinerary.

Small notepad and pen. A tiny notepad in your back pocket is a great organizer, reminder, and communication aid (for sale in European stationery stores).

OPTIONAL BRING-ALONGS

*Indicates items available through our Back Door Catalog (call 425/771-8303 or visit www.ricksteves.com).

Robe or nightshirt. Especially for women.

Sunscreen.

*Inflatable pillow (or "neck nest") for sun snoozing.

Pillowcase. It's cleaner and possibly more comfortable to stuff your own.

Hair drier. People with long or thick hair appreciate a travel hair drier in the off-season, when hair takes a long time to dry and it's cold outside (see Electricity, below). These are generally provided in $100+ hotel rooms.

Light warm-up suit. Use for pajamas, evening lounge outfit, instant modest street wear, smuggling things, and going down the hall.

Teva-type sandals or thongs.

Leather-bottomed slippers. These are great for the flight and for getting cozy in your hotel room.

*Small flashlight. Handy for reading under the sheets after "lights out" in the hostel, late night trips down the hall, exploring castle dungeons, and hypnotizing street thieves.

Stronger light bulbs. You can buy these in Europe to give your cheap hotel room more brightness than the 25- to 40-watt norm.

A good paperback. There's plenty of empty time on a trip to either be bored or enjoy some good reading.

Radio, Walkman, or recorder. Partners can bring a Y-jack for two sets of earphones. Some travelers use microcassette recorders to record pipe organs, tours, or journal entries. Some recorders have radios, adding a new dimension to your experience.

Collapsible cup.

Office supplies. Bring paper, an envelope of envelopes, and some sticky notes such as Post-Its to keep your place in your guidebook.

Small roll of duct tape.

Mailing tube. Great for art lovers, this protects the posters and prints you buy along your trip. Trim it to fit inside your backpack.

Collapsible umbrella.

*Tiny lock. Use it to lock your rucksack zippers shut.

Spot remover. Bring Shout wipes or a dab of Goop in a film canister.

Bug juice. Especially for France and Italy.

Gifts. Local kids love T-shirts and hologram cards, and gardeners appreciate flower seeds.

Poncho. Hard-core vagabonds use a poncho as protection in a rainstorm, a ground cloth for sleeping, or a beach or picnic blanket.

*Hostel sheet. Hostels require one. Bring your own (sewn up like a sleeping bag), buy one, or rent a sheet at hostels (about $4 per stay). It doubles as a beach or picnic blanket, comes in handy on overnight train rides, shields you from dirty blankets in mountain huts, and will save you money in other dorm-type accommodations, which often charge extra for linen or don't provide it at all.

*Adapters (electrical plugs). See below.

ELECTRICITY

Try to go without electrical gear. Travelers requiring electricity need a converter to let their American appliance work on the European current and an adapter to allow the American plug to fit into the European wall. Many travel accessories come with a built-in converter. Look for voltages marked 120 (U.S.) and 240 (Europe). Often, buying a new travel appliance with a built-in converter can be cheaper than buying a separate converter (often $30) to use with your old appliance. Regardless, you'll still need an adapter. Secure your adapter to your appliance plug with duct tape; otherwise it'll stay in the outlet (and get left behind) when you pull out the plug.

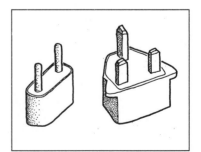

Two prongs for the Continent, three for Britain

British plugs have three big flat prongs, and continental European plugs have two small round prongs. Many sockets in Europe are recessed into the wall. Your adapter should be small enough to fit into this hole in order for your prongs to connect. Cheap converters with built-in adapters have prongs that are the right size but are unable to connect.

Many budget hotel rooms have only one outlet, occupied by the lamp. Hardware stores in Europe sell cheap three-bangers that let you keep the lamp on and still plug in your toothbrush and Game Boy.

PLANNING YOUR ITINERARY

5. When to Go

In travel industry jargon, the year is divided into three seasons: peak season (roughly late June, July, and August), shoulder season (May, early June, September, early October), and off-season (mid-October through April). Each has its pros and cons.

PEAK SEASON STRATEGIES

Except for the crowds, summer is a great time to travel. The sunny weather, long days, and exuberant nightlife turn Europe into a powerful magnet. I haven't missed a peak season in 25 years. Here are a few crowd-minimizing tips that I've learned:

Arrange your trip with crowd control in mind. Consider, for instance, a six-week European trip beginning June 1, half with a Eurailpass to see the famous sights and half visiting relatives in Scotland. It would be wise to do the Eurail section first, enjoying those precious last three weeks of relatively uncrowded shoulder season, and then spend time with the family during the last half of your vacation, when Florence and Salzburg are teeming with tourists. Salzburg on June 10 and Salzburg on July 10 are two very different cities.

Seek out places with no promotional budgets. Keep in mind that accessibility and promotional budgets determine a place's fame and popularity just as much as its worthiness as a tourist attraction. For example, Zurich is big and famous—with nothing special to offer the visitor. The beaches of Greece's Peloponnesian Peninsula enjoy the same weather and water as the highly promoted isles of Mykonos and Ios but are out of the way, not promoted, and wonderfully deserted. If you're traveling by car or bike, take advantage of your mobility by leaving the well-worn tourist routes. The Europe away from the train tracks seems more peaceful and relaxed. Overlooked by the Eurail mobs, it's one step behind the modern parade.

Hit the back streets. So many people energetically jockey themselves into the most crowded square of the most crowded city in the most crowded month (St. Mark's Square, Venice, July) and complain about the crowds. You could be in Venice in July and walk six blocks behind St. Mark's Basilica, step into a café, and be greeted by Venetians who act as though they've never seen a tourist.

Spend the night. Popular daytrip destinations near big cities and resorts such as Toledo (near Madrid), San Marino (near huge Italian beach resorts),

St. Mark's Square in July—no wonder Venice is sinking.

and San Gimignano (near Florence) take on a more peaceful and enjoyable atmosphere at night, when the legions of daytrippers retreat to the predictable plumbing of their big-city hotels. Small towns normally lack hotels big enough for tour groups and are often inaccessible to large buses. So they will experience, at worst, midday crowds.

Be an early bird. Walk around Rothenburg's ancient wall at breakfast time, before the tour buses pull in and turn the town into a medieval theme park. Crack-of-dawn joggers and walkers enjoy a special look at wonderfully medieval cities as they yawn and stretch and prepare for the daily onslaught of the 21st century.

See how the locals live. Residential neighborhoods rarely see a tourist. Browse through a department store. Buy a copy of the local *Better Homes and Thatches* and use it to explore that particular culture. Dance with the locals. Play street soccer with the neighborhood gang.

Plan your museum sightseeing carefully. Avoid museums on their weekly free days, when they're most crowded. And because nearly all Parisian museums are closed on Tuesday, nearby Versailles, which is open, is predictably crowded—very crowded. And it follows that Parisian museums are especially crowded on Monday and Wednesday. While crowds at the Louvre can't be avoided altogether, leaving home with a thoughtful itinerary can help. (For more tips, see Chapter 23: Museum Strategies.)

Arrive at the most popular sights early or late in the day to avoid tour groups. Germany's fairy-tale Neuschwanstein Castle is cool and easy with relaxed guides and no crowds at 8:30 or 9:00 in the morning. And very late in the day—when most tourists are long gone, exhausted in their rooms or searching for dinner—I linger alone, taking artistic liberties with some of Europe's greatest art in empty galleries.

London fog is a good day . . . dress for rain.

It's Tuesday at Versailles, and these people now have time to read their guidebooks, which warn: On Tuesday, most Paris museums are closed, and Versailles has very long lines.

Be aware of the exceptions. Although Europe's tourist crowds can generally be plotted on a bell-shaped curve peaking in July and August, there are odd glitches. For instance, Paris is relatively empty in July and August but packed full in June (air show) and September (fashion shows). Hotels in Scandinavia are cheapest in the summer, when travel—which, up there, is mostly business travel—is down.

In much of Europe (especially Italy and France), cities are partially shut down in July and August, when local urbanites take their beach break. You'll hear that these are terrible times to travel, but it's really no big deal. You can't get a dentist and many Laundromats are shut down, but tourists are basically unaffected by Europe's mass holidays. Just don't get caught on the wrong road on the first or 15th of the month (when vacations often start or finish) or try to compete with all of Europe for a piece of French Riviera beach in August.

SHOULDER SEASON

For many, "shoulder season"—April, May, early June, September, and early October—offers the best mix of peak-season and off-season pros and cons. In shoulder season you'll enjoy decent weather, long days, fewer crowds, and a local tourist industry that is still eager to please and entertain.

The main itinerary concerns between spring and fall: The Mediterranean region is generally greener in spring and parched in summer. For hikers, the Alps are best in summer and early fall, because many good hiking trails stay snowed-in through the spring. The cooler months during spring and fall are peak season for Italy.

OFF-SEASON EUROPE

Each summer, Europe greets a stampede of sightseers and shoppers with erect postcard racks. Before jumping into the peak-season pig pile, consider an off-season trip.

The advantages of off-season traveling are many. Off-season airfares are often hundreds of dollars cheaper. With fewer crowds in Europe, you'll sleep cheaper. Many fine hotels drop their prices, and budget hotels will have plenty of vacancies. And, while many of the cheap alternatives to hotels will be closed, those still open are usually empty and, therefore, more comfortable.

Fit in: Which one is the tourist?

David C. Hoerlein

Off-season adventurers loiter all alone through Leonardo's home, ponder unpestered in Rome's Forum, kick up sand on virgin beaches, and chat with laid-back guards by log fires in French châteaus. In wintertime Venice you can be alone atop St. Mark's bell tower, watching the clouds of your breath roll over the Byzantine domes of the church to a horizon of cut-glass Alps. Below, on St. Mark's Square, pigeons fidget and wonder, "Where are the tourists?"

Off-season adventurers enjoy step-right-up service at banks and tourist offices and experience a more European Europe. Although many popular tourist-oriented parks, shows, and tours will be closed, off-season is in-season for the high culture: Vienna's Boys Choir, opera, and Spanish Riding School are in their crowd-pleasing glory.

But winter travel has its drawbacks. Because much of Europe is in Canadian latitudes, the days are short. It's dark by 5 p.m. The weather can be miserable—cold, windy, and drizzly—and then turn worse. But just as summer can be wet and gray, winter can be crisp and blue, and, even into mid-November, hillsides blaze with colorful leaves.

Off-season hours are limited. Some sights close down entirely, and most operate on shorter schedules (such as 10 a.m.–5 p.m. rather than 9 a.m.–7 p.m.), with darkness often determining the closing time. Winter sightseeing is fine in big cities, which bustle year-round, but it's more frustrating in small tourist towns, which often shut down entirely. In December many beach resorts are shut up as tight as canned hams. While Europe's wonderful outdoor evening ambience survives year-round in the south, wintertime streets are empty in the north after dark. English-language tours, common in the summer, are rare during the off-season, when most visitors are natives. Tourist information offices normally stay open year-round but with shorter hours in the winter. A final disadvantage of winter travel is loneliness. The solo traveler won't have the built-in camaraderie of other travelers that she would find in peak season.

To thrive in the winter, you'll need to get the most out of your limited daylight hours. Start early and eat a quick lunch. Tourist offices close early, so call ahead to double-check hours and confirm your plans. Pack for the cold and wet—layers, rainproof parka, gloves, wool hat, long johns, waterproof shoes, and an umbrella. Dress warmly. Cold weather is colder when you're outdoors trying to enjoy yourself all day long. And cheap hotels are not always adequately heated in the off-season. Use undershirts to limit the washing of slow-drying heavy shirts.

Empty beds abound in the off-season. I led an 18-day November tour of Germany, Italy, and France with 22 people and no room reservations. We'd amble into town around 5 p.m. and always found 22 beds well within our budget.

Most hotels charge less in the winter. To save some money, arrive late, notice how many empty rooms they have (keys on the rack), let them know you're a hosteler (student, senior, artist, or whatever) with a particular price limit, and bargain from there. The opposite is true of big-city business centers (especially in Berlin, Brussels, and the Scandinavian capitals), which are busiest and most expensive off-season.

Regardless of when you go, if your objective is to "meet the people," you'll find Europe filled with them 365 days a year.

6. Itinerary Skills

If you have any goals at all for your trip, make an itinerary. I never start a trip without having every day planned out. Your reaction to an itinerary may be, "Hey, won't my spontaneity and freedom suffer?" Not necessarily. Although I always begin a trip with a well-thought-out plan, I maintain my flexibility and make plenty of changes. An itinerary forces you to see the consequences of any spontaneous change you make while in Europe. For instance, if you spend two extra days in the sunny Alps, you'll see that you won't make it to, say, the Greek Isles. With the help of an itinerary, you can lay out your goals, maximize their potential, avoid regrettable changes...and impress your friends.

ITINERARY CONSIDERATIONS

If you deal thoughtfully with issues such as weather, culture shock, health maintenance, fatigue, and festivals, you'll travel happier.

Moderate the weather conditions you'll encounter. Match the coolest month of your trip with the warmest area, and vice versa. For a spring and early summer trip, enjoy comfortable temperatures throughout by starting in the southern countries and working your way north. If possible, avoid the midsummer Mediterranean heat. Spend those weeks in Scandinavia or the Alps. Scandinavia and Britain have miserable weather and none of the crowd problems that plague Italy and France. Ideally, forget crowd concerns and visit Britain and Scandinavia in the peak of summer. (See the appendix for climate charts.)

Mix in cities and villages. Alternate intense big cities with villages and countryside. For example, break a tour of Venice, Florence, and Rome with an easygoing time in the hill towns or on the Italian Riviera. Judging Italy by Rome is like judging America by New York City.

Join the celebration. Hit as many festivals, national holidays, and arts seasons as you can. This takes some study (for a starter, go to www .ricksteves.com/festivals). Ask the national tourist office of each country you'll visit (addresses listed in Chapter 2: Gathering Informaton) for a calendar of events. An effort to hit the right places at the right time will drape your trip with festive tinsel.

Save your energy for the biggies. Don't overestimate your powers of absorption. Rare is the tourist who doesn't become somewhat jaded after several weeks of travel. At the start of my trip, I'll seek out every great painting and cathedral I can. After two months, I find myself "seeing" cathedrals with a sweep of my head from the doorway, and I probably wouldn't cross the street for a Rembrandt. Don't burn out on mediocre castles, palaces, and museums. Sightsee selectively.

Establish a logical flight plan. It's been years since I flew in and out of the same city. You can avoid needless travel time and expense by flying "open-jaw"—into one port and out of another. You usually pay just half the round-trip fare for each port. Even if your open-jaw flight plan is more expensive than the cheapest round-trip fare, it may save you lots of time and money when surface connections are figured in. For example, you could fly into London, travel east through whatever interests you in Europe, and fly home from Athens. This would eliminate the costly and time-consuming return to London. Your travel agent will know where flying open-jaw is economical.

See countries in order of cultural hairiness. If you plan to see Britain, the Alps, Greece, and Turkey, do it in that order so you'll grow steadily into the more intense and crazy travel. England, compared to any place but the United States, is pretty dull. Don't get me wrong—it's a great place to travel. But go there first, when cream teas and roundabouts will be exotic. And you're more likely to enjoy Turkey if you work gradually east.

Save your good health. Visit countries that may be hazardous to your health (North Africa or the Middle East) at the end of your trip, so you won't needlessly jeopardize your healthy enjoyment of the safer countries. If you're going to get sick, do it at the end of your trip so you can recover at home, missing more work—not vacation.

Minimize one-night stands. Even the speediest itinerary should be a series of two-night stands. I'd stretch every other day with long hours on the road or train and hurried sightseeing along the way in order to enjoy the sanity of two nights in the same bed. Minimizing hotel changes saves time and money and gives you the sensation of actually being comfortable in a town on the second night.

Leave some slack in your itinerary. Don't schedule yourself too tightly (a common tendency). Everyday chores, small business matters, transportation problems, constipation, and planning mistakes deserve about one day of slack per week in your itinerary.

Punctuate a long trip with rest periods. Constant sightseeing is grueling. Schedule a peaceful period every two weeks. If your trip is a long one, schedule a vacation from your vacation in the middle of it. Most people need several days in a place where they couldn't see a museum or take a tour even if they wanted to. A stop in the mountains or on an island, in a friendly rural town, or at the home of a relative is a great way to revitalize your tourist spirit.

Assume you will return. This Douglas MacArthur approach is a key to touristic happiness. You can't really see Europe in one trip. Don't even try. Enjoy what you're seeing. Forget what you won't get to on this trip. If you worry about things that are just out of reach, you won't appreciate what's in your hand. I'm planning my 28th three-month European adventure, and I still need more time. I'm happy about what I can't get to. It's a blessing that we can never see all of Europe.

YOUR BEST ITINERARY IN EIGHT STEPS

1. Read up on Europe and talk to travelers. Do some reading, get a guidebook or two, take a class, write to the tourist offices. You must have some friends who'd love to show you their slides. What you want to see is determined by what you know (or don't know). Identify your personal interests: WWII buffs study up on battle sites; McGregors locate their clan in Scotland. This is a time to grow a forest of ideas from which you'll harvest the dream trip.

2. Decide on the places you want to see. Start by listing everything you'd like to see. Circle your destinations on a map. Have a reason for every stop. Don't go to Casablanca just because it's famous.

Minimize redundancy. On a quick trip, focus on only one part of the Alps. England's two most well-known university towns, Oxford and Cambridge, are redundant. Choose one (Cambridge).

Example: Places I want to see: London, Alps, Bavaria, Florence, Amsterdam, Paris, Rhine, Rome, Venice, Greece.

3. Establish a route and timeline. Figure out a logical geographical order and length for your trip. Pin down any places that you have to be on a certain date (and ask yourself if it's really worth the stifle). Once you've settled on a list, be satisfied with your efficient plan, and focus any more study and preparation only on places that fall along your proposed route.

4. Decide on the cities you'll fly in and out of. If your route is linear (like London to Athens), fly open-jaw. If it's circular, fly round-trip. Ask your travel agent about the cheapest, most convenient dates and ports.

Example: I can escape for 23 days.
Cheapest places to fly to: London, Frankfurt, Amsterdam.

5. Determine the mode of transportation. Do this not solely on economical terms but by analyzing what is best for the trip you envision.

Example: Since I'm traveling alone, going so many miles, and spending the majority of my time in big cities, I'd rather not mess with a car. I'll use a train pass.

6. Rough in an itinerary. Write in the number of days you'd like to stay in each place. Carefully consider travel time. Driving, except on superfreeways, is slower than in the U.S. Borrow a Thomas Cook Timetable from your travel agent or library or study Web sites (such as http://reiseauskunft.bahn.de /bin/query.exe/en) to get an idea of how long various train journeys will take. Learn which trains are fast, and avoid minor lines in southern countries. Use night trains (NT) or boats (NB) to save time and money whenever possible.

Sample Itinerary

Example: Logical order and desired time in each place:
Days
  3 *London*
  5 *Paris (NT)*
  3 *Alps (NT)*
  2 *Florence*
  3 *Rome (NT)*
  7 *Greece (NB or flight)*
  2 *Venice (NT)*
  3 *Munich/Bavaria*
  3 *Romantic Road/Rhine Cruise*
  <u>4</u> *Amsterdam*
35 *Notes: I have 23 days for my vacation. If I eliminate Greece, I'll still*
need to cut five days. Flying open-jaw into London and out of Amsterdam is eco-
nomical. "Logical" order may be affected by night-train possibilities.

**7. Adjust by cutting, streamlining, or adding to fit your timeline or
budget.** Minimize travel time. When you must cut something, cut to save
the most mileage. For instance, if Amsterdam and Berlin are equally important to you and you don't have time for both, cut the destination that saves
the most miles (in this case, Berlin).

Minimize clutter. A so-so sight (San Sebastian) breaking a convenient
night train (Paris–Madrid) into two half-day journeys is clutter.

Consider economizing on car rental or a Eurailpass. For instance, try
to manage a 23-day trip on a 15-day train pass by seeing London, Paris,
and Amsterdam before or after you use the pass.

Example: Itinerary adjusted to time limitations:
Days
  4 *London*
  3 *Paris (NT)*
  3 *Alps (NT)*
  1 *Florence*
  2 *Rome (NT)*
  2 *Venice (NT)*
  3 *Munich/Bavaria*
  2 *Romantic Road/Rhine Cruise*
  <u>3</u> *Amsterdam*
23 *Get a 15-day Eurailpass (valid from last day in Paris until first day*
in Amsterdam).

8. Fine tune. Study your guidebook. Maximize festival and market days.

SAMPLE ITINERARY

SEPTEMBER

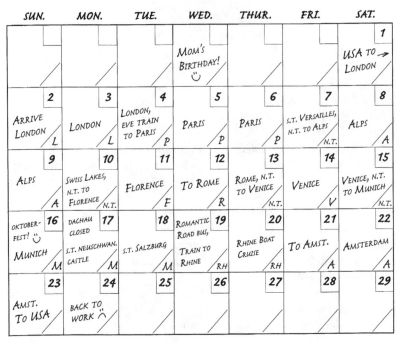

SUN.	MON.	TUE.	WED.	THUR.	FRI.	SAT.
			MOM'S BIRTHDAY! ☺			**1** USA TO → LONDON
2 ARRIVE LONDON / L	**3** LONDON / L	**4** LONDON, EVE TRAIN TO PARIS / P	**5** PARIS / P	**6** PARIS / P	**7** S.T. VERSAILLES, N.T. TO ALPS / N.T.	**8** ALPS / A
9 ALPS / A	**10** SWISS LAKES, N.T. TO FLORENCE / N.T.	**11** FLORENCE / F	**12** TO ROME / R	**13** ROME, N.T. TO VENICE / N.T.	**14** VENICE / V	**15** VENICE, N.T. TO MUNICH / N.T.
16 OKTOBER-FEST! ☺ MUNICH / M	**17** DACHAU CLOSED S.T. NEUSCHWAN. CASTLE / M	**18** S.T. SALZBURG / M	**19** ROMANTIC ROAD BUS, TRAIN TO RHINE / RH	**20** RHINE BOAT CRUISE / RH	**21** TO AMST. / A	**22** AMSTERDAM / A
23 AMST. TO USA /	**24** BACK TO WORK ⌢ /	**25** /	**26** /	**27** /	**28** /	**29** /

INITIAL IN THE BOTTOM RIGHT INDICATES WHERE TO SPEND EACH NIGHT.

N.T. = NIGHT TRAIN   **S.T.** = SIDE TRIP

Be sure crucial sights are open the day you'll be in town. Remember that most cities close many of their major tourist attractions for one day during the week. It would be a shame to be in Madrid only on a Monday when the Prado is *cerrado*. Monday is also bad in Brussels, Munich, Lisbon, and Florence. Paris closes the Louvre and many other sights on Tuesday. Write out a day-by-day itinerary.

Example: According to the guidebooks, I must keep these points in mind as I plan my trip. London: Theaters closed on Sunday, Speaker's Corner is Sunday only. Paris: Most museums are closed on Tuesdays. Versailles and the Orsay Museum are closed on Monday. Florence: Museums are closed on Monday. Dachau: Closed on Monday. Note that I'm choosing to pay a little extra on my flight to let my trip stretch over the weekends and minimize lost work time. Yes, I may be a zombie on that first Monday back, but, hey, what's more important?

*My Favorite Home-Base Cities
and Their Best Daytrips:*

Madrid: Toledo, Segovia, El Escorial, and even Sevilla and
Córdoba with the AVE bullet trains

Amsterdam: Alkmaar, Enkhuisen's Zuiderzee Museum,
Arnhem's Folk Museum and Kröller-Müller Museum,
Scheveningen, Delft, and most of the Netherlands

Copenhagen: Frederiksborg Castle, Roskilde, Helsingør,
Odense, and Malmo (Sweden)

Paris: Versailles, Chartres, Fontainebleau, Chantilly,
Giverny, Reims

London: Bath, Stonehenge, Stratford, Cambridge, York,
and many others

Arles: Pont du Gard, Nîmes, Avignon, and all of Provence

Florence: Siena, Pisa, San Gimignano, and many small towns

Venice: Padua, Vicenza, Verona, and Ravenna

Munich: Salzburg, King Ludwig's castles (Neuschwanstein,
Linderhof, and Chiemsee), Wies Church, Oberammergau,
and other small Bavarian towns

Sorrento: Naples, Pompeii, Herculaneum, Mount Vesuvius,
Amalfi Coast, Paestum, and Capri

Dublin: Newgrange, the Wicklow Mountains, and Belfast

THE HOME-BASE STRATEGY

The home-base strategy is a clever way to make your trip itinerary
smoother, simpler, and more efficient. Set yourself up in a central location and use that place as a base for daytrips to nearby attractions.

The home-base approach minimizes set-up time (usually an hour).
Searching for a good hotel can be exhausting, frustrating, and time-
consuming. And hotels often give a better price, or at least more smiles, for
longer stays. Many private homes don't accept those staying only one night.

You are freed from your luggage. Being able to leave your luggage
in the hotel lets you travel freely and with the peace of mind that you are
set up for the night.

You feel "at home" in your home-base town. This comfortable
feeling takes more than a day to get, and when you are changing locations
every day or two, you may never enjoy this important rootedness. Home-
basing allows you to sense the rhythm of daily life.

Daytrip to a village, enjoy the nightlife in a city. The home-base

approach lets you spend the evening in a city, where there is some exciting nightlife. Most small countryside towns die after 9 p.m. If you're not
dead by 9 p.m., you'll enjoy more action in a larger city.

Transportation is a snap. Europe's generally frequent and punc-
tual train and bus systems (which often operate out of a hub anyway) make
this home-base strategy practical. With a train pass, trips are "free"; otherwise, the transportation is reasonable, often with reductions offered for
round-trip tickets.

Resources: My country guidebooks are made to order for this home-
base approach. They give you the necessary step-by-step details for all of
Europe's best home bases. The king of the daytrippers, Earl Steinbicker,
has written an entire series of *Daytrips* books for London, Holland/
Belgium/Luxembourg, France, Italy, Germany, and Switzerland. Earl's
sidekick, Norman Renouf, wrote the Spain/Portugal edition of *Daytrips*
(published by Hastings House). For Ireland, try Patricia Preston's *Daytrips
Ireland*. Drivers might opt for Frommer's *Best-Loved Driving Tours* for Western Europe, Britain, France, Germany, Ireland, Italy, Scotland, and Spain.

HIGH-SPEED TOWN-HOPPING

When I tell people that I saw three or four towns in one day, many think,
"Insane! Nobody can really see several towns in a day!" Of course, it's
folly to go too fast, but many stop-worthy towns take only an hour or two
to cover. Don't let feelings of guilt tell you to slow down and stay longer
if you really are finished with a town. There's so much more to see in the
rest of Europe. Going too slow is as bad as going too fast.

If you're efficient and use the high-speed town-hopping method,
you'll amaze yourself at what you can see in a day. Let me explain with
an example.

You wake up early in Town A. Checking out of your hotel, you have
one sight to cover before your 10 a.m. train. (You checked the train schedule the night before.) After the sightseeing and before getting to the station, you visit the open-air market and buy the ingredients for your brunch
and pick up a Town B map and tourist brochure at Town A's tourist office.

From 10 to 11 a.m. you travel by train to Town B. During that hour
you have a restful brunch, enjoy the passing scenery, and prepare for
Town B by reading your literature and deciding what you want to see.
Just before your arrival, you put the items you need (camera, jacket, tourist
information) into your small daypack and, upon arrival, check the rest of
your luggage in a locker. Virtually every station has storage lockers or a
baggage check desk.

Before leaving Town B's station, write down on a scrap of paper the departure times of the next few trains to Town C. Now you can sightsee as much or as little as you want and still know when to comfortably catch your train.

Town B is great. After a snack in the park, you catch the train at 2:30 p.m. By 3 p.m. you're in Town C, where you repeat the same procedure you followed in Town B. Town C just isn't what it was cracked up to be so, after a walk along the waterfront and a look at the church, you catch the first train out.

You arrive in Town D, the last town on the day's agenda, by 5:30 p.m. The man in the station directs you to a good budget pension two blocks down the street. You're checked in and unpacked in no time, and, after a few horizontal moments, it's time to find a good restaurant and eat dinner. After a meal and an evening stroll, you're ready to call it a day. Writing in your journal it occurs to you: This was one heck of a sightseeing day. You spent it high-speed town-hopping.

7. Itinerary Issues and Sample Routes

After years of designing bus tours, brainstorming with my guides, and helping travelers plan their itineraries, I've come up with some fun and efficient three-week plans. These itineraries are the routes covered in my various country guidebooks. Each of these guidebooks gives you all the details you'll need for successful navigation.

This chapter also offers tips on crossing the Channel via the Chunnel; traveling through Belgium, Germany, and Italy; long-jumping to Greece; and seeing the best (and missing the worst) of Europe.

"The Chunnel"—Getting from
Great Britain to France

The fastest and most convenient way to travel between Big Ben and the Eiffel Tower is now by rail. Eurostar, a joint service of the Belgian, British, and French railways, is the speedy passenger train that zips you (and up to 800 others in 18 TGV-type cars) between downtown London and downtown Paris (15 trains/day, 3-hour ride) or Brussels (10/day, 3 hours) faster and easier than flying. The train goes 100 mph in England and 160 mph on the Continent. The actual tunnel crossing is a 17-minute black, silent, 100 mph nonevent. Your ears won't even pop.

Chunnel fares are affordable—particularly the cheaper Leisure Tickets. You'll pay essentially the same whether your destination is Brussels, Paris, or London. Note that a round-trip ticket is sometimes cheaper than a one-way ticket. (You can forget to return.)

For the latest fares, call Rail Europe at 800/EU-ROSTAR. The following fares (one-way unless otherwise noted) are U.S. prices from 2001:

First class: A regular first-class ticket costs $279 (including a meal on board—a dinner departure nets you more grub than breakfast). Tickets are fully refundable even after your departure date. You can save money by getting a first-class Leisure Ticket for $219, though it's

Crossing the English Channel

only 50 percent refundable up to three days before departure. Unless you're Bill Gates, skip Premium First Class for $369 (Eurostar lounge privileges, exclusive compartment, taxi on arrival).

Second class: Second ("standard") class is $199 (fully refundable even after departure date) or only $139 for a Leisure Ticket (50 percent refundable up to 3 days before departure).

Discounts: Discounted fares are available for travelers holding railpasses that include France, Belgium, or Britain ($155 for first class, $75 for second); youths under 26 ($79 in second class); and children under 12 (about half fare). Seniors over 60 pay $189 for a regular first-class ticket. Passholder, youth, and senior tickets are fully refundable up to three days before departure.

Round-Trip: Leisure Round-Trip tickets ($248 for first class and $158 for second) are nonrefundable and cannot be changed.

Buying tickets: Cheaper seats can sell out. Ideally, buy a ticket before leaving home. Compare fares sold by U.S. rail agents (www.raileurope.com) and British agents (www.eurostar.co.uk). If you're ready to commit to a date, time, and U.S. prices, you can book by calling 800/EUROSTAR, visiting www.raileurope.com, or having your travel agent do it all for you (prices do not include cost of FedEx ticket delivery). If you prefer the British prices, book by calling 44/1233-617575 or visiting www.eurostar.co.uk; inexpensive but nonrefundable round-trip Apex tickets are available with 7- or 14-day advance purchase (pick up ticket at station). For maximum spontaneity, buy your tickets in Europe at any major train station.

Bus option: Riding the bus through the Chunnel takes more than twice as long as the Eurostar train at about half the cost. Round-trips are a bargain (London to Paris by Eurolines bus: $45 one-way, $75 round-trip, 9 hours, call 44/8705-143-219 outside the U.K. or 08705-143-219 inside the U.K., or visit www.eurolines.com).

Belgium

Anyone taking the six-hour train ride from Paris to Amsterdam will stop in Brussels, but few even consider getting out. Each train stops in Brussels, and there's always another train coming in an hour or so. Leave an hour early, arrive an hour late, and give yourself two hours in one of Europe's underrated cities. Luckily for the rushed tourist, Brussels Central Station has easy money-changing and baggage-storage facilities and puts you two blocks (just walk downhill) from the local and help-

Belgium's little squirt

David C. Hoerlein

ful tourist office, a colorful pedestrian-only city core, Europe's greatest city square (Grand Place), and its most overrated and tacky sight, the *Manneken Pis* (a much-photographed statue of a little boy who thinks he's a fountain). Brussels has three stations: Nord, Midi, and Central. Ask if your train stops at Central (middle) Station. If you have to get off at Nord or Midi, there are local subwaylike connecting trains every few minutes. You'll have no trouble finding English-speaking help.

The Best of Germany

The most interesting sightseeing route through Germany follows the most prosperous trade route of medieval Germany: down the Rhine, along the "Romantic Road" from Frankfurt to Munich, and through Bavaria near the Austrian border. While this can be done in two days, it's worth up to a week.

While many travelers spend too much time cruising the Rhine and not enough time in castles, I'd cruise just the best hour (St. Goar to Bacharach) and get some hands-on castle experience crawling through what was once the Rhine's mightiest fortress, Rheinfels (see Chapter 58).

From the end of this most impressive section of the Rhine, it's a short train ride to Frankfurt, the launching pad for a train or bus ride along the Romantic Road (Chapter 43) through Germany's medieval heartland.

From there, the old trading route crossed the Alps (today's Brenner Pass) and headed into Italy, which makes sense for today's travelers as well.

How Much Italy?

Italy is Europe's richest cultural brew. Get out of the Venice-Florence-Rome crush and enjoy its hill towns and Riviera ports. Italy intensifies as you go south. If you like Italy as far south as Rome, go farther. It gets better. If Italy is getting on your nerves by the time you get to Rome, don't go farther south. It gets worse. For most first-timers, after a week in Italy, Switzerland starts looking really good. The travelers I respect most count Italy as one of their favorite countries.

By train, you might consider seeing everything except Venice on your way south. Enjoy a romantic day in Sorrento before catching the overnight train from Naples, arriving in Venice for brunch, canalside.

Sailing from Italy to Greece

Italy to Greece

Brindisi, the spur on the Italian boot, is at the end of a funnel where thousands of Eurailers, backpackers, and various other travelers fall out to catch the boat for a 21-hour overnight passage to Patras, Greece. Getting on the boat is no problem without reservations except at peak season (Italy to Greece from late July to mid-August; Greece to Italy from about August 11 to September 3), when it's a mob scene.

Making reservations at a travel agency in Italy or Greece: Prices for the Italy–Greece connection vary, depending on which Italian port you choose (Brindisi, Bari, or Ancona) and whether you have a railpass.

The Eurailpass, Europass, and Eurail Selectpass cover all three routes. Hellenic Mediterranean Lines runs between Brindisi and Patras on alternate days year-round (schedules at a travel agency's site at www.ferries.gr /hml). The Superfast Attika Line operates the Bari–Patras and Ancona–Patras routes (www.superfast.com). Traveling on Superfast shaves several hours off your journey (e.g., 15.5 hours from Ancona to Patras compared with 21 hours on the more popular Brindisi–Patras route). Bari and Ancona may offer fewer crowds and ticket hawkers than Brindisi. For more schedule info, see www.youra.com/ferry/intlferries.html.

I'll cover the popular Brindisi–Patras route here. Tickets cost about $25 (low season) to $50 (high season) for basic deck class. On some ships "deck" is taken literally, and it's chilly at night, even in summer; vagabonds can spend the night in the bar or in the restaurant after hours. An airplane-type seat indoors costs about $20. For more comfort, pay $40 to $75 for a bed in a four-person stateroom. During the mid-June to mid-September rush, crossing prices are $20 higher. Students under 30 and anyone under 26 saves about $10. Cars cost $50 (high season), and bikes go for free.

A Eurailpass, Europass, or Eurail Selectpass gives you free deck-class passage, but you'll have to pay a reservation fee, a $7 port tax, and, if traveling in the summer, a $20 peak-season supplement. You can get a stopover halfway on the lush and popular island of Corfu for the mere cost of two sets of port taxes ($14). Just get "S.O. Corfu" marked on your ticket when you buy it.

For a summer crossing (particularly in August), make a reservation at least three days in advance from an Italian or Greek travel agency (easy but with varying service charges) or, ideally, go direct to a Hellenic Mediterranean Line office.

On arrival in Brindisi, follow the mob on the half-mile stampede from the train station down the city's main drag to the dock. You can walk, taxi, take a city bus, or see if you can hop a shuttle bus offered by the boat lines for ticket holders.

You'll see several agencies along the way that sell tickets and handle boat-related business such as reserving staterooms, collecting port taxes and Eurail supplements, and distributing boarding passes. Be wary of thieves. Expect con artists to tell you your railpass doesn't work on today's boat or some similar nonsense. At the port, check in at the boat office two hours before departure or face the (slight) risk of being turned away. Then board your boat. The crossing from Patras to Brindisi features similar touts and headaches. Off-season, I'd go to the port and bargain. Student discounts are often given to anyone who asks for them.

The Patras-to-Athens connection is a four- to five-hour train ride or a frightening three-hour bus ride. (The fear welds some special friendships on the bus.) Even with a railpass, I'd buy the $15 bus ticket with the boat ticket. Buses meet the boat—don't dally. Upon arrival in Athens, expect a welcoming committee of hotel runners and locals with rooms to rent. Consider putting off Athens and hooking south through the fascinating Peloponnesian Peninsula. Start with the hour-long bus ride (leaving Patras every two hours) to Olympia.

Brindisi is well connected by night trains from Rome, Milan, and Venice. Overnight trains arrive in Brindisi in the morning, and the boats to Greece leave in the evening, so you'll likely have time to kill in Brindisi. Consider spending it in Lecce, a hot, noble, but sleepy city of lovely Baroque facades and Roman ruins; pick up a map of this confusing town at the three-star hotel in front of the Lecce train station (just 30 minutes south of Brindisi). For one last Italian beach, try Apani (30 minutes north of Brindisi on the Adriatic coast). The beach is fair and the water is clean.

To Greece or Not to Greece?

Many itineraries are really stressed by people who underestimate the travel time involved and wrongly plug in Greece. By car or train, it takes two days of solid travel—if all goes well—to get from Rome to Athens, and two days to get back. If all you've got is a week for Greece, I question the sanity of traveling four days for a couple of days in huge, overrated, and polluted Athens and a quick trip to an island, especially when you consider that 500 years before Christ, southern Italy was called Magna Graecia (Greater Greece). You can find excellent Greek ruins at Paestum, just south of Naples. Greece is great, but it needs more time or an open-jaw plan that lets you fly out of Athens.

In the summer, Greece is the most touristed, least explored country in Europe. It seems that nearly all of its tourists are in a few places, while the rest of the country casually goes about its traditional business.

The Britain/Europe/Greece Plan

Here's an efficient overall plan for a six-week introduction to Europe: Fly into London and spend four days. Rent a car for a week in England (Bath, Cotswolds, Blenheim, Warwick, Ironbridge Gorge, North Wales). Drop the car in North Wales. Catch the boat to Dublin and take a look at West Ireland. Begin your 21-day Eurailpass to catch the discounted 20-hour boat ride from southeast Ireland to France. Spend three weeks touring central Europe (Paris, Benelux, Rhine, Romantic Road, Bavaria, Swiss Alps, Italy, boat to Athens, where train pass expires). Relax in the Greek Isles before flying home from Athens.

The Best and Worst of Europe—With No Apologies

Good travel writers should make hard choices and give the reader solid opinions. Just so nobody will accuse me of gutlessness, I've assembled a pile of spunky opinions. Chances are that you have too many stops on your trip wish list and not enough time. To make your planning a little easier, heed these warnings. These are just my personal feelings after 100 months of European travel. And, if you disagree with any of them, you obviously haven't been there.

Let's start with the dullest corner of the British Isles, south Scotland. It's so boring the Romans decided to block it off with Hadrian's Wall. Hadrian's Wall, near the town of Haltwhistle, is far more intriguing than the area beyond it. Like Venice's St. Mark's Square at midnight and Napoleon's tomb in Paris, this sight covers history buffs with goose bumps.

London, York, Bath, and Edinburgh are the most interesting cities in Britain. Belfast, Liverpool, and Glasgow are quirky enough to be called interesting. Oxford pales next to Cambridge, and Stratford is little more than Shakespeare's house—and that's as dead as he is.

The west coast of Ireland (the Dingle Peninsula), Snowdon National Park, and the Windermere Lakes District are the most beautiful natural regions of Great Britain and Ireland. The York Moors disappoint all creatures great and small.

Italy's island of Capri, the German town of Berchtesgaden, Ireland's Blarney Stone (kissed by countless tourists to get the "gift of gab"), and the French Riviera in July and August are Europe's top tourist traps. The tackiest souvenirs are found next to Pisa's tower and in Lourdes.

Extra caution is merited in southwest England, a minefield of tourist traps. The British are masters at milking every conceivable tourist attraction for all it's worth. Here are some booby traps: the Devil's Toenail (a rock that looks just like . . . a toenail), Land's End (pay, pay, pay), and cloying Clovelly (a one-street town lined with knickknack shops selling the same goodies—like "clotted cream that you can mail home"). While Tintagel's castle, famous as the legendary birthplace of King Arthur, offers thrilling windswept and wave-beaten ruins, the town of Tintagel does everything in its little power to exploit the profitable Arthurian legend. There's even a pub in town called the Excali Bar.

Sognefjord is Norway's most spectacular fjord. The Geiranger fjord—while famous as a cruise-ship stop—is a disappointment. The most boring countryside is Sweden's (I am Norwegian), although Scandinavia's best medieval castle is in the Swedish town of Kalmar.

Zurich and Geneva, two of Switzerland's largest and most sterile cities, share the "nice place

Geneva's newspaper objects to my denigrating its dull city on the Internet.

to live but I wouldn't want to visit" award. Both are pleasantly situated on a lake—like Buffalo and Cleveland. And both are famous, but name familiarity is a rotten reason to go somewhere. If you want a Swiss city, see Bern, but it's almost criminal to spend a sunny Swiss day anywhere but high in the Alps.

Bordeaux must mean boredom in some ancient language. If I were offered a free trip to that town, I'd stay home and clean the fridge. Connoisseurs visit for the wine, but Bordeaux wine country and Bordeaux city are as different as night and night soil. There's a wine-tourist information bureau in Bordeaux that, for a price, will bus you out of town into the more interesting wine country nearby.

Andorra, a small country in the Pyrenees between France and Spain, is as scenic as any other chunk of those mountains. People from all over Europe flock to Andorra to take advantage of its famous duty-free shopping. As far as Americans are concerned, Andorra is just a big Spanish-speaking Radio Shack. There are no bargains here that you can't get at home. Enjoy the Pyrenees with less traffic elsewhere.

Germany's famous Black Forest disappoints more people than it excites. If that's all Germany offered, it would be worth seeing. For Europeans, any large forest is a popular attraction. But I'd say the average American visitor who's seen more than three trees in one place would prefer Germany's Romantic Road and Bavaria to the east, the Rhine and Mosel country to the north, the Swiss Alps to the south, and France's Alsace region to the west—all high points that cut the Black Forest down to stumps.

Norway's Stavanger, famous for nearby fjords and its status as an oil boom town, is a large port that's about as exciting as, well, put it this way... emigrants left it in droves to move to the wilds of Minnesota. Time in western Norway is better spent in and around Bergen.

Bucharest, the capital of Romania, has little to offer. Its top-selling postcard is of the Intercontinental Hotel. If you're heading from eastern Europe to Greece, skip Thessaloníki, which deserves its place in the Bible but doesn't belong in travel guidebooks.

Europe's most scenic train ride is across south Switzerland from Chur to Martigny. The most scenic boat ride is from Stockholm to Helsinki—countless islands and blondes. Europe's most underrated sight is Rome's ancient seaport Ostia Antica, its most misunderstood wine is Portugal's *vinho verde* (green wine), and its most overrated and polluted city is Athens.

Nineteenth-century Athens was a sleepy town of 8,000 people with a pile of ruins in its backyard. Today it's a giant mix of concrete, smog, noise, tourists, and four million Greeks. See the four major attractions (the Acropolis, Agora, Plaka, and great National Archaeological Museum) and get out to the islands or countryside.

THE BEST OF GREAT BRITAIN
in 22 days

Day 01 Arrive in London,
        bus to Bath

Day 02 Bath

Day 03 Pick up car, Avebury,
        Wells, Glastonbury

Day 04 South Wales, St. Fagans,
        Tintern

Day 05 Explore the Cotswolds,
        Blenheim

Day 06 Stratford, Warwick,
        Coventry

Day 07 Ironbridge Gorge,
        Ruthin banquet

Day 08 Highlights of
        North Wales

Day 09 Liverpool, Blackpool

Day 10 Southern Lake District

Day 11 Northern Lake District

Day 12 Drive up west coast
        of Scotland

Day 13 Highlands, Loch Ness,
        Scenic Drive

Day 14 More Highlands or
        Edinburgh

Day 15 Edinburgh

Day 16 Hadrian's Wall, Beamish,
        Durham evensong

Day 17 York Moors, York,
        turn in car

Day 18 York

Day 19 Early train to London

Day 20 London

Day 21 London

Day 22 Side trip to Cambridge or
        Greenwich, London

While this itinerary is designed to be done by car, it can be done by train and bus, or, better yet, with a rail 'n' drive pass (best car days: Cotswolds, North Wales, Lake District, Scottish Highlands, Hadrian's Wall). For three weeks without a car, I'd probably cut back on the recommended sights with the most frustrating public transportation (South and North Wales, Ironbridge Gorge, the Highlands). Lacing together the cities by train is very slick. With more time, everything is workable without a car.

For all the specifics, see *Rick Steves' Great Britain 2002*.

THE BEST OF IRELAND
in 14 days

Day 01 Arrive in
         Dublin

Day 02 Dublin

Day 03 Dublin

Day 04 Dublin to
         Kilkenny via
         Glendalough

Day 05 Kilkenny to
         Dingle via
         Cashel

Day 06 Dingle
         Peninsula

Day 07 Easy day in
         Dingle town

Day 08 Dingle to
         Galway via
         Cliffs of Moher
         and the Burren

Day 09 Galway or daytrip to Aran
         Islands

Day 10 Galway to Portrush, with
         stop in Londonderry

Day 11 Antrim Coast: Giant's
         Causeway, Bushmills, and
         Portrush

Day 12 Portrush to Belfast

Day 13 Belfast

Day 14 Belfast to Dublin via
         Newgrange

While this itinerary is designed to be done by car (picked up on Day 4 as you leave Dublin), it could be done with public transportation. Without a car, you might loop back to Dublin after Galway and do the north as a side trip from Dublin (taking advantage of the speedy Dublin–Belfast express train). It may be efficient to end the trip in Belfast and connect from there to Scotland, London, or back home.

For all the specifics, see *Rick Steves' Ireland 2002*.

THE BEST OF FRANCE
in 22 days

Day 01 Arrive in Paris
Day 02 Paris
Day 03 Paris
Day 04 Paris
Day 05 Into Normandy
Day 06 Bayeux, D-Day
        beaches
Day 07 Mont St. Michel,
        Brittany, Loire
        Valley
Day 08 Château hopping
Day 09 Sarlat, Dordogne
Day 10 Dordogne Valley
Day 11 Albi and
        Carcassonne
Day 12 To Arles
Day 13 Provence
Day 14 To the Riviera
Day 15 Beaches
Day 16 To Alps
Day 17 Alps admiration

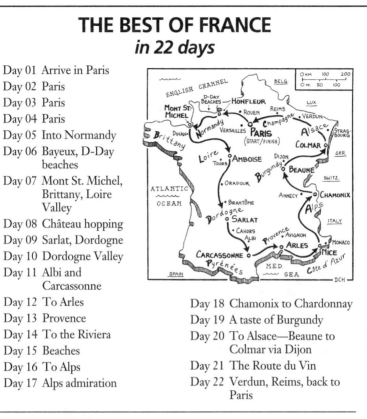

Day 18 Chamonix to Chardonnay
Day 19 A taste of Burgundy
Day 20 To Alsace—Beaune to
        Colmar via Dijon
Day 21 The Route du Vin
Day 22 Verdun, Reims, back to
        Paris

While this itinerary is designed to be done by car, it can be done by train with a few modifications. A France Flexipass with nine train days works well. For a three-week trip *sans* car, I'd modify it by skipping Honfleur and going straight to Bayeux. Base in Sarlat in the Dordogne, and skip Cahors and Albi on your way to Carcassonne. In Provence stay in Arles—or Isle sur la Sorgue if you prefer a smaller town still accessible by rail. Take a night train from the Riviera to Chamonix (via St. Gervais-les-Bains). Choose Reims or Verdun on your way back to Paris from Colmar, but Verdun is tricky without a car. A France rail 'n' drive pass is another good option—a car is especially efficient in Normandy, the Dordogne, and Provence. *Bonne route!*

For all the specifics, see *Rick Steves' France, Belgium & the Netherlands 2002.*

THE BEST OF SCANDINAVIA
in 22 days

Day 01 Arrive in
        Copenhagen

Day 02 Copenhagen

Day 03 Sightsee in
        Copenhagen

Day 04 Frederiksborg
        Castle, N. Zealand

Day 05 Växjö, Kalmar,
        glass country

Day 06 To Stockholm

Day 07 Stockholm

Day 08 Stockholm,
        evening cruise

Day 09 Helsinki, Finland

Day 10 Stockholm,
        Uppsala, to Oslo

Day 11 Oslo

Day 12 Oslo

Day 13 Peer Gynt country

Day 14 Glacier hike, Sognefjord

Day 15 Fjord cruise: "Norway
        in a Nutshell"

Day 16 Bergen

Day 17 To Setesdal Valley

Day 18 Evening sail to Denmark

Day 19 Jutland, Århus

Day 20 Ærø Island

Day 21 Ærø, Odense,
        Roskilde, Copenhagen

Day 22 Fly home from
        Copenhagen

While this itinerary is designed to be done by car, it can be done by train and bus. Scandinavia in 22 days by train is most efficient with a little reworking: I'd go overnight whenever possible on any train ride six or more hours long. Streamline by doing North Zealand, Odense, and Ærø as a three-day side trip from Copenhagen. Take the overnight train from Copenhagen to Stockholm, skipping Växjö and Kalmar. The Bergen/Setesdal/Århus/Copenhagen leg is possible on public transit, but Setesdal (between Bergen and Kristiansand) is not worth the trouble if you don't have the freedom a car gives you. Consider flying out of Bergen.

For all the specifics, see *Rick Steves' Scandinavia 2002*.

THE BEST OF SPAIN & PORTUGAL
in 22 days

Day 01 Arrive in
        Madrid and
        set up

Day 02 Madrid

Day 03 Madrid

Day 04 Segovia

Day 05 Salamanca to
        Coimbra,
        Portugal

Day 06 Nazaré

Day 07 Nazaré

Day 08 Óbidos, Lisbon

Day 09 Lisbon

Day 10 Lisbon and
        nearby beach towns

Day 11 Salema

Day 12 Salema and beaches

Day 13 Sevilla

Day 14 Sevilla

Day 15 Arcos, Tarifa

Day 16 Tarifa

Day 17 Morocco

Day 18 Gibraltar

Day 19 Costa del Sol

Day 20 Granada and Moorish
        Alhambra

Day 21 Toledo

Day 22 Madrid

While this itinerary is designed to be done by car, it can be done by train and bus (seven to eight bus days and four to five train days). For three weeks without a car, I'd modify it to start in Barcelona and finish in Lisbon: From Barcelona, fly or take the night train to Madrid (see Toledo, Segovia, El Escorial); take the night train to Granada; bus along Costa del Sol to Tarifa (see Morocco); bus to Arcos, Sevilla, and Algarve; and take the train to Lisbon. This skips Coimbra and Salamanca and assumes you'll fly open-jaw into Barcelona and out of Lisbon. If catching the train back to Europe from Lisbon, you can sightsee your way there in three days (via Coimbra and Salamanca) or catch the night train to Madrid.

For all the specifics, see *Rick Steves' Spain & Portugal 2002*.

THE BEST OF GERMANY, AUSTRIA & SWITZERLAND
in 22 days

Day 01 Arrive Frankfurt, to Rothenburg

Day 02 Rothenburg

Day 03 Romantic Road to Tirol

Day 04 Castle day

Day 05 To Munich

Day 06 Munich

Day 07 To Salzburg

Day 08 Hallstatt, Lakes District

Day 09 To Vienna

Day 10 Vienna

Day 11 To Hall in Tirol

Day 12 Into Switzerland

Day 13 Interlaken and up into the Alps

Day 14 Alps hiking day, Gimmelwald

Day 15 French Switzerland

Day 16 Chocolate and Mürten

Day 17 Bern

Day 18 Black Forest

Day 19 Baden-Baden to the Rhineland

Day 20 Rhine and castles

Day 21 Mosel Valley, Köln

Day 22 Berlin

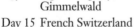

This itinerary is designed to be done by car, but it works by train and bus with a few modifications. A 10-days-within-two-months Eurail Selectpass works best. Fly into Frankfurt and start on the Rhine. The Mosel is great, but tricky without a car. From Rothenburg take the Romantic Road bus to Füssen and base there, not Reutte for Castle Day. Train up to Munich. Then on to Switzerland, basing in the Interlaken area. Skip Appenzell, Mürten, and the Black Forest. Stay in Hall one night en route to Salzburg to spend two nights. From Vienna night train back to Frankfurt to fly home or add Prague or Berlin. If considering a rail/drive option, the Mosel and Bavaria are *wunderbar* places to have wheels. *Gute Reise!*

For all the specifics, see *Rick Steves' Germany, Austria & Switzerland 2002.*

THE BEST OF ITALY
in 22 days

Day 01 Arrive in Milan

Day 02 Milan to Lake Como

Day 03 Lake Como

Day 04 To the Dolomites via Verona (pick up car in Lakes)

Day 05 Dolomites

Day 06 To Venice

Day 07 Venice

Day 08 To Florence

Day 09 Florence

Day 10 To Cinque Terre

Day 11 Cinque Terre

Day 12 To Siena

Day 13 Siena

Day 14 To Orvieto or Assisi

Day 15 Orvieto or Assisi

Day 16 To Sorrento via Pompeii

Day 17 Sorrento

Day 18 To Paestum

Day 19 To Roma, drop car

Day 20 Roma

Day 21 Roma

Day 22 Roma, fly home

This trip is designed to be done by car but works fine by rail with a few modifications. The Kilometric Ticket (3,000 km) or the eight-day-in-one-month Italy Rail Card pass work well (pay out of pocket for short runs like Milan to Varenna). While you can fly into Milan or Roma, I'd choose Milan and work my way south, flying out of Roma. Upon landing in Milan, go directly to Lake Como to relax and get over jet lag. Then see Milan for a half day but sleep in cozier Verona. Consider basing in Bolzano in the Dolomites. From Venice go straight to Cinque Terre (2 direct trains/day), then do Florence and Siena. Sorrento makes a great home base for the Naples Bay sights. A car is handy in the hill towns of Tuscany and Umbria, but is a headache elsewhere. *Buon viaggio!*

For all the specifics, see *Rick Steves' Italy 2002.*

THE BEST OF EUROPE
in 22 days

Day 01 Arrive in
        Amsterdam,
        stay in Haarlem
Day 02 Amsterdam
Day 03 To Rhine,
        Bacharach
Day 04 Cruise Rhine,
        tour Rheinfels
        Castle
Day 05 Rothenburg
Day 06 Munich
Day 07 Castle Day in
        Bavaria and
        Tirol, Reutte
Day 08 To Venice
Day 09 Venice
Day 10 Florence
Day 11 Florence
        (Siena)
Day 12 Rome
Day 13 Rome
Day 14 Rome
Day 15 Italian Riviera, Cinque
        Terre, Vernazza
Day 16 Beach time or hiking
        Riviera trails

Day 17 To the Alps, Gimmelwald
Day 18 Alps Appreciation Day
Day 19 To Beaune in Burgundy
Day 20 Versailles, drop car
Day 21 Paris
Day 22 Paris

While this itinerary is designed to be done by car, with a few small modifications, it works great by train. Stay in Füssen in Bavaria rather than Reutte in Tirol. Consider skipping Beaune if you'd prefer to take an overnight train from Switzerland to Paris. Do Versailles as an easy daytrip from Paris.

For all the specifics, see
Rick Steves' Best of Europe 2002.

Itinerary Priorities, Country by Country

Use this chart to get ideas on how speedy travelers can prioritize limited sightseeing time in various countries. Add places from left to right as you build plans for the best of that country in 3, 5, 7, 10, or 14 days. (In some cases the plan assumes you'll take a night train.) So, according to this chart, the best week in Britain would be spread between London, Bath, Cambridge, and the Cotswolds.

Country	3 days	5 days	7 days	10 days	14 days
Europe	Forget it	London, Paris	Amsterdam	Rhineland, Swiss Alps	Rome, Venice
Britain	London	Bath	Cambridge, Cotswolds	York	Edinburgh, N. Wales
France	Paris, Versailles	Loire, Chartres	Normandy	Provence, Nice, Riviera	Chamonix, Burgundy
Germany	Rhine Munich	Romantic Road, Rothenburg	Bavarian sights	Berlin	Black Forest, Mosel, Köln
Austria	Salzburg, Vienna	Hallstatt	Danube Valley	Prague	—
Switzerland	Bern and the Berner Oberland	French Switzerland, Murten	Appenzell, Luzern	Zermatt	—
Italy	Rome	Florence, Venice	Italian Riviera	Hill towns	Milan and Lake Como
Scandinavia	Copenhagen, Stockholm	Oslo, "Norway in a Nutshell"	More time in capitals	Helsinki, Tallinn	Ærø, more fjords
Spain & Portugal	Madrid, Toledo	Lisbon	Barcelona	Andalucía, Sevilla	Algarve

The best French château is Chantilly near Paris. The best look at Gothic is the Sainte-Chapelle church in Paris. The top two castles are Germany's Burg Eltz on the Mosel River and Italy's Reifenstein near the Brenner Pass border in the north. Lisbon, Oslo, Stockholm, and Brussels are the most underrated big cities. For romance, Varenna on Italy's Lake Como murmurs "honeymoon."

The biggest mistakes that tourists make: packing too heavily, relying on outdated guidebooks, not wearing a money belt, leaving home with too many hotel reservations, and taking other people's opinions too seriously. Happy travels!

8. The Whirlwind Tour: Europe's Best Two-Month Trip

Let's assume you have two months, plenty of energy, and a desire to see as much of Europe as is reasonable. Fly into London and travel around Europe with a two-month Eurailpass. You'll spend two months on the Continent and use any remaining time in Great Britain, before or after you start your railpass (because Eurailpasses don't cover Great Britain). Budgeting for a $900 round-trip ticket to London, around $1,260 for a two-month first-class Eurailpass, and $95 a day for room, board, and sightseeing, the entire trip will cost about $7,900. It can be done. Rookies on a budget do it all the time—often for less.

If I were planning my first European trip and wanted to see as much as I comfortably could in two months (and I had the experience I now have to help me plan), this is the trip I'd take. I'll have to admit, I itch just thinking about this itinerary.

London and Side Trips—5 days

London is Europe's great entertainer; it's wonderfully historic. Mild compared to anything but the United States, it's the best starting point for a European adventure. The English speak English, but their accents will give you the sensation of understanding a foreign language.

From London's airports, you'll find easy train or subway access to the hotels. Consider the Aster House Hotel (hotelesque splurge, 3 Sumner Place, tel. 020/7581-5888, www.asterhouse.com), Winchester Hotel (17 Belgrave Road, tel. 020/7828-2972), or Woodville House (homey, small rooms; 107 Ebury Street, tel. 020/7730-1048, www.woodvillehouse.co.uk). To get your bearings, catch a "Round London" orientation bus tour (departs every 20 min) from the park in front of Victoria Station. Give the London Eye Ferris Wheel a spin and tour the spiffed-up British Museum. Every day will be busy and each night filled with a play and a pub.

Europe's Best Two-Month Trip

Spend your remaining time in the English countryside: Bath (see chapter 49), the Cotswolds (see chapter 52), York (see chapter 50), and the university city of Cambridge. But the Continent beckons. Paris is only three hours away by Eurostar train (15 trains/day). Cheaper seats can sell fast. To save money, order your tickets from home (tel. 800/EUROSTAR). If you'll be ending your trip in London, plan for your return: Reserve a good B&B and get tickets to a hot play.

Paris—3 days

Ascend the Eiffel Tower to survey a Paris studded with architectural gems and historical one-of-a-kinds. You'll recognize the Louvre, Notre-Dame, Arc de Triomphe, Sacré-Coeur, and much more.

Take a walk covering Paris' biggies. From the Latin Quarter, head to Notre-Dame, the Deportation Monument to Nazi victims, and Sainte-Chapelle. Take the Pont-Neuf bridge over to the Samaritaine department store for a self-serve lunch and a great rooftop view. Walk by the Louvre, through the Tuileries Gardens, and up the Champs-Elysées to the Arc de Triomphe.

Be sure to visit Napoleon's Tomb, the Rodin Museum (*The Thinker* and *The Kiss*), the great Orsay Museum (Impressionism), a jazz club, and Latin Quarter nightlife. Spend an evening on Montmartre soaking in the spiritual waters of the Sacré-Coeur and browsing among the tacky shops and artists of the Place du Tertre. Pick up the *Pariscope* entertainment guide. Most museums are closed on Tuesday.

Paris' Eiffel Tower

Learn the Paris subway—it's fast, easy, and cheap. Stay near the Eiffel Tower at Hotel Leveque (29 rue Cler, tel. 01 47 05 49 15, www.hotel-leveque.com) or in the Marais neighborhood at Hotel Jeanne-d'Arc (elegant, 3 rue Jarente, tel. 01 48 87 62 11) or Hotel Castex (cheap, friendly, 5 rue Castex, tel. 01 42 72 31 52). Ask your hotelier to recommend a small family-owned restaurant for dinner.

Side-trip to Europe's greatest palace, Louis XIV's Versailles (take the RER-C train to the end of the line: Versailles R.G.). Another great side trip is the city of Chartres with its great Gothic cathedral (lectures by Malcolm Miller at noon and 2:45 p.m.).

Start your Eurailpass when you leave Paris. Take the overnight train to Madrid (16 hours), or take a detour ...

Loire Valley—2 days

On the way to Spain, explore the dreamy châteaus of the Loire Valley. Make Amboise or Tours your headquarters. Consider an all-day bus tour of the châteaus. For the simplest approach to château sightseeing, skip the Loire and see Chantilly, the epitome of a French château, just a 30-minute side trip from Paris.

Madrid—2 days

On arrival, reserve your train out. Reservations on long trains are required in Spain (and Norway), even with Eurail.

Take a taxi or the subway to Puerto del Sol to find a central hotel. Try Hotel Europa (comfortable, just off Puerta del Sol, Calle del Carmen 4, tel. 91-521-2900, www.hoteleuropa.net) or Hostal Residencia Miami (cheap, 8th floor, at Gran Vía 44, tel. 91-521-1464).

Bullfights, shopping, and museums will fill your sunny days. Madrid's three essential sights are the Prado Museum (Goya, El Greco, Velázquez, Bosch), Reina Sofia (*Guernica*), and the Royal Palace (one of Europe's most lavish interiors). Bullfights are on Sundays through the summer (check at hotel, buy tickets at arena). Tourists and pickpockets alike enjoy the sprawling El Rastro flea market every Sunday.

From Madrid, side-trip to Toledo (75 min by train, bus, or shared taxi).

Toledo—1 day

Save a day for this perfectly preserved historic capital, home of El Greco and his masterpieces. Back in Madrid, take the night train to Lisbon (about 9 hours). Night trains make sense in Iberia—long distances are boring and hot on crowded, slow day trains. But, remember, domestic shuttle flights cost less than $100.

Lisbon—2 days

Lisbon, Portugal's friendly capital, can keep a visitor busy for days. Its highlight is the Alfama. This salty old sailors' quarter is a photographer's delight. You'll feel rich here in Europe's bargain basement. (See chapter 36: Lisbon.)

Side-trip to Sintra for its eclectic Pena Palace and mysterious ruined Moorish castle. Circle south for a stop on Portugal's south coast, the Algarve (train to Lagos, about 7 hours).

Algarve—2 days

Settle down in Salema, the best beach village on the south coast of Portugal (see Chapter 37). Cross into Andalucía for flamenco, hill towns, and Sevilla.

Sevilla and Andalucía—3 days

After strolling the paseo of Sevilla, the city of flamenco, head for the hills and explore Andalucía's Route of the Whitewashed Hill Towns. Arcos de la Frontera is a good home base. Ride the speedy AVE train back to Madrid. Fly or catch the night train to Barcelona.

Barcelona—2 days

Tour the Picasso Museum, relax, shop, and explore the Gothic Quarter. Stay in the simple Hotel Jardi (Plaça Sant Josep Oriol 1, tel. 93-301-5900, e-mail: sgs110sa@retemail.es), the homey Hosteria Grau (Ramelleres 27, tel. 93-301-8135, www.intercom.es/grau), or the palatial but affordable Hotel Gran Vía (Gran Vía de les Corts Catalanes 642, tel. 93-318-1900). Catch a night train to Arles, France (about 11 hours).

Provence or French Riviera—2 days
Your best home base for Provence is Arles (Hotel Regence, 5 rue Marius Jouveau, tel. 04 90 96 39 85). Tour the Papal Palace in Avignon and ramble among Roman ruins in Nîmes and Arles.

Most of the Riviera is crowded, expensive, and stressful, but if you're set on a Riviera beach, Nice is where the jet set lies on rocks. Tour Nice's great Chagall Museum and stay at Hotel Clemenceau (3 avenue Clemenceau, tel. 04 93 88 61 19). Then dive into intense Italy.

Cinque Terre— 2 days
The Cinque Terre is the best of Italy's Riviera. You will find pure Italy in these five sleepy, traffic-free little villages between Genoa and Pisa. Unknown to many tourists, it's the ultimate Italian coastal paradise. (See chapter 30.)

Finishing a day-long Riviera hike, your home village, Vernazza, comes into view.

Florence—1 day
Florence is steeped in history and art. Europe's Renaissance art capital is packed in the summer but worth the headaches. Stay at Hotel La Scaletta (rooftop garden, Via Guicciardini 13, tel. 055-283-028, www.lascaletta.com) or Casa Rabatti (cheap, homey, near station, Via San Zanobi 48, tel. 055-212-393).

Hill Towns of Tuscany and Umbria—2 days
This is where dreams of Italy are fulfilled. Visit Siena and Civita di Bagnoregio. (See chapters 31 and 32.)

Rome—3 days
Devote your first day to Classical Rome: Tour the Colosseum, Forum, Capitol Hill (and its museum), and Pantheon. Linger away the evening at Piazza Navona. *Tartufo* ice cream is mandatory.

For your second day, visit Vatican City and St. Peter's (climb the dome), and tour the Vatican Museum and Sistine Chapel (follow *Rick Steves' Mona Winks* or rent an audioguide). Take advantage of the Vatican's post office, much better than Italy's. Picnickers will find a great open-air produce market three blocks in front of the Vatican Museum entry. Spend your third morning at Ostia Antica, ancient Rome's seaport (like Pompeii, but just a subway ride away from Rome). In downtown Rome, visit Piazza Barberini for its Bernini fountain and Cappuccin crypt (thousands of bones in the first church up Via Veneto). In the early evening, do the Dolce Vita stroll from Piazza del Popolo to the Spanish Steps. Have dinner on Campo dei Fiori. Explore Trastevere, where yesterday's Rome lives out a nostalgic retirement.

Stay near the Vatican Museum at Hotel Alimandi (Via Tunisi 8, tel. 06-3972-6300, www.alimandi.org), near the train station at Hotel Oceania (Via Firenze 38, tel. 06-482-4696, www.hoteloceania.it), or even cheaper at Hotel Magic (Via Milazzo 20, 3rd floor, tel. & fax 06-495-9880). Take a train to Venice (about 7 hours, night trains sometimes available).

Venice—2 days

Cruise the colorful canals of Venice. Grab a front seat on boat #82 for an introductory tour down the Canale Grande. Stay at Albergo Guerrato (near Rialto Bridge at Calle drio la Scimia 240a, tel. & fax 041-522-7131, e-mail: hguerrat@tin.it) or near the train station at Hotel Marin (San Croce 670b, tel. 041-718-022, www.hotelmarin.it). The Accademia Gallery showcases the best Venetian art. Tour the Doge's Palace, St. Mark's, and catch the view from the Campanile bell tower. Then wander, leave the tourists, and get as lost as possible. Don't worry, you're on an island and you can't get off. Catch the night train to Vienna (about 8 hours).

Vienna—2 days

Savor the Old World elegance of Hapsburg Vienna, Paris' eastern rival. This grand capital of the mighty Hapsburg Empire is rich in art history, Old World charm, and elegance. You'll find a great tourist information office behind the impressive Opera (fine tours). Stay at tidy Pension Hargita (Andreasgasse 1, tel. 01/526-1928, www.hargita.at) or the classier Pension Suzanne (near Opera, Walfischgasse 4, tel. 01/513-2507, www.pension-suzanne.at). Side-trip east for a look at Prague.

Prague—2 days

Prague, a magnificently preserved city, is a happening place. Visas are no longer required, and Prague is five hours from Vienna by train. If you're on a budget, arrive without hotel reservations and use the AVE room-booking service in the station (tel. 02/2422-3226, e-mail: ave@avetravel.cz).

Salzburg—1 day

Mozart's gone, but you'll find his chocolate balls everywhere. Baroque Salzburg, with its music festival and *Sound of Music* delights, is touristy in a way most love. Sleep cheap at Institute San Sebastian (Linzergasse 41, tel. 0662/871-386) or fancier at Gasthaus zur Goldenen Ente (Goldgasse 10, tel. 0662/845-622, www.ente.at).

Tirol and Bavaria—2 days

Tour "Mad" King Ludwig's fairy-tale castle at Neuschwanstein and Bavaria's heavenly Wies Church. Visit the Tirolean town of Reutte and its forgotten—unforgettable—hill-crowning, ruined castle. Running along the overgrown ramparts of the Ehrenberg ruins, your imagination works itself loose, and suddenly you're notching up your crossbow and ducking flaming arrows. (See chapter 58: Dungeons and Dragons.)

Switzerland—3 days

Pray for sun. For the best of the Swiss Alps, establish a home base in Switzerland's rugged Berner

Surrounded by Ehrenburg ruins

Oberland, south of Interlaken. The traffic-free and quiet village of Gimmelwald in Lauterbrunnen Valley is everything an Alp-lover could possibly want. (See chapter 45: Gimmelwald.)

Switzerland's best big city is Bern and best small town is Murten. Europe's most scenic train ride is across southern Switzerland from Chur to Martigny. Be careful: Mixing sunshine and a full dose of alpine beauty can be intoxicating.

King of the Alps, high above Gimmelwald

Munich—2 days

Munich, the capital of Bavaria, has a great palace, museums, and the world's best street singers. But they probably won't be good enough to keep you out of the beer halls. You'll find huge mugs of beer, bigger pretzels, and even bigger beer maids! The Hofbräuhaus is the most famous (near Marienplatz in the old town center). Good places to stay include Hotel Pension Utzelmann (elegant, near station, Pettenkoferstrasse 6, tel. 089/594-889) and Hotel Münchner Kindl (simple, in old center, Damenstiftstrasse 16, tel. 089/264-349). The Romantic Road bus tour ($28 with a Eurailpass) is a handy daylong way to get from Munich to Frankfurt.

Romantic Road—1 day

The Romantic Road bus rolls through the heart of medieval Germany, stopping for visits at Dinkelsbühl and the always-popular queen of quaint German towns, Rothenburg (see Chapter 43). Consider an overnight stop in Rothenburg at Hotel Goldene Rose (simple, Spitalgasse 28, tel. 09861/4638). Or head straight to the Rhine.

Rhine/Mosel River Valleys and Köln—2 days

Take a Rhine cruise (free with Eurail, Europass, Selectpass, or German railpass) from Bingen to Koblenz to enjoy a parade of old castles. The best hour of the cruise is from Bacharach to St. Goar. In St. Goar, hike up to the Rheinfels castle (see Chapter 58: Dungeons and Dragons). Stay in Bacharach at the Hotel Kranenturm (Langstrasse 30, tel. 06743/1308, e-mail: hotel-kranenturm@t-online.de) or up at the Castle Youth Hostel (Jugendherberge Stahleck, tel. 06743/1266, e-mail: jh-bacharach@djh -info.de, $14 beds) with panoramic Rhine views.

Cruise along the sleepy Mosel Valley and tour Cochem's castle, Trier's Roman ruins, and the impressive medieval castle, Burg Eltz. From Köln, catch the night train (about 8 hours) to Germany's capital, ever-vibrant Berlin.

Berlin—2 days

Berlin, capital of a united Germany, with its great art and stunning Reichstag dome, is worth two busy days. For accommodations try homey Pension Peters (Kantstrasse 146, tel. 030/3150-3944, e-mail: penspeter@aol.com) or the classy Hotel Astoria (Fasanenstrasse 2, tel. 030/312-4067). Catch the night train from Berlin to Copenhagen (about 9 hours).

Copenhagen—1 day

Finish your continental experience with a blitz tour of the capitals of Scandinavia: Copenhagen, Stockholm, and Oslo. To save money and time, sleep on trains. Scandinavia's capitals are a convenient 10 hours apart, the train rides are boring and sleepable, and hotels are expensive. Leave your bags at the Copenhagen train station. Tour the city during the day and spend the evening at Tivoli, just across the street from the train station. Catch the night train to Stockholm (about 9 hours). If you'd like to stay overnight in Copenhagen, try a comfortable B&B (Annette and Rudy Hollender's home, Wildersgade 19, tel. 32 95 96 22, e-mail: hollender@adr.dk).

Stockholm—2 days
With its ruddy mix of islands, canals, and wooded parks studded with fine sights such as the 350-year-old *Vasa* warship, Europe's best open-air folk museum at Skansen, and gas-lamped old town, Stockholm is a charmer. Catch an afternoon train to Oslo (6 to 10 hours, depending on the train and connections).

Oslo—1 day
After a busy day wandering through Viking ships, the *Kon-Tiki*, the Nazi Resistance Museum, and climbing the ski jump for a commanding view of the city and its fjord, you'll be famished. It's Rudolph with lingonberries for dinner! Sleep cozy near the palace at Ellingsen's Pensjonat (Holtegata 25, tel. 22 60 03 59), right downtown at the Rainbow Hotel Astoria (Dronningensgate 21, tel. 22 42 00 10, e-mail: astoria@rainbow-hotels.no), or cheap in the suburbs with the Caspari family's B&B (Heggelbakken 1, tel. 22 14 57 70).

Scenic Train, Fjord Country, and Bergen—2 days
For the best look at the mountainous fjord country of west Norway, do "Norway in a Nutshell," a combination of spectacular train, boat, and bus rides. Catch the morning train from Oslo over the spine of Norway to Bergen. Stay overnight on the fjord near Flam in Aurland at the funky Aabelheim Pension or the basic Vangen Motel (same tel. 57 63 35 80, e-mail: vangsgas@online.no). Enjoy a day in salty Bergen. Stay downtown at the Heskja home (good budget beds, Skivebakken 17, tel. 55 31 30 30, e-mail: mail@skiven.no) or catch the night train back to Oslo (about 8 hours).

Oslo—1 day
Take a second day in Oslo. There's plenty to do. (See Chapter 56.) Hop a night train back to Copenhagen (about 9 hours).

> **Excursions You May Want to Add**
> England—Bath, York, Cambridge, the Cotswolds
> French Alps—Chamonix, Aiguille du Midi, Aosta
> Morocco and South Spain
> South Italy or Greece
> Finland or the Arctic
> Eastern Europe or Russia
> A day for showers and laundry
> Visiting, resting, and a little necessary slack
> Travel days to avoid sleeping on the train

Copenhagen—1 day
Another day in Copenhagen. Yes! Smörgåsbords, Viking *lur* horns, and healthy, smiling blondes are the memories you'll pack on the night train south to Amsterdam (about 12 hours).

Amsterdam—2 days
The Dutch Golden Age sparkles in Amsterdam's museums, but the streets can be a bit seedy for many Americans' tastes. Consider daytripping into Amsterdam from small-town Haarlem (Hotel Amadeus, Grote Markt 10, tel. 023/532-4530, www.amadeus-hotel.com; or the homey bed-and-breakfast House de Kiefte, Coornhertstraat 3, tel. 023/532-2980, two-night minimum stay). You'll discover great side trips in all directions.

After touring crazy Amsterdam and biking through the tulips, sail for England (about 11 hours). Or, to avoid a surface return to London, consider flying out of Amsterdam (arrange this open-jaw flight before you leave home).

This 61-day Whirlwind Tour is just a sampler. There's plenty more to see, but I can't imagine a better first two months in Europe. The itinerary includes 14 nights on the train (saving about $600 in hotel costs) and 14 days for doing more interesting things than sitting on a train.

A Eurailpass is good for two calendar months (e.g., May 15 through midnight July 14). If you validate when you leave Paris and expire (the Eurailpass, not you) on arrival in Amsterdam, you'll spend 53 days, leaving eight days of railpass time to slow down or add options.

RECOMMENDED BOOKS FOR THE WHIRLWIND TOUR
My various country guides offer details on sights, hotels, and restaurants. For one fat book detailing most of the stops mentioned in this chapter,

consider this year's *Rick Steves' Best of Europe*. See also this book's "Part Two: Back Doors" for in-depth descriptions of some of the cities. For art history, read *Rick Steves' Europe 101* before you go and take *Rick Steves' Mona Winks* for self-guided museum tours. My French/Italian/German and Spanish/Portuguese phrase books will help you leap over the language barrier. (All of my books are published by Avalon Travel Publishing.)

TRANSPORTATION

9. Travel Agents and Flights

The travel industry is considered the second biggest industry and employer on the planet (after armaments and the military). To travel, you need to deal with it, so it's good to know how, when, and where. Here are some ideas to help you consume with a little savvy.

OUR TRAVEL INDUSTRY

Travel is a huge business. Most of what the industry promotes is decadence: Lie on the beach and hedonize those precious two weeks to make up for the other 50; see if you can eat five meals a day and still snorkel when you get into port. That's where the money is, and that's where most of the interest is. With recent caps on airline commissions, agents are pushing organized travel more than ever. Obviously they'd prefer you spend your money for Europe here rather than over there. Independent travelers fit the industry like a snowshoe in Mazatlán.

Understand what shapes the information that shapes your travel dreams. As a newspaper travel columnist, I've learned that it takes a bold travel editor to run articles that may upset advertisers. Travel newspaper sections are possible only with the support of travel advertisers. And advertisers are more interested in filling cruise ships or tour buses than in turning people free to travel independently. In fact, when I first started running my weekly travel column, it was called "The Budget Traveler." Within a month of its appearance, that travel section's major advertisers met with the editor and explained they would no longer buy ads if he continued running a column with that name. Hastily, the editor and I found a new name. To save the column we called it "The Practical Traveler"—same subversive information but with a more palatable title.

Many travel agents don't understand travel "through the Back Door." The typical attitude I get when I hobnob with bigwigs from the industry in Hilton Hotel ballrooms is: "If you can't afford to go first class, save up and go next year." I'll never forget the bewilderment I caused when I turned down a free room in Bangkok's most elegant Western-style hotel in favor of a cheap room in a simple Thai-style hotel.

Of course, these comments are generalizations. There are many great travelers in the travel industry. They understand my frustration because they've also dealt with it.

Travel can mean rich people flaunting their affluence, taking snapshots of black kids jumping off white ships for small change. Or it can promote understanding, bending out our hometown blinders and making our world more comfortable in its smallness. What the industry promotes is up to all of us—writers, editors, agents, and travelers.

YOU NEED A TRAVEL AGENT

I'm not "anti–travel agent." I *am* "anti–*bad* travel agent." My travel agent is my vital ally. I've never gone to Europe without her help. Travel agency recommendations from other travelers provide excellent leads, but the right agency doesn't guarantee the right agent. You need a particular person— someone whose definition of "good travel" matches yours. Ask for the agency's "independent Europe specialist." Once you find the right agent, nurture your alliance. Be loyal. Send her a postcard.

Travel agents save you money. These days it takes a full-time and aggressive travel professional to keep up with the constantly changing airline industry. I don't have time to sort through all the frustrating, generally too-good-to-be-true ads that fill the Sunday travel sections. I rely on the experience of an agent who specializes in budget European travel.

Some travel agents do charge modest fees. Agents used to earn most of their income from airline commissions, but now a 5 percent rate cap ($100 maximum) per round-trip international ticket has caused some agents to start charging a $10 to $20 fee per ticket.

You can't save money by buying directly from the airlines. Most airline representatives barely know what they're charging, much less their competitors' rates and schedules. Only your agent would remind you that leaving two days earlier would get you in on the end of shoulder season— and save you $100.

An agent can get you almost any ticket. Dumping your agent for a $30 savings from a discount agent down the street is a bad move. These days, many people milk good agents for all they're worth and then buy tickets from their sister's friend's agency around the corner. Because of this, it's tough to get good advice over the phone, and "browsers" usually get no respect. I enjoy the luxury of sitting down with my agent, explaining travel plans, getting a briefing on my options, and choosing the best flight.

Use your agent only for arranging transportation. Although many agents can give you tips on Irish B&Bs and sporadic advice on biking in Holland, assume you'll do better if you use your travel agent only to get you to your destination. After that, rely on a good guidebook. Travel agents handle their clients with kid gloves. Don't let their caution clamp a ball and chain onto your travel dreams. I use an agent for my plane ticket, train pass or car rental, advice on visa and health precautions, and nothing else.

Car rentals are cheaper when arranged before departure through your agent. Eurailpasses and most country railpasses must or should be purchased before you leave home. To get good service on small, tedious items like these, do all your trip business through the agent who made a commission on your air ticket.

Check student travel agencies—even if you're not a student. Any city with a university probably has a student travel agency. Council Travel (with 75 offices in the U.S., tel. 800/2-COUNCIL, www.counciltravel.com) and STA Travel (50 stateside offices, tel. 800/777-0112, www.statravel.com) offer budget fares even to nonstudents. Most big campuses also have a more independent agency that is a member of the University Student Travel Network (USTN, www.ustn.org). These agencies sell Council and STA tickets as well as their own discounted tickets.

If your schedule's flexible, consider flying standby. Air-Tech (tel. 212/219-7000, www.airtech.com) or 4Standby (tel. in NY 800/326-2009, in CA 800/397-1098, www.4standby.com) offer unsold seats at bargain prices (e.g., one-way from Los Angeles to Paris for $249, year-round). However, a short list of departure cities in the U.S. (such as Boston, New York, and Chicago) and an equally limited number of European destinations (such as Amsterdam, London, and Copenhagen) make arranging these flights tricky. And in the summer prepare to be bumped—two or three times.

FLYING TO EUROPE

Flying to Europe is a great travel bargain—for the well-informed. The rules and regulations are confusing and always changing, but when you make the right choice, you get the right price.

Dollars saved = discomfort + restrictions + inflexibility. There is no great secret to getting to Europe for next to nothing. Assuming you know your options, you get what you pay for. There's no such thing as a free lunch in the airline industry. Regular fare is very expensive. You get the ultimate in flexibility, but I've never met anyone spending his or her own money who flew that way.

Rather than grab the cheapest ticket to Europe, go with your agent's recommendation for the best combination of reliability, economy, and flexibility for your travel needs. Buy your ticket when you're ready to firmly commit to flight dates and ports. As you delay, dates sell out and prices generally go up. Special fares are limited to a few seats to jump-start departures.

Consider open-jaw. I always fly "open-jaw": into one city and out of another. The fare is figured simply by taking half of the round-trip fare for each of those ports. I used to fly into Amsterdam, travel to Istanbul, and (having rejected the open-jaw plan because flying home from Istanbul costs $200 more than returning from Amsterdam) pay $200 to ride the train for two days back to Amsterdam to catch my "cheap" return flight. Now I see the real economy in spending more for open-jaw. Open-jaw is cheapest when the same airline covers each segment of the round-trip journey.

A good agent will check both consolidator and airline fares, then offer you the best deal. Consolidator tickets are generally cheapest, but sometimes fare wars can make an airline's prices unbeatable. Consolidators (or wholesalers) negotiate with airlines to get deeply discounted fares on a huge number of tickets; they offer these tickets to your travel agent, who then marks them up and still sells you a cheaper flight to Europe than the airline itself can. An airline's ticket prices in a drawn-out fare war, however, can drop to bargain-basement levels. A good travel agent will offer both consolidator and regular airline fares. If not, specifically ask the agent to check consolidator rates.

With consolidator tickets, you usually have 7 to 10 days to pay after booking, and credit cards are becoming more acceptable (a fee of 4 percent or so is charged for payment in plastic). If, after you buy an airline ticket, the airline's price drops yet again, you can exchange your ticket and save some money—if the discount is greater than the change fee (generally $75–250). Consolidator tickets, however, won't get any cheaper; the price, once established, stays the same. Ask about cancellation policies: What is the fee? Will you receive a refund or credit? Consolidator tickets are usually refundable prior to departure minus a fee of $200 to $300.

Consolidator tickets often waive the normal advance-purchase and minimum- and maximum-stay requirements that come with other budget tickets. But consolidator tickets are cheap because they come with disadvantages: They are "nonendorsable," meaning that no other airline

Know Thy Travel Agent—A Quiz

One way to be sure your travel agent is enthusiastic about European travel and properly suited to helping you with your trip is to ask him or her a few questions. Here's a little quiz—complete with answers.

1. What is "open-jaw"?
a) Yet another shark movie sequel.
b) A tourist in awe of the *Mannekin Pis*.
c) A special-interest tour of Romania's dental clinics.
d) An airline ticket that allows you to fly into one city and out of another.

2. Which international boat rides are covered by the Eurailpass?
a) Poland to Switzerland.
b) All of them.
c) Sweden to Finland, Italy to Greece, Germany to Denmark, and Sweden to Denmark.

3. What's the age limit to sleep in a Youth Hostel?
a) Five.
b) As high as 30 if you like rap music.
c) There is none, except in Bavaria, where it's 26.

4. What is the most economical way to get from London's Heathrow Airport into London?
a) Walk.
b) Ask the queen for a lift.
c) Don't. Spend your whole vacation at Heathrow.
d) By subway or airbus.

5. What is an ISIC card?
a) A universal way to tell foreigners you're not feeling well.
b) It beats three-of-a-kind.
c) The International Student Identity Card, good for many discounts at sights and museums.

6. Is there a problem getting a bed and breakfast in England's small towns without a reservation?
a) Not if you live there.
b) Yes. Carry No-Doz in England.
c) No.

7. How much does a Hungarian visa cost?
a) $45.
b) You can just charge it on your Visa card.
c) More than a Grecian urn.
d) It's not required.

Answers: The last answer to each question is the correct one.

is required to honor that ticket if your airline is unable to get you home (though in practice this is rarely a problem). Sometimes you may not get frequent-flyer miles (particularly with British Airways and American). And, if the airline drops its prices (which often happens), you are stuck with what was, but no longer is, a cheap fare.

Chartered flights can save you money. A charter company offers flights on certain days in and out of the same city. In return for fitting into their limits, you can fly cheaper than on scheduled airlines.

However, charter companies can cancel flights that don't fill. Anyone selling charters promotes an air of confidence, but at the last minute any flight can be "rescheduled" if it won't pay off. Those who "saved" by booking onto that charter are left all packed with nowhere to go. Get an explicit answer to what happens if the flight is canceled. "It won't be canceled" is not good enough. Some charter companies are reliable. Ask about their track record: How many flights did they cancel last year?

Scheduled airlines are most reliable. If for some reason (such as a strike) they can't fly you home, they find you a seat on another airline. You won't be stranded in Europe—unless you have a discounted ticket marked "nonendorsable."

Courier flights usually sound better than they are. Courier flights can get some travelers to Europe with deeply discounted tickets (30–80 percent off). Couriers, whose luggage is limited to carry-ons, are required to transport shipping documents. Upon landing, they turn the documents over to a courier company representative, who checks the cargo through customs.

For most, these cheap flights are a pipe dream. The number of bargain courier flights to Europe has diminished over the past several years. You need to be able to fly on short notice and live in the key "departure cities" (such as New York, Miami, or San Francisco). Lately, courier services have started charging a percentage of the ticket value, making the whole notion less exciting.

If you think courier flights could work for you, do a little research. Consider the books *Air Courier Bargains—How to Travel Worldwide for Next to Nothing* by Kelly Monaghan (The Intrepid Traveler) and *The Courier Air Travel Handbook* by Mark Field (Perpetual Press). You won't find out much from the Air Courier Association (tel.800/282-1202, www.aircourier.org) or the International Association of Air Travel Couriers (tel. 561/582-8320, www.courier.org) until you pay a membership fee of around $50.

Budget flights are restrictive. Most are nonchangeable and nonrefundable, but some offer changes on the return dates for a penalty of about $100 to $200. If you need to change your return date in Europe, telephone your airline's European office. If that fails, I've found airlines become more lenient if you go to their office in person with a good reason for your need to change the return date. If you must get home early, go to the airport. If you're standing at the airport two days before your ticket says you can go home—and seats are available—regardless of the rules, they may let you fly home early. They win a happy customer and gain two more days to try to sell an empty seat. Besides, at that point, it's the easiest way to get rid of you.

Be wary of using electronic tickets. More airlines are pushing electronic tickets, even awarding extra frequent flyer miles to customers who use them. The advantages to you are that the tickets can't be lost or stolen. However, if the airline loses the e-record of your transaction, if their computers go down, or if you need to switch your flight (due to a strike or cancellation) to another airline, you've got nothing to show but air . . . without a plane.

If you have the time and interest, comparison shop on the Web. Some travelers like to research fares on the Web, using the information to either book online or arrive prepared at the travel agent's office. Occasionally you'll find amazing deals online, but usually only after hours of digging.

Consider the following before buying a ticket on the Web:

Other than the rare deal and the convenience of arranging a flight when travel agencies are closed, the only real benefit to online booking is the first-time bonus of frequent-flyer miles (up to 5,000) awarded by airlines if you book on their site. Subsequent bookings garner fewer miles (1,000).

Whichever Web site you use, make sure it lists a phone number. You'll need to speak to a person if you have a problem. Read the fine print. Most tickets are nonrefundable. Check for additional fees, especially those tacked on to ticket changes and requests for paper tickets.

To shop around for flights, check the travel Web sites. Stick with the big names, such as Travelocity (www.travelocity.com) and Expedia (www.expedia.com), which are built upon conventional reservation systems used by travel agents. The new Orbitz site (www.orbitz.com), owned by the five largest domestic airlines, boasts that it offers travelers the lowest fares and the most flights.

Discount sites such as www.cheaptickets.com, www.bestfares.com, and www.1travel.com offer many restrictions, inconvenient itineraries, and few possibilities for frequent-flyer miles.

If you're interested in booking your flight through an airline's Web site to get frequent-flyer bonus miles, check Travelocity or Expedia first to find out which airline offers the most competitive prices to your destination. Then go to that airline's Web site to book your flight and get your bonus. Be aware that deals and even flight availability can differ between travel Web sites and the airlines' sites. You could come up with a super deal, say, on an SAS flight through Travelocity that SAS doesn't offer on its site.

Personally, I'd rather have my travel agent do the work.

FLIGHTS WITHIN EUROPE

Flying is now a realistic option for budget travelers. Airfares within Europe have plunged due to European Union reforms and deregulation, and new no-frills airlines are taking off. And some well-established carriers continue to offer discounts (or air passes) for flights within Europe to travelers who fly with them from North America.

An affordable flight beats a long train ride.

These days, before buying any long-distance train ticket, drop by a travel agency (either at home or in Europe) to check out budget airfares. Some round-trip fares are cheaper than one-way, but you won't be told unless you ask. Always ask.

Flight versus Train? While airfares have dropped, a railpass is still usually a lot cheaper than flying. But if you're short on time or have long distances to cover, flying is worth considering. By taking a quick flight, you can easily visit two countries far apart from each other (say, a week in Norway and a week in Italy). For cities close together, the train is more practical. From London to Paris, the Eurostar Chunnel train can be faster than flying when you consider the train zips you directly from downtown to downtown (800/EUROSTAR, www.eurostar.com). While the actual flight between the cities is faster than the train, you must factor in the time it takes to get between downtown and the airports, and the extra time needed for check-in and security. Train and car travel, unlike flights, keep you close to the scenery, to Europe, and to Europeans. Ground transportation is also less likely to be disrupted by bad weather or mechanical problems. But if the distance from Point A to Point B is long, flying is an attractive, affordable option.

Budget Flights: Budget airlines offer cheap fares within Europe. Count on booking inexpensive flights yourself (via phone and credit card) rather than through a travel agent. To get the best fares, book long in advance. Cheap seats sell out fast, leaving the pricier seats for latecomers.

If you're flying into or out of London, consider British Midland. Their "Discover Europe Air Pass" costs from $109 to $159 (depending on the distance, plus tax) for European flights that originate or terminate in London. (British Midland flights that require a transfer in London, say a Paris–Amsterdam flight, cost double: $109 per segment or a total of $218 plus tax—not a great deal.) Sometimes bigger savings—and more restrictions—are possible if you fly round-trip without the Air Pass—ask (U.S. tel. 800/788-0555, British tel. 0870-607-0555, www.britishmidland.com). For more information on cheap airfares for flights originating within the United Kingdom, visit Cheap Flights at www.cheapflights.co.uk.

Virgin Express offers flights starting at around $100 between London, Rome, Madrid, Barcelona, and more (British tel. 020/7744-0004, www.virgin-express.com). Other budget airlines worth considering include Ryan Air (Irish tel. 01/609-7881, www.ryanair.ie), Easy Jet (British tel. 0870-600-0000, www.easyjet.com), and Buzz (British tel. 0870-240-7070, www.buzzaway.com).

European airlines such as Lufthansa, Air France, Alitalia, SAS, KLM, and British Air also offer competitive fares. There's a catch: Often you must buy your transatlantic flight from the airline in order to take advantage of its intra-European budget fares. But it can be worth an extra $100 for an overseas flight in order to save on flights within Europe. In some cases, you purchase an "air pass" (for $300–400)—a set of three or more flight coupons, each good for one nonstop flight. Be aware that with any air pass, a flight will "cost" two coupons if you need two connecting flights to reach your destination. Check with your travel agent for details.

Some flight passes are valid on several different airlines. The most flexible is the Europe by Air pass, offering flights between nearly 100 European cities in 20 countries. Each coupon for a nonstop flight costs $99 plus tax. But if you make a connection through one of Europe by Air's four hubs (Brussels, Rome, Berlin, and Zagreb, Croatia), you pay double—$99 for each flight to and from the hub. Ask if you must buy a minimum number of coupons (U.S. tel. 888/387-2479, www.europebyair.com).

Bucket Shops: London, Amsterdam, Paris, and Athens have bucket shops that sell plane tickets at superdiscounted prices. If your travel plans fit the tickets available and you're flexible enough to absorb delays, these can be a great deal. *Let's Go: Europe* lists a few of the bigger bucket shops. Your hometown library should have a London newspaper; look in the classifieds under "Travel" to see what's available. Tickets from London to the Mediterranean can be incredibly—and reliably—cheap. Athens also has some great buys on tickets to London, Western Europe, and the Middle East.

THE FEAR OF FLYING

Like many people, I'm afraid to fly. I always think of the little rubber wheels splashing down on a rain-soaked runway and then hydroplaning out of control. Or the spindly landing gear crumbling. Or, if not that, then the plane tilting just a tad, catching a wing tip, and flipping into flames.

Despite my fears, I still fly. I remind myself that every day 60,000 planes take off and land safely in the U.S. alone. The pilot and crew fly daily, and they don't seem to be terrified. They let an important guy like Bill Clinton fly all over the place, and nothing happened to him.

I guess it's a matter of aerodynamics. Air has mass, and the plane maneuvers itself through that mass. I can understand a boat coming into a dock—maneuvering through the water. That doesn't scare me. So I tell myself that a plane's a boat with an extra dimension to navigate, and its "water" is a lot thinner. Also, the pilot, who's still "flying" the plane after it lands, is as much in control on the ground as in the air. Only when he's good and ready does he allow gravity to take over.

Turbulence scares me, too. A United pilot once told me that he'd have bruises from his seat belt before turbulence really bothered him. Still, every time the plane comes in for a landing, I say a prayer, close my eyes, and take my pen out of my shirt pocket so it won't impale me if something goes wrong. And every time I stick my pen back in my shirt pocket, I feel thankful.

Wondering which airline to choose? For me, it doesn't matter. If I arrive in Europe safely on the day I had hoped to, it was a great flight.

10. Train and Railpass Skills

The European train system makes life easy for the visitor. The great trains of Europe shrink that already small continent, making the budget whirlwind or far-reaching tour a reasonable and exciting possibility for anyone.

Generally, European trains go where you need them to go and are fast, frequent, and inexpensive.

Eurail Countries

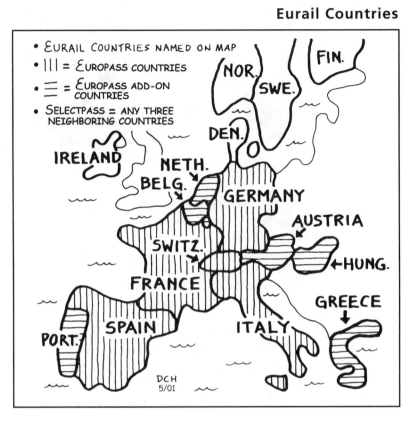

- EURAIL COUNTRIES NAMED ON MAP
- ||| = EUROPASS COUNTRIES
- ☰ = EUROPASS ADD-ON COUNTRIES
- SELECTPASS = ANY THREE NEIGHBORING COUNTRIES

DCH
5/01

(They're faster and more frequent in the north and less expensive but slower in the south.) You can easily have dinner in Paris, sleep on the train, and have breakfast in Rome, Munich, or Madrid.

You can buy train tickets as you travel or, depending on your trip, save money by buying a railpass.

RAILPASSES AND POINT-TO-POINT TICKETS

With a railpass, you can travel virtually anywhere, anytime without reservations. Just step on the proper train, sit in an unreserved seat, and, when the uniformed conductor comes, flash your pass. More and more fast trains are requiring reservations, but, despite that chore, a railpass is still a joy.

The train pass scene has become complex. It used to be just Eurail. But digging the English Channel Tunnel, building a bridge between Denmark and Sweden, and adding slick trains all over Europe aren't cheap. Consequently railpass prices have gone up faster than car rental rates.

First class   *Second class*
First class costs 50 percent more than second.

The 17-country, consecutive-day Eurailpasses are now harder to afford. Rather than lowering the price, the railpass companies are offering us ways to save money by consuming with more focus. Instead of just a consecutive-day Eurailpass, we now have "flexipasses" allowing us to travel a day here and a day there when we like; a core-of-Europe, five-country Europass; a three-country Eurail Selectpass; individual country passes; partner passes (giving two traveling together a 15 percent savings); and rail and drive passes. Let me explain:

Eurailpasses offer you unlimited first-class travel on all public railways in 17 European countries. These popular passes give you Western Europe (except Britain) by the tail. Choose between the consecutive-day pass (ranging from 15 days to three months) or the cheaper flexipass (any 10 or 15 individual days in two months). Travel partners (from 2 to 5 companions) save 15 percent with Eurail Saverpasses, available in consecutive-day and flexipass versions. Youths under 26 travel cheaper with second-class passes.

For the average independent first-timer planning to see lots of Europe (from Norway to Portugal to Italy, for instance), the Eurailpass is usually the best way to go. In a nutshell, you need to travel from Amsterdam to Rome to Madrid and back to Amsterdam to justify the purchase of a one-month Eurailpass. Two people on a three-week car trip (3,000 miles) and two people each using a three-week, first-class Eurailpass will spend about the same, around $600 per person.

Europasses are cheaper, mini–Eurail-type passes giving you 5, 6, 8, 10, or 15 "flexi" days in five core countries: France, Germany, Switzerland, Italy, and Spain. Neighboring regions can be added for an additional cost.

Eurail Selectpasses allow you to choose three adjoining countries, whether connected by land or ferry (for instance, Germany, Denmark,

Europe by Rail: Time and Cost

Connect the dots, add up the cost, and see if a railpass is right for your trip.

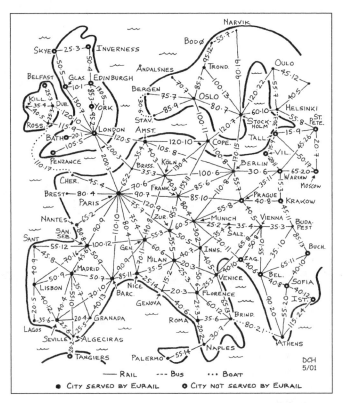

Map designed by Dave Hoerlein

The **first number** between cities = cost in $US for a 1-way, 2nd class ticket.

The **second number** = number of **hours** the trip takes.

●   = Cities served by Eurailpass.

○   = Cities **not** served by Eurailpass (for example, if you want to go from Munich to Prague, you'll need to pay extra for the portion through the Czech Republic).

…   = Boat crossings free or discounted with Eurailpass.

….   = Boat crossings **not** included with Eurailpass.

Important: These fares and times are based on the Eurail Tariff Guide. Actual prices may vary due to currency fluctuations and local promotions. Local competition can cut the actual price of some boat crossings (from Italy to Greece, for example) by 50% or more. Ireland - France boat is half-price for Eurailpass holders. For approx. 1st class rail prices, multiply the prices shown by 1.5. In some cases faster trains (like the TGV in France) are available, cutting the hours indicated on the map. Travelers under age 26 can receive up to 1/3 off the 2nd class fares shown. Carefully read the railpass descriptions in the back of this book to see which countries are included.

Guide to European Railpasses

Railpass details are confusing and tedious, but if you're planning to do Europe by rail on limited money, this book's "Guide to European Railpasses" (in the appendix) is very important. It's the only information source where you'll find rail deals available in the U.S. compared with rail deals available in Europe. My staff and I research and produce this guide annually. Our goal is to create smart consumers (as well as sell a few passes). It covers everything you need to know to order the best train pass for your trip, or to order nothing at all and save money by buying a pass or tickets in Europe. For our free updated 2002 Guide to European Railpasses, go to www.ricksteves.com or call 425/771-8303.

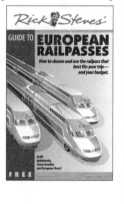

and Finland). With this flexipass, you can tailor the pass to your trip instead of trying to make your trip fit a pass. Discounts are available for youth and traveling companions.

Country passes focus on a single country—virtually every European country has such a pass. If you're limiting your travels to one country, this is your best bet. Because short passes cost much more per day than long passes, if you're considering patching together several country passes, you're probably better off with a Europass or the Eurail Selectpass.

Rail and drive passes are popular varieties of many of these passes. Along with a railpass (Eurail, Euro, or country), you get vouchers for Hertz or Avis car rental days (billed at the economical weekly rate). These allow travelers to do long trips by train and enjoy a car where they need the freedom to explore.

Point-to-point tickets can be your best budget bet. Many Eurail travelers would save lots of money by buying tickets as they go. While you can buy individual train tickets through your hometown travel agent, tickets are easy to buy—and cheaper—in Europe. You can buy tickets in train stations or, more comfortably, in the travel agency near your hotel. While most railpasses come only in first-class, travelers of any age can save 33 percent over first-class prices by purchasing second-class point-to-point tickets.

EUROPE'S TRAIN STATIONS

Train stations can be one of the independent traveler's best and most helpful friends. Take advantage of the assistance they can offer.

Train information: Every station has a train information office eager (or at least able) to help you with your scheduling. I usually consult the timetables myself first and write down my plan, then confirm this with the information desk. Written communication is easiest and safest. Computer terminals offering all the train schedules are becoming more common. They are multilingual and can be a real time-saver.

Eurail freedom: My idea of good travel is being on this platform in Hamburg. In five minutes, the train on track 7 is going to Berlin. In six minutes, a train will leave from track 8 for Copenhagen. And I've yet to decide which train I'll be on.

Tourist information and room-finding services: These are usually either in the station (in the case of major tourist centers) or nearby. Pick up a map with sightseeing information and, if you need it, advice on where to find budget accommodations.

Money changing: Most sizable stations have ATM machines offering great rates 24 hours a day. Often the station's money-changing office is open long after others have closed (though the rates aren't great).

Lockers: Virtually every station has storage lockers and/or a luggage-checking service where, for about $2 to $5 a day, you can leave your luggage. People traveling light can fit two rucksacks into one storage locker, cutting their storage costs in half.

Waiting rooms: Most stations have comfortable waiting rooms. Those with fancy tickets often enjoy fancy business or VIP lounges. The bigger stations are equipped with day hotels for those who want to shower, shave, rest, and so on. If, for one reason or another, I ever need a free, warm, and safe place to spend the night, a train station (or an airport) is my choice. Some stations boot everyone out from about midnight to 6 a.m. Ask before you bed down. Thieves work the stations in the wee hours. Be on guard.

Bus connections: Train stations are major bus stops, so connections from train to bus are generally no more difficult than crossing the street. Buses go from the stations to nearby towns that lack train service. If you have a bus to catch, be quick, since many are scheduled to connect with the train and leave promptly. If there's an airport nearby, you'll find bus or rail shuttle services (usually well marked) at the train station.

GETTING ON THE RIGHT TRACK

Armed with a train pass or a ticket, the independent traveler has Europe as a playground. Most will master the system simply by diving in and learning from their mistakes. To learn quicker—from someone else's mistakes—here are a few tips:

Many cities have more than one train station. Paris has six, Brussels has three, and even Switzerland's little Interlaken has two. Be sure you know whether your train is leaving from Interlaken East or Interlaken West, even if that means asking what might seem like a stupid question. A city's stations are generally connected by train, subway, or bus. When arriving in a city (especially on a milk-run train), you may stop at several suburban stations with signs indicating your destination's name with the name of the neighborhood (e.g., Madrid Vallecas or Roma Tiburtina). Don't jump out until you've reached the central station (Madrid Chamartin or Roma Termini). You can also avoid arrival frustrations by finding out if your train stops at a city's main station rather than a suburban one. For instance, several trains to "Venice" leave you at Venice's suburban station (Venezia Mestre), where you'll be stranded without a glimpse of a gondola. (You'll have to catch another train to reach the main "Venezia S. Lucia" station.)

Ask for help and pay attention. Managing on the trains is largely a matter of asking questions, letting people help you, and assuming things are logical. I always ask someone on the platform if the train is going where I think it is. (Point to the train or track and ask, "Roma?") Uniformed train personnel can answer any question you can communicate. Speak slowly, clearly, and with caveman simplicity. Be observant. If the loudspeaker comes on, gauge by the reaction of those around you if the announcement concerns you. If, after the babble, everyone dashes over to track 15, assume your train is no longer arriving on track 7.

This train started in Istanbul and will end in Wien Südbahnhof—Vienna's South Train Station.

The train on track 4 will stop at three Berlin stations. It was due to leave ten minutes ago, but the sign notes it's 20 minutes später.

Scope out the train ahead of time. The configuration of many major trains is charted in little display cases on the platform next to where your train will arrive. As you wait, study the display to note where the first-class and sleeping cars are, whether there's a diner, and which cars are going where. Some train schedules will say, in the fine print, "Munich-bound cars in the front, Vienna-bound cars in the rear." Knowing which cars you're eligible for can be especially handy if you'll be competing with a mob for a seat. When expecting a real scramble, I stand on a bench at the far end of the track and study each car as the train rolls by, noting where the most empty places are. If there are several departures within an hour or so and the first train looks hopeless, I'll wait for the next.

Never assume the whole train is going where you are. For long hauls, each car is labeled separately, because cars are usually added and dropped here and there along the journey. I'll never forget one hot afternoon in the middle of Spain. My train stopped in the middle of nowhere. There was some mechanical rattling. Then the train pulled away leaving me alone in my car . . . in La Mancha. Ten minutes later another train came along, picked up my car, and I was on my way. To survive all of this juggling easily, be sure that the city on your car's nameplate is your destination. The nameplate lists the final stop and some (but not all) of the stops in between.

Every car has plenty of room for luggage. In 25 years of train travel, I've never checked a bag. Simply carry it on and heave it up onto the racks above the seats. I've seen Turkish families moving all their worldly goods from Germany back to Turkey without checking a thing. People complain about the porters in the European train stations. I think they're great—I've never used one. People with more luggage than they can carry deserve porters.

Luggage is never completely safe. There is a thief on every train (union rules) planning to grab a bag (see Chapter 22: Outsmarting Thieves). Don't be careless. Before leaving my luggage in a compartment, I establish a relationship with everyone there. I'm safe leaving it among mutual guards.

Many train travelers are ripped off while they sleep. A $20 *couchette* (berth in a compartment, see below) is safer because an attendant monitors who comes and goes. Those sleeping for free in regular cars should exercise extreme caution. Keep your valuables in a money belt or at least securely attached to your body. I clip and fasten my rucksack to the luggage rack. If one tug doesn't take the bag, a thief will usually leave it rather than ask, "*Scusi*, how is your luggage attached?" You'll hear stories of entire train cars being gassed and robbed in Italy and Spain. It happens—but I wouldn't lose sleep over it.

Women need to be careful on all overnight rides. Women should use discretion when choosing a compartment. Sleeping in an empty compartment in southern Europe is an open invitation to your own private Casanova. Choose a room with a European granny or nun in it. That way you'll get a little peace, and he won't even try. A *couchette* (berth) is your best bet.

Use train time wisely. Train travelers, especially Eurailers, spend a lot of time on the train. This time can be dull and unproductive, or you can make a point to do whatever you can on the train to free up time off the train. It makes no sense to sit bored on the train and then, upon arrival, sit in the station for an hour reading your information and deciding where to go for hotels and what to do next.

Spend train time studying, reading, writing postcards or journal entries, eating, organizing, or cleaning. Talk to local people or other travelers. There is so much to be learned. Europeans are often less open and forward than

Andrea Hagg

Making friends on the trains

Americans. You could sit across from a silent but fascinating and friendly European for an entire train ride, or you could break the ice by asking a question, quietly offering some candy or a cigarette (even if you don't smoke), or showing your Hometown, USA postcards. This can start the conversation flowing and the friendship growing.

TRAIN SCHEDULES—BREAKING THE CODE

Learning to decipher train schedules makes life on Europe's rails easier. These list all trains that come to and go from a particular station each day, and are clearly posted in two separate listings: departures (the ones we're concerned with, usually in yellow) and arrivals (normally in white). You'll also find airport-type departure schedules that flip up and list the next 8 or 10 departures. These often befuddle travelers who don't realize that all over the world the same four easy-to-identify columns are listed: destination, type of train, track number, and departure time. I don't care what language they're in, without much effort you can accurately guess which column is what.

Train schedule computers (in most Italian stations and spreading across Europe) will save you many long waits in station information lines. Use them to understand all your options. Indicate your language, departure and arrival points, and rough time of departure, and all workable connections will flash on the screen.

If you want to check schedules before you go to Europe, the Internet is your best resource. Try www .reiseauskunft.bahn.de/bin /query.exe/en for all of Europe, including tiny towns, though its info on Spain is limited (supplement with www.renfe.es); note that you only need to fill in "From" and "To" before clicking on "Search Connections." Other Web timetables include www .raileurope.com (for links

In this French train station, arrivals and departures are clearly listed. Who says you can't read French? The small schedule in the middle lists trains that are about to depart. The Tabac stand sells candy, phone cards, newspapers, and often subway and bus tickets.

to each country's rail site) and http://mercurio.iet.unipi.it. If you prefer a book format, consider *The Thomas Cook Continental Timetable*. Published several times a year (because schedules change with the season), it contains nearly every European train time-table, complete with maps ($33 postpaid, tel. 800/FORSYTH or www.forsyth.com.) Although I don't carry the bulky "Cook Book" with me, those who do find it handy.

Learn to use the 24-hour clock used in European timetables. After 12:00 noon, the Europeans keep going—13:00, 14:00, and so on. To convert to the 12-hour clock, subtract 12 and add p.m. (16:00 is 4 p.m.).

Scoping Out Schedules

Let's crack the code in the Thomas Cook Book. You'll find these confusing-looking charts and maps in the Cook Timetable. Find the trip you want to take on the appropriate train map. Your route will be numbered, referring you to the proper timetable. That table is the schedule for the trains traveling along that line, in both directions (a. = arrivals, d. = departures).

As an example, let's go from Turin to Venice (the local spellings are always used, in this case, Torino and Venezia). This is #350 on the map. So refer to table 350. Locate your starting point, Torino. Reading from left to right, you will see that trains leave Torino for Venezia at 7:08, 9:06, 15:08, 15:50, and 22:50. Those trains arrive in Venezia at 11:55, 13:59, 19:55, 21:25, and 5:08, respectively. Note that Venezia has two stations (Mestre and the more central Santa Lucia). As you can see, not all Torino departures go all the way to Venezia. For example, the 8:50 train only goes to Milan, arriving at 10:40. From there, the 10:50 train will get you to Venezia SL by 13:59. The 15:08 departure stops at Venezia Mestre, not actually in Venice. That's an inconvenience but not a big problem, since you can assume there are frequent connections from outlying stations to downtown. This schedule shows an overnight train. You could leave Torino at 22:50 and arrive in Venezia by 5:08.

Train schedules are helpful in planning your stopovers. For instance, this table shows a train leaving Torino at 8:50 and arriving in Milan at 10:40. You could spend two hours touring Milan's cathedral, catch the 13:05 train for Verona (arrive at 14:27, see the Roman Arena and Juliet's balcony), and hop on the 19:10 train to arrive in Venezia by 20:35.

Each table has three parts: a schedule for each direction (only one is shown here) and a section explaining the many exceptions to the rules (not shown here). You never know when one of those confusing exceptions might affect your train. Schedule symbols also indicate problem-causing exceptions, such as which trains are first-class or sleepers only, or charge supplements. An X means you'll have to change trains, crossed hammers indicate the train goes only on workdays (daily except Sundays and holidays), a little bed means the train has sleeping compart-

Table 350 — TORINO - MILANO - VENEZIA

km		IC 645	IR 2007	IR 2009	IC 649	IR 2097	E 351	IC 651	EC 39	IC 657	IR 2107	EC 13	IR 2019	IR 2031	E 869
0	Torino Porta Nuova 353 ...d.	0708	0750	(0850)	0906	...	...	1108	...	1508	...	...	1550	2150	2250
6	Torino Porta Susa 353 ...d.	0718	0800	(0900)	0915	...	...	1118	...	1518	...	...	1600	2200	2300
29	Chivasso 353 ...d.		0816	0916	0933	...	...		...		...	...	1616	2216	2316
60	Santhia ...d.		0834	0934		...	...		...		...	...	1634	2234	2334
79	Vercelli ...d.	0802	0846	0946	1002	...	...	1202	...	1602	...	...	1646	2246	2346
101	Novara ...d.	0818	0901	1001	1018	...	...	1218	...	1618	...	...	1701	2301	0001
153	Milano Centrale ...a.	0850	0940	(1040)	1050	...	...	1250	...	1650	...	...	1740	2340	0040

| | | | | | IC 647 | | | | | | IR 2109 | | | | |

km		IC 645			IC 647	IR 2097	E 351	IC 651	EC 39	IC 657	IR 2109	EC 13	IR 2019	IR 2031	E 869
153	Milano Centrale ...d.	0905	...	...	1105	1110	1210	.	(1305)	1705	1710	...	1810	..	0110
187	Treviglio ...d.		...	...		1135	1235	...			1735	...	1835	...	0150
236	Brescia ...d.	0952	...	...	1152	1206	1306	...	1352	1752	1806	...	1906	...	0239
263	Desenzano del Garda ...d.		...	...		1224	1324	...			1824	...	1924	...	0257
278	Peschiera del Garda ...d.		...	...		1235	1335	...			1835		1935	...	0309
300	Verona Porta Nuova ...d.	1027	...	...	1227	1254	1354	...	(1427)	1827	1854	(1910)	1954	...	0331
325	San Bonifacio ...d.		...	...		1311	1411	...			1911		2011	...	0347
351	Vicenza ...d.	1100	...	...	1300	1332	1432	...	1500	1900	1932	1945	2032	...	0410
382	Padova ...d.	1122	...	...	1323	1353	1453	...	1522	1922	1953	2004	2053	...	0433
411	Venezia Mestre ...a.	1140	...	...	1346	1413	1513	...	1540	1940	2013	2024	2113	...	0454
411	Venezia Mestre ...d.	1155	...	...	1349	1416	1516	...	1543	1955	2016	2026	2116	...	0459
420	Venezia Santa Lucia ...a.		...	...	1359	1425	1525	...	1552		2025	(2035)	2125	...	0508
	Trieste Centrale 376 ...a.	1345	...	...	...	...	...	...	...	2145	...	...	...	...	0910b

taken from Cook Timetable

ments, an *R* in a box means reservations are required for that departure, and a cross means the train goes only on Sundays and holidays. Remember that each table shows just some of the trains that travel along that track. Other tables feed onto the same line.

City Name Variations

American Name	European Name	American Name	European Name
Athens (Gre.)	*Athinai*	Lisbon (Port.)	*Lisboa*
Bolzano (Italy)	*Bozen* in German	London	*Londres* in French
Bruges (Bel.)	*Brugge*	Munich (Ger.)	*München* (in Italian, *Monaco di Baviera*)
Brussels (Bel.)	*Bruxelles*		
Cologne (Ger.)	*Köln*		
Copenhagen (Den.)	*København*	Naples (Italy)	*Napoli*
Florence (Italy)	*Firenze*	Padua (Italy)	*Padova*
Geneva (Switz.)	*Genève*	Pamplona (Spain)	*Iruña* in Basque
Genoa (Italy)	*Genova* (not *Geneva*)	Paris (Fr.)	*Parigi* in Italian
		Prague (Czech.)	*Praha*
Gothenburg (Swe.)	*Göteborg*	Venice (Italy)	*Venezia*
The Hague (Neth.)	*Den Haag, S'Gravenhage*	Vienna (Aus.)	*Wien*
Helsinki (Fin.)	*Helsingfors* in Swedish	Warsaw (Pol.)	*Warszawa*

Train schedules are a great help to the traveler—if you can read them. Many rail travelers never take the time to figure them out. In this chapter, you'll find a sample map and schedule to practice on. Understand it. You'll be glad you did.

Confirm your plans at the station. The person who knows for sure what's going on is the one at the train station information window. Let that person help you. He can fix mistakes and save you many hours. Just show your plan on a scrap of paper (e.g., Torino→ Milano, 8:50–10:40; Milano→ Verona, 13:05-14:27) and ask, "OK?" If your plan is good, he'll nod, direct you to your track, and you're on your way. If there's a problem, he'll solve it. Uniformed train employees on the platforms or on board the trains can also help.

HOW TO SLEEP ON THE TRAIN

The economy of night travel is tremendous. Sleeping while rolling down the tracks saves time and money, both of which, for most travelers, are limited resources. The first concern about night travel is usually, "Aren't you missing a lot of beautiful scenery? You just slept through half of Sweden!" The real question should be, "Did the missed scenery matter, since you gained an extra day for hiking the Alps, biking through tulips, or island-hopping in the Greek seas?" The answer: No. Maximize night trips.

Couchettes

To assure a safer and uninterrupted night's sleep, you can usually reserve a sleeping berth that's known as a *couchette* (pronounced koo-SHET) at least a day in advance from a travel agency, at the station ticket counter, or, if there are any available, from the conductor on the train. For about the cost of a cheap hotel bed ($20), you'll get sheets, pillow, blankets, a fold-out bunk bed in a compartment with three to five other people, and, hopefully, a good night's sleep.

For $20, you can rent a couchette *(bunk bed) on your overnight train. Top bunks give you a bit more room and safety—but B.Y.O.B.&B.*

As you board, you'll give the attendant your *couchette* voucher, railpass or ticket, and passport. He deals with the conductors and customs officials and keeps the thieves out so you can sleep soundly and safely. While some trains (especially in France) have cushier first-class *couchettes* (double rather than triple bunks for $35 apiece if you have a first-class ticket), most *couchettes* are the same for both classes. While the top bunk gives you more privacy and luggage space, it can be hotter and stuffier than lower bunks and a couple of inches shorter (a concern if you're 6'2" or taller). While compartments are usually coed, you can request smoking or nonsmoking, and top, middle, or bottom berths.

Sleepers: Sleepers are beds in two-bed or three-bed compartments, ranging from about $50 to $100 per person. They are ideal though pricey for couples who want privacy.

Hotel Trains: If you're on a budget, avoid the fancy hotel trains. Increasingly common between Spain and France, Italy, and Switzerland, these overnight hotels-on-wheels are comfortable and, though discounted with a railpass, still expensive. Cheaper options exist and involve changing trains at the Spanish border.

A Typical Train Compartment

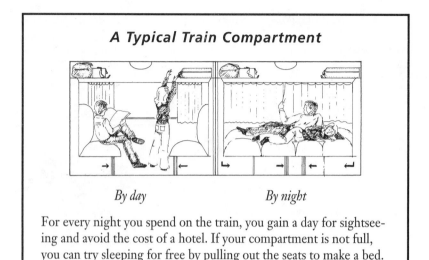

By day   *By night*

For every night you spend on the train, you gain a day for sightseeing and avoid the cost of a hotel. If your compartment is not full, you can try sleeping for free by pulling out the seats to make a bed.

Sleeping Free in Compartments

Shoestring travelers avoid a $20 *couchette* and just sack out for free, draping their tired bodies over as many unoccupied seats as possible. But trying to sleep overnight without a bed can be a waking nightmare.

One night of endless head bobbing, swollen toes, and a screaming tailbone, sitting up straight in a dark eternity of steel wheels crashing along rails, trying doggedly—yet hopelessly—to get comfortable, will teach you the importance of finding a spot to stretch out for the night. This is an art that vagabond night travelers cultivate. Those with the greatest skill at this game sleep. Those not so talented will spend the night gnashing their teeth and squirming for relief.

A traditional train car has about 10 compartments, each with six or eight seats (three or four facing three or four). Most have seats that pull out and armrests that lift, turning your compartment into a bed on wheels. But this is possible only if you have more seats than people in your compartment. A compartment that seats six can sleep three. So if between 30 and 60

They didn't rent a couchette.

people choose your car, some will sleep and some will sit. Your fate depends on how good you are at encouraging people to sit elsewhere. There are many ways to play this game (which has few rules and encourages creativity). Here are my favorite techniques.

The Big Sleep: Arrive 30 minutes before your train leaves. Walk most of the length of the train but not to the last car. Choose a car that is going where you want to go and find an empty compartment. Pull

Car #126 from Copenhagen to Paris' North Station is second-class (indicated by the large number 2), no smoking (the crossed out cigarette), and filled with couchettes (the flat bed under the number 2).

two seats out to make a bed, close the curtains, turn out the lights, and pretend you are sound asleep. It's amazing. At 9 p.m. everyone on that train is snoring away! The first 30 people to get on that car have room to sleep. Number 31 will go into any car with the lights on and people sitting up. The most convincing "sleepers" will be the last to be "woken up." (The real champs put a hand down their pants and smile peacefully.)

The Hare Krishna Approach: A more interesting way that works equally well and is more fun is to sit cross-legged on the floor and chant religious-sounding, exotically discordant harmonies, with a faraway look on your face. People will open the door, stare in for a few seconds, and leave, determined to sit in the aisle rather than share a compartment with the likes of you. You'll probably sleep alone, or end up chanting the night away with five other religious fanatics.

Using reservation cards to your advantage: Each compartment will have a reservation board outside the door. Never sit in a seat that is reserved because you'll be "bumped out" just before the train leaves. Few people realize that you can determine how far the people on a train will travel by reading their reservation tags. Each tag explains which segment of the journey that seat is reserved for. Find a compartment with three or four people traveling for just an hour or two, and for the rest of the night you will probably have that compartment to yourself.

Remember that trains add and lose cars throughout the night. A train could be packed with tourists heading for Milan, and at 1 a.m. an empty

Milan-bound car could be added. The difference between being packed like sardines and stretching out in your own fishbowl could be as little as one car away.

These tricks work not to take advantage of others but to equal out the trainload. When all compartments are lightly loaded and people continue to load in, let the air out of your inflatable travel partner and make room for your new roommates. To minimize the misery on a full train, sit opposite your partner, pull out the seats, and share a single bed (and the smell of your feet).

BUS VERSUS TRAIN

Except in Ireland, Greece, Turkey, Portugal, parts of Spain, and Morocco, the trains are faster, more comfortable, and have more extensive schedules than buses. Bus trips are usually less expensive (especially in the British Isles) and are occasionally included on your railpass (where operated by the train companies, as many are in Germany, Switzerland, and Belgium).

There are some cheap, long-haul buses, such as Eurolines (www .eurolines.com) and more hippie-type "magic buses" such as Busabout (www.busabout.com). These can save you plenty over train fares. For example, Eurolines' one-way bus fare from Amsterdam to Paris is $33 (compared to $100 second-class by train); from Paris to Barcelona it's $75 ($110 by train); and from Paris to Rome it's $80 ($145 by train); you get price breaks for round-trips and advance booking.

Use buses mainly to pick up where Europe's great train system leaves off. Buses fan out from the smallest train stations to places too small for the train to cover. For towns with train stations far from the center (e.g., hill towns), buses are often scheduled to meet each arrival and shuttle passengers to the main square (often for no extra cost). Many bus connections to nearby towns not served by train are timed to depart just after the train arrives.

11. Driving Europe Crazy

Behind the wheel you're totally free. You go where you want to, when you want to. You're not limited by tracks and schedules. And driving's great for those who don't believe in packing light...you can even rent a trailer.

Driving can be economical. Solo car travel is expensive, but three or four people sharing a rented car usually travel cheaper than three or four using train passes.

The super mobility of a car saves you time in locating budget accommodations in small towns and away from the train lines. This savings helps to rationalize the "splurge" of a car rental. You can also play it riskier in peak season, arriving in a town late with no reservation. If the hotels are full, you simply drive to the next town.

Every year, as train prices go up, car rental becomes a better option for budget travelers in Europe. While most travel dreams come with choo-choo noises, and most first trips are best by rail, you should at least consider the convenience of driving.

RENTING A CAR

Cars are economical when rented by the week with unlimited mileage through your travel agent or directly with the rental company in the United States. (There are a few decent three-day deals.) There is no way to chart the best car rental deals. Rates vary from company to company, month to month, and country to country. The cheapest company for rental in one country might be the most expensive in the next. After shopping for half an hour via the toll-free phone numbers listed below, you'll know who has the best deal for your travel plans. Rentals arranged from major companies in Europe are so expensive that you'd save money by having someone arrange your rental for you back in the United States.

In Europe cars are rented for a 24-hour day with a 59-minute grace period. Daily rates are ridiculously high. That's why the various rail 'n' drive passes are a good deal (see the Guide to European Railpasses in the appendix). They basically allow you to rent a car one day at a time at one-seventh the cheap weekly rate.

Car or Train?

While you should travel the way you like, consider these variables when deciding if your European experience might be better by car or train:

Concern	By Car	By Train
• packing heavy?	• no problem	• must go light
• scouring one area	• best	• frustrating
• all over Europe	• too much driving	• great
• big cities	• expensive/worthless	• ideal
• camping	• perfect	• more like boot camp
• one or two people	• expensive	• probably cheaper
• three or more	• probably cheaper	• more expensive
• traveling with young kids	• survivable	• miserable

Car vs. Train—
Rough Costs of Sample Trips per Person

Mode of Transportation	3 weeks 1,600 mi.	3 weeks 3,000 mi.	2 months 3,000 mi.	2 months 8,000 mi.
Eurailpass (first class, consecutive day travel)	$718*	$718*	$1,260*	$1,260*
Second-class individual train tickets	$385	$570	$570	$1,500
Subcompact car (two people)	$450	$560	$890	$1,225
Midsized car (four people)	$280	$330	$540	$700

Sample trips:
- Munich–Paris–Florence–Munich = 1,600 miles.
- Amsterdam–Munich–Rome–Barcelona–Paris = 3,000 miles.
- Amsterdam–Copenhagen–Stockholm–Oslo–Copenhagen–Berlin–Vienna–Athens–Rome–Nice–Madrid–Lisbon–Madrid–Paris–Amsterdam = 8,000 miles.

Train tickets cost about 18 cents per mile in the south and east, 25 cents per mile in the north. Car rates based on typical rentals (for 3 weeks) or leases (for 2 months), including collision damage waiver (CDW) supplements and figuring $4 per gallon and 30 mpg. Rates vary wildly from company to company and from country to country.

*Cheaper alternatives exist: Saverpasses (for two or more travelers), Flexipasses (5, 10, or 15 days of travel within two months), or Europasses (flexipasses for core European countries).

Cost of Car Rental: About $560 a Week

A rough estimate for weekly rental with unlimited mileage plus collision damage waiver (CDW) insurance. Two people in a car for three weeks pay around $560 each...less than the cost of a three-week consecutive day Eurail Saverpass (about $610).

Ford Fiesta:	$200–300
Tax:	15–25 percent extra
CDW:	$10–25/day
Gas:	$130/week ($4/gallon, 30 mpg, 140 miles/day)
Parking in big cities:	$20/day
Freeway tolls (France and Italy only):	$5–7/hour

While ages vary from country to country and company to company, those who are at least 25 years old should have no trouble renting a car. (Younger renters can get stuck with extra costs, like being required to buy CDW insurance.) Only Ireland has a maximum age limit (75). If you're considered too young or too old, look into leasing (see below), which has less stringent age restrictions. Council Travel (800/2-COUNCIL, www.counciltravel.com) and car companies advertising in Let's Go guidebooks are seeking young renters.

Small car, big scenery

Rhonda Pelikan

Rental cars come with the necessary insurance and paperwork to cross borders effortlessly in all of Western Europe. If you plan to drive your rental car from Western to Eastern Europe, keep these tips in mind: State your travel plans up front to the rental company. Some won't allow any of their rental cars to enter Eastern European countries due to the high theft rate. Some won't allow certain types of cars: BMWs, Mercedes, and convertibles. Ask about extra fees—some companies automatically tack on theft and collision coverage for an eastward excursion. To avoid hassles at the border, ask the rental agent to mark your contract with the company's permission to cross.

Some rental companies allow you to take a rental car from Britain to the Continent or to Ireland, but be prepared to pay extra fees (e.g., $165 to drop off a car in London that you picked up in Paris). Hertz offers a unique "Le Swap" program—you get a round-trip Chunnel Passage and a right-hand car rental for Britain that's swapped for a left-hand rental on the Continent. If you want to drive in Britain and Ireland, it's usually cheaper to rent two separate cars than one because of the high ferry costs (two single weeks of car rental usually cost the same as two weeks in a row).

Some companies charge 10 percent or more if you pick up your car at the airport. When you're calling about prices, rental agents usually quote you this pricier airport pickup rate. Ask if they have a cheaper, downtown-pickup price. Some companies deliver the car to your hotel for free.

Take advantage of open-jaw possibilities to save rental days and avoid big-city driving. You can normally pick up and drop off a car at any of your rental company's offices in one country. They don't care if you change your expected drop-off city. (For maximum options, pick up a list of all the offices in that country.) Typically there is a $200 fee to drop in another country. You'll find some happy and some outrageous ($700) exceptions. If expecting an expensive drop fee in another country, you can call the car rental company every few days to see if they have a car that needs to be returned to the country where you're planning on dropping the car. If so, you can swap cars and avoid the drop fee. Or ask to survey the lot to see if they have a car with your drop-off country's plates. You'll do them a favor and save yourself some money by driving this car "home" for them.

Your American driver's license is all you need in most European countries. An international driver's permit provides a translation of your American license—making it easier for the cop to write out the ticket. Exactly where you need one depends on whom you talk to. People who sell them say you should have them almost everywhere. People who rent cars say you need them almost nowhere. Police can get mad (their concern is in finding the expiration date) and fine you if you don't have one. Those traveling in Portugal, Spain, Italy, Austria, Germany, Greece, and Eastern Europe should probably get an international driver's permit (at your local AAA office—$10 plus the cost of two passport-type photos).

Note that most rental cars in Europe have manual transmissions. Renting an automatic can tack on an extra $100 per week. Brush up on your shifting skills. It's better to lurch through your hometown parking lot than grind your gears over the Alps.

COST OF CAR RENTAL

To really compare car costs with train costs, figure your weekly unlimited mileage rental rate plus:

- **Tax**, which is clear and consistent within each country, generally 18 to 25 percent (less in Spain, Germany, Ireland, and Luxembourg, and only 8 percent in Switzerland—but Swiss rental rates are that much higher)
- **CDW insurance supplement** (figure $10–25 a day, see below)
- **Gas** ($130 a week, giving you about 1,000 miles)
- **Tolls** for superfreeways in France and Italy (about $5–7 per hour), $25 for the highway permit decal as you enter Switzerland, $8 for Austria
- **Parking** ($20 a day in big cities, free otherwise)
- **Theft protection** (required in Italy, at about $12–15/day)

Leading Car Rental Companies

Big companies (the first 4 listings below) offer more reliability and flexibility, but consolidators and wholesalers (the last 4) can be cheaper. All can be arranged directly or through your travel agent.

Avis	800/331-1084	www.avis.com
Dollar	800/800-6000	www.dollar.com
Budget	800/472-3325	www.budget.com
Hertz	800/654-3001	www.hertz.com
Auto Europe	800/223-5555	www.autoeurope.com
DER Tours*	800/782-2424	www.dertravel.com
Europe by Car	800/223-1516	www.europebycar.com
Kemwel	800/678-0678	www.kemwel.com

*best for German/Czech

Before you commit, ask about whatever's applicable to your situation:
• weekly unlimited mileage rate
• age restrictions
• insurance cost
• CDW options
• theft insurance (required in Italy)
• cost of adding another driver
• drop-off costs within a country or in another country
• a listing of offices in the countries you're visiting (consider the most efficient pick-up and drop-off points)
• if it's cheaper to pick up the car at the airport or downtown
• if there is a covered trunk
• availability of automatics and car seats
• any restrictions on driving the car in all countries (particularly in Eastern Europe)
• any special "match the competition" deals for a better price
• any additional charges or local taxes such as VAT (value added tax)

Before you drive away, ask about:
• changing a tire
• how to use the radio, lights, etc.
• location of insurance green card
• making repairs and emergency roadside services

The Collision Damage Waiver (CDW) Racket

When you rent a car, you are generally liable for the entire value of that car. For peace of mind, get a collision damage waiver (CDW) supplement. This costs from $10 to $25 a day, depending on the country, the car, and the company. Figure roughly $150 a week for CDW. Travel Guard sells CDW at a much better rate of $6 a day; it's recognized throughout Europe except in the Republic of Ireland or Italy (tel. 800/826-1300, www.travelguard.com).

While some credit cards promise to give you free CDW coverage if you charge the rental on their card, you'll go without CDW as far as the rental company is concerned (and they'll often lie to you, saying your credit-card coverage is no good). Check with your credit-card company. Ask if the amount of coverage is limited to your credit limit on the card, and ask to have the worst-case scenario explained to you.

Luckily, he paid extra for full insurance.

Unscrupulous rental companies will put a hold on your credit card for the value of the car, which can cause problems if you plan on using your card during your trip. If you have an accident, you may have to settle with the rental company and then fight to get reimbursed by your credit-card company when you get home. Note that big American-based car rental companies are easier to work with if you have a problem.

Many rental companies have all-inclusive plans that include a more reasonable CDW. Ask your travel agent about this. Those renting a car for more than three weeks should ask their agent about leasing (see below), which skirts many tax and insurance costs.

CDW is most expensive when purchased at the car rental desk. If you do pay the car company, remember that the rental rates are so competitive that, to make a reasonable profit, these companies have had to make a killing on the CDW. If it's any consolation, think of your CDW fee as half for CDW and half money that you should have paid on the rental fee.

Regardless of how tough CDW is on the pocketbook, I get it for the peace of mind. Note that CDW doesn't cover damage caused by reckless driving. But if you drive responsibly, you'll be able to hold your own on the autobahn (German freeway) with Europe's skilled maniac drivers, knowing you can return your car in an unrecognizable shambles with an apologetic shrug, say "S-s-s-sorry," and lose no money.

LEASING AND BUYING

Leasing (technically, buying the car and selling it back) gets around many tax and insurance costs and is a good deal for people needing a car for three weeks or more. Europe by Car now leases cars in France for as few as 17 days for $500. Lease prices include all taxes and CDW insurance. Germany, France, Belgium, and the Netherlands are also particularly good for leasing.

Although Americans rarely consider this budget option, Aussies and New Zealanders routinely buy used cars for their trips and sell them when they're done. The most popular places to buy cars are Amsterdam, Frankfurt, London, and U.S. military bases. In London, check the used-car market on Market Road (Caledonian Road Tube) and look in London periodicals such as *TNT*, *Loote*, and *New Zealand-UK News*, which list used cars as well as jobs, flats, cheap flights, and travel partners.

Campers: Consider the advantage of a van or motor home, which gives you the flexibility to drive late and just pull over and camp for free. For all the details, including information on insurance and registration issues, see *Road Trip Europe: How to Rent, Buy, Ship, and Enjoy Campers and Motor Homes Abroad* by David Shore and Patty Campbell (2002, 250 pages, $18 postpaid, 1842 Santa Margarita Drive, Fallbrook, CA 92028, tel. 800/659-5222, tel. & fax 760/723-6184, e-mail: shorecam@aol.com). Campanje, a Dutch company, specializes in used VW campers fully loaded for camping through Europe. Rates run about $500 per week for a four-person camper van (minimum 4 weeks), including tax and insurance. Ask about discounts for early booking and off-season and long-term rental. (For a brochure, write to P.O. Box 9332, 3506 GH Utrecht, Netherlands, tel. 31/30-244-7070, fax 31/30-242-0981, www.xs4all.nl/~campanje.)

BEHIND THE EUROPEAN WHEEL

Horror stories about European traffic abound. They're fun to tell, but driving in Europe is really only a problem for those who make it one. Any good American driver can cope with European traffic.

Europe is a continent of frustrated race-car drivers. The most dangerous creature on the road is the timid American. Be aggressive, observe, fit in, avoid big-city driving when you can, wear your seat belt, and pay extra for CDW insurance.

Drive European. After a few minutes on the autobahn, you'll learn that you don't cruise in the passing lane. Cruise in the right-hand lane.

And drive defensively. Be warned that some Europeans, particularly

Standard European Road Signs

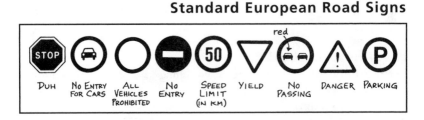

Italians, make up their own rules of the road. In Rome, my cabbie went through three red lights. White-knuckled, I asked, "*Scusi*, do you see red lights?" He said, "When I come to light, I look. If no cars come, red light *stupido*, I go through. If policeman sees no cars—*no problema*—red light *stupido*."

Learn the signs. All of Europe uses the same simple set of road symbols. Just take a few minutes to learn them. Many major rest stops have free local driving almanacs (or cheap maps) explaining such signs, roadside facilities, and exits.

You can drive in and out of strange towns fairly smoothly by following a few basic signs. Most European towns have signs directing you to the "old town" or the center (such as *centrum*, *centro*, *centre ville*, *stadtmitte*). The tourist office, normally right downtown, will usually be clearly signposted (*i*, *turismo*, *VVV*, or various abbreviations that you'll learn in each country). The tallest church spire often marks the center of the old town. Park in its shadow and look for the tourist information office. To leave a city, look for freeway signs (distinctive green or blue, depending on the country) or "all directions" (*toutes directions*) signs. Avoid heavy traffic times. Big cities are great fun and nearly traffic-free for Sunday drives. Mediterranean resort areas are extremely congested on summer weekends.

Much of Europe uses "parking clocks" instead of parking meters. These cardboard clocks often come with rental cars or can be bought cheap at gas stations, newsstands, or tobacco shops. After parking, you can set the clock for the current time and leave it on your dashboard. A street sign indicates how much time you have and the clock establishes when you arrived. In Germanic countries, where they're widely used, ask for a Parkscheibe.

Get the necessary stickers for Switzerland and Austria. You'll pay about $25 for the highway permit decal as you enter Switzerland, $8 for Austria (sold at border crossings). If you don't get the decal, you'll soon meet your first local—in uniform.

To save time, use the freeway. The shortest distance between any two European points is found on the autobahn/strada/route. Although tolls can be high in Italy and France ($7/hr in Italy, $40 to get from Paris to the French Riviera—priciest around Monaco), the gas and time saved on European superfreeways justifies the expense. Some prefer the more scenic and free national highway systems (*route nationale* in France). Small roads can be a breeze, or they can be dreadfully jammed up. To study ahead, consult www.viamichelin.com.

Passing is essential. Americans are timid about passing. Be bold but careful. On winding, narrow roads, you'll notice a turn-signal sign language from the slower car ahead of you indicating when it's OK to pass. This is used inconsistently. Don't rely on it blindly.

Don't use a car for city sightseeing. Park it and use public transportation (or taxis). City parking is a pain. Find a spot as close to the center as possible, grab it, and keep it. For overnight stops, it's crucial to choose a safe, well-traveled, and well-lit spot. A tourist's car parked overnight in a bad urban neighborhood will almost certainly be vandalized. In cities where traffic is worst, look for huge government-sponsored (cheap) parking lots on the outskirts, where a bus or subway will zip you easily into the center. It's often worth parking in a garage ($10–30 a day). Ask your hotel receptionist for advice.

Go metric. On the continent you'll be dealing with kilometers. To convert kilometers to miles, drop the last digit, then multiply by six (90 km/hr: 9 x 6 = 54 mph; 120 km/hr: 12 x 6 = 72 mph). To convert miles to kilometers, divide by six and add zero (50 miles ÷ 6 = 8, add zero to make 80 kilometers). Britain uses miles instead of kilometers. Gas is sold by the liter (4 to a gallon).

Explore Britain's roundabouts. Instead of intersections with stoplights, the British have roundabouts. These work wonderfully if you yield to cars already inside the circle. For many, roundabouts are high-pressure circles that require a snap decision about something you really don't completely understand—your exit. To replace the stress with levity, make it standard operating procedure to take a 360-degree case-out-your-options circuit, discuss the exits with your navigator, go around again if necessary, and then confidently wing off on the exit of your choice.

GAS

The cost of gas in Europe—$3 to $5 a gallon—sounds worse than it is. Distances are short, the petite puddle-jumpers get great mileage, and, when compared to costly train tickets (for the price of a two-hour train ride you can fill your tank), expensive gas is less of a factor. You'll be impressed by how few miles you need to travel to enjoy Europe's diversity.

Pumping gas in Europe is as easy as finding a gas station ("self-service" is universal), sticking the nozzle in, and pulling the big trigger. Gas prices are listed by the liter (about a quart). Don't get confused: Gas is called *petrol* or *benzine*, while diesel is known as *gasoil*. Super is *super* and normal is *normal* (or *essence*) and increasingly rare. In Eastern Europe, use the highest octane available. Unleaded gas (look for the green pump) is standard throughout Western Europe. Freeway stations are more expensive than those in towns, but during siesta only freeway stations are open. Giant suburban supermarkets often offer the cheapest gas.

JOYRIDING

The British Isles are good for driving—reasonable rentals, no language barrier, exciting rural areas, and fine roads; and after one near head-on collision scares the bloody heck out of you, you'll have no trouble remembering which side of the road to drive on.

Other good driving areas are Scandinavia (call for free reservations to avoid long waits at ferry crossings); Belgium and the Netherlands (yield to bikes—you're outnumbered); Spain and Portugal (explore out-of-the-way villages and hill towns); and Germany, Switzerland, and Austria (driving down sunny alpine valleys with yodeling on the tape deck is auto ecstasy). The whirlwind, see-Europe-from-top-to-bottom-type trip is best by train.

12. Biking, Hitching, Walking, and Hiking

BIKING IN EUROPE

Biking is big in Europe. Many cities such as Amsterdam, Copenhagen, and Munich are great by bike. Riverside bike paths from Salzburg, Luxor, and along the Rhine have left me with top-notch memories. Within cities, bikes cut transportation times in half, giving you more time to spend at the sites. Wherever it's worth biking, you'll find a bike rental shop. Bikes are bargains at $10 to $15 a day.

Bikes are a fun change of pace if you're traveling by car or train. In many countries (especially France, Germany, Austria, Belgium, and the Netherlands), the train sta-

Bike-rental shops offer deals on wheels.

Dominic Bonuccelli

tions rent bikes (30 percent discount in Austria for those with train tickets or passes) and sometimes have easy "pick up here and drop off there" plans. For mixing train and bike travel, ask at stations for information booklets: *Bahn & Bike* (Germany/Austria), *Train + Velo* (France), *Velo und Bahn* (Switzerland), and *Treins en Fiets* (Netherlands).

Guided bike tours, ranging from two to five hours, are popular in Europe's cities (such as Amsterdam, Bruges, Paris, Munich, and Vienna). You'll get an entertaining, sometimes informative guide who will show you the back streets and treats of the city or countryside. Tours are fun, reasonable (about $15–30), good exercise, and an easy way to meet other travelers as well as get a fresh angle on an old city.

Some people travel almost exclusively by bike and wouldn't have it any other way. Rich Sorensen and Edwin McCain, who for years have gotten their travel thrills crisscrossing Europe by bike, helped me assemble the following tips on bicycle touring in Europe.

Bicycle touring is cheap and rewarding. To see Europe on $20 a day, you don't need a time machine. What you need is a bike, farmers' markets, and campgrounds or hostels. Traveling this way, you'll not only save money and keep fit, but you'll experience a quieter side of Europe that travelers rarely see.

While bicycle touring is one of the cheapest ways to see Europe, most bikers choose to pedal for the sheer joy of it. Imagine low-gearing up a beautiful mountain road on a bike (smell the freshly mown hay), then picture an air-conditioned Mercedes with the windows closed and the stereo on (smell the upholstery). The driver might think, "Masochistic nut!" but he also might notice the biker's smiling face—the face of a traveler who can see clearly from mountain to village and hear the birds singing while anticipating a well-earned and glorious downhill run.

Determine if a bike is the best transportation for your trip. Define what part of Europe you want to experience, and then ask yourself some basic questions to see whether your bicycle will be your key to freedom or an albatross around your neck. Remember that it takes an entire day to travel the same distance by bicycle that you could cover in a single hour by train or car. Sixty miles per day is a high average. With bakery stops, Rich averages about 40. For example, if you have the entire summer free, you and your bike can cover a lot of ground through, say, France, Germany, Benelux, Switzerland, and Italy. But if you have a month or less, will you be content to focus on a single country or region? Given what you want to see in the time you have, is the slow pace of bicycling a worthwhile trade-off for the benefits? And finally, do you want to spend much more of your time in rural and small-town Europe than in cities?

Europe is made for biking.

Dominic Bonuccelli

Read a biking guidebook. Consider Lonely Planet's *Cycling France* and *Cycling Britain*; the Mountaineers' *Ireland by Bike;* and *Cycling the Netherlands, Belgium, and Luxembourg,* by Katherine and Jerry Widing. Adventure Cycling Association's *Cyclists Yellow Pages* is a good resource directory, and their *Cyclosource* catalog contains first-rate books, clothing, maps, and bike gear (tel. 800/721-8719, www.adv-cycling.org).

Take practice trips. Make sure you really enjoy taking long rides weighted down with loaded panniers. Try some 60-mile-a-day rides (5 hours at 12 mph) around home. If possible, take a weekend camping trip with everything you'll take to Europe. Know which tools to bring and learn basic repair work (like repairing flat tires, replacing broken spokes, and adjusting brakes and derailleurs). Ask about classes at your local bike shop.

Decide whether to go solo, with a partner, or with a tour. You can go it alone, with occasional pick-up pals on the way. As a loner, you'll go where, when, and as far and fast as you want. Traveling with a companion or two is more cost-effective and can be more fun, but make sure your partner's cycling pace and temperament are compatible with yours. Organized tours, which usually have sag wagons to carry gear, average an easy 30 to 40 miles a day. For information, check out Europeds (tel.

800/321-9552, www.europeds.com), Euro-Bike and Walking Tours (tel. 800/321-6060, www.eurobike.com), Backroads (tel. 800/462-2848, www.backroads.com), or the ads in *Bicycling* magazine. **When to go depends on where you go.** Ideal biking temperatures are between 50 and 70 degrees Fahrenheit, so May is a good time to bike in the Mediterranean countries. Edwin started his five-week trip in Greece in May before it got too hot and then pedaled up through the Balkans to England. He had good temperatures all the way, but he also had headwinds (the prevailing westerlies). Rich and his wife, Risa, set out from Barcelona on a more leisurely spring-to-fall route that took them through France, England, Germany, Switzerland, Italy, and Greece, and they had not only ideal temperatures but also fewer headwinds. **Bring your bike from home.** Although you can buy good touring bikes in Europe, they're no cheaper than here, and you're better off bringing a bike that you're sure is the right fit for you, your racks, and your panniers. Cyclists debate whether to tour on a thick-tired mountain bike or a touring bike with skinnier tires. Mountain-bike tires are much more forgiving on the occasional cobblestone street, but they are more durable than necessary for most European roads and the chunky tread design will slow you down. In addition, straight mountain-bike handlebars will limit your hand positions, increasing fatigue on long riding days. If you already have a mountain bike, go ahead and take it, but add some bolt-on handlebar extensions.

Some airlines will ship your bike for free. To determine the airline's bike-checking policy, call the airline directly. More airlines are charging a fee for your bike and for the "bike box" they provide. Some airlines will fly it to Europe free, considering it to be one of your two allotted pieces of checked baggage. Most airlines require that bikes be partially disassembled and boxed. Get a box from your local bike shop, the airline, or from Amtrak (which sells cavernous bike boxes). Reinforce your box with extra cardboard, and be sure to put a plastic spacer between your front forks (any bike shop will give

Dominic Bonuccelli

Geared up for cycling

you one). You can also toss in your panniers, tent, and so on for extra padding, as long as you stay under the airline's weight limit. Or consider a folding bike, which packs neatly into a suitcase (Green Gear Cycling Inc. makes a nifty "Bike Friday," tel. 800/777-0258, www.bikefriday.com). Bring the tools you'll need to get your bike back into riding form so you can ride straight out of your European airport.

Be prepared. Expect rain and bring good bikers' rain gear. A Gore-Tex raincoat can double as a cool-weather windbreaker. You'll also be exposed to the sun, so plan on using plenty of sunscreen. A bell is generally required by law in Europe, so you should have one on your bike—for giving a multilingual "Hi!" to other bikers as well as a "Look out, here I come!" Even if you never ride at night, you should at least bring a strobe-type taillight for the many long and unavoidable tunnels. Smaller Presta tire valves are standard in most of Europe, so if your bike has the automotive-type Shraeder valves, take along an adapter. To guard against unsightly road rash (and worse), always wear a helmet and biking gloves.

Obey Europe's traffic rules. Bikers generally follow the same rules as drivers. Some countries, such as the Netherlands, have rules and signs just for bikers: A bike in a blue circle indicates a bike route; a bike in a red circle indicates bikes are not allowed. Be alert, follow the blue bike signs, and these required bike paths will get you through even some of the most complicated highway interchanges. Beware of the silent biker who might be right behind you, and use hand signals before stopping or turning. Stay off the freeways. Little roads are nicer for biking, anyway.

Use good maps. Michelin's Europe and individual country maps are fine for overall planning. In Europe, use local maps for day-to-day navigation. Michelin and Die Generalkarte 1:200,000 maps reveal all the quiet back roads and even the steepness of hills. Don't be obsessed with following a preplanned route. Delightful and spontaneous side trips are part of the spirit and joy of biking.

Taking your bike on a train greatly extends the reach of your trip. Every hour by rail saves a day that would have been spent in the saddle (and there's nothing so sweet as taking a train away from the rain and into a sunny place). To make sure you and your bike can travel on the same train, look for trains marked in timetables with little bicycle symbols, or ask at the station's information window. In some countries, trains that allow bikes require advance reservations.

Bike thieves abound in Europe. Use a good Kryptonite-style bike lock to secure your bike to something sturdy. Never leave your pump, handlebar bag, panniers, water bottle, or computer on your bike when you can't see it. Keep your bike inside whenever possible. At hostels, ask if there is a locked bike room, and, if not, ask or even plead for a place to put your bike inside overnight. Remember that hotels and many pensions don't really have rules against taking a bike up to your room. Just do it unobtrusively. You can even wheelie it into the elevator. Rich and Risa found campgrounds to be safe, but they always locked their bikes together. **Travel light... or camp.** Unless you really love camping, staying in hostels or hotels makes more sense, since it frees you from lugging around a tent, sleeping bag, and cooking equipment. European campgrounds tend to be more crowded than American ones, so if you're willing to sacrifice privacy in order to mix with Europeans, camping can add a fun dimension to your trip. **A bike makes you more approachable.** The most rewarding aspect of bicycling in Europe is meeting people. Europeans love bicycles, and they are often genuinely impressed when they encounter that rare American who rejects the view from the tour-bus window in favor of huffing and puffing through their country on two wheels. Your bike provides an instant conversation piece, the perfect bridge over a maze of cultural and language barriers.

HITCHHIKING—RULES OF THUMB

Hitching, sometimes called "auto-stop," is a popular and acceptable means of getting around in Europe. After picking up a Rhine riverboat captain in my rental car and running him back to his home port, I realized that hitchhiking doesn't wear the same hippie hat in Europe that it does in the United States.

Without a doubt, hitching is the cheapest means of transportation. It's also a great way to meet people. Most people who pick you up are genuinely interested in getting to know an American.

The farther you get from our culture's determination to be self-sufficient, the more volunteerism you'll encounter. Bumming a ride is a perfect example. In the Third World—rural Europe in the extreme— anything rolling with room will let you in. You don't hitch, you just flag the vehicle down.

Hitching is risky. Although hitching in Europe is safer than hitching in the United States, there is an ever-present danger any time you get into a stranger's car. That, coupled with the overabundance of lawyers in the United States, means I cannot recommend it. Personally, I don't hitchhike at home, and I wouldn't rely solely on my thumb to get me through Europe. But I never sit frustrated in a station for two hours because there isn't a bus or train to take me 15 miles down the road. Riding my thumb out of train and bus schedule problems, I can usually get to my destination in a friendly snap.

Hitching can be time-consuming. Some places have 20 or 30 people in a chorus line of thumbs, just waiting their turns. Once I said what I thought was goodbye forever to an Irishman after breakfast. He was heading north. We had dinner together that night, and I learned a lot about wasting a day on the side of a road. You'll find that Germany, Norway, Ireland, and Great Britain offer generally good hitchhiking, while southern countries are less reliable.

Hitchhiking at the Bulgaria–Greece border, or wherever the train and bus schedules leave you stranded.

Learn the gestures. The hitchhiking gesture is not always the outstretched thumb. In some countries, you ring an imaginary bell. In others, you make a downward wave with your hand. Observe and learn.

Crank up your good judgment. Feel good about the situation before you commit yourself to it. Keep your luggage on your lap, or at least out of the trunk, so if things turn sour, you can excuse yourself quickly and easily. Women should not sit in the back seat of a two-door car. A fake wedding ring and modest dress are indications that you're interested only in transportation.

Consider your appearance. Look like the Cracker Jack boy or his sister—happy, wholesome, and a joy to have aboard. Establish eye contact. Charm the driver. Smile. Stand up. Don't walk and hitch. Pick a good spot on the road, giving the driver plenty of time to see you and a safe spot to pull over. Look respectable and a little gaunt. Arrange your luggage so it looks as small as possible. Those hitching with very little or no luggage enjoy a tremendous advantage.

A man and a woman make the perfect combination. A single woman maximizes speed and risk. Two women travel more safely and nearly as fast. A single man with patience will do fine. Two guys go slow, and three or more should split up and rendezvous later. Single men and women are better off traveling together; these alliances are easily made at hostels. A man and a woman traveling together have it easy. If the woman hitches and the guy steps out of view around the corner or into a shop, they should both have a ride in a matter of minutes. (Dirty trick, but it works.)

Create pity. When I'm doing some serious hitching, I walk away from town and find a very lonely stretch of road. It seems that the sparser the traffic, the quicker I get a ride. On a busy road, people will assume that I'll manage without their ride. If only one car passes in five minutes, the driver senses that he may be my only chance.

Go the distance. To get the long ride, take a local bus out of town to the open country on the road to your destination. Make a cardboard sign with your destination printed big and bold in the local language, followed by the local "please." At borders, you might decide to choose only a ride that will take you entirely through that country. Use decals and license plates to determine where a car is from (and therefore likely heading). Every car has to have a large decal with a letter or two indicating in which country the car is registered. And in some countries (such as Germany and Italy), hometowns are indicated by the first few letters on the license plate.

Try to meet the driver directly. Find a spot where cars stop, and you can encounter the driver face to thumb. A toll booth, border, gas station, or—best of all—a ferry ride gives you that chance to smile and convince him that he needs you in his car or truck. Although it's easy to zoom past a hitchhiker at 60 mph and not feel guilty, it's much more difficult to turn down an in-person request for a ride.

Share-a-ride organizations match rides and riders. Start with To Share (www.toshare.org), which lists ride possibilities in over a dozen European countries. Look for Mitfahrzentralen in Germany (www.mitfahren.org, in German), FreeWheelers in Britain (www.freewheelers.co.uk), Taxistop in Belgium (www.taxistop.be), and Allostop in France (www.ecritel.fr/allostop, in French). You pay a small amount to join, and you help with gas expenses, but it works well and is much cheaper than train travel. Also ask about rides at student tourist information centers. Informal ride services are posted on college and hostel bulletin boards all over Europe.

Hitching can become the destination. With the "hitch when you can't get a bus or train" approach, you'll find yourself walking down lovely rural roads and getting rides from safe and friendly small-town folk. I can recall some "it's great to be alive and on the road" days riding my thumb from tiny town to waterfall to desolate Celtic graveyard to coastal village and remembering each ride as much as the destinations. Especially in Ireland, I've found so much fun in the front seat that I've driven right by my planned destination to carry on with the conversation. In rural Ireland, I'd stand on the most desolate road in Connemara and hitch whichever way the car was coming. As I hopped in the driver would ask, "Where you goin'?" I'd say, "Ireland."

WALKING (AND DODGING)

You'll walk a lot in Europe. It's a great way to see cities, towns, and the countryside. Walking tours offer the most intimate look at a city or town. A walker complements the place she walks through by her interest and will be received warmly. Many areas, from the mountains to the beaches, are best seen on foot. Travelers who make walking a focus of their trip will find series of books just for them, published by Lonely Planet (on Britain, France, Ireland, Italy, Switzerland), Interlink Books (Independent Walker's guides to France, Italy, Spain, and Switzerland), and Cicerone Press (trekking guides for many European countries).

Be careful—walking in cities can be dangerous. Annually, more than 300 pedestrians are run down on the streets of Paris. (And mom was worried about terrorism!) The drivers are crazy, and politeness has no place on the roads of Europe. Cross carefully, but if you wait for a break in the traffic, you may never get a chance to cross the street. Look for a pedestrian underpass or, when all else fails, find a heavy-set local person and just follow him like a shadow—one busy lane at a time—across that seemingly impassable street.

Joggers can enjoy a good early morning tour as well as the exercise. Hotel receptionists usually know a good jogging route. Remember to carry identification and your hotel card with you.

HIKING

Imagine hiking along a ridge high in the Swiss Alps. On one side of you, lakes stretch all the way to Germany. On the other sprawls the greatest mountain panorama in Europe—the Eiger, Monch, and Jungfrau. And then you hear the long legato tones of an alp horn, announcing that a helicopter-stocked mountain hut is just ahead, and the coffee schnapps is on.

Hiking in Europe is a joy. Travelers explore entire regions on foot. Switzerland's Jungfrau is an exciting sight from a hotel's terrace café, but those who hike the region enjoy nature's very own striptease as the mountain reveals herself in an endless string of powerful poses.

Romantics commune with nature from Norway's

Alpine trail signs show where you are, the altitude in meters, and how long in hours and minutes it takes to hike to nearby points.

A firsthand look at fairy-tale alpine culture is just a hike away (Walderalm, above Hall in Tirol, See Chapter 46: Offbeat Alps).

fjords to the English lakes to the Alps to the Riviera. Trails are generally well-kept and carefully marked. Very precise maps (scale 1:25,000) are readily available.

You could walk through the Alps for weeks—sleeping in mountain huts—and never come out of the mountains. You're never more than a day's hike from a mountain village, where you can replenish your food supply or enjoy a hotel and a restaurant meal. Most alpine trails are free of snow by July, and lifts take less rugged visitors to the top in a sweat-free flash. Good hiking books include the Walking Easy guide to the Swiss and Austrian Alps (published by Globe Pequot) and *A Hundred Hikes in the Alps* (Mountaineers).

Throughout the Alps, trail markings are both handy and humiliating. Handy, because they show hours to hike rather than miles to walk to various destinations. Humiliating, because these times are clocked by local senior citizens. You'll know what I mean after your first hike.

If you prefer organized walks, look for Volksmarches. These 10-kilometer-or-longer walks are particularly popular in Germanic countries, involve lots of locals, and end with refreshments and socializing (one of many Web sites: www.ava.org/clubs/germany).

Do some research before you leave. Buy the most appropriate hiking guidebook. Ask for maps and advice from the National Tourist Offices (for a list of tourist offices, see Chapter 2: Gathering Information).

MONEY AND YOUR BUDGET

13. Money

I changed my last traveler's check years ago. Now ATM cards and debit cards offer better ways to convert your dollars into European currency.

EUROS!

The new euro currency is big news for 2002. Twelve European countries—and about 300 million people—are using the euro as their currency. In January 2002, the first euro bills and coins appear. For the first two months of 2002, you can carry out transactions with either euros or the traditional currencies. Then in March 2002, no more marks, no more francs, and no more of those pesky lire. Just euros. Once euros rule, tourists and locals will be able to easily compare prices of goods between countries. And you won't lose money or time changing money at borders. For the latest on the euro, see the European Central Bank's Web site at www.euro.ecb.int.

Not all European countries are switching to euros. As of now, major holdouts include Britain, Denmark, Norway, Sweden, and Switzerland.

€uroland

The Euro is big news in 2002! Use euros in €uroland: Austria, Belgium, Finland, France, Germany, Greece, Ireland, Italy, Luxembourg, Netherlands, Portugal, and Spain.

CASH MACHINES (ATMS)

Throughout Europe, cash machines are the standard way for American travelers to change money. European ATMs work like your hometown machine and usually have English-language instructions. An ATM withdrawal takes dollars directly from your bank account at home and gives you that country's cash. You'll pay a fee, but you'll get a better rate than you would for traveler's checks. I take entire trips with just an ATM card—and never stand in a bank line.

Know your personal identification number (PIN). Since European keypads have only numbers, you'll want a four-digit PIN with numbers and no letters (derive the numbers from your hometown bank's keypad).

Confirm with your home bank that your card will work in Europe. Ask about fees. Plan on being able to withdraw money only from your checking account. You might be able to dip

How to use a European cash machine: Insert card, pull out cash.

into your savings account or transfer funds between accounts, but don't count on it.

Debit cards are more versatile than ATM cards. You can use a debit card to purchase items from stores. And in case you run across a non-functioning ATM machine, debit cards issued by Visa or MasterCard can be used for over-the-counter cash advances (with a fee) at banks that accept those credit cards.

Bringing two cards gives you a handy backup if one is demagnetized or eaten by a machine. Make sure the validity period of your card won't expire before your trip ends.

Ask your banker how much you can withdraw per 24 hours. Note that foreign ATMs may not let you withdraw your daily limit. Many machines have a small maximum, forcing you to make several withdrawals and incur several fees to get the amount you want. When choosing how much to withdraw from a cash machine, request a big amount on the small chance you'll get it. If you're lucky and the machine complies, you'll save on fees. If you're denied, try again, requesting a smaller amount.

Few ATM receipts list the exchange rate, and some machines don't dispense receipts at all. If it's important to you to have the complete rundown on the fees you're paying and rate you're getting, you're better off cashing traveler's checks at a bank. You'll get a worse deal but better documentation.

ATMs may not be as good a deal in the future, as overseas ATM vendors and U.S. banks add a 2 percent or so fee to each transaction, but, right now, they're the best way to go.

CASH ADVANCES

Many travelers, using credit cards at banks throughout Europe, fund their trips by relying solely on cash advances. (Note that ATM cards are good only for withdrawing cash.) Visa is the most commonly accepted credit card for cash advances. The problem with using a credit card is that you are immediately into the 18 percent interest category with your new credit-card debt.

CASH-TO-CASH MACHINES

There are 24-hour money munchers in big cities all over Europe. These machines look like ATM machines, but you feed in cash instead of a card. At midnight in Florence, you can push in a $20 bill (or any major European currency) and, assuming the president (or royalty) is on the right side, the correct value of local currency will tumble out. They are handy, open all the time, and usually offer bad rates. These are more of a novelty than anything else, useful only if you want a new experience or if you're too tired to find a regular cash machine.

BUYING ON PLASTIC

Charge cards work fine throughout Europe (at hotels, shops, travel agencies, and so on), although more and more merchants are establishing a $30 minimum. Visa and MasterCard are the most widely accepted. American Express is less commonly accepted but is popular with travelers for its extra services (such as receiving and holding clients' mail).

Plastic fans gloat that you get a better exchange rate by using your card. While it is true that plastic transactions are processed at the best possible exchange rate, card users are buying from businesses that have enough slack in their prices to absorb the bank's fee for the charge service. Those who travel on their plastic may be getting a better rate, but on a worse price. (As more and more consumers believe they are getting "free use of the bank's money," we're all absorbing the 3 percent the banks are making in higher purchase prices.)

I use my credit card for booking hotel reservations by phone, making major purchases (such as car rentals and plane tickets), and paying for things near the end of my trip to avoid another visit to the cash machine. But a dependence on plastic reshapes the Europe you experience. Pedro's Pension, the friendly guide at the cathedral, and most merchants in the market don't take credit cards. Going through the Back Door requires hard local cash.

THEFT PREVENTION

Your ATM, credit, and debit cards can be stolen as easily in Europe as in the U.S. There is no surefire protection, but you can take a few precautions. Keep all bank cards safely in your money belt.

Memorize your PIN; you'd be surprised at how many people write it on their card. Talk to your bank about setting a daily withdrawal limit for your ATM card. Carry your bank's phone number (make photocopies of the front and back of your cards). If your card is lost or stolen, report it immediately.

Scams are commonplace. When you pay in plastic, understand the numbers and keep the receipts. Banks charge a maximum $50 liability fee if thieves go on a shopping spree with your card.

A thief using your debit card could conceivably empty your account. Verify with your bank what would happen in this worst-case scenario. There's likely just a maximum $50 liability fee, but it makes good sense to minimize your risks. The best precaution is to contact your bank and set up a separate account, linked with a new debit card, to cover your trip. Keep your savings safe in your main account. If you run out of money in your trip account, call your bank (or access it online) to transfer money from your main account. Although a thief could empty your trip account, your savings would be safe. As an extra precaution, minimize spreading your debit card number around. Use your debit card only for cash-machine withdrawals. To make purchases, use cash or your credit card. (If an unscrupulous shopkeeper uses your credit card number for his purposes, he's spending "nonexistent" money rather than real money out of your account.) Upon returning home, call your debit and credit card vendor to verify your balance and bill.

TRAVELER'S CHECKS

Traveler's checks function almost like cash but are replaceable if lost or stolen. You need to choose the company, the currency, and denominations.

Choose a well-known company. Use whichever big company's checks (American Express, Thomas Cook, Visa) you can get without the typical 1.5 percent fee. Ask around. There are plenty of ways to avoid that extra charge (your own bank might waive it). Any legitimate check is good at banks, but it's helpful when you're in a jam to have a well-known check that private parties and small shops will recognize and honor.

If you're traveling only in England, go with Barclays—a British bank with a branch in every town. They waive the $2- to $5-per-transaction service charge for their checks.

The American Express Company, or AmExCo, is popular for its centrally located "landmark" offices (listed at www.americanexpress.com), travel service, and clients' mail service. AmExCo checks, which normally come with a 1.5 percent charge, are free through AAA for its members. While

AmExCo offices offer mediocre exchange rates, they usually change their checks without the customary $2 to $5 fee. AmExCo's fee relief can make up for their bad rates if you're exchanging less than several hundred dollars. **Understand the refund policy.** Lost or stolen traveler's checks are replaceable only if you keep track of the serial numbers and know exactly which checks you've cashed and lost. Leave a photocopy of all your check numbers (along with photocopies of your passport, plane ticket, and bankcards) with someone at home, in your luggage, and in your wallet. Your original traveler's checks receipt is an important document. Keep it handy but separate from your checks. Use checks in numerical order and update your list regularly as you cash them. Get a police report after any theft, and report the loss to your issuing bank within 24 hours. (Travel with their emergency phone numbers.) You'll hear many stories about slow or fast refunds. None of them matter. The delay is always too long. Would someone please hand Karl Malden a money belt?

For most trips, buy checks in U.S. dollars. Traveler's checks come in U.S. dollars, euros, Swiss francs, British pounds, and Japanese yen. Get traveler's checks in U.S. dollars because it's simpler. We think in dollars.

Get a mix of denominations. Large checks ($100, $500) save on signing and bulk. Since many banks—especially in Scandinavia—are charging a $2 to $4 fee per check rather than per transaction, cashing large denominations can save money. Also bring a few small checks ($20, $50), which can be easier to cash. If you're out of money and the banks are closed, it's easy to find a merchant or another traveler who will change a $20 check.

CHANGING TRAVELER'S CHECKS AT BANKS

You'd be appalled if you knew how much money you'll lose in banks over the course of your trip. You can't avoid these losses, but you can minimize them by understanding how the banks make their money. In spite of their ads, no bank really likes people. They like your money. Banks change money only to make money.

Look for fees and rates. Banks make money from fees and from rates. Banks with great rates have high fees. Others have lousy rates and no fees. Any place advertising "no fees" should complete the equation with "and lousy rates." For a small exchange, you don't care about the rate as long as there's no fee. For a large exchange, the fee doesn't matter—you want a good rate.

Study this example: Krankbank offers €0.90 per dollar and charges a small €1 fee. Riverbank offers a better rate at €0.93 per dollar, but charges a €6 fee. For $100 I'll get €89 at Krankbank (100 x 0.90 less €1) and only €87 at Riverbank (100 x 0.93 less €6). But if I change $500, I'll get €449 at Krankbank (500 x 0.90 less €1) and €459 at Riverbank (500 x 0.93 less €6). For a small exchange, Krankbank gives me more euros. For a $500 exchange, I get €10 extra at Riverbank—about $9 more.

Change only at places showing both rates. Every decent place that changes money displays both its buying and selling rates. After all the traveling I've done, I still can't conceptualize what's what here. Who's getting pounds? Who's giving dollars? It doesn't matter. We lose. For maximum clarity when comparing banks, ask how much you'll get for $200 (or whatever) in traveler's checks. Tellers will quickly figure the fees and rates and give you a hard bottom line to compare with the next place.

Avoid "one-rate" exchange bureaus. Places that show only one rate are hiding something—an obscene profit margin. Check it out. Every rip-off exchange desk at every border crossing, casino, and nightclub in Europe shows only one rate . . . and it's a lousy one.

Beware of an exchange bureau scam directed at naive tourists: They have a great rate and advertise a fair 2 percent fee—but it's only for buying the local currency. The fine print explains that their fee for *selling* the local currency is a whopping 9.5 percent.

Minimize trips to the bank. It's expensive and time-consuming to change money. Bring your passport, find a decent bank, estimate carefully what you'll need, and get it all at once. Keep it safe in your money belt.

CASH

Carry plenty of cash. American cash in your money belt comes in handy for emergencies, such as when banks go on strike. I've been in Greece and Ireland when every bank went on strike, shutting down without warning. Some places (such as Russia) make life with traveler's checks or an ATM card very difficult. But hard cash is cash. People always know roughly what a dollar is worth, and you can always sell it.

Use local money. Many Americans exclaim gleefully, "Gee, they accept dollars! There's no need to change money." Without knowing it, they're changing money—at a lousy rate—every time they buy something with their dollars. Anyone on a budget will stretch it by using hard local cash. Local hotels and small businesses—which suffer big bank fees when they take your credit card, dollars, or traveler's checks—prefer cash.

Figure out the money. To "ugly Americans," foreign money is "funny money." They never figure it out, get no respect from the locals, and are constantly ripped off. Local currencies are all logical. Each system is decimalized just like ours. There are a hundred "little ones" (cents, pence, stotinki) in every "big one" (euro, pound, leva). Only the names have been changed—to confuse the tourist. Get a good sampling of coins after you arrive, and in two minutes you'll be comfortable with the "nickels, dimes, and quarters" of each new currency. A currency-converting calculator isn't worth the trouble.

Very roughly, figure out what the unit of currency (euro, kroner, Swiss franc, or whatever) is worth in American cents. For example, if there are €1.10 in a dollar, each euro is worth $0.90. If a hot dog costs €5, then it costs five times $0.90 or $4.50. If mustard costs €0.10 (a tenth of $0.90), it costs the equivalent of $0.09. Ten euros is $9, and €250 = $225 (250 x 0.90, or 250 less one-tenth). Quiz yourself. Soon it'll be second nature. Survival on a budget is easier when you're comfortable with the local currency.

Assume you'll be shortchanged. In banks, restaurants, at ticket booths, everywhere—assume you'll be shortchanged if you don't do your own figuring. People who spend their lives sitting in booths for eight hours a day taking money from strangers often have no problem stealing from dumb tourists who don't know the local currency. For 10 minutes I observed a man in the Rome metro shortchanging half of the tourists who went through his turnstile. Half of those shortchanged caught him and got their correct change with apologies. Overall, about 25 percent didn't notice and went home saying, "Boy, Italy is really expensive."

Paper money of any Western country is good at banks anywhere. Dollars are not sacred. If you leave Norway with paper money, that 100-kroner note is just as convertible as dollars at any European bank or exchange office. Many people change excess local money back to dollars before they leave a country, then change those dollars into the next country's currency (e.g., they change euros to dollars in France, then dollars to pounds in Britain). This double changing is unnecessary and expensive. It can be handy, however, to change your remaining local currency into the next country's currency before leaving a country.

Coins are generally worthless outside their country. Since big-value coins are common in Europe, exporting a pocketful of change can be an expensive mistake. Spend them (on postcards, newspaper, a phone call home, or food or drink for the train ride), change them into bills, or give them away. Otherwise, you've just bought a bunch of souvenirs.

Some Eastern European currencies are worthless outside their country. While paper money from any Western country is good at banks in every other country, some Eastern European currencies are still "soft"—kept at unrealistically high rates. You can't avoid buying this money when you're in Bulgaria, Romania, the Baltics, or Turkey. But it's worthless (or nearly so) in Western Europe. Until Eastern currency becomes hard, exchange it, spend it, buy candles in churches, or ice-cream cones for strangers. Give it away if you have to—but don't take it out of its country.

Getting back to dollars at the end of your trip. At your final European country, gather any leftover bills and change them into that last currency to help fund your trip. If you have any foreign cash left before you fly home, change it into dollars at the European airport or simply spend it at the airport. You might get a few more dollars for that last smattering of foreign bills from your hometown bank, but it's clean and convenient to simply fly home with nothing but dollars in your pocket.

14. Your Budget

Most of today's Europe is more expensive than the United States, and the sloppy traveler can blow a small fortune in a hurry. If you travel like a big shot, you'd better be loaded. You can live well in Europe on a budget, but it will take some artistry.

I'm cautious about sending people to Europe with too much confidence and not enough money. The tips in this book are tried and tested in the worst circumstances every year. And my feedback from Back Door travelers makes it clear: Enjoying Europe through the Back Door can be done—by you.

BUDGET BREAKDOWN

Airfare: Flying to Europe is a bargain. Get a good agent, understand all your options, and make the best choice. Traveling outside of peak season will save you several hundred dollars.

Surface Transportation: Transportation in Europe is reasonable if you take advantage of a railpass or split a car rental between three or four people. Transportation expenses are generally fixed. People who spend $8,000 for their vacation spend about the same on transportation as do those whose trips cost half as much. Your budget should not dictate how freely you travel in Europe. If you want to go somewhere, do it, taking advantage of whatever money-saving options you can. You came to travel.

Sightseeing/Entertainment: Sightseeing costs have risen faster than anything else. Admissions to major attractions are now $5 to $10; smaller sights are $2 to $3. Concerts, plays, and bus tours cost around $25. Don't skimp here. This category directly powers most of the experiences all the other expenses are designed to make possible.

Shopping/Miscellany: Figure about $2 each for coffee, beer, ice cream, soft drinks, and bus and subway rides. Shopping can vary in cost from nearly nothing to a small fortune. Good budget travelers find that this category has little to do with assembling a trip full of lifelong and wonderful memories.

Trip Costs

In 2002, you can travel comfortably for a month for around $4,000—not including your airfare ($700–1,000). If you have extra money, it's more fun to spend it in Europe.

Allow:

$700	for a 15-days-in-two-months Eurailpass or split car rental
600	for sightseeing
300	for entertainment/shopping/miscellany
+2,400	for room and board ($70 a day)
$4,000	

Students or rock-bottom budget travelers can enjoy a month of Europe at least as much for about a third less—$2,150 plus airfare.

Allow:

$600	for a one-month youth Eurailpass
300	for sightseeing
200	for entertainment/shopping/miscellany
+1,050	for room and board ($35 a day)*
$2,150	

*$20 for a dorm bed or a bed in a private home with breakfast, $5 for a picnic lunch, $10 for dinner.

Room and Board: The area that will make or break your budget—where you have the most control—is in your eating and sleeping expenses. In 2002, smart travelers can thrive on $80 a day (less if necessary) for room and board. Figure on $50 per person in a $100 hotel double with breakfast, $10 apiece for lunch, and $15 for dinner. That leaves you $5 for cappuccino and *gelato*.

The key is finding budget alternatives to international-class hotels and restaurants, and consuming only what you want to consume. If you want real tablecloths and black-tie waiters, your tomato salad will cost 20 times what it costs in the market. If you want a suite with fancy room service and chocolate on your pillow, you'll pay in a day what many travelers pay in a week.

My idea of "cheap" is simple but not sleazy. My budget morality is to never sacrifice safety, reasonable cleanliness, sleep, or nutrition to save money. I go to safe, central, friendly, local-style hotels, shunning swimming pools, people in uniforms, and transplanted American niceties in favor of an opportunity to travel as a temporary European. Unfortunately, simple is subversive these days, and the system is bullying even cozy Scottish bed-and-breakfast places into more and more facilities, more and more debt, and higher and higher prices.

I traveled every summer for years on a part-time piano teacher's income (and, boy, was she upset). I ate and slept great by learning and following these guidelines.

EATING AND SLEEPING ON A BUDGET

You can get eight good, safe hours of sleep and three square meals in Europe for $30 a day if your budget requires it. If your budget is tight, remember these rules of thumb.

Minimize the use of hotels and restaurants. Enjoying the sights and culture of Europe has nothing to do with how much you're spending to eat and sleep. Take advantage of each country's many alternatives to hotels and restaurants. If your budget dictated, you could have a great trip without hotels and restaurants—and probably learn, experience, and enjoy more than most tourists.

Budget for price variances. Prices as much as double from south to north. Budget more for the north and get by on less than your daily allowance in Spain, Portugal, and Greece. Exercise those budget alternatives where they'll save you the most money. A hostel saves $3 in Crete and $30 in Finland. In Scandinavia I picnic, walk, and sleep on trains, but I live like a king in southern Europe, where my splurge dollars go the farthest. And if your trip will last only as long as your money does, travel fast in the north and hang out in the south (but famous places in Italy can be as expensive as the north).

Swallow pride and save money. This is a personal matter, depending largely on how much pride and money you have. Many people cringe every time I use the word "cheap"; others appreciate the directness. I'm not talking about begging and groveling around Europe. I'm talking about drinking tap water at restaurants ($3 saved) and choosing a hotel room with a shower down the hall ($20 saved).

Find out the complete price before ordering anything, and say "no thanks" if the price isn't right. Expect equal and fair treatment as a tourist. When appropriate, fight the price, set a limit, and search on. Remember, even if the same thing would cost much more at home, the local rate should prevail. If you act like a rich fool, you're likely to be treated as one.

Two lunches for $10, no problema

Avoid the tourist centers. The best values are not in the places that boast in neon: "We Speak English." Find places that earn a loyal local following. You'll get more for your money. If you do follow the tourists, follow the savvy Germans; never follow tour groups.

Patronize family-run places. Small family-run places have cheaper labor (mom, pop, and the kids) and care more about their customers. For these reasons, they generally offer the best values for eating and sleeping.

Adapt to European tastes. Most unhappy people I meet in my travels could find the source of their problems in their own stubborn desire to find the United States in Europe. If you accept and at least try doing things the European way, besides saving money you'll be happier and learn more on your trip. You cannot expect the local people to accept you warmly if you don't accept them. Things are different in Europe—that's why you go. European travel is a package deal. Accept the good with the "bad." If you require the comforts of home, that's where you'll be happiest.

Be a good guest. To Europeans, Americans occasionally act as though they "just got off the boat" (putting shoes on the train seats, chilling grapes in the bidet, talking loudly in restaurants, using flash attachments and camcorders during Mass, hanging wet clothes out the hotel window, and consuming energy like it's cheap and ours to waste). The Europeans you'll deal with can sour or sweeten your experience, depending on how they react to you. When you're in good favor with the receptionist or whomever, you can make things happen that people whose bucks talk can't.

Each year as I update my books, I hear over and over in my recommended hotels and private homes that my *Back Door* readers are the most considerate and fun-to-have guests. Thank you for traveling sensitive to the culture and as temporary locals. It's fun to follow you in my travels.

15. Sleeping

Hotels are the most expensive way to sleep and, of course, the most comfortable. With a reasonable budget, I spend most of my nights in hotels, but they can rip through a tight budget like a grenade in a dollhouse.

I always hear people complaining about that "$250 double in Frankfurt" or the "$200-a-night room in London." They come back from their vacations with bruised and battered pocketbooks, telling stories that scare their friends out of international travel and back to Florida or Hawaii one more time. True, you can spend $200 for a double, but I never have. That's three days' accommodations for me.

Andrea Hagg

As far as I'm concerned, spending more for your hotel just builds a bigger wall between you and what you traveled so far to see. If you spend enough, you won't know where you are. Think about it. "In-ter-con-ti-nent-al." That means the same everywhere—designed for people who deep down inside wish they weren't traveling, people spending someone else's money, people who need a strap over the toilet telling them no one's sat there yet. It's uniform sterility, a lobby full of Stay-Press Americans with tiny wheels on their hard suitcases, English menus, and lamps bolted to the tables.

Europe's small hotels and guest houses may have no room service and offer only a shower down the hall, but their staffs are more interested in seeing pictures of your children and helping you have a great time than in thinning out your wallet.

Europe is full of traditional old hotels—dingy, a bit run-down, central, friendly, safe, and government regulated, offering good-enough-for-the-European-good-enough-for-me beds for $30 to $40 a night ($40–80 doubles). No matter what your favorite newspaper travel writer or travel agent says, this is hardcore Europe: fun, cheap, and easy to find.

WHAT'S A CHEAP ROOM?

In a typical budget European hotel, a double room costs an average of $50 a night. You'll pay about $40 at a pension in Madrid, $50 at a simple guest house in Germany or a one-star hotel in Paris, and $60 for a private room in Bergen.

A typical room in a low-end hotel has a simple bed (occasionally a

springy cot, so always check);
a rickety, old, wooden or new
plastic chair and table; a free-
standing closet; a small window; old wallpaper; a good
sink under a neon light; a
mysterious bidet; a view of
another similar room across
a tall, thin courtyard; peeling
plaster; and a tiled or wood
floor. The light fixtures are
very simple, often with a weak
and sometimes even bare and
dangling ceiling light bulb.
Some travelers B.Y.O.B.
when they travel. A higher

A typical hotel room: tidy, small, affordable

wattage kills a lot of dinginess. Naked neon is common in the south. While
Britain has many smoke-free places, nearly all rooms on the Continent
come with ashtrays. You won't have a TV or telephone, and, while more
and more European hotels are squeezing boat-type prefab showers and toilets into their rooms, the cheapest rooms offer only a WC and shower or
tub down the hall, which you share with a half dozen other rooms.

Rooms often come with a continental breakfast (usually served from
about 7:30 to 10 a.m. in the breakfast room near the front desk): coffee,
tea, or hot chocolate, and a roll that's firmer than your mattress.

In the lobby there is nearly always a living room with a good TV, a
couple of phones, and a person at the desk who is a good information
source. You'll climb lots of stairs, as a hotel's lack of an elevator is often
the only reason it can't raise its prices. You'll be given a front-door key
because the desk is not staffed all night.

Cheap hotels usually have clean-enough-but-depressing shower
rooms, with hot water normally free and constant (but occasionally available only through a coin-op meter or at certain hours). The WC, or toilet, has toilet paper but is often missing its lid or has a cracked or broken
plastic lid. In some hotels, you pay $2 to $5 for a towel and a key to the
shower room. The cheapest hotels are run by and filled with people from
the Two-thirds World.

I want to stress that there are places I find unacceptable. I don't mind
dingy wallpaper, climbing stairs, and "going down the hall," but the place
must be clean, central, friendly, safe, quiet enough for me to sleep well,
and equipped with good beds.

1977: It slowly dawns on Rick that cheap beds aren't always good beds.

The cheap hotel described above is appalling to many Americans; it's charming, colorful, or funky to others. To me, "funky" means spirited and full of character(s): a caged bird in the TV room, grandchildren in the backyard, a dog sleeping in the hall, no uniforms, singing maids, a night-shift man tearing breakfast napkins in two so they'll go farther, a handwritten neighborhood history lesson on the wall, different furniture in each room, and a willingness to buck the system when the local tourist board starts requiring shoeshine machines in the hallways. An extra $15 or $20 per night will buy you into cheerier wallpaper and less funkiness.

As Europe becomes more and more affluent, a powerful force is pushing hotels up in price and comfort. Land in big cities is so expensive that cheap hotels can't survive and are bought out, gutted, and turned into modern hotels. More and more Europeans are expecting what, until lately, have been considered American standards of plumbing and comfort. A great value is often a hardworking family-run place that structurally can't fit showers in every room or an elevator up its spiral staircase. Prices are regulated, and, regardless of how good it is, with no elevator and a lousy shower-to-room ratio, it's a cheap hotel.

MAKING RESERVATIONS

I used to travel with absolutely no reservations. A daily chore was checking out several hotels or pensions and choosing one. Europe was ramshackle, things were cheap, hotel listings were unreliable and unnecessary. Now, like hobos in a Jetson world, budget travelers need to think one step ahead.

Use a good guidebook. Choose a guidebook whose travel philosophy matches yours. These days, those who rely on the tourist office or go potluck are likely to spend $50 more than necessary and get a lousy room. That's why I give hotel listings a very high priority in researching and writing my eight country guidebooks.

Call ahead. My standard room-finding tactic (assuming I know where I want to be) is to telephone in the morning to reserve my room for the night. I travel relaxed, knowing a good place is holding a room for me until late afternoon. A simple phone call a little in advance assures me a good-value room. Lately, I've been getting aced out by my own readers. So when I want to be certain to get my first choice, I call two or three days in advance. For big popular cities (such as London, Paris, Madrid, and so on), make your reservations as soon as you can pin down a date.

Remember, a hotel prefers a cash deposit with a reservation unless there's not enough time to mail it in. In this case, most hotels will hold a room without a deposit if you promise to arrive early. The earlier you promise, the better your chances of being trusted. If you'll be a little late, call again to assure them you're coming. Also, cancel if you won't make it. If someone cancels after 5 p.m. and the room-finding service is closed, the room will probably go unfilled that night. When that happens too often, hotel managers and B&B owners start to get really surly and insist on cash deposits.

It's generally unnecessary to reserve long in advance. Reserving your hotels months in advance through your travel agent or room-booking agency is a needless and expensive security blanket. You won't know what you're getting. You'll destroy your itinerary flexibility. And you'll pay top dollar.

I make reservations from the United States only for my first night's accommodations, when huge crowds are anticipated, and in places (in cities big or small) in which I know for certain where I want to stay and exactly when I'll be there.

Try to e-mail or fax your long-distance reservations. Getting reservations by e-mail is preferred by European hoteliers. An e-mail in simple English communicates clearly, minimizes the language barrier (especially helpful in southern Europe, where, because of the language barrier, a phone call will accomplish little), and gives your hotel a quick and easy way to respond. Whenever possible, reserve by e-mail.

Hotels, pensions, and B&Bs that lack e-mail likely have a fax number. Photocopy and use the handy fax form included in this chapter (online

Rich Sorensen

In a Back Door–style hotel, you get more by spending less. Here, the shower's down the hall, and the Alps are in your lap.

at www.ricksteves.com/reservation). If you don't get a response, assume the hotel received and understood your request and has no room available for you (some hotels get 30–40 faxes a day and would go broke returning them all). You can also make a reservation by telephone (about $1 a minute from the U.S.).

In your e-mailed or faxed request, always list your dates (with date and expected time of arrival, number of nights you'll stay, and date of departure), your room needs (number of people, the facilities you require), and your budget concerns (of course, a trade-off with facilities), and ask for mercy on their deposit requirements (either by promising to telephone a day in advance to reconfirm or giving them your credit-card number with expiration date as security). Including your credit-card information avoids an extra volley of faxes. Request a written confirmation with the price quoted.

Ideally your credit-card number will be accepted as a deposit. If a cash deposit is required, you can mail a bank draft or, easier, a signed $100 traveler's check. (Leave the "pay to" line blank and encourage them to avoid bank fees by just holding the check as security until you arrive and can pay in cash.)

Pack the hotel's written confirmation (in case of a dispute) and reconfirm your reservation a day or two before your arrival.

Don't panic. If, after several tries, it seems that every hotel in town is full, don't worry. Hotels take only so many long-distance advance reservations. They never know how long guests will stay and like to keep a few beds for their regulars. Call between 8 and 10 a.m. the morning you plan to arrive. This is when the receptionist knows exactly who's leaving and which rooms he needs to fill. He'll be eager to get a name for every available room. Those who are there in person are more likely to land a room. Many simple hotels don't bother with reservations more than a couple of weeks in advance, and some very cheap hotels take no reservations at all. Just show up and sleep with your money belt on.

Making Your Hotel Reservation

Most hotel managers know basic "hotel English." Faxing or e-mailing are the preferred methods for reserving a room. They're more accurate and cheaper than telephoning and much faster than writing a letter. Use this handy form for your fax (or find it online at www.ricksteves.com/reservation). Photocopy and fax away.

One-Page Fax

To: _____ @ _____
    hotel   *fax*

From: _____ @ _____
      name   *fax*

Today's date: ____ /____ /____
              day   month   year

Dear Hotel _____,
Please make this reservation for me:
Name: _____

Total # of people: _____   # of rooms: _____   # of nights: _____

Arriving: ____ /____ /____   My time of arrival (24-hr clock): _____
          day   month   year   (I will telephone if I will be late)

Departing: ____ /____ /____
           day   month   year

Room(s): Single___ Double___ Twin___ Triple___ Quad___

With: Toilet___ Shower___ Bath___ Sink only___

Special needs: View___ Quiet___ Cheap___ Ground Floor___

Credit card: Visa___ MasterCard___ American Express___

Card #: _____

Expiration date:_____

Name on card: _____

You may charge me for the first night as a deposit. Please fax, e-mail, or mail me confirmation of my reservation, along with the type of room reserved, the price, and whether the price includes breakfast. Thank you.

_____
Signature

_____
Name

_____
Address

_____
City   **State**   **Zip Code**   **Country**

_____
E-mail Address

BASIC BED-FINDING

In more than a thousand unreserved nights in Europe, I've been shut out three times. That's a 99.7 percent bedding average earned in peak season and very often in crowded, touristy, or festive places. What's so traumatic about a night without a bed anyway? My survey shows those who have the opportunity to be a refugee for a night have their perspectives broadened and actually enjoy the experience—in retrospect.

The cost of a wonderfully reservation-free trip is the remote chance you'll end up spending the night on a bench in the train station waiting room. Every year, I travel peak season (lately, with my wife and kids or a television film crew), arrive early or call a day or so in advance, and manage fine by using the few tricks listed here.

Travel with a good list of hotels. I spend more time in Europe finding and checking hotels (for my country guidebooks) than anything else. I can spend a day in Amsterdam, scaling the stairs and checking out the rooms of 20 different hotels, all offering double rooms from $70 to $150 a night. After doing the grand analysis, what's striking to me is how little correlation there is between what you pay and what you get. You are just as likely to spend $150 for a big impersonal place on a noisy highway as you are to spend $80 for a charming family-run guest house on a bikes-only stretch of canal.

These days, to sleep well and inexpensively on a big-city bed, you need a good guidebook's listing of hotels and budget alternatives. These lists are reliable and work well (but prices have likely gone up since the book was printed). In the last few years, I've expanded my country guides to include all the room listings you'll need for the parts of Europe I cover.

Use room-finding services if necessary. Popular tourist cities usually have a room-finding service at the train station or tourist information office. They have a listing of that town's "acceptable" available accommodations. For a fee of a few dollars, they'll get you a room in the price range and neighborhood of your choice. Especially in a big city (if you don't have a guidebook's listings), their service can be worth the price when you consider the time and money saved by avoiding the search on foot.

I avoid room-finding services unless I have no listings or information of my own. Their hotel lists normally make no quality judgments, so what you get is potluck. The stakes are too high for this to be acceptable (especially when you consider how readily available good hotel listings are in guidebooks). Also, since many room-finding services profit from taking a "deposit" that they pocket, many managers of the best budget places tell the room-finding service they're full when they aren't. They know they'll fill up with travelers coming direct, allowing them to keep 100 percent of the room cost.

Recently many tourist information offices have lost their government funding and are now privately owned. This creates the absurdity of a profit-seeking tourist information "service." Their previously reliable advice is now colored with a need to make a kickback. Some room-finding services work for a group of supporting hotels. Room-finding services are not above pushing you into their "favored" hotels, and kickbacks are powerful motivators. Only if you insist will you get information on cheap sleep options—dormitory, hostel, and "sleep-in" (circus tents, gyms with mattresses on the floor, and other $10-a-night alternatives to the park or station). And beware, many "tourist information offices" are just travel agencies and room-booking services in disguise.

Use the telephone. If you're looking on your own, telephone the places in your guidebook that sound best. Not only will it save the time and money involved in chasing down these places with the risk of finding them full, but you're beating all the other tourists—with the same guidebook—who may be hoofing it as you dial. It's rewarding to arrive at a hotel when people are being turned away and see your name on the reservation list because you called first. If the room or price isn't what you were led to believe it would be, you have every right to say, "No, thank you." If you like and trust the values of your guidebook's author, track down his recommendations by phone. In peak times, a guidebook's top hotel listings are likely to be full. Don't hesitate to jump way down the list where available rooms may abound. Use the tourist office only as a last resort.

Consider hotel runners. As you step off the bus or train, you'll sometimes be met by hotel runners wielding pictures of their rooms for rent. My gut reaction is to steer clear, but these people are usually just hard-working entrepreneurs who lack the location or write-up in a popular guidebook that can make life easy for a small hotel owner. If you like the guy and what he promises, and the hotel isn't too far away, follow him to his hotel. You are obliged only to inspect the hotel. If it's good, take it. If it's not, leave. You're probably near other budget hotels anyway. Establish the location very clearly, as many of these people have good places miserably located way out of town.

"Welcome! I have rooms."

The early bird gets the room. If you anticipate crowds, go to great lengths to arrive in the morning when the most (and best) rooms are available. If the rooms aren't ready until noon, take one anyway. Leave your luggage behind the desk; they'll move you in later and you're set up—free to relax and enjoy the city. I would leave Florence at 7 a.m. to arrive in Venice (a crowded city) early enough to get a decent choice of rooms. Consider the advantage of overnight train rides—you'll arrive, if not bright, at least early.

Ask your friend who runs today's hotel to call tomorrow's hotel to make you a reservation in the local language.

Your approach to room finding will be determined by the market situation—if it's a "buyer's market" or a "seller's market." Sometimes you can arrive late, be selective, and even talk down the price. Other times you'll happily accept anything with a pillow and a blanket. A person staying only one night is bad news to a hotel. If, before telling you whether there's a vacancy, they ask you how long you're staying, be ambiguous.

Leave the trouble zone. If the room situation is impossible, don't struggle—just leave. An hour by car, train, or bus from the most miserable hotel situation anywhere in Europe is a town—Dullsdorf or Nothingston—with the Dullsdorf Inn or the Nothingston Gasthaus just across the street from the station or right on the main square. It's not full—never has been, never will be. There's a guy sleeping behind the reception desk. Drop in at 11 p.m., ask for 14 beds, and he'll say, "Take the second and third floors, the keys are in the doors." It always works. Oktoberfest, Cannes Film Festival, St. Tropez Running of the Girls, Easter at Lourdes—your bed awaits you in nearby Dullsdorf. If you anticipate trouble, stay at the last train stop before the crowded city.

Follow taxi tips. A great way to find a place in a tough situation is to let a cabbie take you to his favorite hotel. They are experts. Cabs are also handy when you're driving lost in a big city. Many times I've hired a cab, showed him that elusive address, and followed him in my car to my hotel.

Let hotel managers help. Have your current manager call ahead to make a reservation at your next destination (offer to pay for the call). If you're in a town and having trouble finding a room, remember that nobody knows the hotel scene better than local hotel managers do. If one hotel is full, ask the manager for help. Often the manager has a list of neighborhood accommodations or will even telephone a friend's

In France each hotel has a plaque next to the door telling you its category.

place that rarely fills up and is just around the corner. If the hotel is too expensive, there's nothing wrong with asking where you could find a "not so good place." The most expensive hotels have the best city maps (free, often with other hotels listed) and an English-speaking staff that can give advice to the polite traveler in search of a cheap room. I find hotel receptionists understanding and helpful.

TO SAVE MONEY...

Think small. Larger hotels are usually pricier than small hotels or B&Bs, partly because of taxes (e.g., in Britain, once a B&B exceeds a certain revenue level, it's required to pay a 17.5 percent VAT tax in addition to its business and insurance taxes). Hoteliers that pay high taxes pass their costs on to you.

Consider a cheap chain hotel. More and more hotel chains— offering cheap or moderately priced rooms—are springing up throughout Europe. The hotels that allow up to four people in a room are great for families. You won't find character at chain hotels, but you'll get predictable, Motel 6–type comfort. Ibis Hotels are the most widespread throughout Europe (www.ibishotel.com, U.S. tel. 800/221-4542). Britain has Travelodge (www.travelodge.co.uk), Travel Inn (www.travelinn.co.uk), and Premier Lodge (www.premierlodge.co.uk). For Ireland, it's Jurys Inn (www.jurys.com).

Know the exceptions. Hotels in northern Europe are pricier than those in the south, but there are exceptions. In Scandinavia, Brussels, and Berlin, fancy "business hotels" are desperate for customers in the summer and on weekends, when their business customers stay away. They offer some amazing deals through the local tourist offices. The later your arrival, the better the discount.

Be a smart consumer—don't stray above your needs. Know the government ratings. A three-star hotel is not necessarily a bad value, but if I stay in a three-star hotel, I've spent $50 extra for things I don't need. You can get air-conditioning, elevators, private showers, room service, a 24-hour reception desk, and people in uniforms to carry your bags. But each of those services adds $10 to your room cost, and, before you know it, the simple $50 room is up to $100.

Avoid hotels that require you to buy meals. Many national governments regulate hotel prices according to class or rating. In order to overcome this price ceiling (especially at resorts in peak season, when demand exceeds supply), hotels often require that you buy dinner in their dining room. Breakfast normally comes with the room, but in some countries it's an expensive, kind-of-optional tack-on. One more meal (demi- or half pension) or all three meals (full pension) is usually uneconomical, since the hotel is skirting the governmental hotel price ceilings to maximize profit. I prefer the freedom to explore and sample the atmosphere of restaurants in other neighborhoods.

Shop around. When going door to door, rarely is the first place you check the best. It's worth 10 minutes of shopping around to find the going rate before you accept a room. You'll be surprised how prices vary as you walk farther from the station or down a street strewn with B&Bs. Never judge a hotel by its exterior or lobby. Lavish interiors with shabby exteriors (blame the landlord who's stuck with rent control, not the hotel) are a cultural trait of Europe. (If there are two of you, let one watch the bags over a cup of coffee while the other runs around.)

Check the prices on the room list to find the best value. Room prices vary tremendously within a hotel according to facilities provided. Most hotels have a room list clearly displayed, showing each room, its bed configuration, facilities, and maximum price for one and for two. Also read the breakfast, tax, and extra-bed policies. By studying this

Formule One is a French-style Motel 6. Fully automated, no-character $25 triples are at nearly every freeway off-ramp.

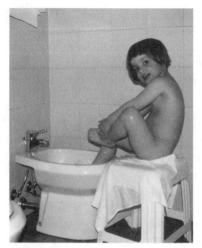

Throughout southern Europe, even the cheapest hotel rooms come with a bidet. Europeans use them to stay clean without a daily shower.

list you'll see that, in many places, a shower is cheaper than a bath, and a double bed is cheaper than twins. In other words, a sloppy couple that prefers a shower and a double bed can pay $20 more for a bath and twins. In some cases, if you want any room for two and you say "double," they'll think you'll only take a double bed. To keep all my options open (twin and double) I ask for "a room for two people." If you want a cheap room, say it. Many hoteliers have a few unrenovated rooms without a private bathroom; they usually don't even mention these, figuring they'd be unacceptable to Americans.

See if there's a discount for a longer stay or payment in cash. If you plan to stay three or more nights at a place, or if you pay in cash rather than by credit card (saving the hotelier the credit-card company's cut), it's worth asking if a discount is available. And if you came direct and point out that the tourist office didn't get their 10 percent, you also have a chance of talking the price down.

If it's off-season, bargain. Prices usually rise with demand during festivals and in July and August. Off-season, try haggling. If the place is too expensive, tell them your limit; they might meet it.

Put more people in a room. Family rooms are common, and putting four in a quad is much cheaper than two doubles. Many doubles come with a small double bed and a sliver single. A third person pays very little. A family with two small children can ask for triples and bring a sleeping bag for the stowaway.

Avoid doing outside business through your hotel. It's better style to go to the bullring and get the ticket yourself. You'll learn more and save money, and you won't sit with other tourists who drown your Spanish fire with Yankee-pankee. So often, tourists are herded together by a conspiracy of hotel managers and tour organizers and driven through gimmicky folk evenings featuring a medley of cheesy cultural clichés kept alive only for the tourists. You can't relive your precious Madrid nights. Do them right—on your own.

CHECK-IN PROCEDURE

Ask to see the room before accepting. Then the receptionist knows the room must pass your inspection. He'll have to earn your business. Notice the boy is given two keys. You asked for only one room. He's instructed to show the hard-to-sell room first. It's only natural for the hotel receptionist to try to unload the most difficult-to-sell room on the easiest-to-please traveler. Somebody has to sleep in it. If you ask to see both rooms, you'll get the better one. When you check out a room, point out anything that deserves displeasure. The price will come down, or they'll show you a better room. Think about heat and noise. I'll climb a few stairs to reach cheaper rooms higher off the noisy road. Some towns never quiet down. A room in back may lack a view, but it will also lack night noise.

Establish the complete and final price of a room before accepting. Know what's included and what taxes and services will be added. More than once I've been given a bill that was double what I expected. Dinners were required, and I was billed whether I ate them or not; so I was told—in very clear Italian.

When checking in, pick up the hotel's business card. In the most confusing cities, the cards come with a little map. Even the best pathfinders get lost in a big city, and not knowing where your hotel is can be scary. With the card, you can hop into a cab and be home in minutes.

If you need help, ask. Although you don't want to be a pest, remember, hotels are in the business of accommodating people. If you didn't get the kind of room you wanted, ask to switch when possible. If you'd like a room farther from a noisy elevator shaft, ask for it. If you need a different pillow, another blanket, mosquito netting, an electrical adapter, advice

---

The Key to Keys

Tourists spend hours fumbling with old skeleton keys in rickety hotel doors. The haphazard, nothing-square construction of old hotels means the keys need babying. Don't push them in all the way. Pull the door in or up. Try a little in, quarter turn, and farther in for full turn. Always turn the top of the key away from the door to open it. Some locks take two key revolutions to open. Leave the key at the desk before leaving for the day. I've never had my room broken into in Europe. Confirm closing time. Some hotels lock up after their restaurant closes, after midnight, or during their weekly "quiet day" and expect you to keep the key to the outside door with you to get in after hours.

on a good restaurant or show, driving instructions for your departure, help telephoning your next hotel, and so on, be sure to ask.

When you pay is up to the hotel and you. Normally I pay upon departure. If they want prepayment, that's fine, but unless I'm absolutely certain I'll be staying on, I pay one night at a time. Don't assume your room is yours once you're in. Make it clear when you check in how long you intend to stay, or you may get the boot.

BED-AND-BREAKFAST PLACES AND PENSIONS

Between hotels and hostels in price and style is a special class of accommodations. These are small, warm, and family-run, and offer a personal touch at a budget price. They are the next best thing to staying with a local family, and, even if hotels weren't more expensive, I'd choose this budget alternative.

Each country has these friendly accommodations in varying degrees of abundance, facilities, and service. Some include breakfast, some don't. They have different names from country to country, but all have one thing in common: They satisfy the need for a place to stay that gives you the privacy of a hotel and the comforts of home at a price you can afford.

While information on some of the more established places is available in many budget travel guidebooks, the best information is often found locally, through tourist information offices, room-finding services, or even from the local man waiting for his bus or selling apples. Especially in the British Isles, each B&B host has a network of favorites and can happily set you up in a good B&B at your next stop.

Many times, the information is brought to you. I'll never forget struggling off the plane on my arrival in Santorini. Fifteen women were begging me to spend the night. Thrilled, I made a snap decision and followed the most attractive offer to a very nice budget accommodation.

Bed-and-breakfasts offer you double the cultural experience for half the price of a hotel.

The "part of the family" element of a B&B stay is determined entirely by you. Chatty friendliness is not forced on guests. Depending on my mood and workload, I am often very businesslike and private during my stay. On other occasions I join the children in the barn for the sheep-shearing festivities.

Don't confuse European bed-and-breakfasts with their rich cousins in America. B&Bs in the United States are usually doily-pretentious places, very cozy and colorful but as expensive as hotels. In a European B&B you don't get seven pillows and a basket of jams.

Britain: Britain's B&Bs are the best of all. Very common throughout the British Isles, they are a boon to anyone touring England, Scotland, or Wales. As the name indicates, a breakfast comes with the bed, and (except in London) this is no ordinary breakfast. Most B&B owners take pride in their breakfasts. Their guests sit down to an

A special bonus when enjoying Britain's great bed-and-breakfasts: You get your own temporary local mother.

elegant and very British table setting and feast on cereal, juice, bacon, sausages,

Never judge a B&B by its name. Like many in Britain, this one is smoke-free and comes with numerous pleasant extras.

eggs, broiled tomatoes, mushrooms, toast, marmalade, and coffee or tea. While you are finishing your coffee, the landlady (who by this time is probably on very friendly terms with you) may present you with her guest book, inviting you to make an entry and pointing out others from your state who have stayed in her house. Your hostess will sometimes cook you a simple dinner for a good price, and, if you have time to chat, you may get in on an evening social hour. When you bid her farewell and thank her for the good sleep and full stomach, it's often difficult to get away. Determined to fill you with as much information as food, she wants you to have the best day of sightseeing possible.

Showers

Showers are a Yankee fetish. A morning without a shower is traumatic to many of us: It can ruin a day. Get used to the idea that you won't have a shower every night. The real winners are those who manage with four showers a week and a few sponge baths tossed in when needed. Here are some tips on survival in a world that doesn't start and end with squeaky-clean hair.

Take quick showers. Americans are notorious (and embarrassing) energy gluttons—wasting hot water and leaving lights on as if electricity is cheap. Who besides us sings in the shower or would even dream of using a special nozzle to take a hot water massage? European electric rates are shocking, and some hotels have had to put meters in their showers to survive. Fifty cents buys about five minutes of hot water. It's a good idea to have an extra token handy to avoid that lathered look. A "navy shower," using the water only to soap up and rinse off, is a wonderfully conservative method, and those who follow you will more likely enjoy some *warm wasser*. (Although starting and stopping the water doesn't start and stop the meter.)

"C" can mean "hot." Half of all the cold showers Americans take in Europe are cold only because they don't know how to turn the hot on. Study the particular system, and, before you shiver, ask the receptionist for help. There are some very peculiar tricks. In Italy and Spain, "C" is *caldo*, or hot. In many British places there's a "hot" switch at the base of the showerbox or even in the hallway. You'll find showers and baths of all kinds. The red knob is hot and the blue one is cold—or vice versa. Unusual showers normally have clear instructions posted.

If the water stays cold, ask, "When is the best time to take a hot shower?" Many cheap hotels have water pressure or hot water only during certain times. Other times, you'll get a shower—but no pressure or hot water. Hot water 24 hours a day is a luxury many of us take for granted.

Try a sponge bath. Nearly every hotel room in Europe comes with a sink and a bidet. Sponge baths are fast, easy, and European. A bidet is that mysterious porcelain (or rickety plastic) thing that looks like an oversized bedpan. Tourists use them as anything from a Laundromat to a vomitorium to a watermelon rind receptacle to a urinal. They are used by locals to clean the parts of the body that rub together when they walk—in lieu of a shower. Give it the old four Ss—straddle, squat, soap up, and swish off.

Bring soap. Many dorm-style accommodations don't provide towels or soap. B.Y.O.S. Towels, like breakfast and people, get smaller as you go south. In simple places, you won't get a washcloth, and bath towels are not replaced every day. Hang them up to dry.

European showers: Each one has its own personality.

Dominic Bonuccelli

Use the hall shower. The cheapest hotels rarely provide a shower or toilet in your room. Each floor shares a toilet and a shower "down the hall." To such a bathoholic people, this sounds terrible. Imagine the congestion in the morning when the entire floor tries to pile into that bathtub! Remember, only Americans "need" a shower every morning. Few Americans stay in these "local" hotels; therefore, you've got a private bath—down the hall. I spend 100 nights a year in Europe—probably shower 80 times—and I have to wait four or five times. That's the price I pay to take advantage of Europe's simple hotels.

In the last decade even the simplest places have added lots of private showers. For example, a hotel originally designed with 20 simple rooms sharing two showers will now be retrofitted with private showers in 14 of its rooms. That leaves a more reasonable six rooms rather than 20 to share the two public showers. Those willing to go down the hall for a shower enjoy the same substantial savings with much less inconvenience.

Try other places to shower. If you are vagabonding or sleeping several nights in transit, you can buy a shower in "day hotels" at major train stations and airports, at many freeway rest stops, in public baths or swimming pools, or even, if you don't mind asking, from hostels or small hotels. Most Mediterranean beaches have free, freshwater showers all the time. I have a theory that after four days without a shower, you don't get any worse, but that's another book.

If you're going to the normal tourist stops, your guidebook will list some good B&Bs. If you're venturing off the beaten British path, you don't need (or want) a listing. The small towns and countryside are littered with places whose quality varies only in degrees of wonderful. I try not to take a B&B until I've checked out three. Styles and atmosphere vary from house to house, and, besides, I enjoy looking through European homes.

Bed-and-breakfast travelers scramble at the breakfast table.

Ireland has essentially the same system of B&Bs. They are less expensive than England's and, if anything, even more "homely." You can expect a big breakfast and comfortable room often in the city center.

Germany, Austria, and Switzerland: Look for *Zimmer Frei* or *Privat Zimmer*. These are very common in areas popular with travelers (such as Austria's Salzkammergut Lakes District and Germany's Rhine, Romantic Road, and southern Bavaria). Signs will clearly indicate whether they have available rooms (green) or not (orange). Especially in Austria, one-night stays are discouraged. Most *Zimmer* cost around $20 per person and include a hearty continental breakfast. *Pensionen* and *Gasthäuser* are similarly priced, small, family-run hotels. Switzerland has very few *Zimmer*. And don't confuse *Zimmer* with the German *Farienwohnung*, which is a self-catering apartment rented out by the week or fortnight.

France: The French have a growing network of *Chambre d'hôte* (CH) accommodations where locals, mainly in the countryside and in small towns, rent double rooms for about the price of a cheap hotel ($50), but they include breakfast. Some CHs post *Chambre* signs in their windows, but most are listed only through local tourist offices. While your hosts will rarely speak English, they will almost always be enthusiastic and a delight to share a home with. For longer stays in the countryside, look into France's popular *gîtes* ($250–675 per week for 4 to 6 people). Pick up regional listings at local tourist offices, or try Gîtes de France, an organization that arranges *gîte* rentals (www.gites-de-france.fr).

Italy: Check out Italy's important alternatives to its expensive hotels: *albergo*, *locanda*, and *pensione*. (While these are technically all bunched together

---

Terms for Private Rooms to Rent

Private rooms throughout Europe cost $15 to $25 per person and come with breakfast in Great Britain, Ireland, Germany, Austria, and Switzerland.

Country	Term for Private Rooms to Rent
Great Britain & Ireland	Bed-and-Breakfast
Norway/Sweden	Rom or Rum
Denmark	Værelser
Germany/Austria/Switzerland	Zimmer
France	Chambre d'hôte
Italy	Affitta Camere
Spain	Casa Particulare
Portugal	Quarto
Greece	Dhomatia
Slovenia	Sobe
Eastern Europe	"Zimmer" or "Rooms"

---

now in a hotel system with star ratings, you'll still find these traditional names, synonymous with simple budget beds.) Private rooms, called *camere libere* or *affitta camere*, are fairly common in Italy's small towns. Small-town bars are plugged into the B&B grapevine. While breakfasts are rarely included, you'll sometimes get a kitchenette in the room. Drivers can try *agriturismo*, rooms in farmhouses in the countryside (weeklong stays are preferred in July and August, shorter stays are possible off-season).

Scandinavia: These usually luxurious B&Bs are called *rom, hus rum*, or, in Denmark, *værelser*. At $25 per bed, these are incredibly cheap (well, not so incredibly, when you figure it's a common way for the most heavily taxed people in Europe to make a little money under the table). Unfortunately many Scandinavian B&Bs are advertised only through the local tourist offices, which very often keep them a secret until all the hotels are full. In my *Rick Steves' Scandinavia* guidebook, I list plenty of wonderful money savers. An evening with a Scandinavian family offers a fascinating look at contemporary Nordic life. If they're serving breakfast, eat it. Even at $12, it's a deal by Nordic standards and can serve as your best big meal of the day.

Spain and Portugal: Travelers get an intimate peek into their small-town, whitewashed worlds by renting out *camas* and *casas particulares* in Spain and *quartos* in Portugal. In rural Iberia, where there's tourism, you'll find these budget accommodations. Breakfast is rarely included.

Greece: You'll find many $20-per-bed *dhomatia*. Especially in touristy coastal and island towns, hard-working entrepreneurs will meet planes, ferries, and buses as they come into town at any hour. In Greek villages with no hotels, ask for *dhomatia* at the town *taverna*. Forget breakfast.

Eastern Europe: This region has always had brave entrepreneurs running underground bed-and-breakfasts. Now, with the hard economic times, the freer atmosphere, and the overcrowded, overpriced, official hotels, you'll find more B&Bs in Eastern Europe than ever before. In Slovenia they're called *Sobe;* otherwise, they seem to go by "room" or the German *Zimmer.* At train stations and around tourist offices, look for hustling hosts with rooms to rent. Many cities now have services that efficiently connect travelers with locals renting rooms.

EUROPE'S 2,000 HOSTELS

Europe's cheapest beds are in hostels. Two thousand hostels provide beds throughout Europe for $10 to $20 per night. The buildings are usually in good, easily accessible locations.

As Europe has grown more affluent, hostels have been remodeled to

Cooking in the hostel members' kitchen, this traveler lives in Europe on $15 a day for his bed plus the price of groceries.

provide more plumbing and smaller rooms. Still, hostels are not hotels— not by a long shot. Many people hate hostels. Others love them and will be hostelers all their lives, regardless of their budgets. Hosteling is a philosophy. A hosteler trades service and privacy for a chance to live simply and communally with people from around the world.

A youth hostel is not limited to young people. You may be ready to jump to the next section because, by every other standard, you're older than young. Well, many countries have dropped the word "youth" from "hostel," and for years the Youth Hostel Association has given "youths" over the age of 54 a discount on the membership card. People of any age can hostel anywhere in Europe (except for Germany's Bavaria, with a strictly enforced 26-year-old age limit). The average hosteler is 18 to 26, but every year there are more seniors and families hosteling. All you need is a hostel membership card ($25 a year, free if you're under 18, and $15 if you're over 54), available at your local student travel office, any hostel office, or Hostelling International (tel. 202/783-6161, or order online at www.hiayh.org).

Hostels provide "no frills" accommodations in clean dormitories. The sexes are segregated, with four to 20 people packed in a room full of bunk beds. Pillows and blankets, but no sheets, are provided. You can bring a regular single bed sheet (sewn into a sack if you like), rent one at each hostel for about $4, or buy a regulation hostel sheet-sack at your first hostel (lightweight, ideal design at a bargain price). Many hostels have a few doubles for group leaders and couples, and rooms for families. Strong, hot showers (often with coin-op meters) are the norm, but simpler hostels have cold showers or even none at all. Hostels were originally for hikers and bikers, but that isn't the case these days.

Many hostels offer meals and meeting places. Hearty, supercheap meals are served, often in family-style settings. A typical dinner is fish sticks and mashed potatoes seasoned by conversation with new friends from Norway to New Zealand. The self-service kitchen, complete with utensils, pots, and pans, is a great budget aid that comes with most hostels. Larger hostels even have a

Hostels: Meet, drink, and be merry

small grocery store. Many international friendships rise with the bread in hostel kitchens.

The hostel's recreation and living rooms are my favorite. People gather, play games, tell stories, share information, marvel at American foreign policy, read, write, and team up for future travels. Solo travelers find a family in every hostel. Hostels are ideal meeting places for those in search of a travel partner. And those with partners do well to occasionally stay in a hostel to meet some new travelers.

Hostels are run by "wardens" or "house parents." They do their best to strictly enforce no-drinking rules, quiet hours, and other regulations. Some are loose and laid-back, others are like Marine drill sergeants, but all

One of Europe's 2,000 hostels—$10 a night, your own kitchen, a million-dollar view of the Jungfrau, and lots of friends. Note the worldwide triangular hostel symbol.

are hostel wardens for the noble purpose of enabling travelers to better appreciate and enjoy that town or region. While they are often overworked and harried, most wardens are great people who enjoy a quiet cup of coffee with an American and are happy to give you some local travel tips or recommend a special nearby hostel. Be sensitive to the many demands on their time and never treat them like hotel servants.

Hostels have drawbacks. Many have strict rules. They lock up during the day (usually from 10 a.m. to 5 p.m.), and they have a curfew at night (10 p.m., 11 p.m., or midnight), when the doors are locked and those that are outside stay there. These curfews are for the greater good—not to make you miserable. In the mountains, the curfew is early because most people are early-rising hikers. In London the curfew is 11:45 p.m., giving you ample time to return from the theater. Amsterdam, where the sun shines at night, has a 1:45 a.m. curfew. The first half hour after "lights out" reminds me of summer camp—giggles, burps, jokes, and strange noises in many languages. Snoring is permitted and practiced openly.

Hostel rooms can be large and packed. Many school groups (especially German) turn hostels upside down (typically weekends during the school year and weekdays in the summer). Try to be understanding (many groups are disadvantaged kids); we were all noisy kids at one time. Get to know the teacher and make it a "cultural experience."

Theft is a problem in hostels, but the answer is simple: Wear your money belt and don't leave valuables lying around (no one's going to steal your tennis shoes or journal). Use the storage lockers that are available in most hostels.

In some hostels in Britain, hostelers are required to do chores (token duties that never take more than a few minutes). It used to be that every hosteler in Europe was assigned a chore. This custom has died out on the Continent, but lives on (barely) in Britain.

Hostel selectively. Hostels come in all shapes and sizes, and some are sightseeing ends in themselves. There are castles (Bacharach, Germany), cutter ships (Stockholm), alpine chalets (Gimmelwald, Switzerland), huge modern buildings (Frankfurt), medieval manor houses (Wilderhope Manor, England), former choirboys' dorms (St. Paul's, London), and former royal residences (Holland Park, London). Survey other hostelers and hostel wardens for suggestions.

Stockholm's floating youth hostel, the af Chapman

I've hosteled most in the north, where hostels are more comfortable and the savings over hotels more exciting. I rarely hostel in the south, where hostels are less common and two or three people can sleep just as cheaply in a budget hotel.

Big-city hostels are the most institutional and overrun by young backpackers. Rural hostels, far from train lines and famous sights, are usually quiet and frequented by a more mature crowd. If you have a car, use that mobility to leave the Eurail zone and enjoy some of Europe's overlooked hostels.

Getting a hostel bed in peak tourist season can be tricky. The most popular hostels fill up every day. Written reservations are possible, but I've never bothered. Most wardens will take telephone reservations. I always call ahead to try to reserve and at least check on the availability of beds. Don't rely solely on the phone, because many hostels hold some beds for drop-ins. Try to arrive early. If the hostel has a lockout period during the day, show up before the office closes in the morning; otherwise, line up with the scruffy gang for the 5 p.m. reopening, when any remaining beds are doled out.

Thankfully, many hostels are putting out envelopes for each available bed, so you can drop by any time of day, pop your card into the reservation envelope and through the slot, and show up sometime that evening. Also, many German hostels have a telex reservation system where, for a small fee, you can reserve and pay for your next hostel bed before you leave the last one.

You can book a European hostel from the U.S. (though I've never found it necessary) by calling Hostelling International at 202/783-6161, www.hiayh.org. For a $5 processing fee, they'll book you a dorm bed at many (but not all) of Europe's hostels. They accept Visa, MasterCard, and Discover, need at least three days' notice, restrict their service to hostel

Dominic Bonuccelli

In hostels there's a dorm room for boys . . . and a dorm for girls.

members, and sell hostel membership cards.

Hostel bed availability is unpredictable. Some obscure hostels are booked out on certain days two months in advance. But I stumbled into Oberammergau one night during the jam-packed Passion Play festival and found beds for a group of eight.

Gung-ho hostelers can get a complete listing. Hostelling International publishes and sells *Hostelling International: Europe* (annually, $13.95

INFORMATION	
YOUNG £3.50	SHEET 80 ₱
JUNIOR £4.40	SHOWERS FREE
SENIOR £5.50	
DINNER £3.00	
BREAKFAST £2.30	
LUNCH PACK £1.60	
DOORS OPENED 7.30 AM	
RISING BELL & OFFICE OPEN 8.00	
BREAKFAST 8.30	
HOSTEL CLOSES 10.00	
HOSTEL REOPENS 5.00 PM	
DINNER 7.00	
HOSTEL CLOSES 11.00	
LIGHTS OUT 11.30	
WARDENS	
KEITH & JOAN BENNETT	
ASSISTANT WARDEN JAN VAN KAAM	
WE HOPE YOU ENJOY YOUR STAY AT	
STOW—ON—THE— OLD	

postpaid, also sold at your local student travel office and most European hostels). This directory lists each of Europe's 2,000 hostels with its number of beds, distance from the train station, directions, address, phone number, and day or season (if any) the hostel is closed. The book comes with a handy map of Europe locating all the hostels. Individual countries have a more accurate and informative directory or handbook (never expensive, often free). England's is especially worthwhile. If you're sticking to the more popular destinations, the Let's Go guidebook (Europe, or individual countries) lists enough hostels to make the *Hostelling International* directory unnecessary.

INDEPENDENT HOSTELS AND STUDENT HOTELS

There seem to be nearly as many unofficial or independent hostels as there are official ones. Many wardens and student groups prefer to run their own show and avoid the occasionally heavy-handed bureaucracy of the IYHF (International Youth Hostel Federation). Unofficial hostels are looser and more casual but not as clean or organized.

Hostels of Europe is a conglomeration of over 300 popular, free-spirited hostels (U.S. tel. 519/251-8821, www.hostelseurope.com). For $16, hostelers of any age may purchase a "discount" card (not required), which provides a 5 to 15 percent discount on hostel, tour, and attraction rates. Travelers can find these hostels on the Web site and book directly with some locations.

Ireland's Independent Holiday Hostels (www.hostels-ireland.com) is a network of 145 independent hostels, requiring no membership and welcoming all ages. All IHH hostels are approved by the Irish Tourist Board.

Many large cities have wild and cheap student-run hostels that are popular with wild and cheap student travelers. If these sound right for you, Let's Go guidebooks and the Internet Guide to Hostelling (www.hostels .com) have good listings.

CAMPING EUROPEAN STYLE

Relatively few Americans take advantage of Europe's 10,000-plus campgrounds. Camping is the cheapest way to see Europe and the middle-class European family way to travel. Campers give it rave reviews.

"Camping" is the international word for campground. Every town has a camping with enough ground to pitch a tent or park a caravan (trailer), good showers and washing facilities, and often a grocery store and restaurant, all for just a few dollars per person per night. Unlike the picturesque, rustic American campground near a lake or forest, European camping is more functional, like spending the night in a park-and-ride. Campings forbid open fires, and you won't find a riverfront lot with a stove, table, and privacy. A camping offers the basics—a place to sleep, eat, wash, and catch a bus downtown. They rarely fill up, and, if they do, the "Full" sign usually refers to trailers (most Europeans are trailer campers). A small tent can almost always be squeezed in somewhere.

Europe's campgrounds mix well with just about any mode of transportation. And very light modern camp gear makes camping without a car easier than ever. Tent and train is a winning combination for many. Nearly every train station has a tourist office nearby. Stop by and pick up a map with campgrounds marked, local camping leaflets, and bus directions. In most cases, buses shuttle campers from station to campground with ease.

Every station has lockers in which those with limited energy can leave unneeded baggage.

Hitchhikers find camping just right for their tender budgets. Many campgrounds are located near the major road out of town, where long rides are best snared. Any hitching camper with average social skills can find a friend driving his way with an empty seat. A note on the camp bulletin board can be very effective.

Tents and bikes also mix well. Bikers enjoy the same we-can-squeeze-one-more-in status as hikers and are rarely turned away.

Camping by car is my favorite combination. A car carries all your camp gear and gets you to any campground quickly and easily. Good road maps always pinpoint campings, and, when you're within a few blocks, the road signs take over. In big cities, the money you save on parking alone will pay for your camping. I usually take the bus downtown, leaving my camper van at the campground.

Learning about campgrounds: Each country's national tourist office in the United States can send you information on camping in its country. Consider getting the *Traveler's Guide to European Camping*, by Mike and Terri Church (1999, $24 postpaid, Rolling Homes Press, P.O. Box 2099, Kirkland, WA 98083, tel. 888/265-6555, www.rollinghomes.com). The Let's Go guide gives good instructions on getting to and from the campgrounds. Campings are well posted, and local tourist information offices have guides and maps listing nearby campgrounds. Every country has good and bad campgrounds. Campgrounds mirror their surroundings. If the region is overcrowded, dusty, dirty, unkempt, and generally chaotic, you're unlikely to find an oasis behind the campground's gates. A sleepy Austrian valley will most likely offer a sleepy Austrian campground.

European sites called "weekend campings" are rented out on a yearly basis to local urbanites. Too often, weekend sites are full or don't allow what they call "stop-and-go" campers (you). Camping guidebooks indicate which places are the "weekend" types.

Prices: Prices vary according to facilities and style. Expect to spend around $5 to $7 per night per person. You'll often pay by the tent, so four people in one tent sleep cheaper than four individual campers.

Registration and regulations: Camp registration is easy. As with most hotels, you show your passport, fill out a short form, and learn the rules. Checkout time is usually noon. English is the second language of campings throughout Europe, and most managers will understand the monoglot American.

European campgrounds generally require you to leave your passport with the office until you pay your bill. But many campgrounds will accept instead a Camping Card International ($10, also called a Camping Carnet). These cards may get you discounts at some campgrounds. The organization Family Campers and RVers sells the card to members ($25 per family for membership plus $10 for the carnet, 4804 Transit Road, Building 2, Depew, NY 14043, tel. 716/668-6242, e-mail: fcrv-nat@pce.net).

Silence usually reigns in European campgrounds beginning at 10 or 11 p.m. Noisemakers are strictly dealt with. Many places close the gates to cars after 11 p.m. If you do arrive after the office closes, set up quietly and register in the morning.

Campground services: European campgrounds have great, if sometimes crowded, showers and washing facilities. Hot water, as in many hostels and hotels, is metered, and you'll learn to carry coins and "douche" quickly. At larger campgrounds, tenters appreciate the in-camp grocery store and café. The store, while high-priced, stays open longer than most, offering latecomers a chance to picnic. The café is a likely camp hangout, and Americans enjoy mixing in this easygoing European social scene. I've scuttled many nights on the town so I wouldn't miss the fun with new friends right in the camp. Camping, like hosteling, is a great way to meet Europeans. If the campground doesn't have a place to eat, you'll find one nearby.

Many campgrounds offer "bungalows" with kitchenettes and four to six beds. Comfortable and cheaper than hotels, these are particularly popular in Scandinavia.

Camping with kids: A family sleeps in a tent a lot cheaper than in a hotel. There's plenty to occupy children's attention, including playgrounds that come fully equipped with European kids. As your kids make European friends, your campground social circle widens.

Safety: Campgrounds, unlike hostels, are remarkably theft free. Campings are full of basically honest middle-class European families, and someone's at the gate all day. Most people just leave their gear zipped inside their tents.

Camping equipment: Your camping trip deserves first-class equipment. Spend some time and money outfitting yourself before your trip. There are plenty of stores with exciting new gear and expert salespeople to get you up-to-date in a hurry.

For Europe, campers prefer a very lightweight "three-season" sleeping bag (consult the climate chart in the appendix for your probable bedroom temperature) and a closed-cell ensolite pad to insulate and soften the ground.

If you bring a stove from home, it should be the butane Gaz variety (but note that you can't take a Gaz cartridge on the plane—buy it there or lose it here). I keep meals simple, picnicking and enjoying food and fun in the campground café. I'd suggest starting without a stove. If you find out you want one, buy it there. In Europe it's much easier to find fuel for a European camp stove than for its Yankee counterpart.

Stoves and all other camping gear are cheaper at large "hypermarkets" (found in Britain, France, or Germany) than at European backpacking stores. In the U.S., the cheap chains (Wal-Mart and Costco) sell cheap equipment. For pricier, fancier gear, consider REI (tel. 800/426-4840, www.rei.com), Campmor (tel. 800/226-7667, www.campmor.com), or L.L. Bean (tel. 800/226-7552, www.llbean.com.)

Commit yourself to a camping trip or to a no-camping trip and pack accordingly. Don't carry a sleeping bag and a tent just in case.

Free camping: Informal camping, or "camping wild," is legal in most of Europe. Low-profile, pitch-the-tent-after-dark-and-move-on-first-thing-in-the-morning free camping is usually allowed even in countries where it is technically illegal. Use common sense, and don't pitch your tent informally in carefully controlled areas such as cities and resorts. It's a good idea to ask permission when possible. In the countryside, a landowner will rarely refuse a polite request to borrow a patch of land for the night. Formal camping is safer than free camping. Never leave your gear and tent unattended without the gates of a formal campground to discourage thieves.

HUT-HOPPING

Hundreds of alpine huts exist to provide food and shelter for hikers. I know a family that hiked from France to Slovenia, spending every night along the way in a mountain hut. The huts are generally spaced four to six hours apart. Most serve hot meals and provide bunk-style lodging. Many alpine huts (like unofficial hostels) require no linen and wash their blankets annually. I'll never forget getting cozy in my top bunk while a German with a "Rat Patrol" accent in the bottom bunk said, "You're climbing into the germs of centuries." Hut-hoppers hike with their own sheets.

In the Alps, look for the word *Lager*, which means they have a coed loft full of $10-a-night mattresses. If you plan to use the huts extensively, consider joining the American alpine Club ($75 a year, $35 if you're under

25, and $50 if you're over 65, 710 10th Street, Suite 100, Golden, CO 80401, tel. 303/384-0110, www.americanalpineclub.org). Membership in the American Alpine Club—plus the purchase of a "hut stamp" (about $55 postpaid from the American Alpine Club, affixed to your membership card)—entitles you to priority over nonmembers and discounts on the cost of your hut stay. Good books on hut-hopping include *Walking Austria's Alps: Hut to Hut* (by Jonathan Hurdle, Mountaineers), *Switzerland Mountain Inns* (Marcia and Philip Lieberman, Countryman Press), and *Walking the Alpine Parks: France and Northwest Italy* (Mountaineers).

SLEEPING FREE

There are still people traveling in Europe on $20 a day. The one thing they have in common (apart from B.O.) is that they sleep free. If even cheap pensions and hostels are too expensive for your budget, you too can sleep free. I once went 29 out of 30 nights without paying for a bed. It's not difficult, but it's not always comfortable, convenient, safe, or legal, either. This is not a vagabonding guide, but any traveler may have an occasional free night. Faking it until the sun returns can become, at least in the long run, a good memory.

Europe has plenty of places to roll out your sleeping bag. Some large cities, such as Amsterdam and Athens, are flooded with tourists during peak season, and many spend their nights dangerously in city parks. Some cities enforce their "no sleeping in the parks" laws only selectively. Big, crowded cities such as London, Paris, Munich, Venice, and Copenhagen run safe, legal, and nearly free "sleep-ins" (tents or huge dorms) during

peak season. Away from the cities, in forests or on beaches, you can pretty well sleep where you like. I have found that summer nights in the Mediterranean part of Europe are mild enough that I am comfortable with just my jeans, sweater, and hostel sheet. I no longer lug a sleeping bag around, but, if you'll be vagabonding a lot, bring a light bag.

Imaginative vagabonds see Europe as one big free

A bench with a view

hotel (barns, churches, buildings under construction, ruins, college dorms, etc.). Just keep your passport with you, attach your belongings to you so they don't get stolen, and use good judgment in your choice of a free bed.

Sleeping in train stations: When you have no place to go for the night in a city, you can always retreat to the station (assuming it stays open all night). It's free, warm, safe, and uncomfortable. Most popular tourist cities in Europe have stations whose concrete floors are painted nightly with a long rainbow of sleepy vagabonds. This is allowed, but everyone is cleared out at dawn before the normal rush of travelers converges on the station. In some cases, you'll be asked to show a ticket. Any ticket or train pass entitles you to a free night in a station's waiting room: You are simply waiting for your early train. Whenever possible, avoid the second-class lounges; sleep with a better breed of hobo in first-class lounges. For safety, lock your pack in a locker.

Sleeping on trains: Success hinges on getting enough room to stretch out, and that can be quite a trick (see Chapter 10: Train and Railpass Skills). It's tempting but quite risky to sleep in a train car that seems to be parked for the night in a station. No awakening is ruder than having your bedroom jolt into motion and roll toward God knows where. If you do find a parked train car to sleep in, check to see when it's scheduled to leave. Some Eurailers get a free if disjointed night by riding a train out for four hours and catching one back in for another four hours. Scandinavia, with Europe's most expensive hotels, offers *couchettes* for a reasonable $20. (Notice that Copenhagen and Stockholm are placed a very convenient overnight train ride apart.)

Sleeping in airports: An airport is a large, posh version of a train station, offering a great opportunity to sleep free. After a late landing, I crash on a comfortable sofa rather than waste sleeping time looking for a place that will sell me a bed for the remainder of the night. Many cut-rate inter-European flights leave or arrive at ungodly hours. Frankfurt airport is served conveniently by the train and is great for sleeping free—even if you aren't flying anywhere. Early the next morning you can book into a hotel and only pay for the following night. If your room is still occupied, leave your bag with the receptionist (she'll move it in later) and get out to see the town.

Some large airports have sterile womblike "rest cabins" which rent for eight hours at the price of a cheap hotel room. (I routinely use the "cocoons" at the Paris and Copenhagen airports.)

FRIENDS AND RELATIVES

There is no better way to enjoy a new country than as the guest of a local family. And, of course, a night with a friend or relative stretches your budget (usually along with your belly). I've had nothing but good experiences (and good sleep) at my "addresses" in Europe. There are two kinds of addresses: European addresses brought from home and those you pick up while traveling.

Before you leave, do some research. Dig up some European relatives. No matter how far out on the family tree they are, unless you're a real jerk, they're tickled to have an American visitor in their nest. I send my relatives a card announc-

The Europeans you visit don't need to be next-of-kin. This Tirolean is the father of my sister's ski teacher. That's close enough.

ing my visit to their town and telling them when I'll arrive. They answer with "Please come visit us" or "Have a good trip." It is obvious from their letter (or lack of one) if I'm invited to stop by.

Follow the same procedure with indirect contacts. I have dear "parents away from home" in Austria and London. My Austrian "parents" are really the parents of my sister's ski instructor. In London they are the parents of a friend of my uncle. Neither relationship was terribly close—until I visited. Now we are friends for life.

This is not cultural freeloading. Both parties benefit from such a visit. Never forget that a Greek family is just as curious and interested in you as you are in them (and the same old nightly family meals are probably pretty boring). Equipped with hometown postcards, pictures of my family, and a bag of goodies for the children, I make a point of giving as much from my culture as I am taking from the culture of my host. I insist on no special treatment, telling my host that I am most comfortable when treated simply as part of the family. I try to help with the chores, I don't wear out my welcome, and I follow up each visit with postcards to share the rest of my trip with my friends. I pay or reimburse my hosts for their hospitality only with a thank-you letter from home, possibly with color prints of all of us together.

The other kind of address is one you pick up during your travels. Exchanging addresses is almost as common as a handshake in Europe. If you have a business or personal card, bring a pile. (Some travelers even print up a batch of personal cards for their trip.) When people meet, they invite each other to visit. I warn my friend that I may very well show up some day at his house, whether it's in Osaka, New Zealand, New Mexico, or Dublin. When I have, it's been a good experience.

SERVAS

Servas is a worldwide organization that connects travelers with host families with the noble goal of building world peace through international understanding. Travelers pay $65 to join. They can stay for two nights (more only if invited) in homes of other members around the world. Arrangements are made after an exchange of letters, and no money changes hands (except to reimburse hosts for telephone calls). This is not a crash-pad exchange. It's cultural sightseeing through a real live-in experience. Plan to hang around to talk and share and learn. Offer to cook a meal or help out around the house. Many travelers swear by Servas as the only way to really travel and build a truly global list of friends. Opening your own home to visitors is not required (but encouraged). For more information, write to Servas at 11 John St. #505, New York, NY 10038, tel. 212/267-0252, fax 212/267-0292, www .usservas.org, e-mail: info@usservas.org.

The Friendship Force offers cultural exchange tours for the purpose of promoting global goodwill (34 Peachtree St., Suite 900, Atlanta, GA 30303, tel. 800/554-6715, www.friendship-force.org). The Globetrotters Club runs a network of hosts and travelers (BCM/Roving, London, WC1N 3XX, United Kingdom, www.globetrotters.co.uk).

HOUSE SWAPPING

Many families enjoy a great budget option year after year. They trade houses (sometimes cars, too, but draw the line at pets) with someone at the destination of their choice. Veteran house-swapper Sydney Brown offers these tips: be triple-sure about where to find the key and how to open the door, find out beforehand how to get to the nearest food store, ensure your host family leaves instructions for operating the appliances, make arrangements in advance to handle telephone charges, and ask about any peculiarities with the car you'll be driving.

For information, contact HomeLink (tel. 800/638-3841, www .swapnow.com), Trading Homes International (tel. 800/877-TRADE, www.trading-homes.com), or Intervac Home Exchange (30 Corte San Fernando, Tiburon, CA 94920, tel. 800/756-HOME, www.intervacus .com). *Vacation Home Exchange and Hospitality Guide* (John Kimbrough) and *Home Exchange Vacationing* (Bill and Mary Barbour) are two guidebooks on the subject.

16. Eating

Many vacations revolve around great restaurant meals, and for good reason. Europe serves some of the world's top cuisine at some of the world's top prices. I'm no gourmet, so most of my experience lies in eating well cheaply. Galloping gluttons thrive on $10 a day—by picnicking. Those with a more refined palate and a little more money can mix picnics with atmospheric and enjoyable restaurant meals and eat just fine for $30 a day.

This $30-a-day budget includes a $5 continental breakfast (usually figured into your hotel bill), a $5 picnic or fast-food lunch, a $15 good and filling restaurant dinner (more with wine or dessert), and $5 for your chocolate, cappuccino, or *gelato* fix. If your budget requires, you can find a satisfying dinner for $10 anywhere in Europe.

BREAKFAST

Only Britain and Scandinavia serve hearty breakfasts. In most of Europe, continental breakfasts are the norm. You'll get a roll with marmalade or jam, occasionally a slice of ham or cheese, and coffee or tea. Even the finest hotels serve the same thing—on better plates. It's the European way to start the day. (Sorry, no Mueslix.)

Supplement your breakfast with a piece of fruit and a wrapped chunk of cheese from your rucksack stash. Orange juice fans pick up liter boxes ($2) in the grocery store and start the day with a glass in their hotel room. If you're a coffee drinker, remember that breakfast is the only cheap time to caffeinate yourself. Some hotels will serve you a bottomless cup of a rich brew only with breakfast. After that, the cups acquire bottoms. Juice is generally available, but you have to ask, and you might be charged.

Breakfast, normally "included" in your hotel bill, can sometimes be skipped and deducted from the price of your room. Ask what the breakfast includes and costs. You can usually save money and gain atmosphere by buying coffee and a roll or croissant at the café down the street or by brunching picnic-style in

The continental breakfast—bread, jam, cheese, and coffee

the park. I'm a big-breakfast person at home. But when I feel the urge for a typical American breakfast in Europe, I beat it to death with a hard roll. You can find bacon, eggs, and orange juice, but it's nearly always overpriced and a disappointment.

Few hotel breakfasts are worth waiting around for. If you need to get an early start, skip it. Many places will fill your thermos with coffee before you go.

PICNICS—SPEND LIKE A PAUPER, EAT LIKE A PRINCE

There is only one way left to feast for $5 anywhere in Europe—picnic. You'll eat better while spending $15 to $20 a day less than those who eat exclusively in restaurants.

I am a picnic connoisseur. While I'm the first to admit that restaurant meals are an important aspect of any culture, I picnic almost daily. This is not solely for budgetary reasons. It's fun to dive into a marketplace and actually get a chance to do business. Europe's colorful markets overflow with varied cheeses, meats, fresh fruits, vegetables, and still-warm-out-of-the-bakery-oven bread. Many of my favorite foods made their debut in a European picnic.

To busy sightseers, restaurants can be time-consuming and frustrating. After waiting to be served, tangling with a menu, and consuming a budget-threatening meal, you walk away feeling unsatisfied, knowing your money could have done much more for your stomach if you had invested it in a picnic. Nutritionally, a picnic is unbeatable. Consider this example:

cheese, thinly-sliced ham, fresh bread, peaches, carrots, a cucumber, a half liter of milk, and fruit yogurt for dessert.

To bolster your budget, I recommend picnic dinners every few nights. At home we save time and money by raiding the refrigerator for dinner. In Europe, the equivalent is the corner deli or grocery store. There are plenty of tasty alternatives to sandwiches. Bakeries often sell little pizzas. Supermarkets, which hide out in the basements of big-city department stores, are getting very yuppie, offering salads, quiche, fried chicken, and fish, all "to go." "Microwave" is a universal word. When staying several nights, I "cozy up" a room by borrowing plates, glasses, and silverware from the hotel breakfast room and stocking the closet with my favorite groceries (juice, fruit and vegetables, cheese, and other munchies).

PICNIC SHOPPING

Every town, large or small, has at least one colorful outdoor or indoor marketplace. Assemble your picnic here. Make an effort to communicate with the merchants. Most markets are not self-service: You point to what you want and let the merchant bag it and weigh it for you. Know what you are buying and what you are spending. Whether you understand the prices or not, act like you do (observing the weighing process closely), and you're more likely to be treated fairly.

Learn the measurements. The unit of measure throughout the

Continent is a kilo, or 2.2 pounds. A kilo has 1,000 grams. One hundred grams (a common unit of sale, in Italy called *un etto*) of cheese or meat tucked into a chunk of French bread gives you about a quarter-pounder.

Food can be priced by the kilo, 100-gram unit, or the piece. Watch the scale when your food is being weighed. It'll show grams and kilos. If dried apples are priced at £2 per kilo, that's $3 for 2.2 pounds, or about $1.25 per pound. If the scale says 400 grams, that means 40 percent of £2 (or 80 pence), which is about $1.

Specialty foods are sometimes priced by 100 grams. If the pâté seems too cheap to be true, look at the sign closely. The posted price is probably followed by "100 gr." Chunky items like cucumbers will be priced by the piece (*Stück* in Germany or *pezzo* in Italy).

If no prices are posted, be wary. Tourists are routinely ripped off by market merchants in tourist centers. Find places that print the prices. Assume any market with no printed prices has a double price standard: One for locals and a more expensive one for tourists.

I'll never forget a friend of mine who bought two bananas for our London picnic. He grabbed the fruit, held out a handful of change, and said, "How much?" The merchant took two pounds (worth $3). My friend turned to me and said, "Wow, London really is expensive." Anytime you hold out a handful of money to a banana salesman, you're just asking for trouble.

If you want only a small amount... You'll likely want only one or two pieces of fruit, and many merchants refuse to deal in small quantities.

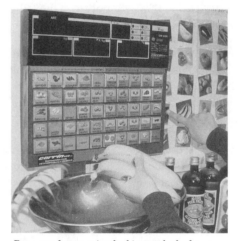

The way to get what you want and no more is to estimate about what it would cost if the merchant were to weigh it and then just hold out a coin worth about that much in one hand and the apple, or whatever, in the other. Have a Forest Gump look on your face that says, "If you take this coin, I'll go away." Rarely will he refuse the deal.

Put your banana in the bin, push the banana button, rip off the price sticker, and stick it on your banana.

In supermarkets, it's a cinch to buy a tiny amount of fruit or vegetables. Most have an easy push-button pricing system: Put the banana on the scale, push the picture of a banana (or the banana bin number), and a sticky price tag prints out. You could weigh and sticker a single grape.

Picnic Drinks
There are plenty of cheap ways to wash down a picnic. Milk is always cheap and available in quarter, half, or whole liters. Be sure it's normal drinking milk. Strange white liquid dairy products in look-alike milk cartons abound, ruining the milk-and-

Picnic on the train—quick, hearty, scenic

cookie dreams of careless tourists. Look for local words for whole or light, such as *voll* or *lett*. Nutritionally, half a liter provides about 25 percent of your daily protein needs. Get refrigerated, fresh milk. You will often find a "long life" kind of milk that needs no refrigeration. This milk will never go bad—or taste good.

European yogurt is delicious and can usually be drunk right out of its container. Fruit juice comes in handy liter boxes (look for "100 percent juice, no sugar" to avoid Kool-Aid clones). Buy cheap by the liter, and use a reusable half-liter plastic mineral-water bottle (sold next to the Coke all over) to store what you can't comfortably drink in one sitting. Liter bottles of Coke are cheap, as is wine in most countries. Local wine gives your picnic a nice touch. Any place that serves coffee has free boiling water. Those who have more nerve than pride get their plastic water bottle (a sturdy plastic bottle will not melt) filled with free boiling water at a café, then add their own instant coffee or tea bag later. Many hotels or cafés will fill a thermos with coffee for about the price of two cups.

Picnic Atmosphere
There is nothing second-class about a picnic. A few special touches will even make your budget meal a first-class affair. Proper site selection can make the difference between just another meal and *le piquenique extraordinaire*. Since you've decided to skip the restaurant, it's up to you to create the atmosphere.

Try to incorporate a picnic brunch, lunch, or dinner into the day's sightseeing plans. For example, I start the day by scouring the thriving market with my senses and my camera. Then I fill up my shopping bag and have breakfast on a riverbank. After sightseeing, I combine lunch and a siesta in a cool park to fill my stomach, rest my body, and escape the early afternoon heat. It's fun to eat dinner on a castle wall enjoying a commanding view and the setting sun. Some of my all-time best picnics have been lazy dinners accompanied by medieval fantasies in the quiet of after-hours Europe.

A quick dashboard picnic halfway through a busy day of sightseeing

Mountain hikes are punctuated nicely by picnics. Food tastes even better on top of a mountain. Europeans are great picnickers. Many picnics become potlucks, resulting in new friends as well as full stomachs.

Table Scraps and Tips

Bring picnic supplies. Pack zip-lock baggies (large and small) and a good knife with a can opener and corkscrew. In addition to being a handy plate, fan, and lousy Frisbee, a plastic coffee can lid makes an easy-to-clean cutting board with a juice-containing lip. A dish towel doubles as a small tablecloth. And a fancy hotel shower cap contains messy food nicely on your picnic cloth.

Kick back and munch a light dinner in your hotel room.

Bring an airline-type coffee cup and spoon for cereal, and a fork for take-out salad and chicken. Some travelers get immersion heaters (buy in Europe for a compatible plug) to make hot drinks to go with munchies in their hotel room.

Stretch your money. Bread has always been cheap in Europe. (Leaders have learned from history that when stomachs rumble, so do the mobs in the streets.) Cheese is a specialty nearly everywhere and is, along with milk, one of the

Continent's cheapest sources of protein. The standard low-risk option any-where in Europe is Emmentaler cheese (the kind with holes that we call "Swiss"). In season, tomatoes, cucumbers, and watermelons are good deals in Italy. Eastern Europe has some of the best and cheapest ice cream any-where. Wine is a great buy in France and Spain. Anything American is usu-ally expensive and rarely satisfying.

Make your big meal of the day a picnic lunch or dinner. Only a glutton can spend more than $10 for a picnic feast. In a park in Paris, on a Norwegian ferry, high in the Alps, on your dashboard at an autobahn rest stop, on your convent rooftop, or in your hotel room, picnicking is the budget traveler's key to cheap and good eating.

FAST FOOD, CAFETERIAS, AND MENSAS

McEurope: Fast-food restaurants are everywhere. Yes, the hamburger-ization of the world is a shame, but face it—the busiest and biggest McDon-ald's in the world are in Tokyo, Rome, and Moscow. The burger has become a global thing. You'll find Big Macs in every language—not excit-ing (and more than the American price), but at least at McDonald's you know exactly what you're getting, and it's fast. A hamburger, fries, and shake are fun halfway through your trip.

American fast-food joints are kid friendly and satisfy the need for a cheap salad bar and a tall orange juice. They've grabbed prime bits of real estate in every big European city. Since there's no cover, this is an oppor-tunity to savor a low-class paper cup of coffee while enjoying some high-class people watching.

Each country has its equivalent of the hamburger stand (I saw a "McCheaper" in Switzerland). What-ever their origin, they're a hit with the young locals and a handy place for a quick, cheap bite.

Cafeterias: "Self-service" is an international word. You'll find self-service restaurants in big cities every-where, offering low-price, low-risk, low-stress, what-you-see-is-what-you-get meals. A sure value for your euro is a department store cafeteria. These places are designed for the shopping housewife who has a sharp

Cafeteria leftovers: even cheaper than picnics . . .

eye for a good value. At a salad bar, grab the small (cheap) plate and stack it like the locals—high.

Mensas: If your wallet is as empty as your stomach, find a "mensa." Mensa is the pan-European word for a government-subsidized institutional (university, fire station, union of gondoliers, etc.) cafeteria. If the place welcomes tourists, you can fill yourself with a plate of dull but nourishing food for an unbeatable price in the company of local students or workers.

University cafeterias (often closed during summer holidays) offer a surefire way to meet educated English-speaking young locals with open and stimulating minds. They're often eager to practice their politics and economics, as well as their English, on a foreign friend. This is especially handy as you travel beyond Europe.

CAFÉS AND BARS

From top to bottom, Europe is into café-sitting, coffee, and people watching. Tourists are often stung by not understanding the rules of the game. You'll pay less to stand and more to sit. In general, if you simply want to slam down a cup of coffee, order and drink it at the bar. If you want to sit awhile and absorb that last museum while checking out

In European cafés, menus are two-tiered: cheaper at the bar, more at a table.

the two-legged art, grab a table with a view, and a waiter will take your order. This will cost you about double. If you're on a budget, always confirm the price for a sit-down drink. While it's never high profile, there's always a price list posted somewhere inside with the two-tiered price system clearly labeled (e.g., cheap at the bar, more at the table). If you pay for a seat in a café with a more expensive drink, that seat's yours for the entire afternoon if you like.

In some coffee bars (especially in Italy), you pay for your drink (or whatever) at the cash register, then take your receipt to the bar, where you'll be served.

RESTAURANTS

Restaurants are the most expensive way to eat. They can pillage and plunder a tight budget, but it would be criminal to pass through Europe without sampling the local specialties served in good restaurants. A country's high cuisine is just as culturally important as its museums. Experience it.

European restaurants are no more expensive than American restaurants. The cost of eating is determined not by the local standard but by your personal standard. Many Americans can't find an edible meal for less than $20 in their hometown. Their neighbors enjoy eating out for half that. If you can enjoy a $10 meal in Boston, Detroit, or Seattle, you'll eat well in London, Rome, or Helsinki for the same price. Last year I ate 100 dinners in Europe. My budget target was $5 to $10 for a simple, fill-the-tank meal; $15 for a memorable restaurant dinner; and $25 for a splurge meal. Forget the scare stories. People who spend $50 for a dinner in Dublin and then complain either enjoy complaining or are fools. Let me fill you in on filling up in Europe.

Average tourists are attracted—like moths to lightbulbs—to the biggest neon sign that boasts, "We speak English and accept credit cards." Wrong! The key to finding a good meal is to find a restaurant filled with loyal, local customers enjoying themselves. Be snoopy. Look at what people are eating—just don't ask for a taste. After a few days in Europe, you'll have no trouble telling a local hangout from a tourist trap.

Restaurants listed in your guidebook are usually fine, but too often when a place becomes famous this way, it goes downhill. You don't need those listings to find your own good restaurant. Leave the tourist center and stroll around until you find a restaurant with a happy crowd of locals. Ask your hotel receptionist, or even someone on the street, for a good place—not a good place for tourists, but a place they'd take a local guest.

Deciphering the Menu
European restaurants post their menus outside. Check the price and selection before entering. If the menu's not posted, ask to see one.

Finding the right restaurant is only half the battle. Then you need to order a good meal. Ordering in a foreign language can be fun, or it can be an ordeal. Ask for an English menu—if nothing else, you might get the waiter who speaks the *goodest* English. Most waiters can give at least a very basic translation—"cheekin, bunny, zuppa, green salat," and so on. A phrase book or menu reader (especially one of Altrainda Publishing's handy little *Marling Menu Masters* for France, Germany, Italy, and Spain) is very helpful for those who want to avoid ordering sheep stomach when all they want is a lamb chop.

If you don't know what to order, go with the waiter's recommendation or look for your dream meal on another table and order by pointing. People are usually helpful and understanding to the poor and hungry monoglot tourist. If they aren't, you probably picked a place that sees too many of them. Europeans with the most patience with tourists are the ones who rarely deal with them.

People who agonize over each word on the menu season the whole experience with stress. If you're in a good place, the food's good. Get a basic idea of what's cooking, have some fun with the waiter, be loose and adventurous, and just order something.

To max out culturally, my partner and I order two different meals: one high risk and one low risk. We share, sampling twice as many dishes. At worst, we learn what we don't like and split the chicken and fries. My tour groups cut every dish into bits, and our table becomes a lazy Susan. If anything, the waiters are impressed by our interest in their food, and very often

they'll run over with a special treat for all of us to sample—like squid eggs.

Common in Italy and France, the "tourist menu" or "menu of the day" is very popular and normally a good value. Look for the posted *menù turistica* or *menù del giorno* in Italy, or the *menu touristique* in France. For a set price, you get the "special of the day,"

Young taste buds having their horizons gently stretched

a multicourse meal complete with bread, service, and sometimes wine. Often you can choose from several appetizers and entrées. When I'm lazy and the price is right, I go for it, and it usually turns out OK. But you'll notice that people in the know (locals) order à la carte.

The best values in entrées are usually chicken, fish, and veal. In Italy, you'll save money by ordering pasta as your main course. Lately my travel partner and I, rather than getting entrées, have shared a memorable little buffet of appetizers—they're plenty filling, less expensive, and more typically local than entrées. Drinks (except for wine in Southern Europe) and desserts are the worst value. Skipping those, you can enjoy some surprisingly classy $15 meals.

Restaurant Drinks

In restaurants, Europeans drink bottled water (for taste, not health). Tap water is normally not served (except in France). You can get free tap water,

A fun neighborhood restaurant: no English menus, no credit cards, but good food, good prices, and a friendly chef.

but you may need to be polite, patient, inventive, and know the correct phrase. There's nothing wrong with ordering tap water, and waiters are accustomed to this American request. But it is a special favor, and while your glass or carafe of tap water is normally served politely, occasionally it just isn't worth the trouble, and it's best to just put up with the bottle of Perrier or order a drink from the menu.

Bottled water is served crisp and cold, either with or without carbonation, usually by happier waiters. Most tourists don't like the bubbly stuff. Learn the phrase–*con/avec/mit/* with gas or *senza/sans/ohne/*without gas (in Italian, French, and German, respectively), and you will get the message across. Acquire a taste for *acqua con gas*. It's a lot more fun (and read on the label what it'll do for your rheumatism).

If your budget is tight and you want to save $5 to $10 a day, never buy a restaurant drink. Scoff if you have the money, but drinks can sink a tight budget. Water is jokingly called the "American champagne" by the waiters of Europe.

Drink like a European. Cold milk, ice cubes, and coffee with (rather than after) your meal are American habits. Insisting on any of these in Europe will get you nothing but strange looks and a reputation as the ugly—if not downright crazy—American. Order local drinks, not just to save money but to experience the culture and to get the best quality and service.

European pubs don't serve minors beer—but many locals do.

The timid can always order the "American waters" (Coke, Fanta, and 7-Up), sold everywhere.

Buying local alcohol is cheaper than your favorite import. A shot of the local hard drink in Portugal will cost a dollar, while an American drink would cost at least the American price. Drink the local stuff with local people in local bars; a better experience than a Manhat-

For restaurant food at halfway-to-picnic prices, visit the local rosticceria or take-out deli.

tan in your hotel with a guy from Los Angeles. Drink wine in wine countries and beer in beer countries. Sample the regional specialties. Let a local person order you her favorite. You may hate it, but you'll never forget it.

Getting the Bill

A continental meal is a leisurely experience, the focus of the evening. At good restaurants, service will seem slow. Meals won't always come simultaneously—it's fine to start eating when served. A European meal is an end in itself. Europeans will spend at least two hours enjoying a good dinner, and, for the full experience, so should you. Fast service is rude service. If you need to eat and run, make your time limits very clear as you order.

To get the bill, you'll have to ask for it (catch the waiter's eye and, with raised hands, scribble with an imaginary pencil on your palm). Before it comes, make a mental tally of roughly how much your meal should cost. The bill should vaguely resemble the figure you expected. It should have the same number of digits. If the total is a surprise, ask to have it itemized and explained. Some waiters make the same "innocent" mistakes repeatedly, knowing most tourists are so befuddled by the money and menu that they'll pay whatever number lies at the bottom of the bill.

Tipping

Tipping is a minuscule concern of mine during a European trip. Front-door travel agents advise going to Europe armed with dollar bills for tipping. They'll advise putting five bucks under your pillow to get extra towels from the maids.

When you're traveling through the Back Door, the only time you'll need to tip is when you're in a restaurant where service isn't included,

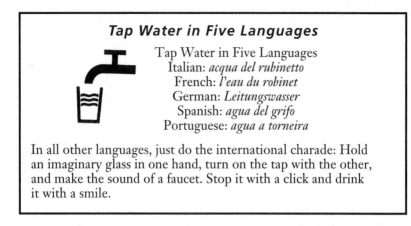

Tap Water in Five Languages

Tap Water in Five Languages
Italian: *acqua del rubinetto*
French: *l'eau du robinet*
German: *Leitungswasser*
Spanish: *agua del grifo*
Portuguese: *agua a torneira*

In all other languages, just do the international charade: Hold an imaginary glass in one hand, turn on the tap with the other, and make the sound of a faucet. Stop it with a click and drink it with a smile.

when you're rounding the taxi bill up, or when someone assists you in seeing a sight and is paid no other way (such as the man who shows people an Etruscan tomb that just happens to be in his backyard).

In restaurants, a service charge of about 15 percent is almost always included in the menu price or added automatically to your bill. If service is not included, the menu will say so (*service non compris* or *s.n.c.*). If it's not included, tip about 5 to 10 percent (by rounding up or leaving the change from your bill). Overtipping is Ugly American. In the days of the big buck, Americans shaped an image that Yankees today are having a hard time living down. If your bucks talk at home, muzzle them in Europe. As a matter of principle, if not economy, the local price should prevail.

Vegetarians

Vegetarians find life a little frustrating in Europe. Very often, Europeans think "vegetarian" means "no red meat" or "not much meat." If you are a strict vegetarian, you'll have to make things very clear. Write the appropriate phrase below, keep it handy, and show it to each waiter before ordering your meal:

German: *Wir sind (Ich bin) Vegetarier. Wir essen (Ich esse) kein Fleisch, Fisch, oder Geflügel. Eier und Käse OK.*

French: *Nous sommes (Je suis) vegetarien. Nous ne mangons (Je ne mange) pas de viande, poisson, ou poulet. Oeufs et fromage OK.*

Italian: *Siamo vegetariani (Sono vegetariano/a). Non mangiamo (mangio) nè carne, nè pesce, nè polli. Uova e formaggio OK.*

Dutch: We are (I am) vegetarian. We (I) do not eat meat, fish, or chicken. Eggs and cheese are OK. (Most Dutch people speak English.)

Vegetarians have no problem with continental breakfasts, which are normally meatless anyway. Meat-free picnic lunches are delicious, since bread, cheese, and yogurt are wonderful throughout Europe. It's in restaurants that your patience may be minced. Big-city tourist offices list restaurants by category. In any language, look under "V." Italy seems to sprinkle a little meat in just about everything. German cooking normally keeps the meat separate from the vegetables. Hearty German salads, with beets, cheese, and eggs, are a vegetarian's delight. Vegetarians enjoy salad bars and ethnic restaurants throughout Europe.

LOCAL SPECIALTIES, ONE COUNTRY AT A TIME

Eating in Europe is sightseeing for your taste buds. Every country has local specialties that are good, memorable, or both. Seek out and eat or drink, at least once, the notorious "gross" specialties: ouzo, horse meat, snails, raw herring, and so on (but not *lutefisk*). All your life you'll hear references to them, and you'll have actually experienced what everyone's talking about. Here are some tips to help you eat, drink, and be merry in Europe.

Belgium

Belgians boast that they eat as heartily as the Germans and as well as the French. This tiny country is into big steaks and designer chocolates. While Godiva's chocolate is considered the finest, most locals will enjoy triple the dose for the same investment by getting their fix at Leonidas. Belgian beer is tops. Connoisseurs arrive with a checklist, hoping to hop from Kriek (a cherry-flavored beer) to Dentergems (with coriander and orange peel) to Trappist (a dark, monk-made brew). The French fries even taste good dunked in mayonnaise, local style. Don't miss mussels in Brussels.

Britain and Ireland

Rather than looking for fine cuisine in Britain and Ireland, settle for decent cuisine in great atmosphere. I'm a sucker for pub grub. The days of starchy microwaved meat pies and mushy peas are over, and pubs actually turn out good, filling, hot meals with crispy fresh vegetables for $8. Locals seem to take great care in keeping up-to-date on which pubs do the best meals. Stow your guidebook and go with the local favorite. Beer snobs appreciate England's ales and bitters. If you're just looking for a cold Bud, ask for a lager. For a change of pace, try Indian food—as popular in Britain as hamburgers are in America.

France

France is famous for its cuisine—and rightly so. Dining in France can be surprisingly easy on a budget, especially in the countryside. Small restaurants throughout the country love their regional cuisine and take great pride in serving it.

The *plat du jour* (daily special), salad plate, and *menu* (fixed-price, three- to six-course meal) are often good deals. To get a complete list of what's cooking, ask for the *carte* (not the *menu*). The cheese boards that come with multicourse meals offer the average American a new adventure in eating. When it comes, ask for "a little of each, please" (*un peu de chaque, s'il vous plaît*). Wine is the cheapest drink, and every region has its own wine and cheese. Order the house wine (*vin du pays*). Classy restaurants are easiest to afford at

Cheers!

lunchtime, when meal prices are usually reduced. France is known for particularly slow (as in polite) service. If you need to eat and run, make it clear from the start. Bars serve reasonable omelets, salads, and the *croque monsieur*—your standard grilled cheese and ham sandwich.

Degustation gratuite is not a laxative but an invitation to sample the wine. You'll find D/G signs throughout France's wine-growing regions. When buying cheese, be sure to ask for samples of the local specialties. Croissants are served warm with breakfast, and baguettes (long, skinny loaves of French bread) are great for budget munching.

Regardless of your budget, picnic for a royal tour of French delicacies. Make a point of visiting the small specialty shops and picking up the finest (most expensive) pâtés, cheeses, and hors d'oeuvres. As you spread out your tablecloth, passersby will wish you a cheery "*Bon appétit!*"

Germany

Germany is ideal for the "meat-and-potatoes" person. With straightforward, no-nonsense food at budget prices, I eat very well in Deutschland. Small-town restaurants serve up wonderful plates of hearty local specialties for $10. The *Würst* is the best anywhere, and *Kraut* is not as *sauer* as the stuff you hate at home. Eat ugly things whenever possible. So many tasty European specialties come in gross packages.

Drink beer in Bavaria and wine on the Rhine, choosing the most atmospheric *Bräuhaus* or *Weinstube* possible.

Browse through supermarkets and see what Germany eats when there's no more beer and pretzels. Try Gummi Bears, the bear-shaped jelly bean with a cult following, and Nutella, a sensuous choco-nut spread that turns anything into a first-class dessert. Fast-food stands are called *Schnell Imbiss*. For budget relief in big-city Germany, find a Greek, Turkish, or Italian restaurant.

Ein Beer, ein Pretzel, und thou

Greece

While the menus are all Greek to most tourists, it's common and accept-able to go into the kitchen and point to the dish you want. This is a good way to make some friends, sample from each kettle, get what you want (or at least know what you're getting), and have a truly memorable meal. (The same is true in Turkey.) Be brave. My favorite Greek snack is a tasty shish kebab wrapped in flat bread—called a *souvlaki* pita. *Souvlaki* stands, offering $1 take-out pita sandwiches, are all over Greece. On the islands, eat fresh seafood and dunk bread into *tzatziki*,

The best snack deal in Europe—a Greek souvlaki

a refreshing cucumber and yogurt dip. Don't miss the creamy yogurt with honey. The feta (goat) cheese salads and the flaky nut 'n' honey dessert called *baklava* are two other tasty treats. If possible, go to a wine festival. *Retsina* is a pine resin–flavored wine that is a dangerous taste to acquire. For American-style coffee, order "Nescafe," but try the potent, grainy Greek coffee for a real kick. Eat when the locals do—late.

Italy

Italians eat huge meals consisting of a first course of pasta, a second plate of meat, plus a salad, fruit, and wine. The pasta course alone is usually enough to fill the average tourist. Some restaurants won't serve just pasta; find one that will, and you'll enjoy a reasonably priced meal of lasagna or minestrone and a salad. Veggie lovers will enjoy the restaurants that have self-serve antipasti buffets. These offer a variety of cooked appetizers spread out like a salad bar (pay per plate, not weight); a plate of antipasti combined with a pasta dish makes a healthy, affordable, inter-

Two fine reasons to savor Italy: gelato *and the* *Riviera*

esting meal. Note that anytime you eat or drink at a table, you'll be charged a cover (*coperto*) of a couple dollars. That, plus service (*servizio*), makes even a cheap, one-course restaurant meal cost $10.

For inexpensive Italian eateries, look for the term *osteria, tavola calda, rosticceria, trattoria, pizzeria,* or "self-service." A meal-sized pizza (sold everywhere for under $7) and a cold beer is my idea of a good, fast, cheap Italian dinner. For a stand-up super bargain meal, look for a *Pizza Rustica* shop, which sells pizza by weight. Just point to the best-looking pizza and tell them how much you want (200 grams is a filling meal). They weigh, you pay. They heat it, you eat it.

The *menù del giorno* (menu of the day, usually a good deal), *pane e coperto* (charge for bread and cover), and *servizio compreso* (service included) are three important phrases to know. But the most important word in your Italian vocabulary is *gelato*—probably the best ice cream you'll ever taste. A big cone or cup containing a variety of flavors costs about $2.

Cappuccino, rich coffee with a frothy head of steamed milk, is very popular, and it should be. Tiny coffee shops are tucked away on just about every street. All have a price list, and most require you to pay the cashier first and then take the receipt to the man who makes the drinks. Experiment. Try coffee or tea *freddo* (cold) or a *frappe* (blended ice). Discover a new specialty each day. Bars sell large bottles of cold mineral water, with or without gas, for about $1. *Panini* (sandwiches), toasted if you ask, are cheap and widely available.

Barhopping is fun. A carafe of house wine serves four or five people for $4. *Corposo* means full-bodied. Many bars have delicious *cicchetti* (cheh-KET-tee), local toothpick munchies. A *cicchetteria* is a great place for an entire meal of these pint-sized taste treats. In big cities many bars offer these munchies free during happy hour.

The Netherlands

My favorite Dutch food is Indonesian. Indonesia, a former colony of the Netherlands, fled the nest, leaving behind plenty of great Indonesian restaurants. The cheapest meals, as well as some of the best splurges, are found in these "Indisch" or "Chinese-Indisch" restaurants. The famous *rijsttafel* (rice table) is the ultimate Indonesian meal, with as many as 36 delightfully exotic courses, all eaten with rice. One meal is plenty for two, so order carefully. In a small-town restaurant, a *rijsttafel* can be a great bargain—two can split 12 exotic courses with rice for $20. *Bami* or *nasi goreng* are smaller and cheaper but still filling versions of a *rijsttafel*.

Other Dutch treats include *nieuwe haring* (raw herring) and *siroop-wafels*—a syrup-filled cookie that's best eaten warm from the bakery.

Portugal

Portugal has some of the most enjoyable and cheapest eating I've found in Europe. Find a local sailors' hangout and fill up on fresh seafood, especially clams, cockles, and the fish soup. While Portuguese restaurants are not expensive, food stands in the fairs and amusement parks are even cheaper. The young *vinho verde* is an addictive local specialty and a favorite of visiting wine buffs. In fishing towns you'll find boiled barnacles (*percebes*) sold on the street and as the Portuguese answer to beer nuts in the bars. Let a local show you how to strip and eat one. A fun excuse to visit the fine bakeries is to go on a quest for the best *pastel del Nata*. These delightful mini–cream pies are sold everywhere but originated near Lisbon in Belém, where you can visit the famous Casa Pasties de Belém and try the original.

Be warned that in restaurants, pricey little appetizers might be placed at your table as if they're free. While fun and tasty, if you nibble even one you'll be charged for the entire lot. To clear out the temptation, ask to have them taken away.

Scandinavia

Most Scandinavians avoid their highly taxed and very expensive restaurants. The cost of alcohol alone is a sobering experience. The key to budget eating in Nordic Europe is to take advantage of the smörgåsbord. For about $15 (cheap in Scandinavia), breakfast smörgåsbords will fill you with plenty of hearty food. Since both meals are, by definition, all-you-can-eat, I opt for the budget breakfast meal over the fancier, more expensive

($25) *middag*, or midday, smörgåsbords. Many train stations and ferries serve smörgåsbords.

For a budget lunch in Denmark, find a *smörre-bröd* (open-face sandwich) shop. These places make artistic and delicious sandwich picnics to go.

All over Scandinavia, keep your eyes peeled for daily lunch specials called *dagens rett*. You can nor-

Enough food to sink a Viking ship: Smörgåsbord

mally have all the vegetables (usually potatoes) you want when you order a restaurant's entrée. Just ask for seconds. Many Scandinavian pizzerias offer amazing all-you-can-eat deals and hearty salad bars. (Your bill will double if you order a beer.) The cheapest cafeterias often close around 5 or 6 p.m.

Fresh produce, colorful markets, and efficient supermarkets abound in Europe's most expensive corner. Liver paste is curiously cheap but tastes powerfully nutritious. The rock-bottom bilge-of-a-Viking-ship cheap meal is a package of cracker bread and a tube of sandwich spread. Handy tubes of cheese, shrimp, and even caviar spread are popular throughout Scandinavia. Save money and get some fresh air—picnic.

Spain

The greatest pleasure in Spanish eating is the price tag. Take advantage of the house wine. Fit the local schedule: Lunch is late (1–3 p.m.), and dinner is later (8:30–11:30 p.m.). Restaurants are generally closed except at meal-times. Two famous Spanish dishes are *gazpacho* (chilled tomato soup) and *paella* (saffron-flavored rice with seafood, chicken, and sausage). *Platos combinados* (combination plates of three or more items) are a reasonable way to sample Spanish cuisine. At other times, bars and coffee spots serve snacks of *bocadillos* (sandwiches), *tortillas* (omelets, great in a bar for a cheap and hearty breakfast), and *tapas* (hors d'oeuvres). On my last trip, I ate at least one easy, quick, and very cheap *tapas* meal a day. It seems that the most popular local bars are the ones with the most litter on the floor.

Switzerland

Swiss restaurant prices will ruin your appetite and send you running to a grocery store. Even locals find their restaurants expensive. The Migros and Co-op grocery stores sell groceries for about the same price as you'd find in American stores—cheap by European standards. Hostels usually serve large family-style dinners at a low price. *Rösti* (a hash-browns-with-onions dish) is a good, hearty standby. *Raclette* (melted cheese, potatoes, and pickles) is also popular. Split a cheese fondue with your hiking partner before filling up on Swiss chocolate. The remote mountain huts offer more than shelter. Many have provisions helicoptered in, are reasonably priced, and bubble with alpine atmosphere. The Swiss wine, *Fendant*, is expensive (sold by the deciliter) but worth every franc. Local beer is cheap by Swiss standards and good.

Turkey

Bring an appetite and order high on the menu in nice restaurants. Eating's cheap in Turkey. The typical eatery is a user-friendly cafeteria with giant bins of lots of delicacies you always thought were Greek. *Kebabs* are a standard meaty snack. *Pide*, fresh out of the oven, is Turkish pizza. *Sutlac* (rice pudding) and *baklava* will satisfy your sweet tooth. Munch pistachios by the pocketful. Tea in tiny hourglass-shaped glasses is served constantly everywhere. A refreshing milky yogurt drink called *ayran*, cheap boxes of cherry juice, and fresh-squeezed orange juice make it fun to quench your Turkish thirst. Or try the *raki* (Turkish ouzo). Let a local show you how to carefully create a two-layered *raki* drink by slowly dribbling in the water. For breakfast, get ready for cucumbers, olives, tomatoes, and lots of goat cheese and bread.

17. Shopping

Gift shopping is getting very expensive. I remember buying a cuckoo clock 20 years ago for $5. Now a "Happy Meal" at the Munich McDonald's costs that much.

SOUVENIR STRATEGIES

Shop in countries where your dollar stretches farthest. Shop in Turkey, Morocco, Portugal, Spain, and Greece. For the price of a four-inch pewter Viking ship in Norway, you can buy a real boat in Turkey.

Shop at flea markets. The most colorful shopping in Europe is at its flea markets. Among the best are Amsterdam's Waterlooplein (Saturday), London's Portobello Market (Saturday), Madrid's El Rastro (Sunday), and Paris' Porte de Clignancourt (runs Saturday through Monday, best on Sunday). Flea markets anywhere have soft prices. Bargain like mad. Pickpockets love flea markets—wear your money belt and watch your day bag.

Check out large department stores. These often have a souvenir section with standard local knickknacks and postcards at prices way below the cute little tourist shops.

Stay in control. Shopping is an important part of the average person's trip, but, all too often, slick marketing and cutesy, romantic window displays can succeed in shifting the entire focus of your vacation toward things in the tourist shops. (It's a lucrative business. Many souvenir merchants in Italy work through the tourist season, then retire for the rest of the year.) This sort of tourist brainwashing can turn you into one of the many people who set out to see and experience Europe but find themselves wandering in a trancelike search for signs announcing Duty-Free Shopping. I've seen half the members of a British Halls of Parliament guided tour skip out to survey an enticing display of plastic "bobby" hats and Union Jack panties. Even if the sign says, "Keep Italy green, spend dollars," don't let your trip degenerate into a glorified shopping spree.

Ask yourself if your enthusiasm is merited. More often than not, you can pick up a very similar item of better quality for a cheaper price at home. Unless you're a real romantic, the thrill of where you bought something fades long before the item's usefulness. My life has more room for a functional souvenir than for a useless symbol of a place I visited. Even thoughtful shoppers go overboard. I have several large boxes in my attic labeled "great souvenirs."

Try to restrict your shopping to a stipulated time. Most people have an idea of what they want to buy in each country. Set aside one day to shop in each country, and stick to it. This way you avoid drifting through your trip thinking only of souvenirs.

To pack light, shop at the end of your trip. Consider enjoying the luxury of not being a shopper for 80 percent of your trip and ending in the best shopping country where you go hog-wild and fly home heavy. One summer I had a 16-pound rucksack and nothing more until the last week of my trip when, in Spain and Morocco, I managed to accumulate two

Boxloads of Davids *await busloads of tourists.*

medieval chairs, two sets of bongos, a camel-hair coat, swords, a mace, and a lace tablecloth.

Good souvenirs: My favorites are books (a great value all over Europe, with many impossible-to-find-in-the-U.S. editions), local crafts (well explained in guidebooks, such as hand-knit sweaters in Portugal or Ireland, glass in Sweden, lace in Belgium), strange stuffed animals (at flea markets), CDs of music I heard live, posters (one sturdy tube stores eight or 10 posters safely), clothing, photographs I've taken, and memories whittled carefully into my journal.

VALUE-ADDED TAX (VAT) REFUNDS

Local European sales taxes vary from 15 to 25 percent. Tourists who buy something new (and expensive) and carry it with them out of the country can often get this tax refunded. And each year more than half a billion dollars of refundable taxes are left unclaimed. Yes, that is exciting. But VAT refunds are generally not worth the trouble.

Each country sets a different limit for the minimum amount you must buy in a store to qualify for a refund. Generally if you're buying something worth over $100 in a country with high taxes (Britain and most of northern Europe), ask about a VAT refund.

Getting a refund: If you shop at a store that participates in the Tax-free Program (look for the sticker in the window or ask a clerk), you'll get a Tax-free Shopping Cheque after you make a major purchase. Get the cheque validated at customs in the airport (when you leave Europe), and then claim your refund at the nearby "Tax-free Refund" booth. You can request cash, check, or charge-card credit. Save up your cheques from various European countries and process them all when you leave Europe. Be prepared to show your purchased goods to customs officials.

Ideally you'll talk your merchants into deducting the VAT from your purchase price and let them process the refund. When VAT refunds are worthwhile, merchants use them in their sales pitch. Local merchants know the VAT ropes and are the best VAT information source for their country.

CUSTOMS FOR AMERICAN SHOPPERS

You are allowed to take $400 of souvenirs home duty-free per person. The next $1,000 is taxed at a flat 3 percent. After that, you pay the individual item's duty rate. You can also bring in duty-free a liter of alcohol, a carton of cigarettes, and up to 100 cigars. To check customs rules and duty rates before you go, visit www.customs.gov.

You can mail one package per person per day worth up to $200 duty-free from Europe to the United States. (If you mail an item home valued at $250, you pay duty on the full $250, not $50.) Mark it "Unsolicited Gift." You'll need to fill out a customs form at the post office. (For details, see Chapter 20: Phones, E-mail, and Mail.)

SUCCESSFUL BARGAINING

In much of the world, the price tag is only an excuse to argue. Bargaining is the accepted and expected method of finding a compromise between the wishful thinking of the merchant and the tourist. Prices are "soft" in much of the Mediterranean world. In Europe bargaining is common only in the south, but you can fight prices at flea markets and with street vendors anywhere.

While bargaining is good for your budget, it can also become an enjoyable game. Many travelers are addicted hagglers who would gladly skip a tour of a Portuguese palace to get the price down on the black-clad lady's handmade tablecloth.

The Ten Commandments of the Successful Haggler

1. Determine if bargaining is appropriate. It's bad shopping etiquette to "make an offer" for a tweed hat in a London department store. It's foolish not to at a Greek outdoor market. To learn if a price is fixed, show some interest in an item but say, "It's just too much money." You've put the merchant in a position to make the first offer. If he comes down even 2 percent, there's nothing sacred about the price tag. Haggle away.

2. Shop around and find out what locals pay. Prices can vary drastically among vendors at the same flea market, and even at the same stall. If prices aren't posted, assume there's a double price standard: One for locals and one for you. If only tourists buy the item you're pricing, see what an Arab, Spanish, or Italian tourist would be charged. I remember thinking I did well in Istanbul's Grand Bazaar, until I learned my Spanish friend bought the same shirt for 30 percent less. Merchants assume American tourists are rich. And they know what we pay for things at home.

3. Determine what the item is worth to you. Price tags can be meaningless and serve to distort your idea of an item's true worth. The merchant is playing a psychological game. Many tourists think that if they can cut the price by 50 percent they are doing great. So the merchant quadruples his prices and the tourist happily pays double the fair value. The best way to deal with crazy price tags is to ignore them. Before you even see the price tag, determine the item's value to you, considering the hassles involved in packing it or shipping it home.

4. Determine the merchant's lowest price. Many merchants will settle for a nickel profit rather than lose the sale entirely. Promise yourself that no matter how exciting the price becomes, you won't buy. Then work the cost down to rock bottom. When it seems to have fallen to a record low, walk away. That last price he hollers out as you turn the corner is often the best price you'll get. If the price is right, go back and buy. Prices often drop at the end of the day when merchants are considering packing up.

5. Look indifferent. As soon as the merchant perceives the "I gotta have that!" in you, you'll never get the best price. He assumes Americans have the money to buy what they really want.

6. Employ a third person. Use your friend who is worried about the ever-dwindling budget or who doesn't like the price or who is bored and wants to return to the hotel. This trick can work to bring the price down faster.

7. Impress the merchant with your knowledge—real or otherwise. He'll respect you, and you'll be more likely to get good quality. Istanbul has very good leather coats for a fraction of the U.S. cost. Before my trip I talked to some leather-coat sellers and was much better prepared to confidently pick out a good coat in Istanbul for $100.

8. Obey the rules. Don't hurry. Bargaining is rarely rushed. Get to know the shopkeeper. Accept his offer for tea, talk with him. He'll know you are serious. Dealing with the owner (no salesman's commission) can lower the price. Bid carefully. If a merchant accepts your price (or vice versa), you must buy the item.

9. Show the merchant your money. Physically hold out your money and offer him "all you have" to pay for whatever you are bickering over. He'll be tempted to just grab your money and say, "Oh, OK."

10. If the price is too much, leave. Never worry about having taken too much of the merchant's time and tea. They are experts at making the tourist feel guilty for not buying. It's all part of the game. Most merchants, by local standards, are financially well-off.

Remember, you can generally find the same souvenirs in large department stores at fair and firm prices. Department-store shopping is quicker, easier, often cheaper—but not nearly as much fun.

CITY SKILLS

18. Getting Oriented

Many Americans are overwhelmed by European big-city shock. Struggling with the Chicagos, New Yorks, and L.A.s of Europe is easier if you take advantage of the local tourist information office, catch some kind of orientation tour, and learn the public transportation system. You can't Magoo Europe's large cities. Plan ahead. Have a directory-type guidebook for wherever you're traveling. Spend the last hour as you approach by train or bus reading and planning. Know what you want to see. To save time and energy, plan your sightseeing strategy to cover the city systematically and efficiently, one neighborhood at a time.

TOURIST INFORMATION OFFICES

No matter how well I know a town, my first stop is the tourist information office. Any place with a tourist industry has an information service for visitors located on the central square, in city hall, at the train station, or at the freeway entrance. You don't need the address—just follow the signs. An often-hectic but normally friendly and multilingual staff will give out sightseeing information, reserve hotel rooms, sell concert or play tickets, and answer questions.

Prepare a list of questions ahead of time. Write up a proposed sightseeing schedule. Find out if it's workable or if you've left out any important sights. Confirm closed days and free-admission days.

Ask for a city map, public transit information, and a list of sights with current hours. Find out about special events and pick up any local periodical entertainment guide. See if walking tours or self-guided walking tour brochures are available. Check on any miscellaneous concerns (such as safety, laundry, Internet access, bike rental, parking, camping, transportation tips for your departure, maps of nearby towns, or help with booking a room for your

Your first stop in a new town—the tourist information office

next destination). If you feel the first person you talk to is rushed or uninterested, browse around for a few minutes and talk to another.

Europe is amazingly well organized. For instance, many tourist offices in major cities sell a "tourist card" for about $20, which includes 24 hours of free entrance to all the sights; free use of all the subways, buses, and boats; a booklet explaining everything; and a map. It's all very straightforward and usually in English.

If necessary, get ideas on where to eat and sleep. But, remember, tourist information offices don't volunteer information on cheap alternatives to hotels, and they pocket any "deposits" collected on big "front door" places they recommend.

If you'll be arriving late, call ahead before the tourist office closes. Good information (in English) is worth a long-distance phone call. Guidebooks list the phone numbers.

MORE INFORMATION SOURCES

Big-hotel information desks, hostel wardens, other travelers, and guidebooks are helpful. To find guidebooks in English, check newsstands and English sections in large bookstores. All big cities have English bookstores, and most general bookstores have local guidebooks in several languages. If you find yourself in a town with no information and the tourist office is closed, a glance through a postcard rack will quickly show you the town's most famous sights.

Youth Centers: Many cities, especially in the north, have industrious youth travel-aid offices. Copenhagen and Oslo have great youth centers called Use It, and several cities publish very practical youth-oriented budget travel magazines (available at the tourist office).

Entertainment Guides: Big European cities bubble with entertainment, festivities, and nightlife. But they won't come to you. New in town and unable to speak the local language, it's easy to be oblivious to a once-in-a-lifetime event erupting just across the bridge. A periodical entertainment guide is the ticket. Every big

At the Oslo tourist office, you can pick up a monthly entertainment guide, list of sights, 24-hour bus pass, telephone card, and city map.

city has one, either in English (such as *This Week in Oslo*) or in the local language but easy to decipher (such as the *Pariscope* weekly). Buy one at a newsstand (if it's not free from the tourist office). In Florence and Rome, the best guides are published monthly by the big, fancy hotels and are available for free at their desks (look like a hotel guest and help yourself). Ask at your hotel about entertainment. Events are posted on city walls everywhere. Read posters. They are in a foreign language, but that really doesn't matter when it reads: Weinfest, Musica Folklorico, 9 Juni, 21:00, Piazza Major, Entre Libre, and so on. Figure out the signs—or miss the party.

MAPS

The best and cheapest map is often the public transit map. Try to get one that shows bus lines, subway stops, and major sights. Many tourist offices and big-city hotels (along with the McDonald's in Paris and Rome) give out free city maps. Study the map to understand the city's layout. Relate the location of landmarks—your hotel, major sights, the river, main streets, and the train station—to each other. Use any viewpoint—such as a church spire, tower, top story of a skyscraper, or hilltop—to look over the city. Retrace where you've been, see where you're going. Back on the ground, you won't be in such constant need of your map.

WALKING TOURS AND LOCAL GUIDES

Walking tours are my favorite introduction to a city. Since they focus on just a small part of a city, generally the old town center, they are thorough. The tours are usually conducted in English by well-trained local people who are sharing their town for the noble purpose of giving you an appreciation of the city's history, people, and culture—not to make a lot of money. Walking tours are personal, inexpensive, and a valuable education. I can't

Guides bring museums and castles to life.

recall a bad one. Many local tourist offices organize the tours or provide a do-it-yourself walking tour leaflet. The avid walking tourist should consider purchasing one of the many "turn right at the fountain"–type guidebooks which are carefully written collections of self-guided walks through major cities.

For the price of three seats on a forgettable quadralingual tape-recorded city bus tour, you can often hire your own private guide through the tourist office for a personalized city tour (most cost-effective if you're traveling with a group). Hiring a private guide is especially easy, cheap, and helpful in Eastern Europe and Russia. The best guides are often those whose tours you can pick up at the specific sight. These guides usually really know their museum, castle, or whatever.

BUS ORIENTATION TOURS

Many cities have fast-orientation bus tours like London's famous "Round London" tour. You'll get a feel for the urban lay of the land as you see the major sights (from the bus window) and hear a live or recorded narration. Many of these tours are "hop-on hop-off," allowing you to get off at a sight, then catch a later bus. They cost around $20, and, if you've got the money and not much time, they provide a good orientation. If I had only one day in a big city, I might spend half of it on one of these tours. Along with London, you'll find bus tours in Bath, York, Edinburgh, Copenhagen, Helsinki, Paris, Berlin, Munich, Vienna, Barcelona, Sevilla, Milan, Rome, and more.

As a popular trend, many cities now offer a public bus (e.g., Berlin's bus #100) or boat route (e.g., Amsterdam's museum boat) that connects all of the city's major sight-seeing attractions. Tourists buy the one-day pass and make the circuit at their leisure.

Bus tours can be worthwhile solely for the ride. Some sights are awkward to reach by public transportation, such as the châteaus of France's Loire, King Ludwig's castles in Bavaria, and the stave church and Grieg's home outside Bergen, Norway. An organized tour not

A minibus tour of Bruges—name your language

only whisks you effortlessly from one hard-to-reach-without-a-car sight to the next, but gives you lots of information as you go.

If you are about to spend $45 anyway for a train ticket, let's say from London to Bath, why not take a $45 one-day tour from London that visits Stonehenge and Bath? You can leave the tour in Bath before it returns to London and enjoy a day of transportation, admissions, and information for the price of a two-hour train ticket.

Fancy coach tours—the kind that leave from the big international hotels—are expensive. Some are great. Others are boring and so depersonalized, sometimes to the point of multilingual taped messages, that you may find the Chinese soundtrack more interesting than the English. These tours can, however, be of value to the budget-minded do-it-yourselfer. Pick up the brochure for a well-thought-out tour itinerary and do it on your own. Take local buses at your own pace and tour every sight for a fraction of the cost.

PUBLIC TRANSPORTATION

Shrink and tame big cities by mastering their subway and bus systems. Europe's public transit systems are so good that many Europeans go through life never learning to drive. Their wheels are trains, buses, and subways.

Save time, money, and energy. Too many timid tourists avoid buses or subways and use up their energy walking or their money on taxis. Subways are speedy and comfortable, never slowed by traffic jams. And with the proper attitude, a subway ride can be an aesthetic experience, plunging you into the people- and advertisement-filled river of local work-a-day life.

Get a transit map. With a map, anyone can decipher the code to cheap and easy urban transportation. Paris and London have the most extensive—and the most needed—subway systems. Both cities come with plenty of subway maps and expert subway tutors. Paris even has maps that plan your route for you. Just push your destination's button, and the proper route lights up.

Find out about specials. Some cities offer deals, such as discounted

Public transit—the European treat

packets of subway tickets (in Paris and London) or tourist tickets allowing unlimited travel on all public transport for a day or several days (in London and elsewhere). These "go as you please" passes may seem expensive, but, if you do any amount of running around, they can be a convenient money saver. And, remember, they are more than economical. With a transit pass you'll avoid the often-long ticket lines.

Ask for help. Europe's buses and subways are run by people who are happy to help lost tourists locate themselves. Confirm with a local that you're at the right platform or bus stop. If a ticket seems expensive, ask what it covers—two dollars may seem like a lot until you learn it's good for a round-trip, two hours, or several transfers. And if you tell them where you're going, bus drivers and passengers sitting around you will gladly tell you where to get off.

Be cautious. While public transportation feels safe, be constantly on guard. Wear your money belt. Thieves—often dressed as successful professionals—thrive underground. Buses that are particularly popular with tourists are equally popular with pickpockets.

TAXIS

Taxis are underrated, scenic time-savers that zip you effortlessly from one sight to the next. Especially for couples and small groups who value their time, a taxi ride can be a good move.

Taxis are especially cheap in southern countries. While expensive for the lone budget traveler, a group of three or four people can frequently travel cheaper by taxi than by buying three or four bus tickets. (You can go anywhere in downtown Lisbon or Athens for $5.)

Don't be bullied by cabbie con men (common in the south and east). Insist on the meter, agree on a rate, or know the going rate. Taxi drivers intimidate too many tourists. If I'm charged a ridiculous price for a ride, I put a reasonable sum on the seat and say good-bye. But don't be too mistrusting. Many tourists wrongly accuse their cabbies of taking the long way around or adding unfair extras. Cabbies are generally honest. There are lots of legitimate supplements (nights, weekends, baggage, extra person, airport ride, etc.), and winding through medieval street plans is rarely even close to direct.

A taxi ride can be a smart intercity bet, too. Last year I rode a taxi from Florence to Siena (50 miles, $100) and from Madrid to Toledo (40 miles, $50). Considering the time saved and the hotel-to-hotel-in-an-hour convenience, the taxi was an affordable splurge.

You or your hotel receptionist can always call for a cab, but the meter may be well under way by the time you get in. It's usually cheaper and easier just to flag one down or ask a local to direct you to the nearest taxi stand. Taxi stands are often listed as prominently as subway stations on city maps; look for the little *T*s.

TRAVELER'S TOILET TRAUMA

Every traveler has one or two great toilet stories. Foreign toilets can be traumatic, but they are one of those little things that can make travel so much more interesting than staying at home. If you plan to venture away from the international-style hotels in your Mediterranean travels and become a temporary resident, "going local" may take on a very real meaning.

Most European toilets are reasonably similar to our own, but some consist simply of porcelain footprints and a squat-and-aim hole. Those of us who need a throne to sit on are in the minority. Most humans sit on their haunches and nothing more.

Toilet paper (like a spoon or a fork) is another Western "essential" that most people on our planet do not use. What they use varies. I won't get too graphic here, but remember that a billion people in south Asia never eat with their left hand. Some countries, such as Turkey, have very frail plumbing, and toilet paper will jam up the WCs. If wastebaskets are full of dirty paper, leave yours there, too.

The WC scene has improved markedly in Western Europe the last few years, but it still makes sense to carry pocket-size tissue packs (easy to buy in Europe) for WCs sans TP.

FINDING A TOILET

Finding a decent public toilet can be frustrating. I once dropped a tour group off in a town for a potty stop, and when I picked them up 20 minutes later, none had found relief. Most countries have few public rest rooms. With a few tips, you can sniff out a biffy in a jiffy.

Restaurants: Any place that serves food or drinks has a rest room. No restaurateur would label his WC so those on the street can see, but you can walk into nearly any restaurant or café, politely and confidently, and find a bathroom. Assume it's somewhere in the back, either upstairs or downstairs. It's easiest in large places that have outdoor seating, because waiters will think you're a customer just making a quick trip inside. Some call it rude—I call it survival. If you feel like it, ask permission. Just smile, "Toilet?" I'm rarely turned down. American-type fast-food places are very common these days and always have a decent and fairly "public" rest room. Timid people buy a drink they don't want in order to leave one. That's unnecessary.

One of Europe's many unforgettable experiences, the squat-and-aim toilet

Public buildings: When nature beckons and there's no restaurant or bar handy, look in train stations, government buildings, and upper floors of department stores. Parks often have rest rooms, sometimes of the gag-a-maggot variety. Never leave a museum without taking advantage of its rest rooms—free, clean, and decorated with artistic graffiti. Large, classy, old hotel lobbies are as impressive as many palaces you'll pay to see. You can always find a royal retreat here and plenty of soft TP.

Coin-op toilets on the street: Some large cities, such as Paris, London, and Amsterdam, are dotted with coin-operated telephone booth–type WCs on street corners. Insert a coin, the door opens, and you have 15 minutes of toilet accompanied by Sinatra Muzak. When you leave, it even disinfects itself.

Trains: Use the free toilets on the train rather than in the station to save time and money. Toilets on first-class cars are a cut above second-class toilets. I go first class even with a second-class ticket. Train toilets are located on the ends of cars, where it's most jiggly. A trip to the train's john always reminds me of the rodeo. Toilets empty directly on the tracks. Never use a train WC while stopped in a station (unless you didn't like that particular town). Train WC cleanliness deteriorates as the journey progresses.

The flush: After you've found and used a toilet, you're down to your last challenge—flushing it. Rarely will you find a familiar handle. Find some protuberance and push, pull, twist, squeeze, step on, or pray to it until the waterfall starts. Sinks and urinals with "electric eyes" are increasingly common.

The tip: Paying to use a public WC is a European custom that irks many Americans. But isn't it really worth a quarter, considering the cost of water, maintenance, and cleanliness? And you're probably in no state to argue, anyway. Sometimes the toilet is free, but the woman in the corner sells sheets of toilet paper. Most common is the tip dish by the entry. The local equivalent of about 25 cents is plenty. Caution: Many attendant ladies leave only bills and too-big coins in the tray to bewilder the full-bladdered tourist. The keepers of Europe's public toilets have earned a reputation for crabbiness. You'd be crabby, too, if you lived under the street in a room full of public toilets. Humor them, understand them, and leave them a coin or two.

Men: The women who seem to inhabit Europe's WCs are a popular topic of conversation among Yankee males. Sooner or later you'll be minding your own business at the urinal and the lady will bring you your change or sweep under your feet. Yes, it is distracting, but you'll just have to get used to it—she has.

Going local

Getting comfortable in foreign rest rooms takes a little adjusting, but that's travel. When in Rome, do as the Romans do—and before you know it…Euro-peein'.

TRAVEL LAUNDRY

I met a woman in Italy who wore her T-shirt frontward, backward, inside-out frontward, and inside-out backward to delay the laundry day. A guy in Germany showed me his take-it-into-the-tub-with-you-and-make-waves method of washing his troublesome jeans. And some travelers just ignore their laundry needs and stink.

One of my domestic chores while on the road is washing my laundry in the hotel room sink. I bring a quick-dry travel wardrobe that either looks OK wrinkled or doesn't wrinkle. I test wash and dry my shirts in the sink at home once before I let them come to Europe with me. Some shirts are fine, others prune up.

Pack a self-service laundry kit. Bring a stretchable "travel clothesline." The cord is double stranded and twisted, so clothespins are unnecessary. Stretch it over your bathtub or across the back of your car, and you're on the road to dry clothes. Pack a concentrated liquid detergent in a small, sturdy, plastic squeeze bottle wrapped in a zip-lock baggie to contain leakage. A large plastic bag with a drawstring is handy for dirty laundry.

Wash clothes in the sink in your room. Every real hotel room in Europe has a sink, usually equipped with a multilingual "no washing clothes in the room" sign. This (after "eat your peas") may be the most ignored rule on earth. Interpret this as an "I-have-lots-of-good-furniture-and-a-fine-carpet-in-this-room-and-I-don't-want-your-drippy-laundry-ruining-things" order. In other words, you can wash clothes carefully, wring them nearly dry, and hang them in a low-profile, nondestructive way. Do not hang your clothes out the window. The maid hardly notices my laundry. It's hanging quietly in the bathroom or shuffled among my dry clothes in the closet. Occasionally a hotel will keep

Whistler's laundry

the stoppers in an attempt to discourage washing. You can try using a wadded-up sock or a film canister cap, or line the sink with your plastic laundry bag and wash in it. Some create their own washing machine with a large, two-gallon zip-lock baggie: soak sudsy an hour, agitate, drain, rinse.

Wring wet laundry as dry as possible. Rolling it in a towel and twisting or stomping on it can be helpful, but many places don't provide new towels every day. Always separate the back and front of hanging clothes to speed drying. Some travelers pack an inflatable hanger. Laid-back hotels will let your laundry join theirs on the lines out back or on the rooftop.

Smooth out your wet clothes, button shirts, set collars, and "hand iron" to encourage wrinkle-free drying. If your shirt or dress dries wrinkled, hang it in a steamy bathroom. A piece of tape is a good ad-lib lint brush. In very hot climates, I wash my shirt several times a day, wring it, and put it on wet. It's clean and refreshing, and in 15 minutes it's dry.

Use a Laundromat occasionally. For a thorough washing, ask your hotel to direct you to the nearest Laundromat. Nearly every neighborhood has one. It takes about $8 and an hour if there's no line. (Many hostels have coin-op washers and dryers or heated drying rooms.) Better Laundromats have coin-op soap dispensers, change machines, and helpful attendants. Others can be very frustrating. Use the time to picnic, catch up on postcards and your journal, or chat with the local crowd. Laundromats throughout the world seem to give people the gift of gab. Full-service places are quicker—just drop it off and come back in the afternoon—but much more expensive. Also pricey—but handiest of all—you can hire your hotel to do your laundry. Regardless of the price, every time I slip into a fresh pair of jeans, I figure it was worth the hassle and expense.

19. Hurdling the Language Barrier

CONFESSIONS OF A MONOGLOT

That notorious language barrier is about two feet tall. It keeps many people out of Europe, but, with a few communication tricks and a polite approach, the English-only traveler can step right over it.

I've been saying this for 25 years, and during that time an entire generation of Europeans has grown up speaking more English than ever. English really has arrived as Europe's second language. Historically, many European signs and menus were printed in four languages: German, French, English and—depending on where you were—Italian or Spanish. In the last few years there's been a shift. Now signs are printed in just two languages: The language for locals ... and English, for everyone else.

While it's nothing to brag about, I speak only English. Of course, if I spoke more languages, I could enjoy a much deeper understanding of the people and cultures I visit, but even with English only, I have no problems getting transportation and rooms, eating, and seeing the sights. While you can manage fine with the blunt weapon of English, you'll get along with Europe better if you learn and use a few basic phrases and polite words.

Having an interest in the local language wins the respect of those you'll meet. Get an English-German (or whatever) phrase book and start your practical vocabulary growing right off the bat. You're surrounded by expert, native-speaking tutors in every country. Let them teach you. Spend bus and train rides learning. Start learning the language when you arrive. Psychologically, it's hard to start later because you'll be leaving so soon. I try to learn five new words a day. You'd be surprised how handy a working vocabulary of 50 words is. A phrase book with a dictionary is ideal; a two-language dictionary is cheap and easy to find.

While Americans are notorious monoglots, Europeans are very good with languages. Make your communicating job easier by choosing a multilingual person to speak with. Business

These days, most signs come in two languages: one for the locals, and English for everyone else.

Europeans: Babel of Tongues

Europe's many languages can be arranged into a family tree. Most of them have the same grandparents and resemble each other more or less like you resemble your brothers, sisters, and cousins. Occasionally, an oddball uncle sneaks in whom no one can explain, but most languages have common roots. An understanding of how these languages relate to one another can help boost you over the language barrier.

LANGUAGE TREE

Romance Countries: Italy, France, Spain, and Portugal

The Romance family evolved out of Latin, the language of the Roman Empire ("Romance" comes from "Roman"). Few of us know Latin, but knowing any of the modern Romance languages helps with the others. For example, your high school Spanish will help you with Italian and Portuguese words.

Germanic Countries: Germany, the Netherlands, and Scandinavia

The Germanic languages, though influenced by Latin, are a product of the native tribes of northern Europe—people the ancient Romans called "barbarians" because of the crude sound of their language.

German is the handiest second language in Northern and Eastern Europe. It's spoken by all Germans and Austrians and most Swiss.

The people of Holland and northern Belgium speak Dutch (called Flemish in Belgium), which is very closely related to German. While Dutch is not Deutsch, a Hamburger or Frankfurter can almost read an Amsterdam newspaper.

The Scandinavians (except the Finns) can read each other's

magazines and enjoy their neighbors' TV shows. And almost any young or educated Scandinavian speaks English.

Multilingual Regions

Switzerland speaks four languages: 67 percent of the people speak Swiss German, 20 percent speak French, 12 percent speak Italian, and 1 percent speak Romansch, a language related to ancient Latin.

Alsace, another bilingual culture, is a French province on the German border. Its people have been dragged through the mud during several French-German tugs-of-war. For the time being, it's a part of France. Still, German often works better than English here.

Belgium waffles, linguistically, with the southern half (the Walloons) speaking French and the other half speaking Flemish, or Dutch. Brussels, like Belgium itself, is legally bilingual, but the French in Belgium, like those in Switzerland and Canada, often feel tongue-tied and linguistically abused.

Dying Tongues

The Basques, struggling to survive in the area where Spain, France, and the Atlantic all touch, are well aware that every year five languages die on our planet and that the cards are stacked against isolated groups like theirs.

England is surrounded by a "Celtic Crescent." In Wales, Scotland, Ireland, and Brittany (western France), the old Celtic language survives, mostly as a symbol of local spirit that refuses to be subjugated culturally (as has occurred politically) by England or France. Seek out these die-hard remnants in militant bookstores (fronts for the autonomy movement in Brittany), Gaelic pubs, and the Gaeltachts (districts, mostly in Western Ireland, where the old culture is preserved by the government).

Small linguistic groups, such as those who speak Flemish or Norwegian, are quicker to jump on the English bandwagon. It's crucial for these cultures to know a major language. These cultures are melting into the English sphere of linguistic influence, while large groups such as the Spanish, French, and Germans can get by without embracing English so readily.

people, urbanites, young well-dressed people, students, and anyone in the tourist trade are most likely to speak English. Most Swiss grow up trilingual. Many young North Europeans speak several languages. People speaking minor languages (Dutch, Belgians, Scandinavians) have more reason to learn German, French, or English since their linguistic world is so small. Scandinavian students of our language actually decide between English and "American." My Norwegian cousin speaks with a touch of Texas and knows more slang than I do.

We English speakers are the one linguistic group that can afford to be lazy. English is the world's linguistic common denominator. When a Greek meets a Norwegian, they speak English. You'd be hard-pressed to find a Greek speaking Norwegian.

Imagine if each of our states spoke its own language. That's the European situation. They've done a great job of minimizing the communication problems you'd expect to find in a small continent with such a Babel of tongues. Most signs that the traveler must understand (such as road signs, menus, telephone instructions, and safety warnings) are printed either in English or in universal symbols. Europe's uniform road sign system enables drivers to roll right over the language barrier. And rest assured that any place trying to separate tourists from their money will explain how to spend it in whatever languages are necessary. English always makes it.

Start every conversation by politely asking, "Do you speak English?", *"Parlez-vous anglais?"*, *"Sprechen Sie Englisch?"*, or whatever. If they say "No," then I do the best I can in their language. Normally, after a few sentences they'll say, "Actually, I do speak some English." One thing Americans do well linguistically is put others at ease with their linguistic shortcomings. Your European friend is doing you a favor by speaking your language. The least we can do is make our English simple and clear.

USING SIMPLE ENGLISH

English may be Europe's lingua franca, but communicating does require some skill. If you have a trip coming up and don't speak French yet, forget it. It's hopeless. Rather than learning a few more French verbs, the best way to increase your ability to communicate is to master what the Voice of America calls "simple English."

Speak slowly, clearly, and with carefully chosen words. Assume you're dealing with someone who learned English out of a book, reading British words, not hearing American ones. They are reading your lips, wishing it was written down, hoping to see every letter as it tumbles out of your mouth. Choose easy words and clearly pronounce each letter. (Crispy pota-to chips.) Use no contractions. When they aren't understood, many

Americans speak louder and toss in a few extra words. Listen to other tourists, and you'll hear your own shortcomings. If you want to be understood, talk like a Dick and Jane primer. For several months out of every year, I speak with simple words, pronouncing every letter. When I return home, my friends say (very deliberately), "Rick, you can relax now, we speak English."

Can the slang. Our American dialect has become a superdeluxe slang pizza not found on any European menu. The sentence "Can the slang," for example, would baffle the average European. If you learned English in school for two years, how would you respond to the American who exclaims, "What a day!" or asks, "Howzit goin'?"

Keep your messages grunt simple. Make single nouns work as entire sentences. When asking for something, a one-word question ("Photo?") is more effective than an attempt at something more grammatically correct. ("May I take your picture, sir?") Be a Neanderthal. Strip your message naked and drag it by the hair into the other person's mind. But even Neandertourists will find things go easier if they begin each request with the local "please" (e.g., "*Bitte*, toilet?").

Use internationally understood words. Some spend an entire trip telling people they're on *vacation*, draw only blank stares, and slowly find themselves in a soundproof, culture-resistant cell. The sensitive communicator notices that Europeans understand the word *holiday* (probably because that's what the English say), plugs that word into her simple English vocabulary, is understood, and enjoys a much closer contact with Europe. If you say rest room or bathroom, you'll get no room. *Toilet* is direct, simple, and understood. If my car is broken in Portugal, I don't say, "Excuse me, my car is broken." I point to the vehicle and say, "Auto kaput."

TIPS ON CREATIVE COMMUNICATION

Even if you have no real language in common, you can have some fun communicating. Consider this profound conversation I had with a cobbler in Sicily:

"Spaghetti," I said, with a very saucy Italian accent.

"Marilyn Monroe," was the old man's reply.

"*Mama mia!*" I said, tossing my hands and head into the air.

"Yes, no, one, two, tree," he returned, slowly and proudly. By now we'd grown fond of each other, and I whispered, secretively, "*Molto buono*, ravioli."

He spat, "Be sexy, drink Pepsi!"

Waving good-bye, I hollered, "*No problema*."

"*Ciao*," he said, smiling.

Risk looking goofy. Even with no common language, rudimentary

International Words

As our world shrinks, more and more words leap their linguistic boundaries and become international. Sensitive travelers develop a knack for choosing words most likely to be universally understood ("auto" instead of "car," "kaput" rather than "broken," "photo," not "picture"). They also internationalize their pronunciation. "University," if you play around with its sound (oo-nee-vehr-see-tay) can be understood anywhere. The average American is a real flunky in this area. Be creative.

Analogy communication is effective. Anywhere in Europe, "Attila" means "crude bully." When a bulky Italian crowds in front of you, say, "*Scusi*, Ah-tee-la" and retake your place. If you like your haircut and want to compliment your Venetian barber, put your hand sensually on your hair and say "Casanova." Nickname the hairstylist "Michelangelo" or "Rambo."

Here are a few internationally understood words. Remember, cut out the Yankee accent and give each word a pan-European sound.

Stop	Kaput	Vino
Restaurant	Ciao	Bank
Hotel	Bye-bye	Rock 'n' roll
Post	Camping	OK
Auto	Picnic	Amigo
Autobus (booos)	Nuclear	English (Engleesh)
Yankee, Americano	Tourist	Mama mia
Michelangelo (artistic)	Beer	Oo la la
Casanova (romantic)	Coffee	Moment
Disneyland (wonderland)	Tea	Hercules (strong)
Coke, Coca-Cola	No problem	Attila (mean, crude)
Sexy	Europa	Self-service
Toilet	Police	Super
Taxi	Telephone	Photo
Photocopy	Central	Information
Mañana	University	Passport
Chocolate	Pardon	Fascist
Rambo	Communist	Hello
America's favorite four-letter words	No	Elephant (a big clod)
	Bon voyage	

communication is easy. Butcher the language if you must, but communicate. I'll never forget the lady in the French post office who flapped her arms and asked, "Tweet, tweet, tweet?" I understood immediately, answered with a nod, and she gave me the airmail stamps I needed. At the risk of getting birdseed, I communicated successfully. If you're hungry, clutch your stomach and growl. If you want milk, "moo" and pull two imaginary udders. If the liquor was too strong, simulate an atomic explosion starting from your stomach and mushrooming to your head. If you're attracted to someone, pant.

Be melodramatic. Exaggerate the local accent. In France communicate more effectively (and have more fun) by sounding like Maurice Chevalier or Inspector Clousseau. The locals won't be insulted; they'll be impressed. Use whatever French you know. But even English, spoken with a sexy French accent, makes more sense to the French ear. In Italy be melodic, exuberant, and wave those hands. Go ahead, try it: *Mama mia!*

Hurdle the language barrier by thinking of things as multiple-choice questions and making educated guesses. This is a sign on a shop in Germany. It lists open times. Hours can only be open or closed. I'd guess it lists hours open from (vom = from, if it rhymes, I go for it) the Fourth of July. Those six words on the left, most of which end in tag, must be days of the week. Things are open from 9:00 to 11:00 and from 16:00 to 18:00 (24-hour clock). On Mittwoch (midweek) afternoon, something different happens. Since it can only be open or closed, and everything else is open, you can guess that on Wednesdays, nach Mittag, this shop is geschlossen!

No. Do it again. *MAMA MIA!* You've got to be uninhibited. Self-consciousness kills communication.

Figure things out. Most major European languages are related, coming from Latin. Knowing that, words become meaningful. The French word for Monday (our "day of the moon") is *lundi* (lunar day). The Germans say the same thing—*Montag*. *Sonne* is sun, so *Sonntag* is Sunday. If *buon giorno* means good day, *zuppa del giorno* is soup of the day. If *Tiergarten* is zoo (literally "animal garden") in German, then *Stinktier* is skunk and *Kindergarten* is children's garden. Think of *Vater*, *Mutter*, *trink*, *gross*, *gut*, *nacht*, *rapide*, *grand*, *economico*, *delicioso*, and you can *comprende mucho*.

Many letters travel predictable courses (determined by the physical way a sound is made) as related languages drift apart over the centuries. For instance, *p* often becomes *v* or *b* in the next language. Italian menus always have a charge for *coperto*—a "cover" charge.

Practice your understanding. Read time schedules, posters, multilingual signs (and graffiti) in bathrooms, and the newspaper headlines. Develop your ear for foreign languages by tuning in to the other languages on a multilingual tour. It's a puzzle. The more you play, the better you get.

A notepad can work wonders. Words and numbers are much easier understood when they're written rather than spoken—and mispronounced. (My back-pocket notepad is my constant travel buddy.) To repeatedly communicate something difficult and important (such as medical instructions, "I'm a strict vegetarian," "boiled water," "well-done meat,"

"your finest ice cream," or "I am rich and single"), have it written in the local language on your notepad.

Assume you understand and go with your educated guess. My master key to communication is to see most communication problems as multiple-choice questions, make an educated guess at the meaning of a message (verbal or written), and proceed confidently as if I understood it correctly. At the breakfast table the

Make an educated guess and go for it. Can you read the Danish: "Sentral Syke Huset"? Too many Americans would bleed to death on the street corner looking for the word "hospital."

waitress asks me a question. I don't understand a word she says, but I say "caffé" and my room number. Faking it like this applies to rudimentary things like instructions on customs forms, museum hours, and menus. With this approach I find that 80 percent of the time I'm correct. Half the time I'm wrong I never know it, so it doesn't really matter. So 10 percent of the time I really blow it. My trip becomes easier—and occasionally much more interesting.

Let's take a border crossing as another example. I speak no Bulgarian. At the border a uniformed guard struts up to my car and asks a question. Not understanding a word he said, but guessing what the average border guard would ask the average tourist, I look at him and answer with a solid "*Nyet.*" He steps back, swings his arm open like a gate, and says, "OK." I'm on my way, quick and easy. I could have gotten out of the car, struggled with the phrase book, and made a big deal out of it, but I'd rather fake it, assuming he was asking if I'm smuggling anything in, and keep things simple. It works.

POLITE PARIS

The "mean Parisian" problem is a holdover from de Gaulle days. It's definitely fading, but France's lingering reputation of rudeness can create a self-fulfilling expectation. You can enjoy the French. Make it your goal.

The French, as a culture, are pouting. They used to be the crème de la crème, *the* definition of high class. Their language was the lingua franca—everyone wanted to speak French. There was a time when the czar of Russia and his family actually spoke better French than Russian. A U.S. passport even has French on it—leftovers from those French glory days.

Modern French culture is reeling—humiliated by two world wars, lashed by Levi's, and crushed by the Big Mac of American culture. And our two cultures aren't natural buddies. The French enjoy subtleties and sophistication. American culture sneers at these fine points. We're proud, brash, and like to think we're rugged individualists. We are a smiley-face culture whose bank tellers are fined if they forget to say, "Have a nice day." The French don't find slap-on-the-back niceness terribly sincere.

Typically, Americans evaluate the

Enjoy the French

Not all French people are formal . . .

French by the Parisians they meet. Big cities anywhere are colder than small towns. And, remember, most of us see Paris at the height of the hot, busy summer, when those Parisians who can't escape on vacation see their hometown flooded with insensitive foreigners who butcher their language and put ketchup on their meat. That's tough to take smiling and, if you're looking for coldness, this is a good place to start.

To make the Parisians suddenly 40 percent friendlier, learn and liberally use these four phrases: *bonjour, s'il vous plaît, merci,* and *pardon*. And to really revel in French friendliness, visit an untouristy part of the countryside and use those four phrases. Oh, and *vive la différence*.

For more tips on etiquette in France and other countries, visit Gestures around the World (www.webofculture.com/worldsmart /gestures.html).

EUROPEAN GESTURES

In Europe, gestures can contribute to the language barrier. Here are a few common gestures, their meanings, and where you are likely to see them:

Fingertips kiss: Gently bring the fingers and thumb of your right hand together, raise to your lips, kiss lightly, and joyfully toss your fingers and thumb into the air. Be careful, tourists look silly when they overemphasize this subtle action. This gesture is used commonly in France, Spain, Greece, and Germany as a form of praise. It can mean sexy, delicious, divine, or wonderful.

Hand purse: Straighten the fingers and thumb of one hand, bringing them all together making an upward point about a foot in front of your face. Your hand can be held still or moved a little up and down at the wrist. This is a common and very Italian gesture for a query. It is used to say "What do you want?" or "What are you doing?" or "What is it?" or "What's new?" It can also be used as an insult to say "You fool." The hand purse can also mean "fear" (France), "a lot" (Spain), and "good" (Greece and Turkey).

Cheek screw: Make a fist, stick out your forefinger, and (without piercing the skin) screw it into your cheek. The cheek screw is used widely and

Tongue Twisters

These are a great way to practice a language—and break the ice with the Europeans you meet. Here are some that are sure to challenge you and amuse your new friends.

German	**Fischer's Fritze fischt frische Fische, frische Fische fischt Fischer's Fritze.**	Fritz Fischer catches fresh fish, fresh fish Fritz Fischer catches.
	Ich komme über Oberammergau, oder komme ich über Unterammergau?	I am coming via Oberammergau, or am I coming via Unterammergau?
Italian	**Sopra la panca la capra canta, sotto la panca la capra crepa.**	On the bench the goat sings, under the bench the goat dies.
	Chi fù quel barbaro barbiere che barberò così barbaramente a Piazza Barberini quel povero barbaro di Barbarossa?	Who was that barbarian barber in Barberini Square who shaved that poor barbarian Barbarossa?
French	**Si ces saucissons-ci sont six sous, ces six saucissons-ci sont trop chers.**	If these sausages are six cents, these six sausages are too expensive.
	Ce sont seize cents sèches dans seize cent sachets secs.	There are 600 dry hyacinths in 600 dry sachets.
Spanish	**Un tigre, dos tigres, tres tigres comían trigo en un trigal. Un tigre, dos tigres, tres tigres.**	One tiger, two tigers, three tigers ate wheat in a wheatfield. One tiger, two tigers, three tigers.
	Pablito clavó un clavito. ¿Qué clavito clavó Pablito?	Paul stuck in a stick. What stick did Paul stick in?
Portuguese	**O rato roeu a roupa do rei de Roma.**	The mouse nibbled the clothes of the king of Rome.
	Se cá nevasse fazia-se cá ski, mas como cá não neva não se faz cá ski.	If the snow would fall, we'd ski, but since it doesn't, we don't.

Excerpted from Rick Steves' phrase books—full of practical phrases, spiked with humor, and designed for budget travelers who like to connect with locals.

HAPPY TALK

English	French	Italian	German	Spanish
Good day.	Bonjour.	Buon giorno.	Guten Tag.	Buenos días.
How are you?	Comment allez-vous?	Come sta?	Wie geht's?	¿Cómo está?
Very good.	Très bien.	Molto bene.	Sehr gut.	Muy bien.
Thank you.	Merci.	Grazie.	Danke.	Gracias.
Please.	S'il vous plaît.	Per favore.	Bitte.	Por favor.
Do you speak English?	Parlez-vous anglais?	Parla inglese?	Sprechen Sie Englisch?	¿Habla usted inglés?
Yes. / No.	Oui. / Non.	Sì. / No.	Ja. / Nein.	Sí. / No.
My name is...	Je m'appelle...	Mi chiamo...	Ich heiße...	Me llamo...
What's your name?	Quel est votre nom?	Come si chiama?	Wie heißen Sie?	¿Cómo se llama?
See you later.	À bientôt.	A più tardi.	Bis später.	Hasta luego.
Goodbye.	Au revoir.	Arrivederci.	Auf Wiedersehen.	Adiós.
Good luck!	Bonne chance!	Buona fortuna!	Viel Glück!	¡Buena suerte!
Have a good trip!	Bon voyage!	Buon viaggio!	Gute Reise!	¡Buen viaje!
OK.	D'accord.	Va bene.	O.K.	De acuerdo.
No problem.	Pas de problème.	Non c'è problema.	Kein Problem.	No hay problema.
Everything was great.	C'était super.	Tutto magnifico.	Alles war gut.	Todo estuvo muy bien.
Enjoy your meal!	Bon appétit!	Buon appetito!	Guten Appetit!	¡Qué aproveche!
Delicious!	Délicieux!	Delizioso!	Lecker!	¡Delicioso!
Magnificent!	Magnifique!	Magnifico!	Wunderbar!	¡Magnífico!
Bless you! (after sneeze)	À vos souhaits!	Salute!	Gesundheit!	¡Salud!
You are very kind.	Vous êtes très gentil.	Lei è molto gentile.	Sie sind sehr freundlich.	Usted es muy amable.
Cheers!	Santé!	Salute!	Prost!	¡Salud!
I love you.	Je t'aime.	Ti amo.	Ich liebe dich.	Te quiero.

almost exclusively in Italy to mean good, lovely, beautiful. Many Italians also use it to mean clever. Be careful—in Southern Spain the cheek screw is used to call a man effeminate.

Eyelid pull: Place your extended forefinger below the center of your eye and pull the skin downward. In France and Greece this means "I am alert. I'm looking. You can't fool me." In Italy and Spain it is a friendlier warning, meaning "Be alert, that guy is clever."

Forearm jerk: Clench your right fist and jerk your forearm up as you slap your right bicep with your left palm. This is a rude phallic gesture that men throughout southern Europe often use the way many

Dominic Bonuccelli

Very delicious!

Americans "give someone the finger." This jumbo version of "flipping the bird" says "I'm superior" (it's an action some monkeys actually do with their penises to insult their peers). This "get lost" or "up yours" gesture is occasionally used by rude men in Britain and Germany as more of an "I want you" gesture about (but never to) a sexy woman.

Chin flick: Tilt your head back slightly and flick the back of your fingers forward in an arc from under your chin. In Italy and France this means "I'm not interested, you bore me," or "You bother me." In Southern Italy it can mean "No."

"Thumbs up," "V for Victory," and more: The "thumbs up" sign popular in the United States is used widely in France and Germany to say "OK." The "V for victory" sign is used in most of Europe as in the United States. (Beware, the V with your palm toward you is the rudest of gestures in England.) "Expensive" is often shown by shaking your hand and sucking in like you just burned yourself. In Greece and Turkey you signal "no" by jerking your eyebrows and head upward. In Bulgaria and Albania "OK" is indicated by happily bouncing your head back and forth as if you were one of those Asian dolls with a spring neck and someone slapped you.

To beckon someone, remember that in northern Europe you bring your palm up, and in the south you wave it down. While most people greet each other by waving with their palm out, you'll find many Italians wave "at themselves" as infants do, with their palm towards their face. *Ciao-ciao.*

EUROPEAN NUMBERS AND STUMBLERS

Europeans do many things different from the way we do. Simple as these things are, they can be frustrating barriers and cause needless, occasionally serious problems.

Numbers: A European's handwritten numbers look different from ours. The ones have an upswing (1). Fours often look like short lightning bolts (4). If you don't cross your 7 (7) it may be mistaken as a sloppy 1, and you could miss your train (and be mad at the French for "refusing to speak English"). Avoid using "#" for "number"—it's not common in Europe and can look like a currency symbol.

Counting: When counting with your fingers, start with your thumb. If you hold up your first finger, you'll probably get two; and making a "peace" sign to indicate the number two may get you a punch in the nose in parts of Britain, where it's an obscene gesture.

Dates and Decimals: Europeans reverse the day and month in numbered dates. Christmas is 25-12-02 instead of 12-25-02, as we would write it. Commas are decimal points and decimals commas, so a dollar and a half is 1,50 and there are 5.280 feet in a mile.

Time: The 24-hour clock is used in any official timetable. This includes bus, train, and tour schedules. Learn to use it quickly and easily. Everything is the same until 12:00 noon. Then, instead of starting over again at 1:00 p.m., the Europeans keep on going—13:00, 14:00, and so on. 18:00 is 6 p.m. (subtract 12 and add p.m.).

Metric: European countries (except Great Britain) use kilometers instead of miles. A kilometer is six-tenths of a mile. To quickly translate kilometers to miles, cut the kilometer figure in half and add 10 percent of the original figure (e.g., 420 km = 210 + 42 = 252 miles). Quick, what's 360 km? (180 + 36 = 216 miles.) "36-26-36" means nothing to a European (or metric) girl watcher. But a "90-60-90" is a real *pistachio*.

Temperatures: Europeans measure temperatures in degrees Celsius. Zero degrees C = 32 degrees Fahrenheit. You can use a formula to convert temperatures in Celsius to Fahrenheit (C x 9/5 + 32 = F), or easier and nearly as accurate,

This is Danish for "tour bus." These days most come with air conditioning.

double the Celsius temperature and add 30. A memory aid: 28° C = 82° F—darn hot.

Addresses: House numbers often have no correlation to what's across the street. While odd is normally on one side and even is on the other, #27 may be directly across from #2.

Floors: Floors of buildings are numbered differently. The bottom floor is called the ground floor. What we would call the second floor is a European's first floor. So if your room is on the second floor (European), bad news—you're on the third floor (American). On the elevator, push whatever's below "1" to get to the ground floor. On an escalator, keep the left lane open for passing. Stand to the right.

A YANKEE-ENGLISH PHRASE BOOK

Oscar Wilde said, "The English have everything in common with the Americans—except, of course, language." On your first trip to England you'll find plenty of linguistic surprises. I'll never forget checking into a small-town bed-and-breakfast, a teenager on my first solo European adventure. The landlady cheerily asked me, "And what time would you like to be knocked up in the morning?" I looked over at her husband, who winked, "Would a fry at half-eight be suitable?" The next morning I got a rap on the door at 8:00 and a huge British breakfast a half hour later.

Traveling through England is an adventure in accents and idioms. Every day you'll see babies in prams, sucking dummies as mothers change wet nappies. Soon the kids can trade in their nappies for smalls and spend a penny on their own. "Spend a penny" is British for a visit to the loo (bathroom). Older British kids enjoy candy floss (cotton candy), naughts and crosses (ticktacktoe), big dippers (roller coasters), and iced lollies (popsicles), and are constantly in need of an elastoplast (Band-Aid).

It's fun to browse through an ironmonger's (hardware store), chemist's shop (pharmacy), or Woolworth's and notice the many familiar items with unfamiliar names. The school supplies section includes sticking plaster (adhesive tape), rubbers (erasers), and scribbling blocks (scratch pads). Those with green fingers (a green thumb) might pick up some courgette (zucchini), swede (rutabaga), or aubergine (eggplant) seeds.

In England, chips are fries and crisps are potato chips. A hamburger is a bomb (success) on a toasted bap. Wipe your fingers with a serviette—never a napkin (sanitary pad).

The English have a great way with names. You'll find towns with names like Upper and Lower Piddle, Once Brewed, and Itching Field. This cute coziness comes through in their language as well. Your car is built with a bonnet and a boot rather than a hood and trunk. You drive on motorways,

Insulting British road signs

and when the freeway divides, it becomes a dual carriageway. And never go anticlockwise (counterclockwise) in a roundabout. Gas is petrol, a truck is a lorry, and when you hit a traffic jam, don't get your knickers in a twist (make a fuss), just queue up (line up) and study your American-English phrase book.

A two-week vacation in England is unheard of, but many locals holiday for a fortnight in a homely (pleasant) rural cottage, possibly on the Continent (continental Europe). They'll pack a face flannel (washcloth), torch (flashlight), hoover (vacuum cleaner), and hair grips (bobby pins) before leaving their flat (apartment). You can post letters in the pillar box and give your bird (girlfriend) a trunk (long distance) call. If you reverse the charges (call collect), she'll say you're tight as a fish's bum. If she witters on (gabs and gabs), tell her you're knackered (exhausted), and it's been donkey's years (ages) since you've slept. On a cold evening it's best to pick up a pimp (bundle of kindling) and make a fire or take a walk wearing the warmest mackintosh (raincoat) you can find or an anorak (parka) with press studs (snaps). After washing up (doing the dishes), you can go up to the first floor (second floor) with a neat (straight) Scotch and a plate of biscuits (sweet cookies) and get goose pimples (goose bumps) just enjoying the view. Too much of that Scotch will get you sloshed, paralytic, bevvied, wellied, popped up, ratted, or even pissed as a newt.

All across the British Isles, you'll find new words, crazy local humor, and colorful accents. Pubs are colloquial treasure chests. Church services, sporting events, the House of Parliament, live plays featuring local comedy, the streets of Liverpool, the docks of London, and children in parks are playgrounds for the American ear. One of the beauties of touring the British Isles is the illusion of hearing a foreign language and actually understanding it—most of the time.

20. Phones, E-mail, and Mail

Communication for travelers in Europe has never been easier. Not only are more and more people speaking English, but telephoning is a cinch, whether you're making local, long distance, or international calls. Most hotels have fax machines, many are able to take reservations online, and cybercafés are catching on fast. Oh, yes, and each country still has a postal system.

SMART TRAVELERS USE THE TELEPHONE

The only way to travel smoothly is to use the telephone. Call tourist offices to check sightseeing plans, train stations to check travel plans, museums to see if an English tour is scheduled, restaurants to see if they're open, hotels to confirm reservations, and so on.

I get earnest letters from readers asking me to drop a hotel from my listings because they made a reservation, got a written confirmation, and still arrived to find no room available. Hotels make mistakes. Call a day in advance to double-check reservations. As we were filming my public television show in Ireland, I took a minute to call Avis in England to reconfirm our car pickup the next day at the ferry dock in North Wales. The man at Avis said, "Right-tee-o, Mr. Steves, we will have your car waiting for you, noon tomorrow, at Heathrow Airport." No, at North Wales! "Oh, sorry, Mr. Steves. It's good you called ahead." I didn't think, "Boy, Avis sure screwed up." I thought, "You can't travel smart without double-checking things by telephone." The more I travel, the more I use the telephone.

Each country's phone system is different, but each one works—logically. The key to figuring out a foreign phone is to approach it without comparing it to yours back home. It works for the locals, and it can work for you. Many people flee in terror when a British phone starts its infamous "rapid pips." (That's just the British way of telling you to pop in a few coins.)

Each country has phone booths with multilingual instructions. If you follow these step by step, the phone will work—usually. Operators generally speak some English and are helpful. International codes, instructions, and international assistance numbers are usually on the wall (printed in several languages) or in the front of the phone book. If I can't manage in a strange phone booth, I ask a nearby local person for help.

PHONE CARDS, COIN-OP PHONES, AND CELL PHONES

The first step is to find the right phone. The increasingly rare coin-op phones are being replaced by more convenient and vandal-resistant phones that accept only phone cards. If you spend time looking for coin-operated phones in Europe, you're still traveling in the '90s. The first thing I purchase upon arrival in a new country is a phone card.

European phone cards: European telephone cards (not to be confused with American phone credit cards) are common throughout Europe. They're easy to use and sold conveniently at post offices, newsstands, street kiosks, and tobacco shops. You just slide your card into a slot in the phone and dial any local or international number. The phone reads your card's magnetic strip, and a display shows you how much money is remaining on your card. The only drawback is that the

Most European phone booths use phone cards rather than coins.

cheapest cards can cost $5, more phone time than you may need in that country. If you're as frugal as I am, you'll lay awake at night wondering how to productively use it up before you cross the next border—a worthwhile exercise. You can always blow the remaining telephone time by calling home.

International PIN phone cards: Calling the U.S. from Europe now costs as little as a dime a minute with the handy international PIN phone cards sold at newsstands and mini-markets throughout Europe. Competing cards offer different rates for different destinations. Some cards work only for local calls. Ask for the best deal for calls to America. While sold in cards ranging from $5 to $40, I'd stick with smaller cards since occasionally a card doesn't work or a company goes out of business.

These cards can be used from virtually any touch-tone phone, even from your hotel room, and allow you to make local, long-distance, and international calls at a much cheaper per-minute rate than regular European phone cards. You don't insert the card into the phone; you simply dial a toll-free access number, your Personal Identification Number (on card, scratch to reveal), then the number you wish to dial. If you're making lots of calls with a PIN card, you can avoid redialing the long access number and PIN code by pressing whatever key (usually the pound sign) that allows you to launch directly into your next call (just follow instructions on the card). While some companies brag that their cards work for calling out of several countries, don't count on it. A PIN card works well only in the country in which you buy it.

Student and Hostel phone cards: Students can turn their International Student Identity Card (available for $22) into a prepaid phone card by paying an additional $20 for ISIConnect service. You'll be able to make calls using a PIN code from any phone in 80 countries. You can even get voice mail, a free e-mail account, and a virtual safety deposit box for your passport and other important documents (you fax photocopies of your documents to a certain fax number, and you can later retrieve them from anywhere in the world in case your originals are lost or stolen). Anyone can recharge your card by using a credit card to pump more money into your account. This is a great service for students and a great relief for parents. For more information, contact Council Travel (tel. 800/2-COUNCIL, www.counciltravel.com) or STA Travel (tel. 800/777-0112, www.statravel.com). Council Travel throws in an extra $5 worth of calls if you buy ISIConnect from them.

Both Hostelling International and Hostels of Europe offer similar phone-card services, packaged as an "eKit," free with the purchase of their hostel card. Hostelling International's card costs $25 and comes with $10 worth of calls (tel. 202/783-6161, www.hiayh.org). Hostels of Europe's card is $16 (tel. 519/251-8821, www.hostelseurope.com).

Coin-operated phones: For coin-op phones, have enough small coins to complete your call. The instructions may say the local minimum, your credit total is generally shown, and only entirely unused coins will be returned. Many phones allow run-on calls, so you won't lose your big-coin credit (if you need to make another call). Look for this (usually black) button and push it rather than hanging up. In countries such as Britain, where you hear tourists in phone booths yelling, "Hello . . . Hello . . . HELLO," your voice won't be heard until you push a button to engage the call.

Cell phones: Affluent travelers buy cell phones (about $60 on up) in Europe for making local and international calls. The cheaper phones generally work only if you're making calls from the country where you bought it. Pricier phones allow you to call from any country, but it costs you about $40 to outfit the phone per country with the necessary chip and prepaid phone time. If interested, stop by any European shop that sells cell phones. Depending on your trip and budget, ask for a phone that works only in that country or one usable throughout Europe. And if you're really on a budget, skip cell phones and use PIN phone cards instead.

DIALING DIRECT

You'll save money if you learn to dial direct.

Making Calls within a European Country: About half of all European countries use area codes (like we do); the other half uses a direct-dial system without area codes.

To make calls within a country that uses a direct-dial system (Belgium, Denmark, France, Italy, Portugal, Norway, Spain, and Switzerland), you

---

PHONE CODES
International Access Codes
When dialing direct, first dial the international access code of the country you're calling from. For virtually all European countries it's "00"; the only exceptions are Finland (990) and Lithuania (810). For America and Canada it's "011."

Country Codes
After you've dialed the international access code, then dial the code of the country you're calling.

Austria:	43	Ireland:	353
Belgium:	32	Italy:	39
Britain:	44	Morocco:	212
Canada:	1	Netherlands:	31
Czech Rep:	420	Norway:	47
Denmark:	45	Portugal:	351
Estonia:	372	Spain:	34
Finland:	358	Sweden:	46
France:	33	Switzerland:	41
Germany:	49	Turkey:	90
Greece:	30	USA:	1

---

dial the same number whether you're calling across the country or across the street.

In countries that use area codes (such as Austria, Britain, Czech Republic, Finland, Germany, Ireland, Netherlands, and Sweden), you dial the local number when calling within a city, and you add the area code if calling long-distance within the country. Example: To call a Munich hotel (tel. 089/264-349) within Munich, dial 264-349; to call it from Frankfurt, dial 089-264-349.

Making International Calls: You always start with the international access code (011 if you're calling from America or Canada, or 00 from virtually anywhere in Europe), then dial the country code of the country you're calling (see chart).

What you dial next depends on the phone system of the country you're calling. If the country uses area codes, drop the initial zero of the area code, then dial the rest of the number. Example: To call the Munich hotel (tel. 089/264-349) from Italy, dial 00, 49 (Germany's country code), then 89-264-349.

Countries that use direct-dial systems (no area codes) vary in how they're accessed internationally by phone. For instance, if you're making an international call to Denmark, Italy, Norway, Portugal, or Spain, simply dial the international access code, country code, and phone number. Example: To call a Madrid hotel (tel. 91-521-2900) from Germany, dial 00, 34 (Spain's country code), then 91-521-2900. But if you're calling Belgium, France, or Switzerland, drop the initial zero of the phone number. Example: To call a Paris hotel (tel. 01 47 05 49 15) from London, dial 00, 33 (France's country code), then 1 47 05 49 15 (phone number without initial zero).

Communication tips: Once you've made the connection, the real challenge begins. With no visual aids, getting the message across in a language you don't speak requires some artistry. Speak slowly and clearly, pronouncing every letter. Keep it very simple—don't clutter your message with anything less than essential. Don't overcommunicate—many things are already understood and don't need to be said (those last six words didn't need to be written). Use international or carefully chosen English words. When all else fails, let a local person on your end (such as a hotel receptionist) do the talking after you explain to him, with visual help, the message. My Rick Steves' Phrase Books predict conversations you'll need to make on the phone and provide the necessary foreign language templates with various options to fill in the blanks.

CALLING HOME

You can call the United States directly from Europe (and say a few things very quickly) for as little as 50 cents—half the cost of a postcard stamp. Rather than write postcards, just call in your "scenery's here, wish you were beautiful" messages.

Phone booths: I normally just get a phone card, PIN card (see Phone Cards, above), or a pile of coins. Then I find a phone booth and dial direct. Nearly all European countries have "dial direct to anywhere" phone booths. Calls to the United States cost less than $1 per minute (and as little as a dime a minute with a PIN card).

First dial the international access code (00 from Europe), then the country code of the U.S. (1), then the area code and the seven-digit number. To call me from France, dial 00-1-425-771-8303. Every country has its quirks. Try pausing between codes if you're having trouble, or dial the English-speaking international operator for help. Off-hours calls are cheaper.

At coin-op phones, I start with a small coin worth 25 to 50 cents to be sure I get the person I need or can say, "I'm calling back in five minutes, so wake him up." (Remember, it's about six hours earlier in New York and nine hours earlier in California.) Then I plug in the larger coins. I keep one

Desperate Telephone Communication

Let me illustrate with a hypothetical telephone conversation. I'm calling a hotel in Barcelona from a phone booth in the train station. I just arrived, read my guidebook's list of budget accommodations, and I like Pedro's Hotel. Here's what happens:

Pedro answers, "Hotel Pedro, grabdaboodogalaysk."

I ask, "Hotel Pedro?" (Question marks are created melodically.)

He affirms, already a bit impatient, "*Si*, Hotel Pedro."

I ask, "*Habla* Eng-leesh?"

He says, "No, dees ees Ehspain." (Actually, he probably would speak a little English or would say "moment" and get someone who did. But we'll make this particularly challenging. Not only does he not speak English—he doesn't want to . . . for patriotic reasons.)

Remembering not to overcommunicate, you don't need to tell him you're a tourist looking for a bed. Who else calls a hotel speaking in a foreign language? Also, you can assume he's got a room available. If he's full, he's very busy and he'd say "complete" or "no hotel" and hang up. If he's still talking to you, he wants your business. Now you must communicate just a few things, like how many beds you need and who you are.

I say, "OK." (OK is international for, "Roger, prepare for the next transmission.") "Two people"—he doesn't understand. I get fancy, "*Dos* people"—he still doesn't get it. Internationalize, "*Dos* pehr-son"—no comprende. "*Dos* hombre"—nope. Digging deep into my bag of international linguistic tricks, I say, "*Dos* Yankees."

"OK!" He understands that you want beds for two Americans. He says, "*Si*," and I say, "Very good" or "*Muy bueno.*"

Now I need to tell him who I am. If I say, "My name is Mr. Steves, and I'll be over promptly," I'll lose him. I say, "My name Ricardo (Ree-KAR-do)." In Italy I say, "My name Luigi." Your name really doesn't matter; you're communicating just a password so you can identify yourself when you walk through the door. Say anything to be understood.

He says, "OK."

You repeat slowly, "Hotel, *dos* Yankees, Ricardo, coming *pronto*, OK?"

He says, "OK."

You say, "*Gracias, ciao!*"

Twenty minutes later you walk up to the reception desk, and Pedro greets you with a robust, "Eh, Ricardo!"

last sign-off coin ready. When my time is done, I pop it in and say good-bye. The digital meter warns you when you're about to be cut off.

Calling collect is sometimes more complicated and always more expensive. It's cheaper (about $1 a minute—and the other end pays) and easier if you have your friend call you back, dialing direct from the States. Call cheap and fast from a phone booth and ask your friend to call you at your hotel (in 10 minutes or so).

You can't count on being able to access your stateside voice mail from Europe via touch-tone phone, particularly in Italy.

Metered phones: Some post offices have metered phone booths. The person who sells stamps will plug you in, assign you a booth, and help you with your long-distance prefixes. You sit in your private sweatbox, make the call, and pay the bill when you're done (same cost as a public phone). Beware of a popular new rip-off: small businesses on main tourist streets that look like telephone company long-distance services but actually charge like hotels. Ask the price per minute (or per unit on the clicking meter) before you take a metered phone booth.

Hotel phones: Telephoning through your hotel's phone system is fine for local calls, PIN card calls, or toll-free USA Direct calls (see below) but an almost-criminal rip-off for long-distance calls. I do this only when I'm feeling flush and lazy for a quick "Call me in Stockholm at this number" message.

USA Direct: USA Direct services offered by Sprint, AT&T, and MCI are handy, popular, and pricey. Each company has a toll-free access number in every European country (listed on the info that comes with your card and included most days in the European edition of the *International Herald Tribune*). Cardholders follow a series of automatic prompts (or sometimes speak with an English-speaking operator), enter their card number and a PIN, and then dial the number they want to reach. The rates are more expensive than if you dialed direct.

The cheapest of the lot, MCI charges about $1 per minute. AT&T charges less per minute, but tacks on surcharges and fees. Sprint is the priciest at $3 for the first minute with a $4.50 connection fee (if you get an answering machine, it'll cost you $7.50 to say "Hi, sorry I missed you."). For less than 25 cents, call first with a coin or European phone card to see if the answering machine is off or if the right person's at home.

If you're choosing between companies, ask about surcharges, monthly fees, the first-minute rate, and the rate for additional minutes (AT&T—tel. 800/224-5610, www.att.com; Sprint—tel. 800/882-7802, www.sprint.com; MCI—tel. 800/286-8052, www.mci.com).

It's outrageously expensive to use USA Direct to call from one

European country to another (it costs more than calling the U.S.). When you're in Europe—calling anywhere, it's far cheaper to simply dial direct using a European phone card.

E-MAIL

Cybercafés, along with the many shops that offer Internet access without the coffee, are popular throughout Europe. Large European chains such as easyEverything (www.easyeverything .com) offer inexpensive access in big cities. In small towns you can usually find Internet access in libraries and youth hostels, and sometimes at bookstores, copy shops, post offices, and

Sending e-mail is e-zee.

video stores. Ask the TI, your hotelier, a young person, or another traveler for the nearest plugged-in place. Or, before you go, compile a list by searching Cybercafes.com (www.cybercafes.com).

You can send and receive e-mail using free services such as Yahoo! Mail (www.mail.yahoo.com) or Hotmail (www.hotmail.com). Although you can set up your e-mail account from anywhere, it's smarter to figure it out at home than in Europe.

Use Backflip (www.backflip.com) to store your favorite Web sites in folders, instead of taking along printed copies. At a cybercafé in Europe, you can access your folders with a password, then do a keyword search to zero in on, say, Renaissance domes or Rome's catacombs.

Be patient with foreign-letter keyboards. It takes time to find the right keys. If you can't locate a special character (such as the @ symbol), simply copy it from a Web page and paste into your e-mail message. Or you can ask the clerk for help.

If you're traveling with a digital camera, you'll want to empty your media storage card from time to time. Many cybercafés will copy your images to a CD-ROM or zip disk. Then you can upload your pictures to an online scrapbook service such as My Yahoo! (www.my.yahoo.com) or send them home as e-mail attachments.

Avoid storing personal information (such as passport and credit-card numbers) online. If you need important documents, e-mail or phone home and have them sent by fax. (Or consider the eKit offered by hostel organizations; see Phone Cards, above.)

For more information on cybercafés and useful European travel Web sites, read our Road Scholars' tips on the Graffiti Wall at www .ricksteves.com/graffiti.

MAIL

Receiving mail: Minimize mail pickups to maximize your flexibility. Arrange your mail stops before you leave. Most American Express offices (listed at www.americanexpress.com) offer a free clients' mail service for those who have an American Express card or traveler's checks (even just one). Have mail marked "Clients' Mail." They'll hold it for 30 days unless the envelope instructs otherwise.

Every city has a general delivery service. Pick a small town where there is only one post office and no crowds. Have letters sent to you in care of "Poste Restante." Tell your friends to print your last name in capitals, underline it, and omit your middle name. If possible, avoid the Italian male, I mean mail.

Friends or relatives in Europe are fine for mail stops. Or, to avoid mail pickup commitments on a long trip, have mail sent to a friend or relative at home. When you know where you'll be, you can telephone them from Europe with instructions on where to mail or FedEx your letters. Second-day USA–Europe services are reliable and reasonable—but allow up to four days for a delivery to a small town. With the ease of phoning these days, I've dispensed with mail pickups altogether.

Sending packages home: Shoppers lighten their load by sending packages home by surface mail. Postage is expensive. A box the size of a small fruit crate costs about $40 by slow boat. Books are much cheaper if they are sent separately.

Customs regulations amount to 10 or 15 frustrating minutes of filling out forms with the normally unhelpful postal clerk's semi-assistance. Be realistic in your service expectations. Remember, European postal clerks are every bit as friendly, speedy, and multilingual as ours in the United States.

You can mail one package per person per day worth up to $200 duty free from Europe to the United States. Mark it "Unsolicited Gift." When you fill out the customs form, keep it simple and include the item's value (contents: clothing, carving, gifts, poster, value $50). For alcohol, perfume containing alcohol, and tobacco valued over $5, you will pay a duty. You are not allowed to send a "gift package" to yourself or one of your traveling companions. You can mail home all the "American Goods

Returned" you like with no customs concerns (but note that these Goods really must be American—not Bohemian crystal or a German cuckoo clock—or you'll be charged a duty).

Post offices usually sell boxes and string or tape for about $2. Service is best north of the Alps and in France. (The fastest way to get a package home from Italy is to use the Vatican post office or take it home in your suitcase.) Small-town post offices can be less crowded and more user-friendly. Every box I've ever mailed has arrived—bruised and battered but all there—within six weeks.

21. Staying Healthy

GET A CHECKUP

Just as you'd give your car a good checkup before a long journey, it's smart to meet with your doctor before your trip. Get a general checkup and ask for advice on maintaining your health. (For tips specific to women, see Chapter 25: The Woman Traveling Alone.)

At the time of this printing, no shots are required for basic European travel, but it's always smart to check. Obtain recommended immunizations and discuss proper care for any preexisting medical conditions while on the road. Bring along a letter from your doctor describing any special health problems and a copy of any pertinent prescriptions. If you have any heart concerns, pack a copy of a recent EKG.

Travel-medicine specialists: While I consider Europe as safe as the United States, those traveling to more exotic destinations should consult a travel-medicine physician. Only these specialists keep entirely up-to-date on health conditions for travelers around the world. Tell the doctor about every place you plan to visit and anyplace you may go. Then you can have the flexibility to take that impulsive swing through Turkey or Morocco knowing that you're prepared medically and have the required shots. Ask the doctor about Havrix (a vaccine that protects against hepatitis A), antidiarrheal medicines, and any extra precautions. The Centers for Disease Control offers (and can fax you) updated information on every country (24-hour info by fax and recorded voice: 888/232-3228; www.cdc.gov/travel/).

Dental checkup: Get a dental checkup well before your trip. (If you get a crown right before you leave, it's timed to start hurting on the plane.) Emergency dental care during your trip is time- and money-consuming, and can be hazardous and painful. I was once crowned by a German dentist who knew only one word in English, which he used in question form—"Pain?"

JET LAG AND THE FIRST DAY OF YOUR TRIP

Anyone who flies through time zones has to grapple with the biorhythmic confusion known as jet lag. When you switch your wristwatch six to nine hours forward, your body says, "Hey, what's going on?" Body clocks don't reset so easily. All your life you've done things on a 24-hour cycle. Now, after crossing the Atlantic, your body wants to eat when you tell it to sleep and sleep when you tell it to enjoy a museum.

Too many people assume their first day will be made worthless by jet lag. Don't prematurely condemn yourself to zombiedom. Most people I've traveled with, of all ages, have enjoyed productive—even hyper—first days. You can't avoid jet lag, but with a few tips you can minimize the symptoms.

Leave home well rested. Flying halfway around the world is stressful. If you leave frazzled after a hectic last night and a wild bon voyage party, there's a good chance you won't be healthy for the first part of your trip. An early-trip cold used to be a regular part of my vacation until I learned a very important trick. Plan from the start as if you're leaving two

Jet lag hits even the very young.

days before you really are. Keep that last 48-hour period sacred, even if it means being hectic before your false departure date. Then you have two orderly, peaceful days after you've packed so that you are physically ready to fly. Mentally, you'll be comfortable about leaving home and starting this adventure. You'll fly away well rested and 100 percent capable of enjoying the bombardment of your senses that will follow.

On the flight, drink plenty of liquids, eat lightly, and rest. Long flights are dehydrating. I ask for "two orange juices with no ice" every chance I get. Help yourself to the juice pitchers in the galley area. Eat lightly and have no coffee and only minimal sugar until the flight's almost over. Alcohol will stress your body and aggravate jet lag. The in-flight movie is good for one thing—nap time. With three hours' sleep during the transatlantic flight, you will be functional the day you land.

Reset your mind to local time. When the pilot announces the local European time, reset your mind along with your wristwatch. Don't prolong jet lag by reminding yourself what time it is back home. Be in Europe.

On arrival, stay awake until an early local bedtime. If you doze off at 4 p.m. and wake up at midnight, you've accomplished nothing. Plan a good walk until early evening. Jet lag hates fresh air, daylight, and exercise. Your body may beg for sleep but stand firm: Refuse. Force your body's transition to the local time. You'll probably awaken very early on your first morning. Trying to sleep later is normally futile. Get out and enjoy a "pinch me, I'm in Europe" walk, as merchants set up in the marketplace and the town slowly comes to life. This will probably be the only sunrise you'll see in Europe.

You'll read about many jet lag "cures." Most are worse than the disease. Just leave unfrazzled, minimize jet lag's symptoms, force yourself into European time, and give yourself a chance to enjoy your trip from the moment you step off the plane.

TRAVELING HEALTHY

Europe is generally safe. All the talk of treating water with purification tablets is applicable only south and east of Europe. Many may disagree with me, but with discretion and common sense I eat and drink whatever I like in Europe. If any area deserves a little extra caution, it is rural areas in Spain, Portugal, Italy, and Greece. As our world becomes more chemical, reasons for concern and caution will increase on both sides of the Atlantic.

I was able to stay healthy throughout a six-week trip traveling from Europe to India. By following these basic guidelines, I never once suffered from Tehran Tummy, Delhi Belly, or the Tegucigallop.

Eat nutritiously. The longer your trip, the more you'll be affected by an inadequate diet. Budget travelers often eat more carbohydrates and less protein to stretch their travel dollar. This is the root of many nutritional problems. Protein helps you resist infection and rebuilds muscles. Get the most nutritional mileage from your protein by eating it with the day's largest meal (in the presence of all those "essential" amino acids). Supplemental supervitamins, taken regularly, help me to at least feel healthy. If you have a serious dietary restriction, have a multilingual friend write it in the local language on the back of a business card and use it to order in restaurants.

Use good judgment. Avoid unhealthy-looking restaurants. Meat should be well cooked and, in some places, avoided altogether. Have "well done" written on a piece of paper in the local language and use it when ordering. Pre-prepared foods gather germs (a common cause of diarrhea). Outside of Europe, be especially cautious. When in serious doubt, eat only thick-skinned fruit...peeled.

Keep clean. Wash your hands often, keep your nails clean, and avoid touching your eyes and mouth.

Practice safe sex. Sexually transmitted diseases are widespread. Obviously, the best way to prevent acquiring an STD is to avoid exposure. Condoms (readily available at pharmacies and from rest-room vending machines) are fairly effective in preventing transmission. (Cleaning with soap and water before and after exposure is also helpful, if not downright pleasurable.) AIDS is also a risk; according to CNN, more than 60 percent of the prostitutes in Amsterdam are HIV positive.

Exercise. Physically, travel is great living—healthy food, lots of activity, fresh air, and all those stairs! If you're a couch potato, try to get in shape before your trip by taking long walks. If you like to keep in shape, you may want to work out during your trip. Jogging, while not as widespread in Europe as it is in the United States, is not considered weird. Traveling joggers can enjoy Europe from a special perspective—at dawn. Swimmers will find that Europe has plenty of good, inexpensive public swimming pools. Whatever your racket, if you want to badly enough, you'll find ways to keep in practice as you travel. Most big-city private tennis and swim clubs welcome foreign guests for a small fee. This is a good way to make friends as well as stay fit.

Give yourself psychological pep talks. Europe can do to certain travelers what south France did to van Gogh. Romantics can get the sensory bends, patriots can get their flags burned, and anyone can suffer from culture shock.

Europe is crowded, smoky, and not particularly impressed by America or Americans. It will challenge givens that you always assumed were above the test of reason, and most of Europe on the street doesn't really care that much about what you, the historical and cultural pilgrim, have waited so long to see.

A break—a long, dark, air-conditioned trip back to California in a movie theater; a pleasant sit in an American embassy reading room surrounded by eagles, photos of presidents, *Time* magazines, and other Yankees; or a visit to the lobby of a world-class hotel, where any hint of the local culture has been lost under a big-business bucket of intercontinental whitewash—can do wonders for the struggling traveler's spirit.

EUROPEAN WATER

I drink European tap water and any water served in restaurants. Read signs carefully, however, because some taps, like those on trains, are not for drinking. If there's any hint of nonpotability—a decal showing a glass with a red "X" over it, or a skull and crossbones—don't drink it.

The water (or, just as likely, the general stress of travel on your immune system) may, sooner or later, make you sick. It's not necessarily dirty. The bacteria in European water is different from that in American water. Our bodily systems—raised proudly on bread that rips in a straight line—are the most pampered on earth. We are capable of handling American bacteria with no problem at all, but some people can go to London and get sick. Some French people visit Boston and get sick. Some Americans travel around the world, eating and drinking everything in sight, and don't get sick, while others spend weeks on the toilet. It all depends on the person.

East of Bulgaria and south of the Mediterranean, do not drink untreated water. Water can be treated by boiling it for 10 minutes or by using purifying tablets or a filter. Bottled water, beer, wine, boiled coffee and tea, and bottled soft drinks are safe as long as you skip the ice cubes. Coca-Cola products are as safe in Syria as they are at home.

TRAVELER'S FIRST-AID KIT
You can buy anything you need in Europe, but it's handy to bring along:
- Band-Aids
- soap or alcohol preps (antiseptic Handiwipes)
- moleskin
- tweezers
- thermometer in a hard case
- Tylenol (or any nonaspirin pain reliever)
- medication for colds and diarrhea
- prescriptions and medications (in labeled, original containers)

Particularly if you'll be hiking in isolated areas, bring a first-aid booklet, Ace bandage, space blanket, and tape and bandages.

For eye care: Those with corrected vision should carry the lens prescription as well as extra glasses in a solid protective case. Contact lenses are used all over Europe, and the required solutions for their care are easy to find. Soft lenses can be boiled like eggs. (Remind your helpful landlady to leave them in their case.) Do not assume that you can wear your contacts as comfortably in Europe as you can at home. I find that the hot, dusty cities and my style of travel make contacts difficult.

BASIC FIRST AID
Travel is a package deal. You will probably get sick in Europe. If you stay healthy, feel lucky.

Headaches and other aches: Tylenol (or any other nonaspirin pain reliever) soothes headaches, sore feet, sprains, bruises, Italian traffic, hangovers, and many other minor problems.

Abrasions: Clean abrasions thoroughly with soap to prevent or control infection. Bandages help keep wounds clean but are not a substitute for cleaning. A piece of clean cloth can be sterilized by boiling for 10 minutes or by scorching with a match.

Blisters: Moleskin, bandages, tape, or two pairs of socks can prevent or retard problems with your feet. Cover any irritated area before it blisters.

Motion sickness: To be effective, medication for motion sickness (Bonine or Dramamine) should be taken several hours before you think you'll need it. This medication can also serve as a mild sleeping pill.

Swelling: Often accompanying a physical injury, swelling is painful and delays healing. Ice and elevate any sprain periodically for 48 hours. A package of frozen veggies works as a cheap ice pack. Use an Ace bandage to immobilize, stop swelling, and, later, provide support. It is not helpful to "work out" a sprain.

Fever: A high fever merits medical attention. A normal temperature of 98.6° Fahrenheit equals 27° Celsius. To give you an idea of fever equivalents in Celsius: 101° F = 38.3° C. And 104° F = 40° C.

Colds: Haste can make waste when it comes to gathering travel memories. Keep yourself healthy and hygienic. If you're feeling run-down, check into a good hotel, sleep well, and force fluids. Stock each place you stay with boxes of juice upon arrival. Sudafed (pseudoephedrine) and other cold capsules are available everywhere.

Diarrhea: Get used to the fact that you might have diarrhea for a day. (Practice that thought in front of the mirror tonight.) If you get the runs, take it in stride. It's simply not worth taking eight Pepto Bismol tablets a day or brushing your teeth in Coca-Cola all summer long to avoid a day of the runs. I take my health seriously, and, for me, traveling in India or Mexico is a major health concern. But I find Europe no more threatening to my health than the USA.

I routinely take groups of 24 Americans through Turkey for two weeks. With adequate discretion, we eat everything in sight. At the end of the trip, my loose-stool survey typically shows that five or six travelers coped with a day of the Big D and one person was stuck with an extended weeklong bout.

To avoid getting diarrhea, eat yogurt. Its helpful enzymes ease your system into the local cuisine.

If you get diarrhea, it will run its course. Revise your diet, don't panic, and take it easy for a day. Make your diet as bland and boring as possible for a day or so (bread, rice, boiled potatoes, clear soup, weak tea). Keep telling yourself that tomorrow you'll feel much better. You will. Most conditions are self-limiting.

If loose stools persist, drink lots of water to replenish lost liquids and minerals. Bananas are effective in replacing potassium, which is lost during a bout with diarrhea.

Do not take antidiarrheals if you have blood in your stools or a fever greater than 101° F (38.3° C). You need a doctor's exam and antibiotics. A child (especially an infant) who suffers a prolonged case of diarrhea also needs prompt medical attention.

I visited the Red Cross in Athens after a miserable three-week tour of the toilets of Syria and Jordan. My intestinal commotion was finally stilled by its recommended strict diet of boiled rice and plain tea. As a matter of fact, after five days on that dull diet, I was constipated.

Constipation: With all the bread you'll be eating, constipation, the other side of the intestinal pendulum, is (according to my surveys) as prevalent as diarrhea. Get exercise, eat lots of roughage—raw fruits, leafy vegetables, prunes, or bran tablets from home—and everything will come out all right in the end.

PHARMACIES AND DOCTORS

Throughout Europe, people with a health problem go first to the local pharmacy, not to their doctor. European pharmacists diagnose and prescribe remedies for most simple problems. They are usually friendly and speak English. If necessary, they'll send you to a doctor.

Serious medical treatment in Europe is generally of high quality. To facilitate smooth communication, it's best to find an English-speaking doctor. Before your trip, consider joining IAMAT, the International Association for Medical Assistance to Travelers. You'll get a list of English-speaking doctors in member countries who provide services at special rates and offer travel medicine advice (membership is free but donation requested, 417 Center Street, Lewiston, NY 14092, tel. 716/754-4883, www.iamat.org). Typical fees for IAMAT–affiliated doctors: $55 for an office call, $75 for a house call, $95 for a house call on nights, holidays, and Sundays.

In Europe get a referral for an English-speaking doctor from the TI or other agencies that deal with Americans (such as embassies, consulates, large hotels, and American Express companies).

Most hotels can generally get an English-speaking doctor to stop by within the same day. As a tour guide, I've been impressed with the quality of the house-call care and the reasonable fees ($50 per visit). You're diagnosed, billed, and you pay on the spot. You'll generally head off to the nearest 24-hour pharmacy with a prescription, and by the next day you're back in sightseeing business.

22. Outsmarting Thieves

Europe is safe when it comes to violent crime. But it's a very dangerous place—if you're an American—from a petty purse-snatching, pickpocketing point of view. Thieves target Americans: Not because they're mean but because they're smart. Loaded down with valuables in a strange new environment, we stick out like jeweled thumbs. If I were a European street thief, I'd specialize in Americans. My card would say "Yanks Я Us." Americans are known as the ones with all the good stuff in their bags and wallets. Last year I met an American woman whose purse was stolen, and in her purse was her money belt. That juicy little anecdote was featured in every street-thief newsletter.

If you're not constantly on guard, you'll have something stolen. One summer, four out of five of my traveling companions lost cameras in one way or another. (Don't look at me.) In more than 25 summers of travel, I've been mugged once (in a part of London where only fools and thieves tread), had my car broken into six times (broken locks and shattered wing windows, lots of nonessential stuff taken), and had my car hot-wired once (it was abandoned a few blocks away after the thief found nothing to take). But I've never had my room rifled and never had any money belt–worthy valuables stolen.

Remember, nearly all crimes suffered by tourists are nonviolent and avoidable. Be aware of the pitfalls of traveling, but relax and have fun. Limit your vulnerability rather than your travels. Leave precious valuables at home and wear your money belt on the road. Most people in every country are on your side. If you exercise adequate discretion, aren't overly trusting, and don't put yourself into risky situations, your travels should be about as dangerous as hometown grocery shopping. Don't travel afraid—travel carefully.

MONEY BELTS

Money belts are your key to peace of mind. I never travel without one. A money belt is a small, nylon-zippered pouch that ties around the waist under your pants or skirt. You wear it completely hidden from sight, tucked in like a shirttail—over your shirt and under your pants. You can protect your fortune at a cost of only $8 (for our free newsletter/catalog, contact us at 425/771-8303 or www.ricksteves.com).

With a money belt, all your essential documents are on you as securely and thoughtlessly as your underpants. Have you ever thought about that? Every morning you put on your underpants. You don't even think about them all day long. And every night when you undress, sure enough, there they are, exactly where you put them. When I travel, my valuables are

Tour of a Moneybelt

Packing light applies to your money belt as well as your suitcase. Here's what to pack in your money belt:

Passport. You're legally supposed to have it with you at all times.

Plane ticket. Put essential pages in your money belt, nonessential pages in your luggage.

Railpass. This is as valuable as cash.

Driver's license. This works just about anywhere in Europe and is necessary if you want to rent a car on the spur of the moment.

Credit card. It's required for car rental and handy to have if your cash runs low.

Cash machine card. A Visa debit card is the most versatile.

Cash. Keep only major bills in your money belt.

Traveler's checks. Keep the receipt, up-to-date log (necessary for replacement if lost), and a few checks in your money belt. Keep bulk of checks (they're replaceable) in your luggage.

Plastic sheath. Money belts easily get slimy and sweaty. Damp plane tickets and railpasses are disgusting and sometimes worthless. Even a plain old baggie helps keep things dry.

Address list. Print small, and include every number of importance in your life.

just as securely out of sight and out of mind, around my waist in a money belt. It's luxurious peace of mind. I'm uncomfortable only when I'm not wearing it.

Operate with a day's spending money in your pocket. You don't need to get at your money belt for every nickel, dime, and quarter. Your money belt is your deep storage—for select deposits and withdrawals. Lately, I haven't even carried a wallet. A few bills in my shirt pocket—no keys, no wallet—I'm on vacation!

Precautions: Never leave a money belt "hidden" on the beach while you swim. It's safer left in your hotel room. You can shower with your money belt (hang it—maybe in a plastic bag—from the nozzle) in sleazy hotel or dorm situations where it shouldn't be left alone in your room. Keep your money belt contents dry and unsweaty with a zip-lock baggie.

Purses and wallets are handy for odds and ends and a day's spending money, but plan on losing them. A button-down flap or a Velcro strip sewn into your front or back pocket slows down fast fingers. Those with nothing worth stealing (cars, video cameras, jewelry, and so on) except what's in their money belt can travel virtually invulnerably.

TIPS ON AVOIDING THEFT

Thieves thrive on confusion, crowds, and other tourist traps. Here's some advice given to me by a thief who won the lotto.

Keep a low profile: Never leave your camera lying around where hotel workers and others can see it and be tempted. Keep it either around your neck or zipped safely out of sight. Luxurious luggage lures thieves. The thief chooses the most impressive suitcase in the pile—never mine. Thieves assume that anyone leaving a bank with their luggage just changed money. Bags are much safer in your room than with you on the streets. Hotels are a relative haven from thieves and a good resource for advice on personal safety.

On trains and at the station: On the train, be alert at stops, when thieves can dash on and off—with your bag. When sleeping on a train (or at an airport or anywhere in public), clip or fasten your pack or suitcase to the chair, luggage rack, or yourself. Even the slight inconvenience of undoing a clip foils most thieves. Women shouldn't sleep in an empty train compartment. You're safer sharing a compartment with a family or a couple of nuns. Be on guard in train stations, especially upon arrival, when you may be overburdened by luggage and overwhelmed by a new location. If you check your luggage, keep the claim ticket or key in your money belt. Thieves know just where to go if they get one of these.

The Métro, subway, and flea markets: Crowding through the Paris

Tourists are often the targets of thieves at major sights in Italy, especially around Rome's Forum and the Florence train station. Some will pose as beggars—using babies or newpapers to distract you while they rip you off.

Métro turnstiles is a popular way to rip off the unsuspecting tourist. Imaginative artful-dodger thief teams create a fight or commotion to distract their victims. Crowded flea markets and city buses that cover the tourist sights (like Rome's notorious #64) are also happy hunting grounds. Thief teams will often block a bus or subway entry, causing the person behind you to "bump" into you. While I don't lock my zippers, most zippers are lockable, and even a wire twisty or key ring is helpful to keep your bag zipped up tight. Don't use a waist (or "fanny") pack as a money belt. Thieves assume this is where you keep your goodies.

Your rental car: Thieves target tourists' cars—especially at night. Don't leave anything even hinting of value in view in your parked car. Put anything worth stealing in the trunk. Leave your glove compartment open so the thief can look in without breaking in. Choose your parking place carefully. (Your hotel receptionist knows what's safe and what precautions are necessary.)

Make your car look local. Take off or cover the rental company decals. Leave no tourist information lying around. Put a local newspaper in the back. More than half of the work that European automobile glass shops get is repairing wings broken by thieves. Before I choose where to park my car, I check if the parking lot's asphalt glitters. If you have a hatchback, leave the trunk covered during the day. At night take the cover off the trunk and lay it on the back seat so the thief thinks you're savvy and can see there's nothing stored in the back of your car. Many police advise leaving your car unlocked at night. Worthless but irreplaceable things (journal, spent film, etc.) are stolen only if left in a bag. Lay these things loose in the trunk. In major cities in Spain, crude thieves reach into windows or even smash the windows of occupied cars at stoplights to grab a purse or camera. In Rome my favorite pension is next to a large police station—a safe place to park, if you're legal.

SCAMS

Many of the most successful scams require a naive and trusting tourist. Be wary of any unusual contact or commotion in crowded public (especially touristic) places. If you're alert and aren't overly trusting, you should have no problem. Here are a few clever ways European thieves bolster their cash flow:

Slow count: Cashiers who deal with lots of tourists (especially in Italian tourist spots) thrive on the "slow count." Even in banks, they'll count your change back with odd pauses in hopes the rushed tourist will gather up the money early and say "*Grazie*." Also be careful when you pay with too large a bill. Waiters have a tough time keeping track of the zeros. Take time to give accurate coins to minimize the complexity of the deal (e.g., give €52.50 for a €12.50 bill and wait for €40 in change).

Oops!: You're jostled in a crowd as someone spills mustard, ketchup, or fake pigeon poop on your shirt. The thief offers greedy apologies while dabbing it up—and pawing your pockets. There are variations: Someone drops something, you kindly pick it up, and you lose your wallet. Or, even worse, someone throws a baby into your arms as your pockets are picked. Assume beggars are pickpockets. And assume any commotion is fake commotion—designed to distract and jostle unknowing victims. If an elderly woman falls down an escalator, stand back and guard your valuables, then . . . carefully . . . move in to help.

The "helpful" local: Thieves posing as concerned locals will warn you to store your wallet safely—and then steal it after they see where you stash it. Some thieves put out tacks and ambush drivers with their "assistance" in changing the tire. Others hang out at subway ticket machines eager to "help you," the bewildered tourist, buy tickets with a pile of your quickly disappearing foreign cash. If using a station locker, beware of the "hood samaritan" who may have his own key to a locker he'd like you to use.

Fake police: Two thieves in uniform—posing as "Tourist Police"—stop you on the street, flash their bogus badges, and ask to check your wallet for counterfeit bills or "drug money." You won't even notice some bills are missing until they leave. Never give your wallet to anyone.

Groups of teenagers, using newspapers to distract their prey, pickpocket tourists strolling the beach promenade in Nice. Not nice.

Young thief gangs: These are common throughout urban southern Europe, especially in the touristed areas of Milan, Florence, and Rome. Groups of boys or girls with big eyes, troubled expressions, and colorful raggedy clothes play a game where they politely mob the unsuspecting tourist, beggar style. As their pleading eyes grab yours and they hold up their pathetic message scrawled on cardboard, you're fooled into thinking that they're beggars. All the while, your purse, fanny bag, or rucksack is being expertly rifled. If you're wearing a money belt and you understand what's going on here, there's nothing to fear. In fact, having a street thief's hand in your pocket becomes just one more interesting cultural experience.

IF YOU'RE RIPPED OFF...

Even the most careful traveler can get ripped off. If it happens, don't let it ruin your trip. (If you'll be making an insurance claim, get a police report immediately. Traveler's check thefts must be reported within 24 hours.) Many trips start with a major rip-off, recover, and with the right attitude and very light bags, finish wonderfully.

Before you leave on your trip, make photocopies of your valuable documents and tickets. It's easier to replace a lost or stolen plane ticket, passport, railpass, or car rental voucher if you have a photocopy proving that you really owned what you lost.

American embassies or consulates are located in major European cities. They're there to help American citizens in trouble but don't fancy themselves as travelers' aid offices. They will inform those at home that you need help, assist in replacing lost or stolen passports, and arrange for emergency funds to be sent from home (or, in rare cases, loan it to you directly).

23. Museum Strategies

CULTURE BEYOND THE PETRI DISH

Europe is a treasure chest of great art. You'll see many of the world's greatest museums. These tips will help you make the most out of your trip.

Study your guidebook. Some museums now require reservations, such as the Alhambra (in Granada, Spain), the church that houses Leonardo's *Last Supper* (Milan), Giotto's Scrovegni Chapel (Padua), and the Borghese Gallery and Nero's Golden House (both in Rome). If you don't reserve in advance, you'll miss out.

At Florence's Uffizi Gallery, the showcase for Italian Renaissance art, it's smart to book ahead. While hundreds of tourists are sweating in the two-hour-long line, you can just show up at your reserved entry time and spend your time in the museum instead of the line.

Know the closed days. Most museums are closed one day during the week (usually Monday or Tuesday). If you've got only one day for the Sistine Chapel, avoid Sunday. It's either closed, or—on the last Sunday of the month—free and terribly crowded, when it feels more like the Sardine Chapel. It can be worth paying the entrance fee to avoid the rampaging hordes on a museum's free day.

At many great galleries, such as the Uffizi in Florence, you can wait in line for two hours . . . or call ahead for an appointment and walk right in.

Arrive early (or late) at popular sights. If you show up by 8:30 in the morning at Neuschwanstein, Bavaria's famous fairy-tale castle, you'll get a ticket. Come later and you'll either wait a long time or find that tickets are sold out—or worse, both.

Some museums are open late a night or two a week. For instance, London's Tate Modern stays open Friday and Saturday evenings—when the crowds disappear and you're glad you came.

Museum passes (such as the Paris museum pass) and combo-tickets allow you to bypass the long admission lines and walk right in. You can wait up to an hour to get into Rome's Colosseum—or buy a combo-ticket (at another participating site) and just scoot inside.

Note that many museums stop selling tickets and start shutting down rooms 30 to 60 minutes before closing. My favorite time in museums is the cool, lazy, last hour. But I'm careful to get to the far end early, see the rooms that are first to shut down, and work my way back toward the entry.

A victim of the Louvre

These tricks aren't secrets. They're in any good, up-to-date guidebook. Just read ahead.

Learn about art. If the art's not fun, you don't know enough about it. I remember touring the National Museum of Archaeology in Athens as an obligation. My mom said it would be a crime to miss it. It was boring. I was convinced that the people who looked like they were enjoying it were actually just faking it—trying to look sophisticated. Two years later, after a class in ancient art history, that same museum was a fascinating trip into the world of Pericles and Socrates, all because of some background knowledge. Some pre-trip study makes the art more fun.

In Europe, it's hard to find art guidebooks in readable English. Before you go, consider getting my art guidebook, *Rick Steves' Mona Winks: Self-Guided Tours of Europe's Top Museums* (co-authored with Gene Openshaw, 2001). This book is a fun collection of take-you-by-the-hand, two-hour tours of Europe's 20 most important (and exhausting) museums and sights. It's just us together with the greatest art of our civilization. Of all of my guidebooks, *Mona Winks*—while far from the best-selling—has the most devoted following. You can study up and figure out what you want to see before you go, and then refer to *Mona* when you're standing before Botticelli's *Birth of Venus*. If you decide to travel without *Mona*, try to make friends and tag along with someone in the big museums who's got it.

Be selective. A common misconception is that a great museum has only great art. A museum such as the Louvre in Paris is so big (the building itself was, at one time, the largest in Europe), you can't possibly cover everything—so don't try. Only a fraction of a museum's pieces are really masterpieces.

With the help of a guide or guidebook, focus on just the museum's top two hours. Some of Europe's great museums provide brief pamphlets recommending the best basic visit. With this selective strategy, you'll appreciate the highlights when you're fresh. If you have any energy left afterwards, you can explore other areas of specific interest to you. For me, museum-going is the hardest work I do in Europe, and I'm rarely good for more than two or three hours at a time. If you're determined to cover a large museum thoroughly, try to tackle one section a day for several days.

Try to get a tour. Phone ahead. Some museums offer regularly scheduled tours in English. If the tour is in French or German only, politely let the guide know at the beginning that there are several English-speaking people in the group who'd love some information.

Audioguide tours are getting more and more popular at museums. These portable devices—which rent for about $4—allow you to dial up dry but worthwhile information in English on particular pieces of art.

Eavesdrop. If you are especially interested in one piece of art, spend half an hour studying it and listening to each passing tour guide tell his or her story about *David* or the *Mona Lisa* or whatever. They each do their own research and come up with different information to share. Much of it is true. There's nothing wrong with this sort of tour freeloading. Just don't stand in the front and ask a lot of questions.

Make sure you don't miss your favorites. On arrival, look through the museum's guidebook index or the gift shop's postcards to make sure you won't miss anything of importance to you. For instance, I love Salvador Dalí's work. One time I thought I was finished with a museum, but as I browsed through the postcards ... Hello, Dalí. A museum guide was happy to show me where this Dalí painting was hiding. I saved myself the disappointment of discovering too late that I'd missed it.

More and more museums offer a greatest-hits plan or brochure. Some (such as London's National Gallery) even have a computer study room where you can input your interests and print out a tailored museum tour.

Miscellaneous tips: Particularly at huge museums, ask if your ticket allows in-and-out privileges. Check the museum map or brochure at the entrance for the location of particular kinds of art, the café, and bathrooms (usually free and clean). Also, note any special early closings of rooms or wings. Get comfortable: Check your bag and coat. (If you want to try to keep your bag with you, carry it low like a purse, not on your back.) Cameras are usually allowed if you don't use a flash or tripod; look for signs or ask.

OPEN-AIR FOLK MUSEUMS

Many people travel in search of the old life and traditional culture in action. While we book a round-trip ticket into the romantic past, those we photograph with the Old World balanced on their heads are struggling to dump that load and climb into our modern world. In Europe, most are succeeding.

The easiest way and, more than ever, the only way to see the "real local culture" is by exploring the open-air folk museums. True, it's culture on a lazy Susan, but the future is becoming the past faster and faster, and in many places it's the only "Old World" you're going to find.

Traditional culture is kept alive in Europe's open-air folk museums.

An open-air folk museum is a collection of traditional buildings from every corner of a country or region carefully reassembled in a park, usually near the capital or major city. These sprawling museums are the best bet for the hurried (or tired) tourist craving a magic-carpet ride through that country's past. Log cabins, thatched cottages, mills, old schoolhouses, shops, and farms come complete with original furnishings and usually a local person dressed in the traditional costume who's happy to answer any of your questions about life then and there.

To get the most out of your visit, start by picking up a list of that day's special exhibits, events, and activities at the information center, and take advantage of any walking tours. In the summer, folk museums buzz with colorful folk dances, live music performances, and young craftspeople specializing in old crafts. Many traditional arts and crafts are dying, and these artisans do what they can to keep the cuckoo clock from going the way of the dodo bird. Some of my favorite souvenirs are those I watched being dyed, woven, or carved by folk-museum artists.

At Stockholm's open-air folk museum you may be entertained by this rare band of left-handed fiddlers.

Popularized in Scandinavia, these sightseeing centers of the future are now found all over the world. The best folk museums are still in the Nordic capitals. Oslo's, with 150 historic buildings and a 12th-century stave church, is just a boat ride across the harbor from the city hall. Skansen, in Stockholm, gets my

Some of Europe's Best Open-Air Folk Museums

Benelux

- Zaanse Schaans near Zaandijk, 30 miles north of Amsterdam. *Windmills, wooden shoes, etc.*
- Dutch Open-Air Folk Museum, in Arnhem, Netherlands. *Holland's first and biggest.*
- Zuiderzee Open-Air Museum, in Enkhuisen, Netherlands. *Lively setting, lots of craftspeople.*
- Bokrijk Open-Air Museum, between Hasselt and Genk, in Belgium. *Old Flemish buildings and culture in a natural setting.*

Denmark

- Funen Village (Den Fynske Landsby), just south of Odense.
- Old Town, Arhus. *Sixty houses and shops show Danish town life from 1580 to 1850.*
- Lyngby Park, north of Copenhagen.

Finland

- Seurasaari Island, near Helsinki. *Reconstructed buildings from all over Finland.*
- Handicraft Museum, Turku. *The life and work of 19th-century craftspeople.*

Germany

- Black Forest Open-Air Museum in Gutach. *A collection of farms filled with exhibits on the local dress and lifestyles.*

Great Britain

- Blists Hill Victorian Town, near Coalport. *Shows life from the early days of the Industrial Revolution.*
- Beamish Open-Air Museum, northwest of Durham. *Life in northeast England in 1900.*
- Welsh Folk Museum, at St. Fagans, near Cardiff. *Old buildings and craftspeople illustrate traditional Welsh ways.*

Ireland

- Bunratty Folk Park, near Limerick. *Buildings from the Shannon area and artisans at work.*
- Irish Open-Air Folk Museum, at Cultra near Belfast. *Traditional Irish lifestyles and buildings from all over Ireland.*
- Glencolumbcille Folk Museum, Donegal. *Thatched cottages show life from 1700 to 1900. A Gaelic-speaking cooperative runs the folk village and a traditional crafts industry.*

Norway

- Norwegian Folk Museum, at Bygdøy near Oslo. *Norway's first, with 150 old buildings from all over Norway and a 12th-century stave church.*
- Maihaugen Folk Museum, at Lillehammer. *Folk culture of the Gubrandsdalen. Norway's best.*

Sweden

- Skansen, Stockholm. *One of the best museums, with more than 100 buildings from all over Sweden, craftspeople at work, live entertainment, and a Lapp camp with reindeer.*
- Kulteren, Lund. *Features southern Sweden and Viking exhibits.*

Switzerland

- Ballenberg Swiss Open-Air Museum, just northeast of Lake Brienz. *A fine collection of old Swiss buildings with furnished interiors.*

first-place ribbon for its guided tours, feisty folk entertainment, and Lapp camp complete with reindeer.

Switzerland's Ballenberg Open-Air Museum, near Interlaken, is a good alternative when the Alps hide behind clouds.

There is no shortage of folk museums in the British Isles. For an unrivaled look at the Industrial Revolution, spend a day at Blists Hill Victorian Town in Ironbridge Gorge, northwest of Stratford. You can cross the world's first iron bridge to see the factories that lit the fuse of our modern age.

Every year new folk museums open. Before your trip, send a card to each country's national tourist office (addresses are listed in Chapter 2: Gathering Information) requesting, among other things, a list of open-air folk museums. As you travel, use a current guidebook and local tourist information centers.

Folk museums teach traditional lifestyles better than any other kind of museum. As our world hurtles past 200 billion McDonald's hamburgers served, these museums will become even more important. Of course, they're as realistic as Santa's Village, but how else will you see the elves?

24. Travel Photography

If my hotel were burning down and I could grab just one thing, it would be my exposed film. Every year I ask myself whether it's worth the worry and expense of mixing photography with my travels. After my film is developed and I relive my trip through those pictures, the answer is always "Yes!" Here are some tips and lessons that I've learned from the photographic school of hard knocks.

BUYING A CAMERA

Good shots are made by the photographer, not the camera. For most people, a very expensive camera is a bad idea. Your camera is more likely to be lost, broken, or stolen than anything else you'll travel with. An expensive model may not be worth the risks and headaches that accompany it.

When buying a camera, get one that will do what you want and a little bit more. You are buying one not only for the trip, but also for use later.

Visit your local camera shops, ask questions, and ask your friends and neighbors what they use. Be careful of what the salespeople try to sell. They make more money if they can sell you the camera that is being promoted for the month, but it may not be what you need. Get a camera built by a well-known company.

At many of Europe's art museums, you can take pictures, but without a flash. Get a camera that will allow you to suppress the flash.

Don't buy a camera a day or two before you fly. Not every camera works perfectly right out of the box. Shoot a roll of 24-exposure film, indoors and outdoors, before you leave. Check your pictures for good exposure and sharp focus. If they're not right, take it back. Do the same checks with the replacement camera. Do your learning on home-town Main Street rather than Piazza San Marco.

A good eye is more important than an extra lens.

TYPES OF CAMERAS

Disposables: The simple choice for an amateur photographer (lacking an environmental conscience) is a disposable or "single-use" camera. These disposables cost as little as $7 for 24 exposures of 400-speed film. A cheap panorama camera, with a very wide–angle lens for 180-degree shots, can be a fun supplement ($15).

Point-and-shoot: Compact little "focus-free" cameras ($25–50) allow minimal creative control but take decent pictures. They're cheap, fragile, and, when broken, usually just tossed out.

The more expensive point-and-shoot cameras ($50–350) have auto focus and a wide-angle 38 mm lens. Models over $100 come with a few helpful bells and whistles and a small adjustable zoom lens of 38 to 70 mm. The pricier cameras have lenses that zoom from 28 to 105 mm.

If you spend less than $100, you'll get a cheap camera that might not last much longer than the trip.

Single lens reflex (SLR): Those shooting slides should stick with a good SLR ($200–1,000). Regardless of advertising claims, there's no real difference between the mind of Minolta and the mind of Pentax, Nikon, or Canon. The trend in SLRs is toward auto-focus lenses, but most of these units have a manual focus–override switch. For traveling, the quick and accurate auto focus is handy, but creative photographers will also want the manual capabilities.

Digital: The latest phenomenon in photography, the digital camera, allows you to edit your pictures and send them by e-mail. And its "film" is reusable. For a primer, visit www.photocourse.com.

Models, ranging in price from $300 to $1,000, come with conventional-camera features such as a zoom lens, flash, and auto and manual focus. They also feature a handy Liquid Crystal Display (LCD), which functions as a viewfinder as well as a "reviewer," showing you photos just taken. Get a camera with both an LCD screen and an "old-fashioned" optical viewfinder (because LCDs tend to drain batteries quicker).

Most digital cameras take AA batteries, which come in three types: regular, rechargeable nickel-metal hydride, and lithium. The regular AA batteries (easily available in Europe) are best for an overseas trip. To use the rechargeable nickel-metal hydride AA batteries, you'd have to lug cumbersome chargers and adapters. Long-lasting lithium batteries are not rechargeable and can be difficult to replace in Europe. Avoid getting a digital camera that works only on its own brand of batteries (such as Canon models that take only Canon batteries); you need more versatility.

Storage media cards (or floppy disks) are the "brains" that store your captured images. The more megabytes the card or disk has, the more photos you can take. Pay attention to the camera's resolution indicators: pixels (or dots) per inch and the megapixel resolution number. The higher the number, the less grainy the photo. Anything over one million pixels produces a clear picture.

When traveling, the trick is finding a place to "empty" your storage media cards. The larger European cybercafés have the technology that allows you to upload your pictures, edit them, or post them to your personal Web site. Some cybercafés can copy your pictures on a zip disk or CD-rom, allowing you to upload your pictures and send them home as e-mail attachments. Still, your safest bet is to take along several storage media cards ($30–100) or one huge one ($300 for 180 high-resolution pictures). These are available in Europe but are more expensive.

LENSES, FILTERS, BATTERIES, AND FILM

Lenses: Your best all-around lens is an f/3.5 28-70 mm or 80 mm "midrange" zoom lens, which range between $120 and $300. No, it's not as fast as an f/1.7, but with the fine-grain ASA-400 films on the market today, it's almost like having an f/1.7 lens.

Filters: Make sure all your lenses have a haze or UV filter ($15) on them. It's better to bang and smudge up your filter than your lens. The only other filter you might use is a polarizer, which eliminates reflections and enhances color separation, but you can lose up to two stops in speed with it. Never use more than one filter at a time.

Batteries: Remember to leave home with fresh batteries in your camera.

Film: When choosing film, I always go with 400-speed film in 36-exposure rolls. Print films are all about the same. You'll see more difference between the print processors than between the films. With slide film, stick with the films that are known as E-6 developing (Ektachrome, Fujichrome, and so on). They can be developed overnight in most large cities and usually cost less, too. Kodak film is cheapest in the United States. In Europe buy film in department stores or camera shops rather than for rip-off prices at the sights. Fuji and Konica are reasonable in Europe.

A GALAXY OF GADGETS

Like many hobbies, photography is one that allows you to spend endless amounts of money on accessories. The following are particularly useful to the traveling photographer:

Gadget bag: The most functional and economical is simply a small nylon stuff bag made for hikers. When I'm taking a lot of pictures, I like to wear a nylon belt pouch (designed to carry a canteen). This is a handy way to have your different lenses and filters readily accessible, allowing you to make necessary changes quickly and easily. A formal camera bag is unnecessary and attracts thieves.

Mini C-clamp/tripod: About five inches high, this great little gadget screws into most cameras, sprouts three legs, and holds the camera perfectly still for slow shutter speeds, timed exposures, and automatic shutter-release shots. (It looks like a small lunar landing module.) The C-clamp works where the tripod won't, such as on a fence or handrail. A conventional tripod is too large to lug around Europe. Those without a mini-tripod use a tiny beanbag (or sock filled with rice) or get good at balancing their camera on anything solid and adjusting the tilt with the lens cap or strap.

Tissue, cleaner, and lens cap: A lens-cleaning tissue and a small bottle of cleaning solution are wise additions to any gadget bag. I leave my protective camera case at home and protect my lens with a cap that dangles on its string when I'm shooting. Carrying film in a lead-lined bag is unnecessary since European airport X-rays these days really are "film safe."

TRICKS FOR A GOOD SHOT

Most people are limited by their skills, not by their camera. Understand your camera. Devour the manual. Shoot experimental shots, take notes, and see what happens. If you don't understand f-stops or depth of field, find a photography class or book and learn (for tips on taking pictures, focus on Photosecrets and its online gallery at www.photosecrets.com). Camera stores sell good books on photography in general and travel photography in particular. I shutter to think how many people are underexposed and lacking depth in this field.

A sharp eye connected to a wild imagination will be your most valuable piece of equipment. Develop a knack for what will look good and be interesting after the trip. The skilled photographer's eye sees striking light, shade, form, lines, patterns, texture, and colors. It's cheaper to weed out dull shots before you take them, not after you get them home. However, if you're using a digital camera, you can shoot like mad, then review and cull out the bad shots each evening.

Look for a new slant to an old sight. Postcard-type shots are boring. Everyone knows what the Eiffel Tower looks like. Find a unique or different approach to sights that everyone has seen. Shoot the bell tower through the horse's legs or lay your camera on the floor to shoot the Gothic ceiling.

Capture the personal and intimate details of your trip. Show how you lived, who you met, and what made each day an adventure (a close-up of a picnic, your leech bite, laundry day, or a local schoolboy playing games with his nose).

Vary your perspective. Shoot close, far, low, high, during the day, and at night. Don't fall into the rut of always centering a shot. Use foregrounds to add color, depth, and interest to landscapes.

Be bold and break rules. For instance, we are told never to shoot into the sun. But some into-the-sun shots bring surprising results. Try to use bad weather to your advantage. Experiment with strange or difficult light situations. Buy a handbook on shooting photos in existing light.

Maximize good lighting. Real photographers get single-minded at the magic hours—early morning and late afternoon—when the sun is very low and the colors glow. Plan for these times. Grab bright colors.

Get close. Notice details. Get closer, real close. Eliminate distractions. Get so close that you show only one thing. Don't try to show it all in one shot. For any potentially great shot, I invest two or three exposures.

People are the most interesting subjects. It takes nerve to walk

Dominic Bonuccelli

Dominic Bonuccelli

up to people and take their picture. It can be difficult, but, if you want some great shots, be nervy. Ask for permission. (In any language, point at your camera and ask, "Photo?") Your subject will probably be delighted. Try to show action. A candid is better than a posed shot. Even a posed candid is better than a posed shot. Give your subject something to do. Challenge the lady in the market to juggle her kiwis. Many photographers take a second shot immediately after the first portrait to capture a looser, warmer subject. If the portrait isn't good, you probably weren't close enough. My best portraits are so close that the entire head can't fit into the frame.

Buildings, in general, are not interesting. It doesn't matter if Karl Marx or Beethoven was born there, a house is as dead as its former resident. As travel photographers gain experience, they take more people shots and fewer buildings or general landscapes.

Be able to take a quick shot. If you're shooting manually, practice setting it. Understand depth of field and metering. In a marketplace situation, where speed is crucial, I preset my camera. I set the meter on the sunlit ground and focus at, let's say, 12 feet. Now I know that, with my depth of field, anything from about 10 to 15 feet will be in focus and, if it's in the sunshine, properly exposed. I can take a perfect picture in an instant, provided my subject meets these preset requirements. It's possible to get some good shots by presetting the camera and shooting from the waist. Ideally, I get eye contact while I shoot from the hip.

Expose for your subject. Even if your camera is automatic, your subject can turn out a silhouette. Meter without the sky. Get those faces in the sun or lit from the side. For slides, you'll get richer tones if you underexpose just a bit. Expose for the highlights.

Don't be afraid to hand hold a slow shot. At most major museums, you're not allowed to use a flash (which ages paintings) or a tripod. Tripods enable you to take professional (profitable) shots that could compete with the museum gift shop's. (Nearly every important museum has a good selection of top-quality slides, cards, and prints at reasonable prices.)

Despite these restrictions, you can take good shots by holding your camera as still as possible. If you can lean against a wall, for instance, you become a tripod instead of a bipod. Use a self-timer, which clicks the shutter more smoothly than your finger can. With these tricks, I get good pictures inside a museum at 1/30 of a second. With ASA-400 film, I manage indoors without a flash.

You'll hear that the focal length of your lens dictates the slowest hand-held shutter speed you can use. For instance, a 50 mm lens should shoot no slower than 1/50 of a second. But you can get decent shots out of the same lens at 1/30 of a second, even 1/15, by using the tricks mentioned above.

Bracket shots when the lighting is tricky. A lot of time-exposure photography is guesswork. The best way to get good shots in difficult lighting situations is to bracket your shots by trying several different exposures of the same scene. You'll have to throw out a few slides that way, but one good shot is worth several in the garbage can. Automatic cameras usually meter properly up to eight or 10 seconds, making night shots easy, but bracketing may still be necessary.

For scrapbook fans: Some scrapbookers buy a book and get their prints developed at their last stop in Europe. Then they happily pass the hours on the long flight home putting together their vacation scrapbook.

Limit your slideshow. Nothing is worse than suffering through an endless parade of lackluster and look-alike shots. If putting together a slideshow, set a limit (maximum two carousels of 140 slides each) and prune your show down until it bleeds. Keep it tight. Keep it moving. Leave the audience crying for more … or at least awake.

TRAVELING WITH A VIDEO CAMERA

With video cameras getting better, smaller, and more affordable, more and more Americans are compromising a potentially footloose and fancy-free vacation to get a memory on videotape. However, to me, a still camera is trouble enough. But thousands of amateur videographers happily seeing Europe through their viewfinders can't all be wrong. Charging your video camera's batteries will be easy, but if your camera doesn't have a built-in converter, you'll have to get one. And, remember, European sockets are different (plugs have two round prongs on the continent, three flat prongs for Britain). Adapters, which can be tough to find in Europe, are available at your hometown travel accessories or electronics store.

STOW THAT CAMERA!

When not using your camera or camcorder, stow it in your day bag. Many go through their entire trip with a camera bouncing on their belly. That's a tourist's badge that puts a psychological wall between you and Europe. To locals, it just screams, "Yodel."

SPECIAL CONCERNS

25. The Woman Traveling Alone

In my classes, women often ask, "Is it safe for a woman to travel alone through Europe?" This is a question best answered by a woman. Europe Through the Back Door tour guide and researcher Risa Laib wrote this chapter based on her solo experience and tips contributed from other travelers: Gail Morse, Peggy Roberts, Suzanne Hogsett, Bharti Kirchner, and Kendra Roth. Collectively, these women have more than five years of solo travel experience in over 30 countries.

Every year, thousands of women, young and old, travel to Europe on their own. You're part of a grand group of adventurers. Traveling alone, you'll have the chance to make your own discoveries and the freedom to do what you like. It becomes habit forming.

As a solo woman, you're more approachable than a couple or a solo man. You'll make friends from all over the world, and you'll have experiences that others can only envy. When you travel with a partner, your focus narrows and doors close. When you're on your own, you're utterly open to the moment.

Solo travel is fun, challenging, vivid, and exhilarating. It's a gift from you to you. Prepared with good information and a positive attitude, you'll dance through Europe. And you'll come home stronger and more confident than ever before. Here's how to make it happen.

GETTING INSPIRED

Read exciting books written by solo women travelers about their experiences (try Dervla Murphy's outrageous adventures). For practical advice, read "how-to" travel guidebooks written by and for women.

Seek out other women travelers. Invite them out for dinner and pepper them with questions.

Take classes. A foreign language course is ideal. Consider a class in European history, art history, or travel skills.

Keep up on international news so you can discuss local politics. Study a map of Europe—get to know your neighbors.

Pretend you're traveling alone before you ever leave America. Practice reaching out. Strike up conversations with people in the grocery line. Consciously become more adaptable. If it rains, marvel at the miracle.

Think hard about what you want to see and do. Create the vacation of your dreams.

FACING THE CHALLENGES

These are probably your biggest fears: vulnerability to theft, harassment, and loneliness. Take heart. You can tackle each of these concerns head-on. If you've traveled alone in America, you're more than prepared for Europe. In America theft and harassment are especially scary because of their connection with violence. In Europe you'll rarely, if ever, hear of violence. Theft is past tense (as in, "Where did my wallet go?"). As for experiencing harassment, you're far more likely to think, "I'm going to ditch this guy  A.S.A.P." than "This guy is going to hurt me."

Loneliness is often the most common fear. But, remember, if you get lonely, you can do something about it.

TRAVELING ALONE WITHOUT FEELING LONELY

Here are some tips on meeting people, eating out, and enjoying your nights.

Meeting people: Stay in hostels, and you'll have a built-in family (hostels are open to all ages, except in Bavaria, where the age limit is 26). Or choose small pensions and B&Bs, where the owners have time to talk with you. Join Servas (see Chapter 15: Sleeping) and stay with local families. Camping is also a good, safe way to meet Europeans.

At most tourist sites you'll meet more people in an hour than you would at home in a day. If you're feeling shy, cameras are good icebreakers; offer to take someone's picture with their camera.

Talk to other solo women travelers and share advice.

Take your laundry and a deck of cards to a Laundromat and turn solitaire into gin rummy. You'll end up with a stack of clean clothes and conversations.

Stop by any American Express office.

Take a walking tour of a city (ask at the tourist information office). You'll learn about the town and meet other travelers, too.

It's easy to meet local people on buses and trains. You're always welcome at a church service; stay for the coffee hour. When you meet locals who speak English, find out what they think—about anything.

Play with kids. Bring along a puppet or a ball-toss game. Learn how to say "pretty baby" in the local language. If you play peek-a-boo with a baby or fold an origami bird for a kid, you'll make friends with the parents.

Call the English department at a university. See if they have an English conversation club you can visit. Or ask if you can hire a student to be your guide (you'll see the city from a local's perspective, give a student a job, and possibly make a friend).

Try pairing up with another solo traveler. Or return to a city you enjoyed. The locals will remember you, you'll know the neighborhood, and it'll feel like home.

Eating out: Consider quick and cheap alternatives to formal dining. Try a self-service café, a local-style fast-food restaurant, or a small ethnic eatery. Visit a supermarket deli and get a picnic to eat in the square or a park (local families often frequent parks). Get a slice of pizza from a take-out shop and munch it as you walk along, people-watching and window-shopping. Eat in the members' kitchen of a hostel; you'll always have companions. Make it a potluck.

A restaurant feels cheerier at noon than at night. Have lunch as your main meal. If you like company, eat in places so crowded and popular that you have to share a table. Or ask other single travelers if they'd like to join you.

If you eat alone, be busy. Use the time to learn more of the language. Practice your verbal skills with the waiter or waitress (when I asked a French waiter if he had kids, he proudly showed me a picture of his twin girls). Read your mail, a guidebook, a novel, or the *International Herald Tribune*. Do trip planning, write or draw in your journal, or scrawl a few postcards to the folks back home.

Most countries have a type of dish or restaurant that's fun to experience with a group. When you run into tourists during the day, make plans for dinner. Invite them to join you for, say, a *rijsttafel* dinner in the Netherlands, a smörgåsbord in Scandinavia, a fondue in Switzerland, a paella feast in Spain, or a spaghetti feed in an Italian trattoria.

At night: Experience the magic of European cities at night. Go for a walk along well-lit streets. With *gelato* in hand, enjoy the parade of people, busy shops, and illuminated monuments. Night or day, you're invariably safe when lots of people are around. Take advantage of the wealth of evening entertainment: concerts, movies, puppet shows, and folk dancing. Some cities offer tours after dark; you can see Paris by night on a river cruise.

If you like to stay in at night, get a room with a balcony overlooking a square. You'll have a front-row seat to the best show in town. Bring along a radio to brighten your room; pull in local music, a friendly voice, maybe even the BBC. Call home, a friend, your family. With the new PIN phone cards, it's actually inexpensive. Read novels set in the country you're visiting. Learn to treasure solitude. Go early to bed, be early to rise. Shop at a lively morning market for fresh rolls and join the locals for coffee.

PROTECTING YOURSELF FROM THEFT

As a woman, you're often perceived as being more vulnerable to theft than a man. Here are tips that'll help keep you safe:

Carry a daypack instead of a purse. Leave expensive-looking jewelry at home. Keep your valuables in your money belt and tuck your wallet (containing only a day's worth of cash) in your front pocket. Keep your camera zipped up in your daypack. In crowded places (buses, subways, street markets), carry your daypack over your chest. Ask at your hotel or the tourist office if there's a neighborhood you should avoid, and mark it on your map.

Avoid tempting people into theft. Make sure any valuables in your hotel room are kept out of sight. Wear your money belt when you sleep in hostels. When you're sightseeing, never set down anything of value (such as a camera or wallet). Either have it in your hand or keep it zipped away. If you're sitting and resting, loop a strap of your daypack around your arm, leg, or chair leg. Remember, you're unlikely ever to be hurt by thieves. They want to separate you from your valuables painlessly.

DEALING WITH MEN

In small towns in continental Europe, men are often more likely to speak English than women. If you never talk to men, you could miss out on a chance to learn about the country. So, by all means, talk to men. Just choose the men and choose the setting.

In northern Europe, you won't draw any more attention from men than you do in America. In southern Europe, particularly in Italy, you'll get more attention than you're used to, but it's nothing you can't handle.

Be aware of cultural differences. In Italy, when you smile and look a man in the eyes, it's considered an invitation. Wear dark sunglasses and you can stare all you want.

Dress modestly to minimize attention from men. Take your cue from what the local women wear. In Italy slacks and skirts (even short ones) are considered more proper than shorts.

Wear a real or fake wedding ring and carry a picture of a real or fake husband. There's no need to tell men that you're traveling alone. Lie unhesitatingly. You're traveling with your husband. He's waiting for you at the hotel. He's a professional wrestler who retired from the sport for psychological reasons.

If you'd like to date a local man, meet him at a public place. Tell him you're staying at a hostel—you have a 10 p.m. curfew and 29 roommates. Better yet, bring a couple of your roommates along to meet him. After the introductions, let everyone know where you're going and when you'll return.

HANDLING HARASSMENT

The way you handle harassment at home works in Europe, too.

In southern Europe men may think that if you're alone, you're available. If a man comes too close to you, say "no" firmly in the local language. That's usually all it takes. Tell a slow learner that you want to be alone. Then ignore him.

If he's obnoxious, solicit the help of others. Ask people at a café or on the beach if you can join them for a while.

If he's well meaning but too persistent, talk openly to him. Turn him into an ally. If he's a northern Italian, ask him about southern Italian men. Get advice from him on how you can avoid harassment when you travel farther south. After you elicit his "help," he'll be more like a brother than a bother to you.

In Europe, sometimes blondes have more trouble.

Usually men are just seeing if you're interested. Only a few are difficult. If a man makes a lewd gesture, look away and leave the scene. Harassers don't want public attention drawn to their behavior. I went out for a walk in Madrid one evening, and a man came up much too close to me, scaring me. I shouted, "Get!" And he was gone. I think I scared him as much as he scared me. Ask a local woman for just the right thing to say to embarrass jerks. Learn how to say it, loudly. (The Rick Steves' phrase books have a whole section on phrases handy for women.)

If you feel the need to carry mace, take a self-defense class instead. Mace can be confiscated at the airport, but knowledge and confidence are yours to keep. And, remember, the best self-defense is common sense.

KEEPING HEALTHY

You can find whatever medications you need in Europe, but you already know what works for you in the U.S. It's easiest to B.Y.O. pills, whether for cramps, yeast infections, or birth control. A few medical insurance companies issue only a month's supply of birth control pills at a time; ask for a larger supply for a longer trip. Condoms are as easy to buy in Europe as in America from pharmacies and vending machines in some women's rest rooms.

Tampons and pads are widely available in Europe, but you'll rarely see a big display of the brands and sizes typical in American supermarkets. If you're used to a particular brand and absorbency, it's simpler and cheaper to bring a supply from home. In Europe, tampons and pads are sold—for more than the U.S. price—at supermarkets (not the smaller groceries) and pharmacies.

Women prone to yeast infections should bring their own over-the-counter medicine (or know the name and its key ingredient to show a pharmacist in Europe). Talk to your doctor about getting a prescription for Diflucan, a powerful pill that cures yeast infections quicker and tidier than creams and suppositories. If you get a yeast infection in Europe and lack medication, go to a pharmacy. Most pharmacists speak English. If you encounter the rare one that doesn't, find an English-speaking local woman to write out "yeast infection" for you in the country's language to avoid the embarrassing charade.

You can treat most urinary tract infections with cranberry juice (available in northern Europe) or with cranberry pills (made from cranberry juice concentrate) sold in America at health food stores.

Traveling when pregnant: Some couples want to time conception to occur in Europe so they can name their child Paris or Siena or wherever. If that's your plan, consider bringing a pregnancy test from home to help you find out when you can celebrate or drink.

If you'll be traveling during your first pregnancy, rip out a few chapters from a book on pregnancy to bring along. It's hard to find basic information on pregnancy in English in much of Europe. If you want certain tests done (such as amniocentesis), ask your doctor when you need to be home.

In the first trimester, climbing all the stairs can be exhausting—packing light is more essential than ever. You might find it easier to travel in the second trimester when your body's used to being pregnant and you're not too big to be uncomfortable. Note that no airline really wants you on board when you're eight months pregnant.

Wear comfortable shoes that have arch supports. If you'll be traveling a long time, bring loose clothing (with elastic waistbands) and shoes a half size larger to accommodate your body's changes. Keep your valuables (cash, passport, etc.) in a neck pouch rather than a constricting money belt.

Pace yourself and allow plenty of time for rest. Contact an English-speaking doctor if you become ill; medical care in most European countries is reassuringly good.

Seek out nutritious food (though some of it may make you nauseated, just as in America). Picnics, with drinkable yogurt, are often healthier than smoky restaurant meals. Pack along baggies for carrying snacks. Bring prenatal vitamins from home, plus a calcium supplement if you're not a milk drinker.

It's actually pleasant to be pregnant in Europe. People are particularly kind to you. And when your child is old enough to understand, she'll enjoy knowing she's already been to Europe—especially if you promise to take her again.

TRAVELING SMART

Create conditions that are likely to turn out in your favor. By following these tips, you'll have a safer, smoother, more enjoyable trip.

Be self-reliant so that you don't need to depend on anybody unless you want to. Always carry local cash, food, water, a map, a guidebook, and a phrase book. When you need help, ask another woman or a family.

If you use cash machines, withdraw cash during the day on a busy street, not at night when it's dark with too few people around.

Walk purposefully. Look like you know where you're going. Use landmarks (such as church steeples) to navigate. If you get lost in an unfriendly neighborhood, go into a restaurant or store to ask for directions or to study your map.

Learn enough of the language to get by. With a few hours' work you'll

Resources

Here are a few books you'll find in travel bookstores: *A Journey of One's Own: Uncommon Advice for the Independent Woman Traveler* and *Adventures in Good Company*, both by Thalia Zepatos; *A Woman's World* and *Gutsy Women: Travel Tips and Wisdom for the Road*, both by Marybeth Bond; *Safety and Security for Women Who Travel*, by Sheila Swan and Peter Laufer; *Women Travel* and *More Women Travel*, published by Rough Guides; and *A Foxy Old Woman's Guide to Traveling Alone Around Town and Around the World*, by Jay Ben-Lesser, Crossing Press. Journeywoman shares travel tips through its Web site: www.journeywoman.com. *Passionfruit: A Woman's Travel Journal* prints women's travel stories from around the world (quarterly, $18 per year, 2917 Telegraph Ave. #136, Berkeley, CA 94705, www.passionfruit.com).

---

know more than most tourists and be better prepared to deal with whatever situation arises. At a bus station in Turkey, I witnessed a female tourist repeatedly asking in English, louder and louder, "When does the bus leave?" The frustrated ticket clerk kept answering her in Turkish, "Now, now, now!" If you know even just a little of the language, you'll make it much easier on yourself and those around you.

Before you leave a city, visit the train or bus station you're going to leave from, so you can learn where it is, how long it takes to reach it, and what services it has. Reconfirm your departure time.

On a bus, if you're faced with a choice between an empty double seat and a seat next to a woman, sit with the woman. You've selected your seat partner. Ask her (or the driver) for help if you need it. They will make sure you get off at the right stop.

If you have to hitchhike, choose people to ask, instead of being chosen. Try your luck at a gas station, restaurant, on a ferry, or in the parking lot of a tourist attraction. Ideally, pair up with another traveler.

When taking the train, avoid staying in empty compartments, especially at night. Rent a *couchette* for overnight trains. Ask for a compartment for women (available in Spain and some other countries). For about $20, you'll stay with like-minded roommates in a compartment you can lock, in a car monitored by an attendant. You'll wake reasonably rested with your belongings intact.

Try to arrive at your destination during the day. Daylight feels safer than night. For peace of mind, reserve a room. If you can't avoid a late-night arrival or departure, consider using the waiting room of the train station or airport as your hotel for the night.

If you're not fluent in the language, accept the fact that you won't always know what's going on. There's a reason why the Greek bus driver drops you off in the middle of nowhere. It's a transfer point, and another bus will come along in a few minutes. You'll discover that often the locals are looking out for you.

The same good judgment you use at home applies to Europe. Start out cautious and figure out as you travel what feels safe to you.

Treat yourself right—get enough rest, healthy food, and exercise. Walking is a great way to combine exercise and sightseeing. I've jogged alone in cities and parks throughout Europe without any problems. If a neighborhood looks seedy, head off in another direction.

Relax. There are other trains, other buses, other cities, other people. If one thing doesn't work out, something else will. Thrive on optimism.

Have a grand adventure!

26. Families, Seniors, and Disabled Travelers

FAMILY TRAVEL—FROM TODDLERS TO TEENS
By Rick and Anne Steves

Travels with Baby Andy—Leashes and Valium?
My wife (Anne), seven-year-old (Andy), and VW van (Vinnie) have spent seven one-month trips with me traveling from Norway to Naples and Dublin to Dubrovnik. It's not hell, but it's not terrific travel, either. Still, when he was a baby, it was more fun to change diapers in Paris than Seattle.

Young European families, like their American counterparts, are traveling, babies and all. You'll find more and more kids' menus, hotel playrooms, and kids-go-crazy zones at freeway rest stops all over Europe. And Europeans love babies. You'll also find that babies are great icebreakers—socially and in the Arctic.

You'll need the proper documents. Even babies need passports. If you're traveling with a child that isn't yours (say, a niece or grandson), bring along a signed, notarized document from the parent(s) to prove to authorities that you have permission to take the child on a trip.

An international adventure is a great foundation for a mountain of memories. Here are some of the lessons we learned whining and giggling through Europe with baby, toddler, and little boy, Andy.

Baby Gear

Since a happy baby on the road requires a lot of gear, a key to survival with a baby in Europe is to have a rental car or stay in one place. Of course, pack as light as you can, but if you figure you'll need it, trust your judgment.

Bring a car seat, buy one in Europe, or see if your car rental company can provide one. If you're visiting friends, with enough notice they can often borrow a car seat and a stroller for you. If you'll be driving long hours while the baby sleeps, try to get a car seat that reclines.

A stroller is essential. Umbrella models are lightest, but we found a heavy-duty model with reclining back worth bringing for the baby. Andy could nap in it, and it served as a luggage cart for the Bataan Death March parts of our trip when we had to use public transportation. Carry the stroller onto the plane—you'll need it in the airport. Big wheels handle cobblestones best.

A small travel crib was a godsend. No matter what kind of hotel, pension, or hostel we ended up in, as long as we could clear a four-by-four-foot space on the floor, we'd have a safe, clean, and familiar home for Andy to sleep and play in. During the day we'd salvage a little space by flipping it up on its side and shoving it against the wall.

If a baby backpack works for you at home, bring it to Europe. (I just use my shoulders.) Rucksacks in general are great for parents who wish they had the hands of an octopus. Prepare to tote more than a tot. A combo purse/diaper bag with shoulder straps is ideal. Be on guard: Purse snatchers target mothers (especially while busy and off-guard, as when changing diapers). Remember, in most of Europe a mother with a small child is given great respect. You'll generally be offered a seat on crowded buses and allowed to go to the front of the line at museums.

There's lots more to pack. Encourage bonding to a blanket or stuffed critter and take it along. We used a lot of Heinz dehydrated food dumped into zip-lock baggies. Tiny Tupperware containers with lids were great for crackers, raisins, and snacks. You'll find plenty of disposable diapers, wipes, baby food, and so on in Europe, so don't take the whole works from home. Before you fly away, be sure you've packed ipecac, a decongestant, acetaminophen, and a thermometer. For a toddler, bring a few favorite books and a soft (easy on hotel rooms) ball, and buy little European toys as you go. As Andy got older, activity books and a Sega Game Gear kept him occupied for what might have been countless boring hours. Also, a daily holiday allowance as a reward for assembling a first-class daily picture journal gave our seven-year-old reasons to be enthusiastic about every travel day. (As an older child, his journal projects have grown.)

In case Andy got lost, he wore a metal Medic Alert bracelet that listed his name, address, home phone, an emergency phone number (of our relatives), and any allergies.

Parenting at 32,000 Feet

Gurgling junior might become an airborne Antichrist as soon as the seat-belt light goes off. You'll pay 10 percent of the ticket cost to take a child under the age of two on an international flight. The child doesn't get a seat, but many airlines have flying baby perks for moms and dads who ask for them in advance—roomier bulkhead seats, hang-from-the-ceiling bassinets, and baby meals. After age two, a toddler's ticket costs 75 to 90 percent of the adult fare—a major financial owie. From age 12 on, kids pay full fare. (Railpasses and train tickets are free for kids under age four. Those under 12 ride the rails for half price.)

Ask your pediatrician about sedating your baby for a 10-hour intercontinental flight. We think it's only merciful (for the entire family). Dimetapp, Tylenol, or Pediacare have also worked well for us.

Prepare to be 100 percent self-sufficient throughout the flight. Expect cramped seating and busy attendants. Bring extra clothes (for you and the baby), special toys, and familiar food. Those colored links are handy for attaching toys to the seat, crib, high chairs, jail cells, and so on. The in-flight headphones are great entertainment for flying toddlers.

Landings and takeoffs can be painful for ears of all ages. A bottle, a pacifier, or anything to suck helps equalize the baby's middle-ear pressure. For this reason, nursing moms will be glad they do when it comes to flying. If your kid cries, remember: Crying is a great pressure equalizer.

Once on foreign soil, you'll find

Siena? We love Siena!

that your footloose and see-it-all days of travel are over for a while. Go easy. Traveling with a tyke is tiring, wet, sticky, and smelly. Your mobility plummets.

Be warned—jet lag is nursery purgatory. On his first night in Europe, baby Andy was furious that darkness had bullied daylight out of his up-until-then-reliable 24-hour body clock cycle. Luckily, we were settled in a good hotel (and most of the guests were able to stay elsewhere).

Accommodations

We slept in rooms of all kinds, from hostels (many have family rooms) to hotels. Until he was five, we were never charged for Andy, and while we always use our own bedding, many doubles have a sofa or extra bed that can be barricaded with chairs and used instead of the crib.

Childproof the room immediately on arrival. A roll of masking tape makes quick work of electrical outlets. Anything breakable goes on top of the free-standing closet. Proprietors are generally helpful to considerate and undemanding parents. We'd often store our bottles and milk cartons in their fridge, ask (and pay) for babysitting, and so on.

Every room had a sink where baby Andy could pose for cute pictures, have a little fun, make smelly bubbles, and get clean. With a toddler, budget extra to get a bath in your room—a practical need and a fun diversion. (Many showers have a six-inch-tall "drain extension," enabling you to create a kid-friendly bathing puddle.) Toddlers and campgrounds— with swings, slides, and plenty of friends—mix wonderfully.

Self-catering flats rented by the week or two-week period, such as *gîtes* in France and villas in Italy, give a family a home on the road. Many families prefer settling down this way and side-tripping from a home base.

Food

We found European restaurants and their customers cool to noisy babies. High chairs are rare. We ate happiest at places with outdoor seating; at the many McDonald's-type, baby-friendly fast-food places; or picnicking. In restaurants (or anywhere), if your infant is making a disruptive fuss, apologetically say the local word for "teeth" (*dientes*–Spanish, *dents*–French, *denti*–Italian, *Zahn*–German), and annoyed locals will become sympathetic.

Nursing babies are easiest to feed and travel with. Remember, some cultures are uncomfortable with public breast-feeding. Be sensitive.

We stocked up on munchies (fruit, pretzels, and tiny boxes of juice— which double as squirt guns). A 7 a.m. banana worked wonders, and a 5 p.m. snack made late European dinners workable. In restaurants we ordered an extra plate for Andy, who just nibbled from our meals. We'd

Resources for Traveling with Kids in Europe

Common sense and lessons learned from daytrips at home are your best sources of information. *Take Your Kids to Europe* is full of practical, concrete lessons from firsthand family travel experience, and the only good book I've seen for those traveling with kids ages 6 to 16 (by Cynthia Harriman, Globe Pequot Press, 2001, 320 pages, $17.95 plus $3.95 shipping, tel. 800/

243-0495). The best book we found on traveling with infants was Maureen Wheeler's *Travel with Children* (Lonely Planet Publications). Though designed for Asian travel, it has good advice for Europe-bound parents. Cadogan now offers six worthwhile books in its *Take the Kids* series covering Amsterdam, England, Ireland, London, Paris, and general travel tips. Or consider Fodor's new guides, *Around London with Kids* and *Around Paris with Kids*.

order "fizzy" (but not sticky) mineral water, call it "pop," and the many spills were no problem. With all the candy and sweet temptations at toddler eye level in Europe, you can forget a low-sugar diet. While gelati and pastries are expensive, Andy's favorite suckers, Popsicles, and hollow, chocolate, toy-filled eggs were cheap and available everywhere.

Plan to spend more money. Use taxis rather than buses and subways. Hotels can get babysitters, usually from professional agencies. The service is expensive but worth the splurge when you crave a leisurely, peaceful evening *sans* bibs and cribs.

With a baby, we arranged our schedule around naps and sleep time. A well-rested child is worth the limitation. Driving while Andy siestaed worked well. As a toddler, however, Andy was up very late, playing soccer with his new Italian friends on the piazza or eating huge ice creams in the hotel kitchen with the manager's kids. We gave up on a rigid naptime or bedtime, and we enjoyed Europe's evening ambience as a family.

OK, you're there—watered, fed, and only a little bleary. Europe is your cultural playpen, a living fairy tale, a sandbox of family fun and adventure. Grab your kid and dive in.

A DECADE LATER: TRAVELING WITH TEENS IN EUROPE

When our kids were still in their single digits, our family travel was consumed with basic survival issues, such as eating and sleeping. Now that Andy is 14 and Jackie is 11, the big challenges are making our trips educational and fun. Our kids are at the age when traveling with mom and dad isn't cool, friends at home are the preferred vacation partners, and being told to "get in the car, we're going on an airplane today" no longer works.

Children in middle school feel that summer break is a vacation they've earned. If this European trip is not their trip...you become the enemy. Ask for their help. Kids can even get excited about a vacation if they're involved in the planning stages. Consider your child's suggestions and make real concessions. "Europe's greatest collection of white-knuckle rides" in Blackpool might be more fun than another ruined abbey. Remember to take it easy at the beginning of your trip, allowing a couple of low-impact days to get over jet lag.

Pretrip study helps get children tuned into and prepared for upcoming experiences. Read books such as *The Diary of Anne Frank* for Amsterdam. Watch movies together such as *The Sound of Music* for Salzburg, and *Brother Sun,*

What's more fun: A museum or Disneyland Paris?

Sister Moon for Assisi. Get a jump on the phrases, learning the top 20 or so before you leave home. Practice at home, wishing your children a cheery *bonjour*, and asking them for a city map, a room with private bath, or well-done meat.

Since a trip is a splurge for the parents, the kids should enjoy a larger allowance, too. Provide ample money and ask your kids to buy their own treats, gelati, batteries, and trinkets within that daily budget. In exchange for the extra allowance, require them to keep a daily journal or scrapbook. Help your kids collect and process their observations. Bring tape, a glue stick, and scissors from home. But if you buy the actual journal at your first stop, it becomes a fun souvenir in itself. Kids like cool books—pay for a nice one. The journal is important, and it should feel that way. Encourage the kids to record more than just a trip log...collect feelings, smells, reactions to cultural differences, and so on.

With older kids, mom and dad have much more freedom. Kids can go to the breakfast room early or late. If they don't want to go out for the evening, they can stay in the hotel. Nearly all rooms have TVs (although be careful, many have pornography channels right next to Monsieur Rogers). To pass time enjoyably with a soothing touch of home, our kids each pack a Gameboy and CD player.

Review the day's plan at breakfast. It should always include a kid-friendly activity. Hands-on tours from cheese making to chocolate factories keep kids engaged. Go to sports or cultural events, but don't insist on staying for the entire event.

Kids need plenty of exercise. Allow time for a few extra runs on the luge. Small towns often have great public swimming pools. And mountain bikes are easily rentable (with helmets), suddenly making the Alps cool.

Help your kids connect with children their own age. Staying in B&Bs or small guesthouses, you'll find it's easy to hook up with other traveling families. When visiting with Europeans, be careful to work your children into the conversation—easier if meeting other families. In hot climates, kids hang out on the squares when it's cooler, until late in the evening. Take your children to the European nightspots to observe—if not actually make—the scene (such as the rollerbladers at Trocadero in Paris or the crowd at Rome's Trevi Fountain). Small-town pubs in Britain and Ireland welcome kids and are filled with family-friendly social opportunities. Many times our children have enjoyed playing pool or throwing darts with new friends in a pub.

Internet cafés and e-mail allow kids to keep in touch with their neighborhood friends and European pals they met on their trip. While Anne and I lingered over a glass of wine or dessert, our kids would run across the street to an Internet café.

Make the consequences of packing heavy perfectly clear—they carry all their stuff all the time. Help your kids pack layers for warmth, clothes that don't show dirt, and sturdy, well-broken-in shoes. Each person should have a day bag for ready access in the car (it keeps down clutter). Stock the car with a trunk pantry for snacks, water, and picnics.

While the train is workable with older kids, we still prefer family vacations by car. With a car, we enjoy doorstep-to-doorstep service with our luggage and can be a little bolder about coming into town without a reserved room. I delegate navigating responsibilities to our kids. Following a map to help dad drive through a new town or leading the family back to the hotel on the Paris metro is a great confidence builder.

An occasional Big Mac or Whopper between all the bratwurst and kraut helps keep our family happy. In a village, we let the kids find dinner on their own. We were in Austria the first time we did this—our kids couldn't believe we'd actually abandon them this way. After Anne and I gave them enough money for pizza and a drink, we took off for a romantic adults-only dinner under the floodlit abbey with a view of the Danube. Our children had no choice but to use their few

Picking green peppers off their pizzas, our kids discover that in Europe, "pepperoni" doesn't mean spicy sausage.

German words and a phrase book, sort through a menu on their own, deal with the waiter, and be careful they understood the bill and had enough money. They did wonderfully and used their spare change to buy ice cream down the street.

In a crowded situation, having a unique family noise (a whistle or call, such as a "woo-woop" sound) enables you to easily get each other's attention. Consider packing walkie-talkies to help you relax when the kids roam. Older children can wear money belts with photocopies of their passport and hotel information.

Most hotels have large family rooms. You need to know the necessary phrases to communicate your needs. When our children were younger, we requested a triple room plus a small extra child's bed. Now we get two rooms for our family of four: A double (one big bed) and a twin (a room with two single beds). In much of Europe a "double" bed is actually two twins put together. These can easily be separated.

Families can hostel very cheaply. Family membership cards are cheap, and there's no age limit except a maximum of 26 in Bavaria (waived for adults traveling with their children). Many hostels have "members' kitchens" where the family can cook for the price of groceries.

Although we enjoy traveling with our family, we've also gone to Europe

without them. Consider leaving your
kids with a trusted family member
or friend, then spending half your
vacation in Europe and the other
half with your kids doing fun activities in your state. See what works
best for you and your kids.

Our two best family trips have
been in Italy and the Alps. Our Italy
trip featured five days in Venice (in
an apartment in the town center) followed by four days in the Cinque
Terre (a Riviera wonderland for

Getting goofy on the Alps

kids). Our 20-daytrip across the Alps—from Vienna to Zurich—included
a few museums and lots of outdoor fun.

Living on the road far from their favorite TV shows and neighborhood friends has broadened our children's outlook. They've learned what
all travelers know: The size of your backyard is up to you.

SAVVY SENIORS

More people than ever are hocking their rockers and buying plane tickets. Many senior adventurers are proclaiming, "Age matters only if you're
a cheese." Travel is their fountain of youth.

I'm not a senior—yet, so I put an appeal on the Graffiti Wall of my
Web site (www.ricksteves.com/graffiti) asking seniors to share their advice.
Thanks to the many who responded, here's a summary of top tips from
seniors who believe it's never too late to have a happy childhood.

Packing: Bring a backpack with wheels or a rolling
suitcase. Whichever you use,
pack light. When you pack
light, you're younger. Two
tops, a pair of lightweight
pants, good shoes, a couple
of changes of underwear and
socks, and you're set. It's
easier to wash out your
clothes in your hotel room
at night than to carry a big
backpack all day.

When to Go: Consider

Their fountain of youth is Europe!

traveling in shoulder season (April, May, September, October). The most exhausting things about European travel are the crowds and heat of summer.

Airports: If you're not flying direct, check your bag—because if you have to transfer to a connecting flight at a huge, busy airport, your carry-on bag will become a lug-around drag. If you're a slow walker, ask the airline or stewardess if they/she can arrange transportation for you to easily make your next flight.

Accommodations: Request a ground-floor room if stairs are a problem. Different locations and types of accommodations offer different advantages. If you stay near the train station, you'll minimize carrying your bag. If you stay outside the big cities and travel in for the day, your hotel room (in the suburbs or nearby small town) will likely be quieter, bigger, and cheaper, with fewer stairs and more ground-floor options. To save money, try hostels, which offer the bonus of ready-made friends. To really relax, rent a cottage, condo, or flat for a week or more. You can settle down and stay awhile, doing side trips if you choose.

Senior Discounts: Just showing your gray hair or passport snares you a discount on many sights and even some events such as concerts. You can get deals on point-to-point rail tickets in Scandinavia, Austria, France, and more (including the Eurostar Chunnel crossing between Britain and France). To get rail discounts in some countries such as Britain, you need to purchase a senior card at a minimal cost at a local train station (don't be put off if these cards are valid for a year—you can save money even on a short trip). Railpasses for Britain, Scandinavia, and the Netherlands give seniors a discount.

City Transportation: Subways involve a lot of walking and stairs (and are a pain with luggage). Consider using city buses or taxis instead. With lots of luggage, definitely take a taxi (better yet, pack light).

Sightseeing: Many museums have elevators—even if these are freight elevators not open to the public, people bend the rules for older travelers. Take advantage of the benches in museums; sit down frequently to enjoy the art and rest your feet. Go late in the day for no crowds and cooler temperatures. Take bus tours (usually 2 hours long) for a painless overview of the highlights. Boat tours—of the harbor, river, lake, or fjord—are a

Resources for Seniors

Good books include *No Problem! Worldwise Tips for Mature Travelers* (by Janice Kenyon; Orca Book Publishers) and *Unbelievably Good Deals and Great Adventures That You Absolutely Can't Get Unless You're Over 50* (by Joan Rattner Heilman; Contemporary Books). You'll find good travel tips at www.retired.com.

Elderhostel, which offers study programs around the world for those over 55, will send you a free catalog listing their educational curriculum, varying in length from one to four weeks (tel. 877/ 426-8056, 11 Avenue de LaFayette, Boston, MA 02111-1746, www.elderhostel.org).

pleasure. Hire an English-speaking cabbie to take you on a tour of a city or region (if it's hot, spring for an air-conditioned taxi). If you're traveling with others but need a rest break, set up a rendezvous point. For easy sightseeing, grab a table at a sidewalk café for a drink and people-watching.

Keep a Record: As you travel, record your experiences on a microcassette recorder to transcribe when you get home. A journal helps capture your trip. Reread, relive, recharge—plan your next trip!

Excerpts from "Senior Savvy" on the Graffiti Wall at www.ricksteves.com

"London is a very good deal for the over-60 crowd. Ask for the senior rate at museums, theaters, and so on. In quite a few places we got reduced rates and, in several, admission was free. You will have to show proof of age."

"On our last trip to Europe we smiled and politely asked if the establishment offered a senior discount, even when it was not posted that one was available. In nearly every instance we got one. Sometimes it saved us as much as half price. Don't be afraid to ask, but remember to smile."

"We just returned from a wonderful trip to Germany with my 79-year-old mother-in-law. It soon became apparent that she was having trouble realizing the fact that we "weren't in Kansas" anymore. My tip to seniors: Please keep an open mind. Your hotel accommodations may not provide washcloths, Kleenex, or more than one wastebasket. If you don't expect things to be like they are in the States, you'll have a much better time and so will your traveling companions."

"There's always one consolation: Whatever you are experiencing will turn out to be a good story. The night in Paris six million rollerbladers skated past our windows at midnight is a wonderful memory, but at the time I was wishing for some boiling oil."

"Don't even consider taking luggage on London's Tube…too many ups and downs on the stairs when you have to change trains. Take a taxi!"

"My wife and I, both seniors, took a tour of Spain, Morocco, and Portugal. After the long transatlantic flight and a day of riding in the bus, my wife's ankles swelled up appreciably. According to the tour guide, this is not unusual. She had my wife keep her legs high the next two nights (by putting a bolster pillow under the foot end of the mattress) and drinking lots of water both days. The swelling was gone by the second day. Moral: Drink lots of water on the way over and during each day!"

"For peace of mind, compile a checklist of all the things you need to do to get your house ready before leaving on vacation. Then, check off the items and take the list with you. This way there is no worrying, 'Did I turn off the stove?'"

"Carry a small notebook to write down things to remember: train reservations to be made, events you want to later record in your journal, and so on."

"Those of us over-60s traveling by train in Great Britain can take advantage of their Senior Railcard obtainable from the station agent for £18 (valid for one year). The 33 percent savings on most rail fares quickly justifies the cost."

"I took my 80-ish mother to London for Christmas. I got excellent help from the Holiday Care Service in London. I found them through the British Tourist Authority Web site: www.bta.org.uk. Click on the link for 'Travellers with disabilities.'"

"At 65+ with bad backs, we hired a taxi in Sorrento to take us sightseeing in Positano, Amalfi, and Ravello, a $150 splurge that was worth every cent."

"Hiking around Loch Lomond, we stopped at a garden shop, where we purchased two long, inexpensive gardening stakes. The salesman kindly cut the sticks off to an appropriate length for each of us & whittled the ends into points. These made perfect walking sticks for the 100-mile trek, and we were delighted to be able to donate them to the last B&B owner where we stayed in Fort William the last night. He was happy to have them for his garden! From now on, we'll leave our walking sticks behind and check out the local gardening stores instead!"

"My partner and I stayed in a 'youth' hostel for the first time by Lake Como and thought we'd be the oldest people there. Not so! This was the wonderful La Primula hostel near Menaggio, Italy, which offers a spectacular view of the lake while you're dining on great food on their outdoor patio. At our table was a 60ish couple from Sydney and a 79-year-old British woman who was backpacking alone through Europe! All three were a delight, but especially the backpacker, who said she stays in hostels for the evening company."

"I went on a trip with a piece of small luggage that also converts into a backpack. I'm in good shape, walk every day, and watch what I eat, but I'm 64 and the backpack eventually made my shoulders ache. The pain lasted for several months. I will use wheeled luggage from now on. I know Rick doesn't like the rolling suitcases, but he isn't 65 yet, so he'll learn."

TRAVELERS WITH DISABILITIES TAKE ON THE WORLD
Thanks to Susan Sygall from Mobility International USA for this article.

More and more people with disabilities are heading to Europe, and more of us are looking for the Back Door routes. We, like so many of our nondisabled peers, want to get off the tourist track and experience the real France, Italy, or Portugal. Yes, that includes those of us who use wheelchairs. I've been traveling the "Rick Steves' way" since about 1973—and here are some of my best tips.

Susan Sygall, on Italy's Cinque Terre

I use a lightweight manual wheelchair with pop-off tires. I take a backpack that fits on the back of my chair and store my daypack underneath my chair in a net bag. Since I usually travel alone, if I can't carry it myself, I don't take it. I keep a bungee cord with me for the times I can't get my chair into a car and need to strap it in the trunk or when I need to secure it on a train. I always insist on keeping MY OWN wheelchair up to the airline gate where I then check it at the gate. When I have a connecting flight I again insist that I use my own chair.

Bathrooms are always a hassle so I have learned to use creative ways to transfer into narrow bathrooms. To be blatantly honest, when there are no accessible bathrooms in sight I have found ways to pee discreetly just about anywhere (outside the Eiffel Tower or on a glacier in a national park). You gotta do what you gotta do, and hopefully one day the access will improve, but in the meantime there is a world out there to be discovered. Bring along an extra pair of pants and a great sense of humor.

I always try to learn some of the language of the country I'm in because it cuts through the barriers when people stare at you (and they will) and also comes in handy when you need assistance in going up a curb or a flight of steps. Don't accept other people's notions of what is possible—I have climbed Masada in Israel and made it to the top of the Acropolis in Greece.

If a museum lacks elevators for visitors, be sure to ask about freight elevators. Almost all have them somewhere, and that can be your ticket to seeing a world-class treasure.

I always get information about disability groups where I am going. See the resources listed at the end of this article for a number of organizations to try. They will have the best access information, and many times they will become your new traveling partners and friends. They can show you the best spots. Remember that you are part of a global family of disabled people.

It can be helpful to contact tourism offices and local transit providers before you travel. Some even include information about accessibility for people with disabilities on their Web sites.

Each person with a disability has her/his own unique needs and interests. Many of my friends use power wheelchairs, or are blind or deaf, or have other disabilities—they all have their own unique travel tips. People who have difficulty walking long distances might want to think of taking or borrowing a sports wheelchair when needed. Whether you travel alone, with friends, or with an assistant, you're in for a great adventure.

Don't confuse being flexible and having a positive attitude with settling for less than your rights. I expect equal access and constantly let people know about the possibility of providing access through ramps or other modifications. When I believe my rights have been violated, I do whatever is necessary to remedy the situation so the next traveler, or disabled people in that country, won't have the same frustrations.

Know your rights as a traveler with a disability. For information regarding travel on U.S. airlines, get the free book *New Horizons: Information for the Air Traveler with a Disability* from the Paralyzed Veterans of America (tel. 888/860-7244, www.pva.org). For more information about your rights, download the *Air Carrier Access Act: Make It Work For You* (www.pva.org). If, under the Americans with Disabilities Act or Air Carrier Access Act, you feel you have been discriminated against (such as not being allowed on a U.S. tour company's tour of Europe), contact the Disability Rights Education and Defense Fund (tel. 800/466-4232 voice and TTY, www.dredf.org).

If you are interested in short-term work, study, research, or volunteering abroad, contact the National Clearinghouse on Disability and Exchange at Mobility International USA (tel. 541/343-1284 voice and TTY, www.miusa.org, e-mail: clearinghouse@miusa.org). Get online and do some investigating. Search for "travel" and "disability."

Hopefully more books like Rick's will include basic access information—which will allow everyone to see Europe through the Back Door. Let's work toward making that door accessible so we can all be there together.

ADDITIONAL RESOURCES

Mobility International USA (MIUSA) sponsors international exchange programs for the disabled, offers membership ($35, includes biannual newsletter), and sells a handy book entitled *A World of Options: A Guide to International Educational Exchange, Community Service, and Travel for Persons with Disabilities* (600 pages, $35 postpaid, P.O. Box 10767, Eugene, OR 97440, tel. 541/343-1284 voice and TTY, www.miusa.org, e-mail: info@miusa.org).

The **National Clearinghouse on Disability and Exchange** (NCDE) helps people with disabilities find out about work, study, volunteer, and research opportunities abroad. NCDE sells a video (*All Abroad!*, $49 postpaid) and publishes the free journal, *A World Awaits You*, about exchange programs for people with disabilities (tel. 541/343-1284 voice and TTY, www.miusa.org).

The **Society for Accessible Travel and Hospitality** (SATH), a non-profit membership organization, publishes a travel magazine and offers travel advice ($45 membership, $30 for students and seniors, includes magazine; $13 for magazine subscription only; tel. 212/447-SATH, fax 212/725-8253, www.sath.org, e-mail: sathtravel@aol.com).

Access Able Travel Source sponsors a useful Web site (www.access-able.com) with access information and resources for travelers with disabilities, as well as a free e-mail newsletter (P.O. Box 1796, Wheat Ridge, CO 80034, tel. 303/232-2979, e-mail: carol@access-able.com). Access Able also runs **Travelin' Talk**, a global organization of disabled people that provides information and assistance to members visiting other members' home

towns ($19.95 lifetime registration fee per family, tel. 303/232-2979, www
.travelintalk.net, e-mail: info@travelintalk.net).

Servas, an organization that enables travelers to stay with families in
other countries, welcomes disabled travelers. Some European Servas
branches list accessibility, or contact your host in advance to ask ($65/year
membership, 11 John Street, #505, New York, NY 10038, tel. 212/267-
0252, fax 212/267-0292, www.usservas.org, e-mail: info@usservas.org).

Hostelling International indicates in its guides which hostels are
accessible (tel. 202/783-6161, www.hiayh.org).

Books: Read firsthand travel accounts in Patrick Simpson's *Wheelchair
Around the World,* which includes an extensive bibliography to help physically challenged travelers plan their own trip ($29.50 postpaid, Pentland Press,
5122 Bur Oak Circle, Raleigh, NC 27612, tel. 919/782-0281). For specifics,
Fodor's Gold Guides always have a section on travel for the disabled.

Tours: If you're interested in taking a tour, these companies offer international travel for the disabled: Accessible Journeys (35 W. Sellers Ave., Rid-
ley Park, PA 19078, tel. 800/846-4537, www.disabilitytravel.com, e-mail:
sales@disabilitytravel.com), Flying Wheels Travel (P.O. Box 382, Owatonna,
MN 55060, tel. 800/535-6790, e-mail: thq@ll.net), and Nautilus Tours and
Cruises (22567 Ventura Blvd., Woodland Hills, CA 91364, tel. 800/797-
6004 outside California, or tel. 818/591-3159, www.nautilustours.com).

Web sites: Several sites offer lists and databases about disability organizations and resources around the world. The **European Union** has
information about accessibility, facilities, tour operators, travel agents,
and more (http://europa.eu.int/comm/enterprise/services/tourism/tourism
-publications/documents/guides.htm). For specific concerns, visit **Reha-
bilitation International** (www.rehab-international.org/directory.html),
the **World Blind Union** (http://umc.once.es/member.htm), the **Royal
National Institute of the Blind** (http://info.rnib.org.uk/Agencies
/allagencies.htm), the **Royal National Institute for the Deaf** (www
.rnid.org.uk/html/info_directory.htm), and the **World Federation of the
Deaf** (www.wfdnews.org/intro/local/index.asp). For a list of **diabetes**
organizations around the world, visit www.childrenwithdiabetes.com
/d_09_800.htm.

27. Bus Tour Self-Defense

Average American tourists see Europe on an organized bus tour and don't
even consider using a guidebook. They pay a guide to show them around.

I'm going to lambaste big bus tours here for a few pages. But first I want
to mention that there are cute little tour companies (like mine) that have a

passion for a particular angle on European travel. By effectively tapping into the efficiency and economy of group travel, they put together a package that is both profitable to them and a good value to the right customer. (We limit the size of our fully guided tours to 26 and provide two guides.)

Many who take an organized bus tour could have managed fine on their own.

But I want to discuss your typical, impossibly cheap, 49-persons-on-a-49-seat-bus tours that are heavily advertised and sold by travel agents for at least a 10 percent commission. These can be a good value, but only if you know how they work.

By understanding the tour business, you can take advantage of a big bus tour, and it won't take advantage of you. Many savvy travelers take escorted coach tours year after year only for the hotels, meals, and transportation provided. Every day they do their own sightseeing, simply applying the skills of independent travel to the efficient, economical trip shell an organized coach tour provides. You can take a tour, and, to a limited degree, still go "on your own."

A typical big bus tour has a professional multilingual European guide and 40 to 50 people on board. The tour company is probably very big, booking rooms by the thousand and often even owning the hotels it uses. Typically, the bus is a luxurious, fairly new 49-seater with a high, quiet ride, comfy seats, air-conditioning, and a toilet on board.

The hotels will fit American standards—large, not too personal, and offering mass-produced comfort, good plumbing, and double rooms. Your hotel's location can make the difference between a fair trip and a great trip. Beware if the tour brochure says you'll be sleeping in the "Florence area"—you may be stuck in the middle of nowhere halfway to Bologna. If this is important to you, get explicit locations in writing before your trip. Most meals are included, generally unmemorable buffets that hotel restaurants require large groups to take. The prices are driven to almost inedible lows by the tour company. A common complaint among tourists is that hotel meals don't match the local cuisine.

Your guide will be happy to spoon-feed Europe to you, but it will be from his or her menu. The sights you'll see are often chosen for their convenience, distorting their importance. Many tours seem to make a big deal

Shopping for Tours

When calling tour companies, here are questions to ask:

Nail down the price.
- What does the price actually include? (How many nights and days? How many meals? Admission to sights? All transportation, including the flight and any ferries or trains?)
- If the tour does not fill up, will the price increase? Are prices lower for off-season tours?
- Do you take credit cards? (A credit-card company can be a strong ally in resolving disputes.)
- Do singles pay a supplement? Can singles request to share rooms?
- Are optional excursions offered? Daily? Average cost?
- Is trip interruption/cancellation insurance included?
- Will the guide and driver expect to be tipped? How much? How often?
- Are there any other costs?
- Do customers receive any freebies for signing up?

Find out how much the guide guides.
- Is the guide also the driver?
- Does the guide give talks on the cities, history, and art?
- What are the guide's qualifications (education, experience, fluency in languages)?

out of a statue in Luzern called the *Dying Lion*, and obedient tourists are impressed on command. The guide declares that this mediocre-at-best sight is great, and that's how it's perceived. What makes it "great" for the guide is that Luzern (which has a hotel the tour company owns but not a lot of interesting sights) was given too much time in the itinerary, and the *Dying Lion* has easy tour bus parking. However, Florence's Uffizi Gallery—with its superb collection of Italian Renaissance art—is often passed over, because its mandatory reservation system makes it inconvenient.

Remember, you can't take 49 people into a "cozy" pub and be cozy. A good stop for a guide is one with great freeway accessibility and bus parking; where guides and drivers are buttered up with free coffee and cakes; where they speak English and accept bank cards; and where 49 people can go to the bathroom at the same time. *Arrivederci, Roma.*

Run a reality check on your dream trip.
- How many tour members will be on the tour?
- Roughly what is the average age and singles-to-couples ratio?
- Are children allowed? What is the minimum age?
- How many seats on the bus? Is there a bathroom on the bus?
- Is smoking allowed?
- Roughly how many hours a day are spent shopping and watching product demonstrations?
- How much free time is usually allotted at each sight, museum, and city?
- Are all the hotels located downtown or are they on the outskirts?
- What's the average length of stay at hotels? One night? Two?
- Does each room have a private bathroom? Air-conditioning?
- What percentage of included meals are eaten at the hotel?

Let's get personal.
- How many years have you been in business?
- Roughly how many tours do you run a year?
- What is your policy if you have to cancel a tour?
- What are your refund policies before and during the tour?

Request:
- The detailed itinerary and location of hotels.
- The names and numbers of satisfied customers.
- Written tour evaluations (if available).

As long as people on board don't think too much or try to deviate from the plan, things go smoothly and reliably, and you really do see a lot of Europe. Note I said "see" rather than "experience." Having escorted several large European coach tours and now owning and operating a tour company of my own, I've learned that you must understand tour guides and their position. Leading a tour is a demanding job with lots of responsibility, paperwork, babysitting, and miserable hours. Very often, guides are tired. They're away from home and family, often for months on end, and are surrounded by foreigners having an extended party that they're probably not in the mood for. Most guides treasure their time alone and, except for romantic side trips, keep their distance from the group socially. Each tourist has personal demands, and a group of 49 can often amount to one big pain in the bus for the guide.

To most guides, the best group is one that lets him do the thinking, is happy to be herded around, and enjoys being spoon-fed Europe.

There are two different ways that a guide is paid: The company pays the guide a low base salary (about $70 a day) that he supplements with a percentage of the optional excursions (daily outings sold to passengers), kickbacks (from merchants that the group patronizes), and trip-end tips from the busload. OR the guide pays the company (a maximum of $240) to let her guide the tour, and she keeps all the money that comes from excursions, kickbacks, and tips. Either way, an experienced guide can make $300 to $500 a day.

The best-selling tours are the ones that promise you the most in the time you have available. But no tour can give you more than 24 hours in a day or seven days in a week. What the "blitz" tour can do is give you more hours on the bus. Choose carefully among the itineraries available. Do you really want a series of one-night stands? Bus drivers call tours with ridiculous itineraries "pajama tours." You're in the bus from 8 a.m. until after dark, so why even get dressed?

HOW TO ENJOY A BUS TOUR

Keep your guide happy. Independent-type tourists tend to threaten guides. It's important to be independent without alienating them. Don't insist on individual attention when the guide is hounded by 48 others. Wait for the quiet moment to ask for advice. If a guide wants to, he can give his entire group a lot of unrequired extras—but only if he wants to. Your objective, which requires some artistry, is to keep the guide on your side without letting him take advantage of you.

Discriminate among options. While some activities are included (such as the half-day city sightseeing tours), each day one or two special excursions or evening activities, called "options," are offered for $30 to $40 a day. Each person decides which options to take and pay for. To make sure you're not being ripped off on excursion prices, ask your hotelier the going rate for a gondola ride, Seine River cruise, or whatever.

Some options are great, others are not worth the time or money. Illuminated night tours of Rome and Paris are marvelous. I'd skip most "nights on the town." On a typical big-bus tour evening, several bus tours come together for the "evening of local color." Three hundred Australian, Japanese, and American tourists drinking sangria and watching flamenco dancing onstage to the rhythm of their automatic rewinds isn't exactly local.

Maintain your independence. Your guide promotes excursions because she profits from it. Don't feel pressured to buy. You are capable of doing plenty on your own. Bring research from home. Tour guides hate guidebooks. They call the dreaded tourist with a guidebook an "informed passenger." But a guidebook is *your* key to travel freedom. Get maps and tourist information from your (or another) hotel desk or a tourist information office. Tour hotels are often located outside the city, where they cost the tour company less and where they figure you are more likely to book the options just to get into town. Ask the

A well-chosen tour can be a fine value, giving you a great trip and a busload of new friends.

person behind the desk how to get downtown using public transportation. Taxis are always a possibility, and, with three or four people sharing, they're affordable. Team up with others on your tour to explore on your own. No city is dead after the shops are closed. Go downtown and stroll.

Don't let your guide intimidate you. In Amsterdam guides are instructed to spend time in the diamond polishing place and not to visit the Van Gogh Museum (no kickbacks on van Gogh). If you want to skip out, your guide will warn you that you'll get lost and the bus won't wait. Keep your travel spirit off its leash and the hotel address in your money belt.

If you shop, shop around. Many people make their European holiday one long shopping spree. This suits your guide and the local tourist industry just fine. Guides are quick to say, "If you haven't bought a Rolex, you haven't really been to Switzerland," or "You can't say you've experienced Florence if you haven't bargained for and bought a leather coat." In Venice, as I orient my groups, merchants are tugging at my arm and whispering, "Bring your groups to *our* glassworks next time. We'll give you 15 percent back on whatever they spend—and a free glass horse!"

Cruise ships don't pay for their Turkish guides. Cruise companies rent their groups out to the local guide who bids the most. That "scholar" who meets you at the dock is actually a carpet salesman in disguise. He'll take you to the obligatory ancient site and then to the carpet shop.

Every tour guide in Europe knows just where to park the bus in Luzern for Swiss clocks. After the shopping spree, the guide steps into the back room and gets a percentage of whatever went into the till. That's good business. And any tour guide in Europe knows that if she's got Americans on board, she's carting around a busload of stark raving shoppers.

Despite this arrangement, don't necessarily reject your guide's shopping tips; just keep in mind that the prices you see often include a 10 to 20 percent kickback. Never swallow the line, "This is a special price available only to your tour, but you must buy now." The sellers who prey on tour buses are smooth. They zero in on the gullible group member who falls for a "good" buy instead of saying "good-bye."

The demonstrations (by carpet sellers, glass merchants, etc.) are usually interesting. Use your new-found knowledge from the demonstration to shop around; you may find an item of equal quality for less elsewhere. Bargain.

Spend time with locals who never deal with tourists. The only locals most tour groups see are hardened business people who know how to make money off tour groups. Going through Italy in a flock of 49 Americans following your tour guide's umbrella, you'll meet all the wrong Italians. Break away. One summer night in Regensburg, I skipped out. While my tour was still piling off the bus, I enjoyed a beer overlooking the Danube and under shooting stars with the great-great-great-grandson of the astronomer Johannes Kepler.

PERSPECTIVES

28. Political Unrest

An awareness of current social and political problems is as vital to smart travel as a listing of top sights. As some popular destinations are entertaining tourists with "sound and light" shows in the old town, they're quelling terrorist and separatist movements in the new. Countries from Great Britain to Italy are dealing with serious or potentially serious internal threats.

Newspaper headlines shape many trips. Many people skip Northern Ireland because of "the troubles," avoid Spain in fear of the militant Basques, and refuse to fly out of Athens or Frankfurt because of a bomb attack years ago. This is like avoiding a particular mall in the United States because it had a robbery last month. Don't let these problems shape your itinerary. Stay up on the news and exercise common sense (don't sing Catholic songs in Ulster pubs). You can travel safely and still experience firsthand the demographic chaos that explains much of what fills the front pages of our newspapers.

Travel broadens your perspective, enabling you to rise above the 6 p.m. entertainment we call news and see things as a citizen of our world. While monuments from the past are worthy of your sightseeing energy, travel can also plug you directly into the present.

There are many peoples fighting the same thrilling battles we Americans won 200 years ago, and, while your globe may paint Turkey orange and Iran green, racial, linguistic, and religious groups rarely color within the lines.

Look beyond the beaches and hotels in your tourist brochures for background on how your vacation target's cultural, racial, and religious makeup is causing problems today or may bring grief tomorrow. With this foundation and awareness, you can enjoy the nearly unavoidable opportunities to talk with involved locals about complex current situations. If you're looking to talk politics, you must be approachable—on your own or away from your tour.

Like it or not, people around the world look at "capitalist Americans" as the kingpins of a global game of Monopoly. (Among deaf people, the international sign language symbol for "American" is the "fat cat"—holding your arms around an imaginary big belly.) Make this a political sightseeing plus by striking up conversations. Young, well-dressed people are most likely to speak (and want to speak) English. Universities are the perfect place to solve the world's problems in English with a liberal, open-minded foreigner over a government-subsidized cafeteria lunch.

Understand a country's linguistic divisions. It's next to impossible to keep everyone happy in a multilingual country. Switzerland has four languages, but *Deutsch ist über alles.* In Belgium there's tension between the Dutch- and French-speaking halves. Like many French Canadians, Europe's linguistic underdogs will tell you their language receives equal treatment only on cornflakes boxes, and many are working on adjustments.

In Ireland "the troubles" are kept at least simmering. At any pub in the Emerald Isle, you'll get an earful of someone's passionate feelings. In Russia and Eastern Europe, whenever you want some political or economic gossip, sit alone in a café. After a few minutes and some eye contact, you'll have company and a fascinating chat.

After your smashingly successful European adventure, you'll graduate to more distant cultural nooks and geographic crannies. If you mistakenly refer to a Persian or Iranian as Arabic, you'll get a stern education on the distinction; and in eastern Turkey you'll learn more about that fiercely nationalistic group of people called Kurds, who won't rest until that orange and green on the globe is divided by a hunk of land called Kurdistan.

TERRORISM

I'd rather not discuss terrorism. But I'm concerned that people are planning their trips thinking they can slip over there and back while there's a lull in the action. There's always been terrorism, and there always will be terrorism. It's in your interest, psychologically, to plan your trip assuming there will be a terrorist event sometime between now and your departure date—most likely in the city into which you're flying. Because, sure enough, as soon as you buy your plane ticket to London, the IRA's going to blow up another pub, and your loved ones will leap into action (as if they've already had a meeting) trying to get you to cancel your trip.

The real enemy: Loved ones and the TV. Your loved ones' hearts are in the right place. But their minds aren't. Your trip's too important for sensationalism and hysteria to get in the way. Understand the risk of

---

Calming Loved Ones with Statistics as You Travel in an Age of Terror

From 1990 to 1999, Americans made about 190 million trips overseas. During that time (according to the State Department's counterterrorism office), fewer than 90 Americans were killed by terrorists. In 2000, Western Europe had the largest decline in international terrorist incidents of any region in the world.

Chance of an American overseas or in the air being killed by a terrorist: 1 in 2,200,000

Chance of being hit by lightning: 1 in 600,000

Chance you'll be killed by a fire this year: 1 in 70,900

Chance you'll be killed by a gun this year: 1 in 18,900

Deaths per year in the U.S.:

  43,600 in car accidents

  14,000 by handguns (vs. less than 100 a year in Britain, France, or Germany)

  3,200 choking on food

  300 pedestrians a year killed by drivers on the streets of Paris

  19 Americans killed by terrorists in 2000 (17 were sailors who died in the attack on the *U.S.S. Cole* in Yemen)

(*Sources: National Safety Council, Tourism Industries-Department of Commerce, and U.S. Department of State*)

---

terrorism in a cold, logical, statistical way. (You take many greater risks without even considering them when you travel.) If you want to take that risk, travel in a way that minimizes that tiny threat. Let me explain.

Terrorism is tailor-made for TV—quick, emotional, and gruesome 90-second spots. Consider the emotional style in which terrorism is covered and how expertly terrorists are milking that, even providing TV news broadcasts with video footage. It's quaint to think that our news media is interested in anything other than ratings and selling advertising. Terrorism sells ads big time. TV news—with the least sophisticated and most lucrative audience—is worst.

Loved ones often take TV news to heart, lack a broad understanding of the world, and may stand between us and our travel dreams—begging and even bribing us not to go. If I'm in Europe and there's a boat hijacked or a train wreck in Italy, I always call to let my mother know I survived. Assure those who'll worry about you that you'll call home every few days. If you're a teenager with worrying parents, hit them up for a $1 per 30-second "I'm doing fine" call, and call home regularly.

Traveling safely. Talking to people about local problems is fine. Dodging bullets isn't. Even in areas that aren't "hot spots," it's wise to be up on the news. English newspapers and broadcasts are available in most of the world. Other tourists can be valuable links with the outside world as well. Most importantly, the nearest American or British consulate can advise you on problems that merit concern.

Take your government's travel advice seriously but don't trust it blindly. I try to weed through State Department travel advisories. While I travel right through advisories designed to stoke domestic hysteria to build support for a presidential adventure (generally terrorist related), others (such as warnings about civil unrest in a country that's falling apart) are grounds to scrub my mission. For the latest U.S. Department of State travel advisories online, check http://travel.state.gov/travel_warnings.html.

I can't remember ever hearing a gun or a bomb in my Mediterranean travels. Many times, however, I've had the thrill of a firsthand experience merely by talking with people who were personally involved. Your tour memories can include lunching with a group of Palestinian college students, walking through Moscow with a diehard Communist, listening to the Voice of America with curious Bulgarians in a Black Sea coast campground, and learning why the Swiss aren't completely comfortable with a unified Germany. Or your travel memories can be built on the blare of your tour guide's bullhorn as he tells you who did the stucco in empty Gothic cathedrals and polished palaces.

Certainly we need to consider the real risk of terrorism, evaluate it, and then travel in a way that minimizes the risk. If you can't accept the risk, settle for a lifetime of *National Geographic* specials.

Comparing risks. Travel is accelerated living and comes with many risks. But statistically the risk of terrorism is much smaller than the chances tourists have always taken without a second thought. Let's look at it in cold unemotional statistics. In 1996, 25 Americans, out of 19 million who traveled, were killed by terrorists. Sure, that's a risk, but in the same year, 14,000 Americans were shot to death in the U.S. Europeans laugh out loud when they read of Americans staying home so they won't be murdered. Statistically, even in the worst times of terrorism, you're much safer in Europe.

Many are also nervous about flying. But in the United States alone more than 60,000 planes take off and land safely every day. In the 1990s, an average of 89 Americans a year died in commercial airplane crashes. There's a one-in-12-million chance that boarding an airplane will result in death. I take the risk and travel.

The stealth tourist. Terrorist targets are predictable. They lash out at the high-profile symbols of our powerful and wealthy society—airplanes, luxury cruise ships, elegant high-rise hotels, posh restaurants, military and diplomatic locations. When you travel through the Back Door, you're melting into Europe, keeping the lowest possible profile. You're staying in simple, local-style places—like Pedro's Pension. Terrorists don't bomb Pedro's Pension. That's where they sleep. And if you just really hate terrorism, the most effective way for you to fight it is to travel a lot, learn about the world, come home, and help our country fit better into this ever-smaller planet.

29. Attitude Adjustment

THE UGLY AMERICAN

Many Americans' trips suffer because they are treated like Ugly Americans. Those who are treated like Ugly Americans are treated that way because they *are* Ugly Americans. They aren't bad people, just ethnocentric.

Even if you believe American ways are better, your trip will go better if you don't compare. Enjoy doing things the European way during your trip, and you'll experience a more welcoming Europe.

Europe sees two kinds of travelers: Those who view Europe through air-conditioned bus windows, socializing with their noisy American friends, and those who are taking a vacation from America, immersing themselves in different cultures, experiencing different people and lifestyles, and broadening their perspectives.

Thank You			
Arabic	*shukran*	Greek	*efharisto*
Bulgarian	*blagodarya*	Iraqi	*shukran*
Danish	*tak*	Italian	*grazie*
Dutch	*dank u wel*	Portuguese	*obrigado*
English	*thank you*	Russian	*spasiba*
Finnish	*kiitos*	Serbo-Croatian	*hvala*
French	*merci*	Spanish	*gracias*
German	*danke*	Turkish	*tesekkurler*

Europeans judge you as an individual, not by your government. A Greek fisherman once told me, "For me, Reagan is big problem—but I like you." I have never been treated like the Ugly American. I've been proud to wear our flag on my lapel. My Americanness in Europe, if anything, has been an asset.

You'll see plenty of Ugly Americans slogging through a sour Europe, mired in a swamp of complaints. Ugly Americanism is a disease, but fortunately there is a cure: A change in attitude. The best over-the-counter medicine is a mirror. Here are the symptoms. The Ugly American:

• criticizes "strange" customs and cultural differences. She doesn't try to understand that only a Hindu knows the value of India's sacred cows, and only a devout Spanish Catholic appreciates the true worth of his town's patron saint.

• demands to find America in Europe. He insists on orange juice and eggs (sunny-side up) for breakfast, long beds, English menus, punctuality in Italy, and cold beer in England. He measures Europe with an American yardstick.

• invades a country while making no effort to communicate with the "natives." Traveling in packs, he talks at and about Europeans in a condescending manner. He sees the world as a pyramid, with the United States on top and the "less developed" world trying to get there.

THE THOUGHTFUL AMERICAN

The Thoughtful American celebrates the similarities and differences in cultures. You:

• seek out European styles of living. You are genuinely interested in the people and cultures you visit.

• want to learn by trying things. You forget your discomfort if you're the only one in a group who feels it.

• accept and try to understand differences. Paying for your Italian coffee at one counter, then picking it up at another may seem inefficient, until you realize it's more sanitary: The person handling the food handles no money.

• are observant and sensitive. If 60 people are eating quietly with hushed conversation in a Belgian restaurant, you know it's not the place to yuk it up.

• maintain humility and don't flash signs of affluence. You don't joke about the local money or overtip. Your bucks don't talk.

• are positive and optimistic in the extreme. You discipline yourself to focus on the good points of each country. You don't dwell on problems or compare things to "back home."

Marijuana in Europe

Compared to the U.S., many European countries have a liberal attitude towards marijuana users. And many Europeans believe marijuana can be enjoyed responsibly by adults.

Still, drugs are not legal in Europe. The use, sale, and possession of any illegal drug can lead to stiff fines or a jail sentence. While laws against the use of drugs such as cocaine, heroin, LSD, and Ecstasy are still strictly enforced, more and more of Europe is reclassifying marijuana as a "soft drug" and tolerating recreational use in private or in certain bars.

Even in the most liberal countries, the sale of marijuana is permitted only in certain places. In Amsterdam and other Dutch cities, "coffeehouses"—often sporting red, green, and yellow Rastafarian flags—are allowed to sell small amounts for personal use to people over 18. In Copenhagen's "free city" Christiania, the sale and use of marijuana is widespread and tolerated. Recently, Switzerland (and to a lesser extent, other countries) has also been liberalizing its approach to marijuana.

Remember that you are subject to the laws of the country in which you travel when abroad, so be sensible and err on the side of caution. People who run coffeehouses warn that even a country "soft on soft drugs" needs to make a few marijuana arrests each year to maintain its "favorable trade status" with the U.S. (which wants European countries to maintain a harder stance on marijuana use).

Be warned that anywhere in Europe, especially in countries adjacent to countries famous for being easy on marijuana, border patrols can be particularly strict. And driving under the influence of any drug is a serious offense that can land you in jail.

For an overview and country-by-country summary of European drug laws, see the Web site of the National Organization for the Reform of Marijuana Laws (NORML) at www.norml.org. Americans interested in "going local" with marijuana in Europe may be interested in the 30-page (and rapidly growing) discussion on the Graffiti Wall at www.ricksteves.com.

• make an effort to bridge that flimsy language barrier. Rudimentary communication in any language is fun and simple with a few basic words. On the train to Budapest, you might think that a debate with a Hungarian over the merits of a common European currency would be frustrating with a 20-word vocabulary, but you'll surprise yourself at how well you communicate by just breaking the ice and trying. Don't worry about making mistakes—communicate!

I've been accepted as an American friend throughout Europe, Russia, the Middle East, and North Africa. I've been hugged by Bulgarian workers on a Balkan mountaintop; discussed the Olympics over dinner in the home of a Greek family; explained to a young, frustrated Irishman that California girls take their pants off one leg at a time, just like the rest of us; and hiked through the Alps with a Swiss schoolteacher, learning German and teaching English.

Go as a guest; act like one, and you'll be treated like one. In travel, too, you reap what you sow.

RESPONSIBLE TOURISM

As we learn more about the problems that confront the earth and humankind, more and more people are recognizing the need for the world's industries, such as tourism, to function as tools for peace. Tourism is a $2 trillion industry that employs more than 60 million people. As travelers become more sophisticated and gain a global perspective, the demand for socially, environmentally, and economically responsible means of travel will grow. Peace is more than the absence of war, and if we are to enjoy the good things of life—such as travel—the serious issues that confront humankind must be addressed now.

Although the most obvious problems relate specifically to travel in the Third World, European travel also offers some exciting socially responsible opportunities. In this chapter are a few sources of information for the budding "green" traveler.

Consume responsibly in your travels—do your part to conserve energy. If your hotel overstocks your room with towels, use just one. Carry your own bar of soap and bottle of shampoo rather than rip open all those little soaps and shampoo packets. Bring a lightweight plastic cup instead of using and tossing a plastic glass at every hotel. Turn the light off when you leave your room. Limit showers to five minutes. Return unused travel information (booklets, brochures) to the tourist information office or pass it on to another traveler rather than automatically relegate it to a European landfill. In little ways, we can make a difference.

Understand your power to shape the marketplace by what you decide to buy (whether in the grocery store or in your choice of hotels). In my travels (and in my writing), whenever possible, I patronize and support small, family-run, locally owned businesses (hotels, restaurants, shops, tour guides). I choose people who invest their creativity and resources in giving me simple, friendly, sustainable, and honest travel experiences—people with ideals.

Resources for Socially Responsible European Travel

Global Volunteers, a nonprofit organization, offers useful "travel with a purpose" trips throughout the world (375 E. Little Canada Road, St. Paul, MN 55117-1628, tel. 800/487-1074, fax 651/482-0915, www.globalvolunteers.org, e-mail: email@globalvolunteers.org). The work varies per country, but if Europe's your goal, you'll likely work with disabled or at-risk youth, help with a renovation project at the peace center in Ireland, or teach conversational English in Italy, Spain, Poland, or Romania.

Volunteers for Peace, a nonprofit organization, runs international work camps to promote goodwill through friendship and community service. European options include historical preservation, festival event planning, conservation projects, AIDS awareness instruction, and social work with disabled or elderly people (1034 Tiffany Road, Belmont, VT 05730, tel. 802/259-2759, fax 802/259-2922, www.vfp.org, e-mail: vfp@vfp.org).

SCI-International Voluntary Service also runs work camps with projects involving children, the elderly, the environment, or local culture and history (814 40th Street N.E., Seattle, WA 98105, tel. 206/545-6585, www.sci-ivs.org).

If you'd like to restore medieval ruins, work in wildlife reserves, or care for refugee children in camps and orphanages, send $21.95 postpaid to Chicago Review Press (814 N. Franklin, Chicago, IL 60610, tel. 800/888-4741, fax 312/337-5985) for **Volunteer Vacations,** which lists 500 options for one- to six-week domestic and foreign volunteer programs.

Other resources: *International Directory of Voluntary Work* (by Victoria Pybus and Louise Whetter; Vacation Work) and *Volunteer Vacations: Short Term Adventures That Will Benefit You and Others* (by Bill McMillon).

Back Door places don't rely on slick advertising and marketing gimmicks, and they don't target the created needs of people whose values are shaped by capitalism gone wild. Consuming responsibly means buying as if your choice is a vote for the kind of world we could have.

MAKING THE MOST OF YOUR TRIP
Accept that today's Europe is changing. Among the palaces, quaint folk dancers, and museums, you'll find a living civilization grasping for

the future while we romantic tourists grope for its past. This presents us with a sometimes painful dose of truth.

Today's Europe is a complex, mixed bag of tricks. It can rudely slap you in the face if you aren't prepared to accept it with open eyes and an open mind. Europe is getting crowded, tense, seedy, polluted, industrialized, hamburgerized, and far from the everything-in-its-place, fairy-tale land I'm sure it used to be.

If you're not mentally braced for some shocks, local trends can tinge your travels. Hans Christian Andersen's statue has four-letter words scrawled across its base. Amsterdam's sex shops and McDonald's share the same streetlamp. In Paris armies of Sudanese salesmen bait tourists with ivory bracelets and crocodile purses. Many a Mediterranean hotel keeper would consider himself a disgrace to his sex if he didn't follow a single woman to her room. Drunk punks do their best to repulse you as you climb to St. Patrick's grave in Ireland, and Greek ferryboats dump mountains of trash into their dying Aegean Sea. An eight-year-old boy in Denmark smokes a cigarette like he was born with it in his mouth, and in a Munich beer hall an old drunk spits *Sieg heils* all over you. The Barcelona shoeshine man will triple charge you, and people everywhere eat strange and wondrous things. They eat next to nothing for breakfast, mud for coffee, mussels in Brussels, and snails in Paris; and dinner's at 10 p.m. in Spain. Beer is room temperature here, flat there, coffee isn't served with dinner, and ice cubes can only be dreamed of. Roman cars stay in their lanes like rocks in an avalanche, and beer maids with huge pretzels pull mustard packets from their cleavage.

Contemporary Europe is alive and groping. Today's problems will fill tomorrow's museums. Feel privileged to walk the vibrant streets of Europe as a sponge—not a judge. Be open-minded. Absorb, accept, and learn.

Don't be a creative worrier. Travelers tend to sit at home before their trip—all alone, just thinking of reasons to be stressed. Travel problems are always there; you just notice them when they're yours. Every year there are air-controller strikes, train wrecks, terrorist attacks, new problems, and deciduous problems sprouting new leaves.

Travel is ad-libbing; incurring and conquering surprise challenges. Make an art out of taking the unexpected in stride. Relax; you're on the other side of the world playing games in a continental backyard. Be a good sport, enjoy the uncertainty, and frolic in the pits.

Many of my readers' richest travel experiences were the result of seemingly terrible mishaps: the lost passport in Slovenia, having to find a doctor in Ireland, the blowout in Portugal, or the moped accident on Corfu.

Expect problems, tackle them creatively. You'll miss a museum or

From comrades to Coke

two and maybe blow your budget for the week. But you'll make some local friends and stack up some memories. And this is the essence of travel that you'll enjoy long after the journal is shelved and your trip is stored neatly in the slide carousel of your mind.

KISS: "Keep it simple, stupid!" Don't complicate your trip. Simplify! Travelers get stressed and cluttered over the silliest things, which, in their nibbly ways, can suffocate a happy holiday: registering your camera with customs before leaving home, standing in a long line at the post office on a sunny day in the Alps, worrying about the correct answers to meaningless bureaucratic forms, making a long-distance hotel reservation in a strange language and then trying to settle on what's served for breakfast, having a picnic in pants that make you worry about grass stains, and sending away for Swedish hotel vouchers.

People can complicate their trips with video cameras, lead-lined film bags, special tickets for free entry to all the sights they won't see in England, inflatable hangers, immersion heaters, instant coffee, 65 Handi-wipes, and a special calculator that figures the value of the franc to the third decimal.

They ask for a toilet in 17 words or more, steal Sweet 'n' Low and plastic silverware off the plane, and take notes on facts that don't matter. Travel more like Gandhi—with simple clothes, open eyes, and an uncluttered mind.

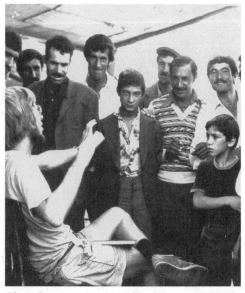

Ask questions. If you are too proud to ask questions, your trip will be dignified but dull. Many tourists are actually afraid or too timid to ask questions. The meek may inherit the earth, but they make lousy travelers. Local sources are a wealth of information. People are

If people stare . . . sing cowboy songs.

happy to help a traveler. Hurdle the language barrier. Use a paper and pencil, charades, or whatever it takes to be understood. Don't be afraid to butcher the language.

Ask questions—or be lost. If you're lost, take out a map and look lost. You'll get help. If you're lonely or in need of contact with a local person, take out a map and look lost. Perceive friendliness and you'll find it.

Be militantly humble—Attila had a lousy trip. All summer long I'm pushing for a bargain, often for groups. It's the hottest, toughest time of year. Tourists and locals clash. Many tourists leave soured.

When I catch a Spanish merchant shortchanging me, I correct the bill and smile, "*Adios.*" When a French hotel owner blows up at me for no legitimate reason, I wait, smile, and try again. I usually see the irate ranter come to his senses, forget the problem, and work things out.

"Turn the other cheek" applies perfectly to those riding Europe's magic carousel. If you fight the slaps, the ride is over. The militantly humble and hopelessly optimistic can spin forever.

Make yourself an extrovert, even if you're not. Be a catalyst for adventure and excitement. Meet people. Make things happen or often they won't. The American casual and friendly social style is charming to Europeans who are raised to respect social formalities. While our "slap-on-the-back" friendliness can be overplayed and obnoxious, it can also be a great asset for the American interested in meeting Europeans. Consider that cultural trait a plus. Enjoy it. Take advantage of it.

I'm not naturally a wild-and-crazy kind of guy. But when I'm shy and quiet, things don't happen, and that's a bad rut to travel in. It's not easy, but this special awareness can really pay off. Let me describe the same evening twice—first with the mild-and-lazy me, and then with the wild-and-crazy me.

The traffic held me up, so by the time I got to that great historical building I've always wanted to see, it was six minutes before closing. No one was allowed to enter. Disappointed, I walked to a restaurant and couldn't make heads or tails out of the menu. I recognized "steak-frites" and settled for a meat patty and French fries. On the way home I looked into a colorful local pub but didn't see any tourists, so I walked on. A couple waved at me from their balcony, but I didn't know what to say, so I ignored them. I returned to my room and did some laundry.

That's not a night to be proud of. A better traveler's journal entry would read like this:

I got to the museum only six minutes before closing. The guard said no one could go in now, but I begged, joked, and pleaded with him. I had traveled all the way to see this place, and I would be leaving early in the morning. I assured him that I'd be out by six o'clock, and he gave me a glorious six minutes in that building. You can do a lot with a Botticelli in six minutes when that's all you've got. Across the street at a restaurant that the same guard recommended, I couldn't make heads or tails out of the menu. Inviting myself into the kitchen, I met the cooks and got a firsthand look at "what's cookin'." Now I could order an exciting local dish and know just what I was getting. Delicioso! On the way home, I passed a local pub, and, while it seemed dark and uninviting, I stepped in and was met by the only guy in the place who spoke any English. He proudly befriended me and told me, in very broken English, of his salty past and his six kids, while treating

When I see a bunch of cute guys on a bench, I ask 'em to scoot over. Twenty-five years later, I'm still one of the gang.

me to his favorite local brew. As I headed home, a couple waved at me from their balcony, and I waved back, saying "Buon giorno!" I knew it didn't mean "Good evening," but they understood. They invited me up to their apartment. We joked around—not understanding a lot of what we were saying to each other—and they invited me to their summer cottage tomorrow. What a lucky break! There's no better way to learn about this country than to spend an afternoon with a local family. And to think that I could be back in my room doing the laundry.

Pledge every morning to do something entirely different today. Meet people and create adventure—or bring home a boring journal.

BECOMING A TEMPORARY EUROPEAN

Most travelers tramp through Europe like they're visiting the cultural zoo. "Ooo, that guy in lederhosen yodeled! Excuse me, could you do that again in the sunshine with my wife next to you so I can take a snapshot?" This is fun. It's a part of travel. But a camera bouncing on your belly tells locals you're hunting cultural peacocks. When I'm in Europe, I'm the best German or Spaniard or Italian I can be. While I never drink tea at home, after a long day of sightseeing in England, "a spot of tea" really does feel right. I drink wine in France and beer in Germany. In Italy I eat small breakfasts. Find ways to really be there. Consider these:

Go to church. Many regular churchgoers never even consider a European worship service. Any church would welcome a traveling American. And an hour in a small-town church provides an unbeatable peek into the local community, especially if you join them for coffee and cookies afterwards. I'll never forget going to a small church on the south coast of Portugal one Easter. A tourist stood at the door videotaping the "colorful natives" (including me) shaking hands with the priest after the service. You can experience St. Peter's by taking photographs . . . or taking a seat at Mass (daily at 5 p.m.).

Root for your team. For many Europeans, the top religion is soccer. Getting caught up in a sporting event is going local. Whether enjoying soccer in small-town Italy, greyhound racing in Scotland, or hurling in Ireland, you'll be surrounded by a stadium crammed with devout locals.

Play where the locals play. A city's popular fairgrounds and parks are filled with local families, lovers, and old-timers enjoying a cheap afternoon or evening out. European communities provide their heavily taxed citizens with wonderful athletic facilities. Check out a swimming center, called a "leisure center" in Britain. While tourists outnumber locals five to one at the world-famous Tivoli Gardens, Copenhagen's other amusement park, Bakken, is enjoyed purely by Danes. Disneyland Paris is great. But Paris' Asterix Park is more French.

Mass with the sun's rays, daily at 5 p.m. in St. Peter's

Experiment. Some cafés in the Netherlands (those with plants in the windows or Rastafarian colors on the wall) have menus that look like a drug bust. Marijuana is less controversial in Holland than tobacco is these days in the United States. For a casual toke of local life without the risk that comes with smoking in the United States, drop into one of these cafés and roll a joint. If you have no political aspirations, inhale.

Take a stroll. Across southern Europe, communities *paseo*, or stroll, in the early evening. Stroll along. Join a *Volksmarch* in Bavaria to spend a day on the trails with people singing "I love to go a-wandering" in its original language. Remember, hostels are the American target, while mountain huts and "nature's friends huts" across Europe are filled mostly with local hikers. Most hiking centers have alpine clubs that welcome foreigners and offer organized hikes.

Get off the tourist track. Choose destinations busy with local holiday-goers but not on the international tourist map. Campgrounds are filled with Europeans in the mood to toss a Frisbee with a new American friend (bring a nylon "whoosh" Frisbee). Be accessible. Accept invitations. Assume you're interesting and do Europeans a favor by finding ways to get invitations.

Challenge a local to the national pastime. In Greece or Turkey drop into a local teahouse or *taverna* and challenge a local to a game of

Connect with the locals. Greeks and Turks love a revealing game of backgammon.

backgammon. You're instantly a part (even a star) of the local café or bar scene. Normally the gang will gather around, and what starts out as a simple game becomes a fun duel of international significance.

Contact the local version of your club. If you're a member of a service club, bridge club, professional association, or international organization, make a point to connect with your foreign mates.

Search out residential neighborhoods. Ride a city bus or subway into the suburbs. Wander through a neighborhood to see how the locals live when they're not wearing lederhosen and yodeling. Visit a supermarket. Make friends at the Laundromat.

Drop by a school or university. Mill around a university and check out the announcement boards. Eat at the school cafeteria. Ask at the English language department if there's a student learning English whom you could hire to be your private guide. Be alert and even a little bit snoopy. You may stumble onto a grade-school talent show.

Join in. When you visit the town market in the morning, you're just another hungry local, picking up your daily produce. You can snap photos of the pilgrims at Lourdes—or volunteer to help wheel the chairs of those who've come in hope of a cure. Traveling through the wine country of

France during harvest time, you can be a tourist taking photos—or you can pitch in and become a local grape picker. Get more than a photo op. Get dirty. That night at the festival, it's just grape pickers dancing—and you're one of them.

If you're hunting cultural peacocks, remember they spread their tails best for people...not cameras. When you take Europe out of your viewfinder, you're more likely to find it in your lap.

Highlights of Central Europe

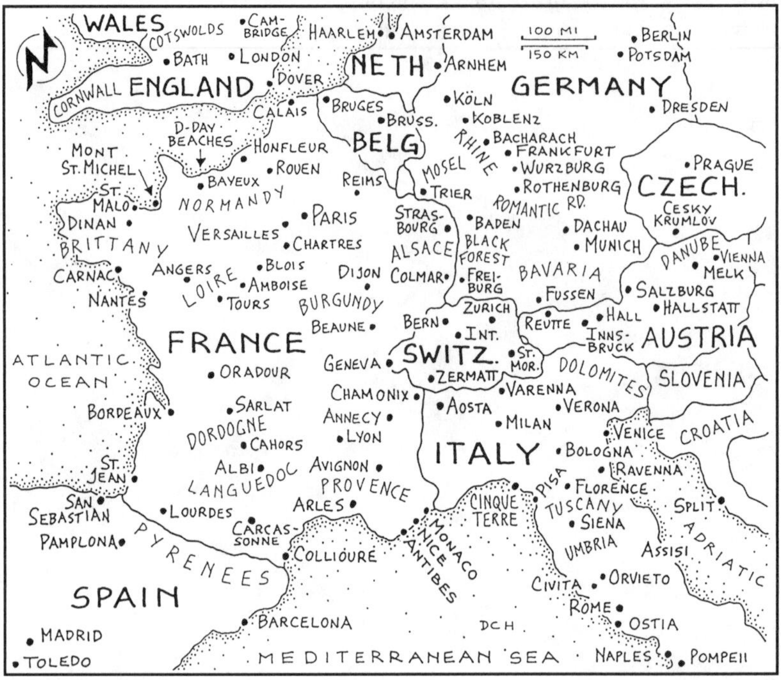

PART TWO

Back Doors

Europe, here you come

CONTENTS

Europe's Back Doors

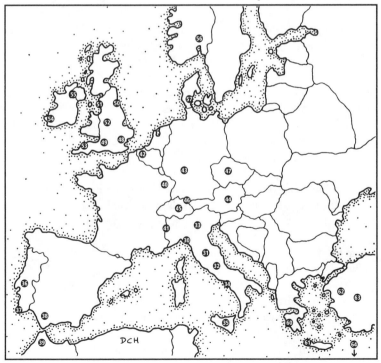

What Is a Back Door, and How Can I Find One of My Own?

The travel skills covered in the first half of this book enable you to open doors most travelers don't even know exist. Now I'd like you to meet my "Back Doors." I'm the matchmaker—and you and the travel bug are about to get intimate. By traveling vicariously with me through these chapters, you'll get a peek at my favorite places. And, just as important, by internalizing this lifetime of magic travel moments, you'll develop a knack for finding your own.

Europe is a bubbling multicultural fondue. A Back Door is a steaming forkful. It could be an all-day alpine ridge walk, a sword-fern fantasy in a ruined castle, or a friendly swing with a church spire bell-ringer. You could jam your camera with Turkish delights or uncover the village warmth hiding in a cold metropolis. By learning where to jab your fork, you'll put together a travel feast exceeding your wildest dreams.

Some of my Back Doors are undiscovered towns that have, for various reasons, missed the modern parade. With no promotional budgets to attract travelers, they're ignored as they quietly make their traditional way through just another century. Many of these places won't hit you with their cultural razzle-dazzle. Their charms are too subtle to be enjoyed by the tour-bus crowd. But, learning from the experiences described in the last half of this book, Back Door travelers make their own fun.

We'll also explore natural nooks and undeveloped crannies. These are rare opportunities to enjoy Europe's sun, beaches, mountains, and natural wonders without the glitz. While Europeans love nature and are fanatic sun worshipers, they have an impressive knack for enjoying themselves in hellish crowds. Our goal is to experience Europe's quiet alternatives: lonesome stone circles, desolate castles, breezy bike rides, and snippets of the Riviera not snapped up by entrepreneurs.

With a Back Door angle on a big city, you can slip your fingers under its staged culture and actually find a pulse. Even London has a warm underbelly, where you'll rumble with a heart that's been beating for 2,000 years.

And finally, to squeeze the most travel experience out of every mile, minute, and dollar, look beyond Europe. Europe is exciting, but a dip into Turkey, Morocco, or Egypt is well worth the diarrhea.

The promotion of a tender place that has so far avoided the tourist industry reminds me of the whaler who screams, "Quick, harpoon it

Lisbon

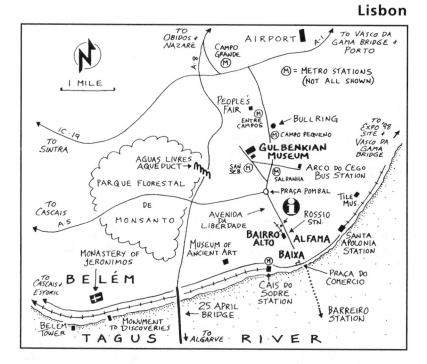

and the country's leading explorers. Across the street, the Monastery of Jerónimos is Portugal's most exciting building—with my favorite cloister in Europe. King Manuel had this giant church and its cloisters built—using "pepper money," a 5 percent tax on spices brought back from India—as a thanks for the discoveries. Sailors would spend their last night here in prayer before embarking on their frightening voyages. The Manueline style of this giant church and cloister combines late Gothic and early Renaissance features with motifs from the sea—the source of the wealth that made this art possible.

Before leaving Belém, take your taste buds sightseeing at a famous pastry shop, Casa Pasties de Belém (a block from the monastery at Rua de Belém 88). This is the birthplace of the wonderful cream tart called *pastel del Nata* throughout Portugal. But in Lisbon, they're called *pastel del Belém*. Since 1837 locals have come here to get them warm out of the oven. Sprinkle on the cinnamon and powdered sugar, get a *café com leite*, and linger.

Spend the early afternoon in your choice of Lisbon's fine museums waiting for the setting sun to rekindle the action in the Alfama. A colorful sailors' quarter, this was the center of the Visigothic town, a rich district during the Arabic period and now the shiver-me-timbers home of Lisbon's fisherfolk. One of the few areas to survive the 1755 earthquake, the Alfama is a cobbled cornucopia of Old World color.

Wander deep. This urban jungle's roads are squeezed into tangled stairways and confused alleys. Bent houses comfort each other in their romantic shabbiness, and the air drips with laundry and the smell of clams and raw fish. Get lost. Poke aimlessly, sample ample grapes, avoid rabid-looking dogs, peek through windows. Make a friend, pet a chicken. Taste the *blanco seco*—the local dry wine.

Gradually zigzag your way up the castle-crowned hill until you reach a viewpoint, the little green square called Miradouro de Santa Luzia. Rest here and survey the cluttered Alfama rooftops below you. A block away is Largo Rodrigues Freitas, a square with several scruffy, cheap, very local eateries. Treat yourself to the special—a plate of boiled clams.

If you climb a few more blocks to the top of the hill, you'll find the ruins of Castelo de São Jorge. From this fortress, which has dominated the city for more than 1,000 years, enjoy the roaming peacocks and a commanding view of Portugal's capital city.

In the late afternoon, for a quintessential Lisbon drink, duck into one of the funky hole-in-the-wall shops throughout town and ask for a *gin-jinha* (zheen-zheen-yah). Sold for about a buck a shot, it's a sweet liquor made from the sour cherry–like ginja berry, sugar, and schnapps. The only choices are: With or without berries (*com* or *sem fruta*) and *gelada* if you want it from a chilled bottle out of the fridge—very nice. In Portugal when someone is impressed by the taste of something they say, "*Sabe melhor que nem ginjas*" (It tastes even better than ginja).

Spend the evening at a Portuguese bullfight. It's a brutal sport, but the bull lives through it and so will you. The fight starts with an equestrian duel—a fast bull against a graceful horse and rider. Then the fun starts. A colorfully clad eight-man team enters the ring strung out in a line as if to play leapfrog. The leader taunts El Toro noisily and, with testosterone sloshing every-where, the bull and the man

In a Portuguese bullfight the matador is brutalized, too.

charge each other. The speeding bull plows into the leader head-on. Then—thud, thud, thud—the raging bull skewers the entire charging crew. The horns are wrapped so no one gets gored—just mashed.

The crew wrestles the bull to a standstill, and one man grabs the bull's tail. Victory is complete when the team leaps off the bull and the man still hanging onto the tail "water-skis" behind the enraged animal. This thrilling display of insanity is repeated with six bulls. After each round, the bruised and battered leader limps a victory lap around the ring.

Portugal's top bullring is Lisbon's Campo Pequeno (fights on Thursdays, mid-June through September; other arenas offer fights most Sundays from Easter to October). Half the fights are simply Spanish-type *corridas* without the killing. For the real slam-bam Portuguese-style fight, confirm that there will be *grupo de forcados*.

For a good lowbrow Lisbon evening out, visit the Feira Popular (open nightly until late, May–September, Avenida da Republica at the Entrecampos metro stop). On summer evenings, this popular fair bustles with Portuguese families at play. I ate dinner surrounded by chattering locals ignoring the ever-present TVs, while great platters of fish, meat, fries, salad, and lots of wine paraded frantically in every direction. A seven-year-old boy stood on a chair and sang hauntingly emotional folk songs. With his own dogged clapping, he dragged applause out of the less-than-interested crowd and then passed his shabby hat. All the while, fried ducks drip, barbecues spit, dogs squirt the legs of chairs, and somehow local lovers ignore everything but each other's eyes.

For good-value accommodations in Lisbon, try Lisboa Tejo (splurge, Rua do Poço do Borratém 4, tel. 21-886-6182, fax 21-886-5163) or Pensão Residencial Gerês (Calçada do Garcia 6, tel. 21-881-0497, fax 21-888-2006). For more hotels, visit www.ricksteves.com/update/intro.htm, and for all the travel specifics, see this year's edition of Rick Steves' Spain & Portugal.

37. Salema, on Portugal's Sunny South Coast

"Let's get the *cataplanas*," said my wife Anne, urging me to try the fish stew at Ze's Carioca Restaurant in Salema.

Overhearing her, Ze came to our table and said, "I have developed a secret recipe for this specialty. If you don't like it, you don't pay."

"What if we don't like anything else we order?" I asked.

"If you don't pay, I break your fingers," Ze said cheerfully.

We ordered the *cataplanas*. Savoring our meal, we savored one of the last true villages on the Algarve—Salema.

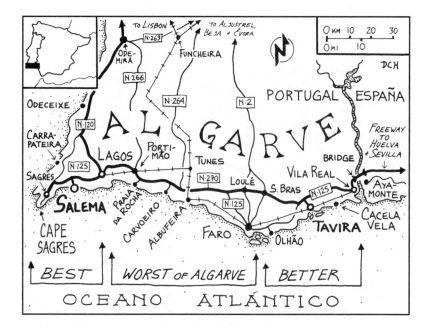

Any place famous as a "last undiscovered tourist frontier" no longer is. But the Algarve of your dreams survives—just barely. To catch it before it goes, find a fringe. It took me three tries. West of Lagos, I tried Lux and Burgano, both offering only a corpse of a fishing village, bikini-strangled and Nivea-creamed. Then, just as darkness turned couples into peaceful silhouettes, I found Salema.

Any Algarve town with a beach will have tourism, but few mix tourism and realism as well as little Salema. It's my kind of resort—an inviting beach with three hotels, lots of quartos (Portuguese bed-and-breakfasts), and four restaurants specializing in fresh fish and *vinho verde* (green wine). Tucked away where a dirt road hits the beach on Portugal's southwestern tip, Salema is an easy 15-mile bus ride or hitch from the closest train station in Lagos. Don't let the ladies hawking rooms in Lagos waylay you into staying in their city by telling you Salema is full.

Salema has a split personality. Half is a whitewashed old town of scruffy dogs, wide-eyed kids, and fishermen who've seen it all. The other half was built for tourists. With the horn-tooting arrival of the trucks, the parking lot that separates the jogging shorts from the black shawls becomes a morning market. The 1812 Overture horn of the fish truck wakes you at 8 a.m. Then the bakery trailer rolls in steaming with fresh bread, followed by a fruit and vegetables truck, and a five-and-dime truck for clothing and other odds and ends. And, most afternoons, the red mobile post office stops by.

Salema is still a fishing village. Unwritten tradition allocates different chunks of undersea territory to each Salema family. While the fishermen's hut on the beach no longer hosts a fish auction, it provides shade for the old-

Salema. Catch the Algarve before it's gone.

timers arm wrestling octopi out of their traps. The pottery jars stacked everywhere are traps. The traps are tied about a meter apart in long lines and dropped offshore. Octopi, looking for a cozy place to set an ambush, climb inside—making their final mistake.

Fishing is important, but Salema's tourist-based economy sits on a foundation of sand. Locals hope and pray that their sandy beach returns after being washed away each winter.

In Portugal, restaurateurs are allowed to build a temporary summer-only beachside restaurant if they provide a lifeguard for swimmers and run a green/yellow/red warning-flag system. The Atlantico Restaurant, which dominates Salema's beach, takes its responsibility seriously—providing lifeguards and flags through the summer . . . and fresh seafood by candlelight all year long.

Locals and tourists pursue a policy of peaceful coexistence at the beach. Tractors pull in and push out the fishing boats, two-year-olds toddle in the waves, topless women read German fashion mags, and old men really do mend the nets. British, German, and Back Door connoisseurs of lethargy laze in the sun, while locals grab the shade.

On the west end of the beach, you can climb over the rocks to Figueira Beach. While the days of black widows chasing topless Nordic women off the beach are gone, nudism is still risqué today. Over the rocks and beyond the view of prying eyes, Germans grin and bare it.

So often tourism chases the sun and quaint folksiness. And the quaint folks can survive only with the help of tourist dollars. Fishermen boost their income by renting spare bedrooms to the ever-growing stream of tan fans from the drizzly north. One year I arrived at 7 p.m. with a group of eight people and no reservations. I asked some locals, *"Quartos?"* (Rooms?) Eyes perked, heads nodded, and I got nine beds in three homes at $15 per person. *Quartos* line Salema's main residential street offering simple rooms with showers, springy beds, and glorious Atlantic views.

If you need to do some touring, drive 15 minutes to the best romantic, secluded beach in the region, Praia da Castelejo—complete with a good restaurant, just north of Cape Sagres.

Closer to home, you could take a two-hour cruise from Salema halfway to Cape Sagres and back with Sebastian, a local English-speaking guide. You'll enjoy a light commentary on the geology and plant and bird life (morning trips are best for bird-watching) and nip into some cool blue natural caves. Kicking back and watching the cliffs glide by, I felt like I was scanning a super-relaxing gallery of natural art. Consider being dropped at the (nude) Figueira Beach just before returning to Salema (a 20-minute walk home to Salema—bring shoes, a picnic, and extra water). Easygoing and gentle Sebastian charges little more than what it costs to run his small boat; ask for him at the beachside fishermen's hut or at Pensión Mare.

But Salema's sleepy beauty kidnaps our momentum, and Anne and I go nowhere. Leaving Ze's restaurant with stomachs full and fingers intact, we take a glass of wine from the Atlantico's waterfront bar and sip it with the sunset in a beached paddleboat. Nearby, a dark withered granny shells almonds with a railroad spike, dogs roam the beach like they own it, and a man catches short fish with a long pole. Beyond him is Cape Sagres—the edge of the world 500 years ago. As far as the gang sipping port and piling olive pits in the beachside bar is concerned, it still is.

For good-value accommodations in Salema, try Pensión Mare (Praia de Salema, tel. 28-269-5165, www.algarve.co.uk) or Casa Duarte (tel. 28-269-5206 or 28-269-5307). For more hotels, visit www.ricksteves.com/update/intro.htm, and for all the travel specifics, see this year's edition of Rick Steves' Spain & Portugal.

38. Andalucía's Arcos de la Frontera and the Route of the White Villages

When tourists head south from Madrid, it's generally for Granada, Córdoba, Sevilla, or the Costa del Sol. The big cities have their urban charms, but the Costa del Sol is a concrete nightmare, worthwhile only as a bad example. The most Spanish thing about the south coast is the sunshine—but that's everywhere. For something different and more authentic, try exploring the interior of Andalucía along the "route of the white villages." The Ruta de Pueblos Blancos, Andalucía's charm bracelet of cute towns, gives you wonderfully untouched Spanish culture.

Spend a night in the romantic queen of the white towns, Arcos de la Frontera. Towns with "de la Frontera" in their names were established on the front line of the Christians' centuries-long fight to recapture Spain from the Muslims, who were slowly pushed back into Africa. Today, these hill towns—no longer strategic and no longer on any frontier—are just passing time peacefully.

Arcos smothers its hilltop, tumbling down all sides like an oversized blanket. While larger than the other Andalusian hill towns, it's equally atmospheric. The labyrinthine old center is a photographer's feast. Viewpoint-hop through town. Feel the wind funnel through the narrow streets as drivers pull in car mirrors to fit around tight corners.

Locals brag that they see only the backs of the birds as they fly. To see why, climb to the viewpoint at the main square high in the old town. Belly up to the railing and look down—the town's suicide departure point. Ponder the fancy cliffside hotel's erosion concerns, orderly orange groves, flower-filled greenhouses, fine views toward Morocco, and the backs of the birds.

The thoughtful traveler's challenge is to find meaning in the generally overlooked tiny details of historic towns such as Arcos. A short walk from its Church of Santa Maria to the Church of St. Peter is littered with fun glimpses into the town's past.

The Church of Santa Maria faces the main square. After Arcos was reconquered from the Moors in the 13th century, this church was built—atop a mosque. In the pavement notice the 15th-century magic circle: 12 red and 12 white stones—the white ones with various constellations marked. When a child came to the church to be baptized, the parents would stop here first for a good Christian exorcism. The exorcist would stand inside the protective circle and cleanse the baby of any evil spirits. This was also a holy place back in Muslim times. While locals no longer use it, Islamic sufis still come here in pilgrimage.

In 1699 an earthquake cracked the church's foundation. Arches were added to prop it against neighboring buildings. Thanks to these, the church survived the bigger earthquake of 1755. All over town, arches support earthquake-damaged structures.

Lately the town rumbles only when the bulls run. Señor Gonzalez Oca's tiny barbershop (behind the church) is plastered with posters of bulls running Pamplona-style through the streets of Arcos during Holy Week. An American from the nearby Navy base at Rota was killed here by a bull in 1994.

A block away, the covered market resides in an unfinished church. Notice the half-a-church wall at the entry. This was being built for the

Jesuits, but construction stopped abruptly in 1767 when King Charles III, tired of the Jesuit appetite for politics, expelled the order from Spain.

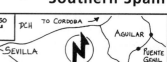

Southern Spain

Look up. The spiky security grill over the window above protects cloistered nuns. Tiny peepholes allow the sisters to look out unseen. Step into the lobby to find a one-way mirror and a blind spinning cupboard. Push the buzzer and a sister will spin some boxes of freshly baked cookies for sale. As I spun back the cookies with a "No, gracias," a Monty Python–esque voice countered, "We have cupcakes as well." I bought a bag of these *magdalanes* both to support their church work and to give to kids as I completed my Arcos walk.

Walking on toward St. Peter's, you pass Roman columns plastered into street corners—protection from reckless donkey carts. Notice also how the walls are scooped out on either side of the windows—a reminder of the days when women stayed inside but wanted the best possible view of any people action in the streets.

Arcos' second church, St. Peter's, really is the second church. It lost an extended battle with Santa Maria for papal recognition as the leading church in Arcos. When the pope finally recognized Santa Maria, pouting parishioners from St. Peter's even changed their prayers. Rather than say "Maria, mother of God" they prayed "Saint Peter, mother of God."

In the cool of the evening, the tiny square in front of the church—about the only flat piece of pavement around—serves as the old town soccer field for neighborhood kids. Join a game and share your cupcakes.

Until a few years ago, this church also had a resident bellman who lived in the spire—notice the cozy balcony halfway up. He was a basketmaker and a colorful character—famous for bringing a donkey into his quarters which grew too big to get back out. Finally, there was no choice but to kill and eat him (the donkey).

From Arcos, the back road to Ronda is spiked with plenty of undiscovered and interesting hill towns. About half the towns I visited were memorable. Only Arcos (by bus) and Ronda (by train) are easily accessible by public transportation. Other towns are best seen by car. Good information on the area is rare but not necessary. Pick up the tourist brochure on the white towns at a nearby big city tourist office, get a good map, and crank your spirit of adventure to high.

Along with Arcos, here are my favorite white villages:

Zahara, a tiny town with a tingly setting under a Moorish castle, has a spectacular view. During Moorish times, Zahara was contained within the fortified castle walls above today's town. It was considered the gateway to Granada and a strategic stronghold for the Moors by the Spanish Christian forces of the *Reconquista*. Locals tell of the Spanish conquest of the Moors'

Zahara, southern Spain

castle as if it happened yesterday: After the Spanish failed several times to seize the castle, a clever Spanish soldier noticed that the Moorish sentinel would toss a rock over the wall to check if any attackers were hiding behind it. If birds flew up, the sentinel figured that no people were there. One night a Spaniard hid there with a bag of pigeons and let them fly when the sentinel tossed his rock. Seeing the birds fly, the guard figured he was clear to enjoy a snooze. The clever Spaniard then scaled the wall, opened the door to let his troops in, and the castle was conquered. That was in 1482. Ten years later Granada fell, the Muslims were back in Africa, and the *Reconquista* was completed. Today the castle is little more than an evocative ruin (always open, free, and worth the climb) with a commanding view. And Zahara is a fine overnight stop for those who want to hear only the sounds of birds, wind, and elderly footsteps on ancient cobbles.

Grazalema, another postcard-pretty hill town, offers a royal balcony for a memorable picnic, a square where you can watch old-timers playing cards, and plenty of quiet, whitewashed streets to explore. Plaza de Andalucía, a block off the view terrace, has several decent little bars, restaurants, and a popular candy store busy with local kids. Grazalema, situated on a west-facing slope of the mountains, catches clouds and is famous as the rainiest place in Spain—but I've had only blue skies on every visit.

Estepa, spilling over a hill crowned with a castle and convent, is a freshly washed, happy town that fits my dreams of southern Spain. It's situated halfway between Córdoba and Málaga, but light years away from either. Atop Estepa's hill is the convent of Santa Clara, worth three stars in any guidebook but found in none. Enjoy the territorial view from the summit, then step into the quiet, spiritual perfection of the church.

In any of these towns, evening is prime time. The promenade begins as everyone gravitates to the central square. The spotless streets are polished nightly by the feet of families licking ice cream. The whole town strolls—it's like "cruising" without cars. Buy an ice-cream sandwich and join in.

For good-value accommodations in Arcos, try Hotel Restaurant El Convento (Maldonado 2, tel. 95-670-2333, fax 95-670-4128) or Hotel Los Olivos (San Miguel 2, tel. 95-670-0811, fax 95-670-2018). For more hotels, visit www .ricksteves.com/update/intro.htm, and for all the travel specifics, see this year's edition of Rick Steves' Spain & Portugal.

39. Morocco: Plunge Deep

Walking through the various souks of the labyrinthine medina, I found sights you could only dream of in America. Dodging blind men and clubfeet, I was stoned by smells, sounds, sights, and feelings. People came in all colors, sizes, temperaments, and varieties of deformities. Milky eyes, charismatic beggars, stumps of limbs, sticks of children, tattooed women, walking mummies, grabbing salesmen, teasing craftsmen, seductive scents, half-bald dogs, and little boys on rooftops were reaching out from all directions.

Ooo! Morocco! Slices of Morocco make the Star Wars bar scene look bland. And it's just a quick cruise from Spain. You can't, however, experience Morocco in a daytrip from the Costa del Sol. Plunge deep and your journal will read like a Dalí painting. While Morocco is not easy traveling, it gets rave reviews from those who plug this Islamic detour into their European vacation.

Catch a boat to Tangier, Morocco, from Gibraltar, or cheaper, from the dreary Spanish town of Algeciras (stay in nearby Tarifa and "commute" to Algeciras). Tarifa also runs boats to Tangier, but currently this crossing is open only to residents of the European Union.

In Morocco, don't linger in Tangier and Tetuan, the Tijuanas of the north coast. Tangier is not really Morocco—it's a city full of con men that thrive on green tourists. Find the quickest connections south to Rabat. At Tangier, power your way off the boat and hop a taxi to the train station. They'll tell you there's no train until tomor-

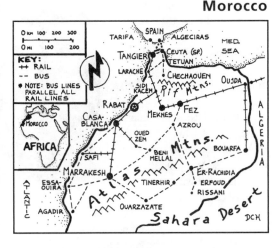

Morocco

row, or "Rabat is closed on Thursdays," anything to get you to stay in Tangier. Believe nothing. Be rude if you have to. Tangier can give you only grief, while the real Morocco lies to the south. Try to make friends with a Moroccan traveler on the boat, who won't be a con man and who'll usually be happy to help you slip through his embarrassingly stressful port of entry.

Rabat, Morocco's capital, is a good first stop. This comfortable, most-European city in Morocco lacks the high-pressure tourism of the towns on the north coast. Or, for a pleasant break on the beach and a relaxing way to break into Morocco, spend a day at Asilah, between Tangier and Larache.

Taxis are cheap and a real bargain when you consider the comfort, speed, and convenience they provide in these hot, dusty, and confusing cities. Eat and drink carefully in Morocco. Bottled water and bottled soft drinks are safe. The extra cautious have "well cooked" written in Arabic on a scrap of paper and flash it when they order meat. I found the couscous, *tajine*, and omelets uniformly good. The Arabs use different number symbols. Learn them. You can practice on license plates, which list the number twice (using their numbers and "ours"). Morocco was a French colony, so French is more widely understood than English. A French phrase book is handy. Travel very light in Morocco. You can leave most of your luggage at your last Spanish hotel for free if you plan to spend a night there on your return from Africa.

After Rabat, pass through Casablanca (great movie, dull city) and catch the Marrakech Express south. You'll hang your head out the window of that romantic old train and sing to the passing desert.

Marrakech is the epitome of exotic. Take a horse-drawn carriage from the station to downtown and find a hotel near the Djemaa el Fna, the central square of Marrakech, where the action is. Desert musicians, magicians, storytellers, acrobats, snake charmers, gamblers, and tricksters gather crowds of tribespeople who have come to Marrakech to do their market chores. As a tourist, you'll fit in like a clown at a funeral. Be very careful, don't gamble, and hang onto your wallet. You're in another world, and

Moroccan road sign: Beware of toboggans

you're not clever here. Spend an entire day in the colorful medina wandering aimlessly from souk to souk. There's a souk for each trade, such as the dyers' souk, the leather souk, and the carpet souk.

In the medina, you'll be badgered—or "guided"—by small boys all claiming to be "a friend who wants to practice English." They are after money, nothing else. If you don't want their services, make two things crystal clear: You have no money for them, and you want no guide. Then completely ignore them. Remember that while you're with a guide, he'll get commissions for anything you buy. Throughout Morocco you'll be pestered by these obnoxious hustler-guides.

I often hire a young and easy-to-control boy who speaks enough English to serve as my interpreter. It seems that if I'm "taken," the other guides leave me alone. And that in itself is worth the small price of a guide.

The market is a shopper's delight. Bargain hard, shop around, and you'll come home with some great souvenirs. Government emporiums usually have the same items you find in the market, but priced fairly. If you get sick of souks, shop there and you'll get the fair price—haggle free.

From Marrakech, consider getting to Fez indirectly by taking an exciting seven-day loop to the south. While buses are reliable and efficient throughout Morocco, this tour is best by car, and it's easy to rent a car in Marrakech and drop it off in Fez. (Car rentals are cheaper when arranged from the U.S.)

Drive or catch the bus south over the rugged Atlas Mountains to Saharan Morocco. Explore the isolated oasis towns of Ouarzazate, Tinerhir, and Er-Rachidia. If time permits, the trip from Ouarzazate to Zagora is an exotic mud-brick pie. These towns each have a weekly "market day," when the tribespeople gather to do their shopping. This is your chance to stock up on honeydew melons and goats' heads. Stay in Tinerhir's Hotel du Todra and climb to the roof for a great view of the busy marketplace below.

Venture out of town into the lush fields, where you'll tumble into an almost Biblical world. Sit on a rock and dissect the silence. A weary donkey carrying a bearded old man in a white robe and turban clip-clops slowly past you. Suddenly, six Botticelli maidens flit like watercolor confetti across your trail and giggle out of sight. Stay tuned. The show goes on.

Bus rides in this part of Morocco are intriguing. I could write pages about experiences I've had on Moroccan buses—good and bad—but I don't want to spoil the surprise. Just ride them with a spirit of adventure, fingers crossed, and keep your bag off the rooftop.

SAHARAN ADVENTURE

Heading south from Er-Rachidia, a series of mud-brick villages bunny-hop down a lush river valley and into the Sahara. Finally the road melts into the sand, and the next stop is, literally, Timbuktu.

The strangeness of this Alice-in-a-sandy-Wonderland world, untempered, can be overwhelming—even frightening. The finest hotel in Erfoud, the region's major town, will provide a much-needed refuge, keeping out the sand, heat waves, and street kids and providing safe-to-eat and tasty local food, reliable information, and a good and affordable bed.

But the hotel is only your canteen and springboard. Explore! If you plan to go deep into the desert, hire a guide. Choose one you can understand and tolerate, set a price for his services, and before dawn head for the dunes.

You'll drive to the last town, Rissani (market days are Tuesday, Thursday, Sunday), and then farther south over 15 miles of natural asphalt to the oasis village of Merzouga. There's plenty of tourist traffic at sunrise and in the early evening, so hitching is fairly easy. A couple of places in Merzouga rent spots on their terrace for those who spend the night. If a civil war is still smoldering in the desert, you may have to show your passport.

Before you glows a chain of sand-dune mountains. Climb one. It's not easy. I seemed to slide farther backward with each step. Hike along a cool and crusty ridge. Observe bugs and their tracks. Watch small sand avalanches you started all by yourself. From the great virgin summit, savor the Sahara view orchestrated by a powerful silence. Your life sticks out like a lone star in a black sky. Try tumbling, rolling, and sloshing down your dune. Look back and see the temporary damage one person can inflict on that formerly perfect slope. Then get back in your car before the summer

Leave Europe and a warm Islamic welcome awaits.

sun turns the sand into a steaming griddle and you into an omelet. Off-season, the midday desert sun is surprisingly mild.

Merzouga is full of very poor people. The village children hang out at the ruins of an old palace. A ragtag percussion group gave us an impromptu concert. The children gathered around us tighter and tighter, as the musicians picked up the tempo. We shared smiles, warmth, and sadness. A little Moroccan Judy Garland saw out of one eye, the other cloudy as rice pudding. One gleaming six-year-old carried a tiny brother slung, sleeping, on her back. His crusty little fly-covered face was too tired to flinch. We had a bag of candy to share and tried to get 40 kids into an orderly line to march past one by one. Impossible. The line degenerated into a free-for-all, and our bag became a piñata.

Only through the mercy of our guide did we find our way back to Rissani. Camels loitered nonchalantly, looking very lost and not caring. Cool lakes flirted, a distant mirage, and the black hardpan road stretched endlessly in all directions.

Then, with a sigh, we were back in Rissani, where the road starts up again. For us, it was breakfast time, and Rissani offered little more than some very thought-provoking irony. My friends and I could find no "acceptable" place to eat. Awkwardly, we drank germ-free Cokes with pursed lips, balanced bread on upturned bottle caps, and swatted laughing legions of flies. We were by far the wealthiest people in the valley—and the only ones unable to enjoy an abundant variety of good but strange food.

Observing the scene from our humble rusted table, we saw a busy girl rhythmically smashing date seeds; three stoic, robed elders with horseshoe beards; and a prophet wandering through with a message for all that he was telling to nobody.

Our Er-Rachidia hotel was Western-style—as dull and comforting as home. We shared the Walkman and enjoyed the pool, resting and recharging before our next Saharan plunge.

SAHARAN NIGHTLIFE

Desert dwellers and smart tourists know the value of a siesta during the hottest part of the day. But a Saharan evening is the perfect time for a traveler to get out and experience the vibrancy of North African village life. We drove 10 miles north of Erfoud to a fortified mud-brick oasis village. There was no paint, no electricity, no cars—only people, adobe walls, and palm trees. Absolutely nothing other than the nearby two-lane highway hinted of the modern world.

We entered like Lewis and Clark without Sacagawea, knowing instantly we were in for a rich experience. A wedding feast was erupting, and the whole town buzzed with excitement, all decked out in colorful robes and their best smiles. We felt very welcome.

The teeming street emptied through the medieval gate onto the field, where a band was playing squawky, oboelike instruments and drums. A circle of 20 ornately dressed women made siren noises with tongues flapping like party favors. Rising dust diffused the lantern light, giving everything the grainy feel of an old photo. The darkness focused our attention on a relay of seductively beautiful, snake-thin dancers. A flirtatious atmosphere raged, cloaked safely in the impossibility of anything transpiring beyond coy smiles and teasing twists.

Then the village's leading family summoned us for dinner. Pillows, blankets, a lantern, and a large, round filigreed table turned a stone cave into a warm lounge. The men of this family had traveled to Europe and spoke some English. For more than two hours, the women prepared dinner and the men proudly entertained their First World guests. First was the ritualistic tea ceremony. Like a mad chemist, the tea specialist mixed it just right. With a thirsty gleam in his eye and a large spike in his hand, he hacked off a chunk of sugar from a coffee can–sized lump and watched it melt into Morocco's basic beverage. He sipped it, as if testing a fine wine, added more sugar, and offered me a taste. When no more sugar could be absorbed, we drank it with cookies and dates. Then, with the fanfare of a pack of Juicy Fruit, the men passed around a hashish pipe. Our shocked look was curious to them. Next, a tape deck brought a tiny clutter of music, from Arab and tribal Berber music to James Brown, reggae, and twangy Moroccan pop. The men danced splendidly.

Finally the meal came. Fourteen people sat on the floor, circling two round tables. Nearby, a child silently waved a palm branch fan, keeping the flies away. A portable washbasin and towel were passed around to start and finish the meal. With our fingers and gravy-soaked slabs of bread, we grabbed spicy meat and vegetables. Everyone dipped eagerly into the delicious central bowl of couscous.

So far, the Moroccan men dominated. Young girls took turns peeking around the corner and dashing off—much like teenyboppers anywhere. Two older women in striking, black-jeweled outfits were squatting attentively in the corner, keeping their distance and a very low profile. Then one pointed to me and motioned in charades, indicating long hair, a backpack, and a smaller partner. I had been in this same village years earlier. I had longer hair and a backpack and was traveling with a short partner. Did she remember us? I scribbled "1978" on a scrap of paper. She scratched it out and wrote "1979." Wow! She remembered my 20-minute stay so long ago! People in remote lands enjoy a visiting tourist and find the occasion at least as memorable as we do. So many more doors open to the traveler who knocks.

After a proud tour of their schoolhouse, we were escorted across the field back to our car, which had been guarded by a silent, white-robed man. We drove away, reeling with the feeling that the memories of this evening would be the prize souvenir of our trip.

Capitalism is working as Adam Smith promised: With a huge demand, the supply is increasing, the price is going up, and budget alternatives are appearing.

The best values in town are rooms in private homes ($25–50, depending on location). You'll meet small-time operators trying to rent rooms to new arrivals at the train station. And, for a small fee, numerous booking services connect travelers with people renting out rooms.

For good-value accommodations in Prague, try AVE (booking service at train station, books private rooms, daily 6 a.m.–11 p.m., tel. 02/2422-3226, fax 02/2423-0783, e-mail: ave@avetravel.cz) or Hotel Julian (Elisky Peskove 11, tel. 02/5731-1150, reception tel. 02/5731-1144, fax 02/5731-1149, www.julian.cz). For more hotels, visit www.ricksteves.com/update/intro.htm, and for all the travel specifics, see this year's edition of Rick Steves' Germany, Austria & Switzerland.

BRITISH ISLES

48. London: A Warm Look at a Cold City

I've spent more time in London than in any other European city. It lacks the grandeur of Rome, the warmth of Munich, and the elegance of Paris, but its history, traditions, people, markets, museums, and entertainment keep drawing me back.

London has changed dramatically in recent years, and many visitors are surprised to find how "un-English" it is. Whites are now a minority in major parts of the city that once symbolized white imperialism. Arabs have nearly bought out the area north of Hyde Park. Chinese take-outs outnumber fish-and-chips shops. Many hotels are run by people with foreign accents (who hire English chambermaids). And outlying suburbs are home to huge communities of Indians and Pakistanis. London is learning—sometimes fitfully—to live as a microcosm of its formerly vast empire. With the English Channel Tunnel complete, many locals see even more foreign threats to the Britishness of Britain.

London is a world in itself, a barrage on all the senses, an urban jungle sprawling over 600 square miles with 9 million struggling people. As a first stop for many travelers, this huge city can be overwhelming. On my first visit I felt like Oliver Twist asking for more soup. Here are a few ideas to soften and warm this hard and cold city.

Have fun seeing the predictable biggies. Blow through the city on the open deck of a double-decker orientation tour bus. Ogle the crown jewels at the Tower of London and see the Houses of Parliament in action. Hobnob with the tombstones in Westminster Abbey. Overfeed the pigeons at Trafalgar Square. Visit with Leonardo, Botticelli, and Rembrandt in the National Gallery. Whisper across the dome of St. Paul's Cathedral and rummage through our civilization's attic at the British Museum. Take a spin on the towering London Eye Ferris wheel. You can enjoy some of Europe's best people-watching at

Dominic Bonuccelli

The London Eye Ferris Wheel towers over Big Ben.

Covent Garden and snap to at Buckingham Palace's Changing of the Guard.

Any guidebook recommends these worthwhile must-sees. But go beyond the big museums, churches, and castles. Take walks (self-guided and with a local guide), hit the off-beat museums, and seek out experiences that come without turnstiles.

Have you tried London lately?

To grasp London comfortably, see it as the old town without the modern, congested, and seemingly endless sprawl. After all, most of the visitors' London lies between the Tower of London and Hyde Park—a great three-mile walk.

On your first evening in London, give yourself a "pinch-me-I'm-in-London" floodlit walking tour. If you just flew in, this is an ideal way to fight jet lag. Catch a bus to the first stop across (east of) Westminster Bridge. Side-trip downstream along the Jubilee Promenade for a capital view. Then, for that "Wow, I'm really in London!" feeling, cross the bridge to view the floodlit Houses of Parliament and Big Ben up close.

To thrill your loved ones (or stoke their envy), call home from a pay phone near Big Ben at about three minutes before the hour. As Big Ben chimes, stick the receiver outside the booth and prove you're in London: ding dong ding dong...dong ding ding dong.

Then cross Whitehall, noticing the Churchill statue in the park. (He's electrified to avoid the pigeon problem that stains so many other great statues.) Walk up Whitehall toward Trafalgar Square. Stop at the barricaded and guarded little Downing Street to see #10, home of the British prime minister. Chat with the bored bobby. From Trafalgar, walk to pop-hopping Leicester Square and continue to youth-on-the-rampage Piccadilly, through safely sleazy Soho (north of Shaftesbury Avenue) up to Oxford Street. From Piccadilly or Oxford Circus you can taxi, bus, or subway home.

To nibble on London one historic snack at a time, take any of the focused two-hour walking tours of the city. For about $8, local historians take small groups through the London story one entertaining page at a time. Choose from London's Plague, Dickens' London, Roman Londinium, Legal London, the Beatles in London, Jack the Ripper's London

London

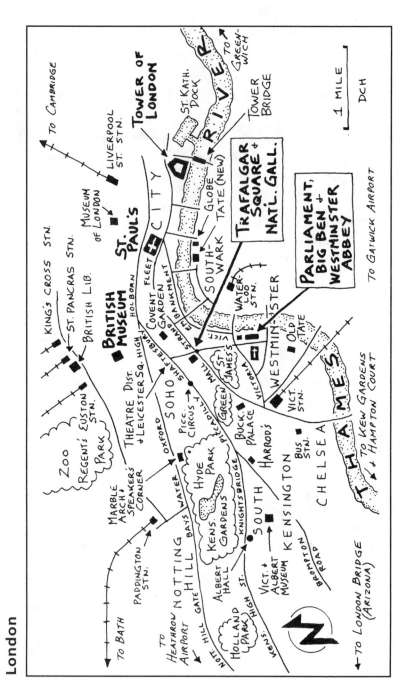

(which, even though guides admit is a lousy walk, is the most popular), and many more. Some walks focus on the various "villages" of London, such as trendy Chelsea and stately, impressed-with-itself Belgravia.

The South Bank of the River Thames, rapidly becoming gentrified, is a thriving arts and cultural center. From Westminster Bridge to the Tower of London bridge, the slick Jubilee Promenade is a trendy jogging, yuppie pub-crawling walk—lined with fun and off-beat sights. The London Eye Ferris wheel, sponsored by British Air, offers the city's highest public viewpoint (450 feet) and a chance to fly British Air without leaving London. Featuring modern art, the striking new Tate Modern is now open in its new South Bank location. The pedestrian Millennium Bridge connects this great Tate with sedate St. Paul's. On the south bank, skip the outrageously amateurish, heavily promoted and over-priced "London Dungeon," but consider the Globe Theater, the Bramah Tea and Coffee Museum, and the Imperial War Museum.

For megatons of things military, the impressive Imperial War Museum covers the wars of the last century. You'll see heavy weaponry, love notes, Varga Girls, Monty's Africa campaign tank, and Schwartzkopf's Desert Storm uniform. Trace the development of the machine gun, push a computer button to watch footage of the first tank battles, and hold your breath through the gruesome "WWI trench experience." You can even buy WWII–era toys. The museum doesn't glorify war, but chronicles the sweeping effects of humanity's most destructive century.

Aficionados of tea or coffee will find the humble little Bramah Tea and Coffee Museum fascinating (just across the bridge from the Tower). It tells the story of each drink almost passionately. The owner, Mr. Bramah, comes from a big tea family and wants the world to know the sad demise of modern tea. The advent of commercial television with breaks not long enough to brew a proper pot of tea required a faster hot drink. In came the horrible English instant coffee. Tea countered with finely chopped leaves in tea bags, and it's gone downhill ever since.

A happier story is the rebuilding of the original Globe Theater. To see Shakespeare in an exact replica of the half-timbered, thatched theater for which he wrote his plays, attend a play at the Globe. This open-air, round theater does the plays as Shakespeare intended, with no amplification ($8 to stand, $16–42 to sit, May–September, usually nightly except Monday, www.shakespeares-globe.org). The $8 "groundling" or "yard" tickets—while open to rain—are most fun. Playing the part of a crude peasant play-goer, you can walk around, munch a picnic dinner, lean your elbows on the stage, and even interact with the actors. I've never enjoyed Shakespeare as much as here, performed as the Bard

intended it... in the "wooden O." The theater is open to tour when there
are no plays; the Shakespeare exhibit is worthwhile (and open even during afternoon plays).

Cheap Globe Theater tip: Plays are long. Many groundlings, who
are allowed to come and go as they please, leave before the end. Peasants
with culture hang out an hour before the finish and beg or buy a ticket
off someone leaving early.

Shakespeare is just the first act here in the world's best theater city.
Choose from the top musicals, comedy, thrillers, sex farces, and more.
Over the years I've enjoyed *Harvey*, starring James Stewart; *The King and
I*, with Yul Brynner; *My Fair Lady*; *A Chorus Line*; *Cats*; *Starlight Express*;
Les Miserables; and *Chicago*. Performances are nightly except Sunday, usu-
ally with one matinee a week. Matinees are cheaper and rarely sell out.
Tickets are cheaper than in New York, ranging from about $12 to $55.
Most theaters are marked on the tourist maps and cluster in the Piccadilly-
Trafalgar area.

Unless you want this year's smash hit, getting a ticket is easy. The
"Theater Guide" (free at any hotel or tourist office) lists everything in
town. Once you've decided on a show, call the theater directly, ask about
seat availability and prices, and book a ticket using your credit card. Pick
up your ticket 20 minutes before show time. You can even book tickets
from the U.S. before your trip. For this month's (and next month's) schedule, call the British Tourist Authority (tel. 800/462-2748, e-mail: travelinfo
@bta.org.uk), photocopy it from the London newspaper at your library,
or visit www.officiallondontheatre.co.uk.

Ticket agencies, which charge a standard 20 to 25 percent booking
fee, are scalpers with an address. Agencies are worthwhile only if a show
you've just got to see is sold out at the box office. Many ticket agencies
speculate, scarfing up hot tickets, in order to make a killing after the show
is otherwise sold out. U.S. booking agencies get their tickets from another
agency, adding to your expense by involving yet another middleman.
With cheap international phone calls and credit cards, there's no reason
not to book direct.

Cheap theater tricks: Most theaters offer "concessions"—indicated
by a "conc" or "s" in the listings—such as cheap returned tickets, standing room, matinee, and senior or student stand-by deals. Picking up a late
return can get you a great seat at a cheap-seat price. Standing room can
be very cheap. If a show is "sold out," there's usually a way to get a seat.
Call and ask how. The famous "half-price booth" in Leicester (pronounced
"Lester") Square sells cheap tickets to shows on the push list the day of
the show only (Monday–Saturday 2:30–6:30 p.m.). While theater box

offices don't discount tickets, they may give you a better seat at a cheap-seat price on a slow day (if you ask).

I buy the second-cheapest tickets directly from the theater box office. Many theaters are so small that there's hardly a bad seat. After the lights go down, "scooting up" is less than a capital offense. Shakespeare did it.

If your play-going puts you in a literary frame of mind, visit the British Library. While the Library contains 180 miles of bookshelves filling London's deepest basement, one beautiful room filled with state-of-the-art glass display cases shows you the printed treasures of our civilization. You'll see ancient maps; early gospels on papyrus; illuminated manuscripts from the early Middle Ages; the Gutenberg Bible; the Magna Carta; pages from Leonardo's notebooks; original writing by the titans of English literature, from Chaucer and Shakespeare to Dickens and Wordsworth; and music manuscripts from Beethoven to the Beatles.

On Sunday enjoy an hour of craziness at Speaker's Corner in Hyde Park. By noon there are usually several soapbox speakers, screamers, singers, Communists, or comics performing to the crowd of onlookers. "The grass roots of democracy" is actually a holdover from when the gallows stood here and the criminal was allowed to say just about anything he wanted to before he swung. I dare you to raise your voice and gather a crowd—it's easy to do. If you catch the London double-decker bus tour from Speaker's Corner Sunday at 10 a.m., you'll return at noon for the prime-time action.

Kew Gardens are lively and open daily. Cruise the Thames or ride the "tube" to London's favorite gardens for plants galore and a breezy respite from the city. While to most visitors, the Royal Botanic Gardens of Kew are simply a delightful opportunity to wander among 33,000 different types of plants, they represent a hardworking organization committed to understanding and preserving the botanical diversity of our planet. Garden-lovers could easily spend all day exploring Kew's 300 acres. For a quick visit, spend a fragrant hour wandering through three buildings. The famous Palm House, built of iron and glass in 1844 and filled with exotic tropical plant life, is a veritable swing through the tropics. Nearby, there's a Waterlily House that Monet would swim for and the Temperate House—a modern greenhouse with many different climate zones growing countless cacti and bug-munching carnivorous plants.

Nearly every morning you can find a thriving market. There are markets for fish, fruit, used cars, antiques, clothing, and on and on. Portobello Road (antiques on Saturday mornings) and Camden Lock (hip crafts and miscellany, Saturday and Sunday 9 a.m.–6 p.m.) are just two of the many colorful markets that offer you great browsing. Don't expect great prices. These days, the only people getting a steal at London's markets are the pickpockets.

Set your taste buds loose at London's trendy restaurants. I like several places in the throbbing Soho district, an easy stroll from the theater district: Belgo Centraal is a space station world overrun with Trappist monks serving hearty Belgian specialties. The classy restaurant section requires reservations, but grabbing a bench in the boisterous beer hall is more fun. Belgians eat as well as the French and as hearty as the Germans. Specialties include mussels, great fries, and a stunning array of dark, blond, and fruity Belgian beers. Belgo actually makes things Belgian trendy—a formidable feat (near Covent Garden tube station, 50 Earlham Street). Soho Spice Indian is where modern Britain meets Indian tradition—fine Indian cuisine in a trendy jewel-tone ambience (north of Piccadilly Circus at 124 Wardour Street). The Wagamama Noodle Bar is a mod, watch-it-boiled, pan-Asian slurpathon where a youthful crowd shares benches, and waiters take orders with walkie-talkies (10a Lexington Street). Yo! Sushi is a futuristic Japanese food extravaganza experience. With thumping rock, Japanese cable TV, a 60-meter-long conveyor-belt sushi bar, automated sushi machines, and a robotic drink trolley, just sipping a sake on a bar stool here is a trip (2 blocks south of Oxford Street, at 52 Poland Street).

Fun as the restaurants are, no visit to London is complete without breathing someone else's smoke in a woody pub. Pubs are an integral part of English culture. You'll find all kinds, each with its own personality. Taste the different beers. If you don't know what to order, ask the bartender for a half pint of his or her favorite. Real ale, pumped by hand from the basement (look for the longest handles on the bar), is every connoisseur's choice. For a basic American-type beer, ask for a lager. Children are welcome in most pubs but will not be served alcohol until they are 18. Order some pub grub and talk to the people: Enjoy a public house. By getting beyond the bobbies and beefeaters—by meeting the people—you see London take on a personality you can't capture on a postcard.

For good-value accommodations in London's Victoria Station neighborhood, try Winchester Hotel (17 Belgrave Road, tel. 020/7828-2972, fax 020/7828-5191) or Woodville House (107 Ebury Street, tel. 020/7730-1048, fax 020/7730-2574, www.woodvillehouse.co.uk). For more hotels, visit www.ricksteves.com/update/intro.htm, and for all the travel specifics, see this year's edition of Rick Steves' London or Rick Steves' Great Britain.

49. Bath: England at Its Elegant and Frivolous Best

Two hundred years ago, this city of 80,000 was the Hollywood of Britain. Today the former trendsetter of Georgian England invites you to take the 90-minute train ride from London and sample its aristocratic charms.

If ever a city enjoyed looking in the mirror, Bath's the one. It has more government-protected buildings per capita than any town in England. The entire city is built of a warm-tone limestone it calls "Bath stone." The use of normal bricks is forbidden, and Bath beams in its cover-girl complexion.

Bath is an architectural chorus line. It's a triumph of the Georgian style (British for neoclassical), with buildings as competitively elegant as the society they housed. If you look carefully, you'll see false windows built in the name of balance (but not used, in the name of tax avoidance) and classical columns that supported only Georgian egos. Two centuries ago, rich women wore feathered hats atop three-foot hairdos. The very rich stretched their doors and ground floors to accommodate this high fashion.

In Bath, even the street musicians play a Georgian beat.

And today many families have a tough time affording the cost of peeling the soot of the last century from these tall walls.

Few towns combine beauty and hospitality as well as Bath. If you don't visit the tourist office, it'll visit you. In summer, a tourist board crew, wearing red, white, and blue "visitor carer" T-shirts, roams the streets in search of tourists to help.

Bath's town square, a quick walk from the bus and train station, is a bouquet of tourist landmarks, including the Abbey, the Roman and medieval baths, the royal "Pump Room," and a Georgian flute player complete with powdered wig.

A good day in Bath starts with a tour of the historic baths. Even in Roman times, when the town was called Aquae Sulis, the hot mineral water attracted society's elite. The town's importance peaked in 973, when the first king of England, Edgar, was crowned in Bath's Anglo-Saxon Abbey.

Bath

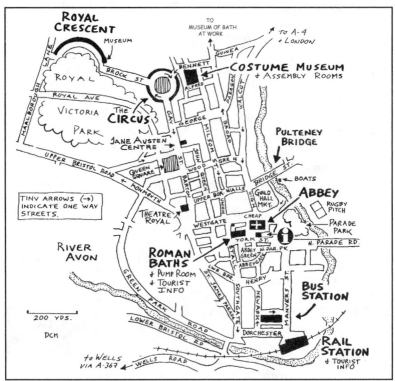

Bath reached a low ebb in the mid-1600s, when the town was just a huddle of huts around the Abbey and a hot springs with 3,000 residents oblivious to the Roman ruins 18 feet below their dirt floors. Then, in 1687, Queen Mary, fighting infertility, bathed here. Within 10 months she gave birth to a son...and a new age of popularity for Bath. The town boomed as a spa resort. Ninety percent of the buildings you see today are from the 18th century. Local architect John Wood was inspired by the Italian architect Palladio to build a "new Rome." The town bloomed in the neoclassical style, and streets were lined with wide "parades" rather than scrawny sidewalks, upon which the women in their stylishly wide dresses could spread their fashionable tails.

For a taste of aristocracy, enjoy tea and scones with live classical music in the nearby Pump Room. For the authentic, if repulsive, finale, have a sip of the awfully curative Bath water from the elegant fountain. To make as much sense as possible of all this fanciness, catch the free city walking tour that leaves from just outside the Pump Room door. Bath's volunteer guides are as much a part of Bath as its architecture. A walking tour gives your visit a little more intimacy, and you'll feel like you actually have a friend in Bath.

In the afternoon, stroll through three centuries of fashion in the Costume Museum. Follow the evolution of clothing styles, one decade at a time, from the first Elizabeth in the 16th century to the second Elizabeth today. The guided tour is excellent—full of fun facts and fascinating trivia. Haven't you always wondered what the line, "Stuck a feather in his cap and called it macaroni," from "Yankee Doodle" means? You'll find the answer (and a lot more) in Bath—the town whose narcissism is justified.

For good-value accommodations in Bath, try Brock's Guest House (32 Brock Street, tel. 01225/338-374, fax 01225/334-245, www.brocksguesthouse.co.uk) or Kennard Hotel (classy, 11 Henrietta Street, tel. 01225/310-472, fax 01225/460-054, www.kennard.co.uk). For more hotels, visit www.ricksteves.com/update /intro.htm, and for all the travel specifics, see this year's edition of Rick Steves' Great Britain.

50. York: Vikings to Dickens

Historians run around York like kids in a candy shop. But the city is so fascinating that even nonhistorians find themselves exploring the past with the same delight they'd give a hall of fun-house mirrors.

York is 200 miles north of London and only two hours by train. For a practical introduction to the city, start your visit by taking one of the free, entertaining, and informative guided walking tours (leaving morning, afternoon, and summer evenings from the tourist office). To keep the day open for museums and shopping and enjoy a quieter tour (with a splash of ghostly gore), take the evening walk. The excellent guides are likeably chatty and opinionated. By the end of the walk, you'll know the latest York city gossip, several ghost stories, and which architectural "monstrosity" the "insensitive" city planners are about to inflict on the public.

With this introductory tour under your belt, you're getting the hang of York and its history. Just as a Boy Scout counts the rings in a tree, you can count the ages of York by the different bricks in the city wall: Roman on the bottom, then Danish, Norman, and the "new" addition—from the 14th century.

The pride of the half-timbered town center is the medieval butcher's street called the Shambles, with its rusty old hooks hiding under the eaves. Six hundred years ago, bloody hunks of meat hung here, dripping into

York

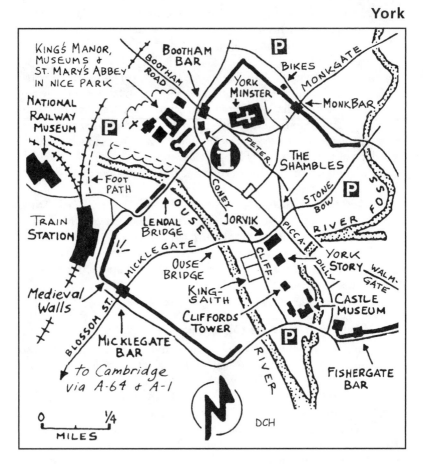

the gutter that still marks the middle of the lane. This slaughterhouse of commercial activity gave our language a new word. What was once a "shambles" is now ye olde tourist shopping mall.

York's four major sights—the York Castle Museum, the Jorvik Viking Museum, the best-in-Europe National Railway Museum, and the huge and historic York Minster church—can keep a speedy sightseer busy for two days.

At York's Castle Museum, Charles Dickens would feel at home. English memorabilia from the 18th and 19th centuries are cleverly displayed in a huge collection of craft shops, old stores, living rooms, and other intimate glimpses of those bygone days.

As towns were being modernized in the 1930s, the museum's founder,

Dr. Kirk, collected entire shops and reassembled them here. On Kirkgate, the museum's most popular section, you can wander through a Lincolnshire butcher's shop, Bath bakery, coppersmith's shop, toy shop, and barbershop. The shops are actually stocked with the merchandise of the day. Eavesdrop on English grannies as they reminisce their way through the museum's displays. The general store is loaded with groceries and candy, and the sports shop has everything you'd need for a game of 19th-century archery, cricket, skittles, or tennis. Anyone for

Fiddling around old York

"whiff-whaff" (Ping-Pong)? In the confectionery, Dr. Kirk beams you into a mouth-watering world of "spice pigs," "togo bullets," "hum bugs," and "conversation lozenges."

In the period rooms, three centuries of Yorkshire living rooms and clothing fashions paint a cozy picture of life centered around the hearth. Ah, a peat fire warming a huge brass kettle and the aroma of freshly baked bread soaking into the heavy, open-beamed ceilings. After walking through the evolution of romantic valentines and unromantic billy clubs, you can trace the development of early home lighting—from simple waxy sticks into the age of electricity. An early electric heater has a small plaque explaining, "How to light an electric fire: Switch it on!"

Dr. Kirk's "memorable collection of bygones" is the closest thing in Europe to a time-tunnel experience, except perhaps for the Jorvik Viking Exhibit just down the street.

A thousand years ago, York was a thriving Viking settlement called Jorvik. While only traces are left of most Viking settlements, Jorvik is an archaeologist's bonanza, the best-preserved Viking city ever excavated.

Sail the "Pirates of the Caribbean" north and back in time 800 years, and you get Jorvik. More a ride than a museum, this exhibit drapes the abundant harvest of this dig in Disney cleverness.

You watch a brief movie showing two people going back in time. Their clothes and the buildings in the background "morph" to fit the passing centuries, which flash by on the screen until...it's A.D. 995. You're in Jorvik.

You climb into a little car and slowly glide through the reconstructed village. Everything—sights, sounds, even smells—has been carefully recreated. You experience a Viking village.

Then your time-traveling train car rolls you into the excavation site, past the actual remains of the reconstructed village you just saw. Stubs of buildings, piles of charred wood, broken pottery—a time-crushed echo of a thriving town.

Your ride ends at the museum filled with artifacts from every aspect of Viking life: clothing, cooking, weapons, clever locks, jewelry, even children's games. The gift shop—the traditional finale of any English museum—capitalized nicely on my newly developed fascination with Vikings in England.

In summer Jorvik's midday lines are more than an hour long. Avoid the line by going very early or very late in the day, or by prebooking (call 01904/543-403). Jorvik's commercial success has spawned a series of similar historic rides that take you into Britain's burly, wax-peopled past. While innovative 10 years ago, Jorvik and its cousins seem tired and gimmicky today. For straightforward Viking artifacts, beautifully explained and set in historical context with no crowds at all, tour the nearby Yorkshire Museum.

York's thunderous National Railway Museum shows 150 fascinating years of British railroad history. Fanning out from a grand roundhouse is an array of historic cars and engines, including Queen Victoria's lavish royal car and the very first "stagecoaches on rails." Even spouses of train buffs will find the exhibits on dining cars, post cars, Pullman cars, and vintage train posters interesting.

York's minster, or cathedral, is the largest Gothic church in Britain. Henry VIII, in his self-serving religious fervor, destroyed nearly everything that was Catholic—except the great York Minster. Henry needed a northern capital for his Anglican church.

The minster is a brilliant example of how the High Middle Ages were far from dark. The east window, the largest medieval glass window in existence, is just one of the art treasures explained in the free hour-long tours given throughout the day. The church's undercroft gives you a chance to climb down, archaeologically and physically, through the centuries to see the roots of the much smaller but still huge Norman church (built in A.D. 1100) that stood on this spot and, below that, the Roman excavations. Constantine was proclaimed Roman emperor here in A.D. 306. The undercroft also gives you a look at the modern concrete and stainless steel save-the-church foundations.

To fully experience the cathedral, go for an evensong service. (No offering plates, no sermon; 5 p.m. on weekdays, 4 p.m. on weekends;

usually spoken, not sung, on Monday.) Arrive early and ask to be seated in the choir. You're in the middle of a spiritual Oz as 40 boys sing psalms— a red-and-white-robed pillow of praise, raised up by the powerful pipe organ. You've got elephant-sized ears as the beautifully carved choir stalls, functioning as giant sound scoops, magnify the thunderous, trumpeting pipes. If you're lucky, the organist will run a spiritual musical victory lap as the congregation breaks up. Thank God for York. Amen.

For good-value accommodations in York, try Airden House (1 St. Mary's, tel. 01904/638-915) or The Sycamore (19 Sycamore Place, tel. & fax 01904/624-712). For more hotels, visit www.ricksteves.com/update/intro.htm, and for all the travel specifics, see this year's edition of Rick Steves' Great Britain.

51. Blackpool: Britain's Coney Island

Blackpool, England's tacky glittering city of fun with a six-mile beach promenade, is ignored by American guidebooks. Located on the coast north of Liverpool, it's the private playground of North England's Anne and Andy Capps.

When I told Brits I was Blackpool-bound, their expressions soured and they asked, "Oh, God, why?" Because it's the ears-pierced-while-you-wait, tipsy-toupee place that local widows and workers go to year after year to escape. Tacky, yes. Lowbrow, OK. But it's as English as can be, and that's what I'm after. Give

British people flock to Blackpool to soak in the seaside resort's atmosphere.

yourself a vacation from your sightseeing vacation. Spend a day just "muckin' about" in Blackpool.

Blackpool is dominated by the Blackpool Tower—a giant fun center that seems to grunt, "Have fun." You pay about $15 to get in, and after that the fun is free. Work your way up through layer after layer of noisy entertainment: circus, bug zone, space world, dinosaur center, aquarium, and the silly house of horrors. Have a coffee break in the elegant ballroom festooned with golden oldies barely dancing to barely live

Blackpool

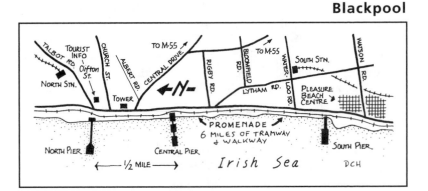

music. The finale at the tip of this 500-foot-tall symbol of Blackpool is a smashing view, especially at sunset. The Tower, a stubby version of its more famous Parisian cousin, was painted gold in 1994 to celebrate its 100th birthday.

Hop a vintage trolley car to survey Blackpool's beach promenade. The cars, which rattle constantly up and down the waterfront, are more fun than driving. Each of the three amusement piers has its own personality. Are you feeling sedate (north pier), young and frisky (central pier), or like a cowboy dragging a wagon full of children (south pier)?

Stroll the Promenade. A million greedy doors try every trick to get you inside. Huge arcade halls advertise free toilets and broadcast bingo numbers into the streets. The randy wind machine under a wax Marilyn Monroe blows at a steady gale, and the smell of fries, tobacco, and sugared popcorn billows everywhere. Milk comes in raspberry or banana in this land where people under incredibly bad wigs look normal. I was told I mustn't leave without having my fortune told by a Gypsy-type spiritualist, but, at $4 per palm, I'll read them myself.

Don't miss an evening at an old-time variety show. Blackpool always has a few razzle-dazzle music, dancing girl, racy humor, magic, and tumbling shows ($12–20 tickets at the door). I enjoy the "old-time music hall" shows. The shows are corny—neither hip nor polished—but it's fascinating to be surrounded by hundreds of partying British seniors, swooning again and waving their hankies to the predictable beat. Busloads of happy widows come from all corners of North England to giggle at racy jokes. The current rage is *Funny Girls*, a burlesque-in-drag show that delights footballers and grannies alike.

Blackpool's "Illuminations" are the talk of England every late September and October. Blackpool (the first city in England to "go electric") stretches its season by illuminating its six-mile waterfront with countless blinking and twinkling lights. The American inside me kept saying, "I've seen bigger and I've seen better," but I stuffed him full with cotton candy and just had some simple fun like everyone else on my specially decorated tram.

British people trying to have fun in the sun at the beach in Blackpool.

For a fun forest of amusements, "Pleasure Beach" is tops. These 42 acres of rides (more than 100, including "the best selection of white-knuckle rides in Europe"), ice-skating shows, cabarets, and amusements attract 6 million people a year, making Pleasure Beach England's most popular single attraction. Their roller coaster is one of the world's highest (235 feet), fastest (85 mph), and least likely to have me on board.

For me, Blackpool's top sight is its people. You'll see England here like nowhere else. Grab someone's hand and a big stick of candy floss (cotton candy) and stroll. Ponder the thought that legions of English dream of actually retiring here to spend their last years, day after day, dog-paddling through this urban cesspool of fun, wearing hats with built-in ponytails.

Blackpool is a scary thing to recommend. Maybe I overrate it. Many people (ignoring the "50 million flies can't all be wrong" logic) think I do. If you're not into kitsch and greasy spoons (especially if you're a nature lover and the weather happens to be good), skip Blackpool and spend more time in nearby North Wales or England's Lake District. But if you're traveling with kids—or still are one yourself—visit Blackpool, Britain's fun puddle where every Englishman goes, but none will admit it.

For good-value accommodations in Blackpool, try Robin Hood Hotel (100 Queens Promenade, tel. 01253/351-599) or Beechcliffe Private Hotel (16 Shaftesbury Avenue, tel. 01253/353-075). For more hotels, visit www.ricksteves.com/update /intro.htm, and for all the travel specifics, see this year's edition of Rick Steves' Great Britain.

52. The Cotswold Villages: Inventors of Quaint

The Cotswold region, a 25-by-50-mile chunk of Gloucestershire, is a sightseeing treat: crisscrossed with hedgerows, raisined with storybook villages, and sprinkled with sheep.

As with many fairy-tale regions of Europe, the present-day beauty of the Cotswolds was the result of an economic disaster. Wool was a huge industry in medieval England, and the Cotswold sheep grew it best. Wool money built lovely towns and palatial houses as the region prospered. Local "wool" churches are called "cathedrals" for their scale and wealth. A typical prayer etched into their stained glass reads, "I thank my God and ever shall, it is the sheep hath paid for all."

With the rise of cotton and the Industrial Revolution, the woolen industry collapsed, mothballing the Cotswold towns into a depressed time warp. Today visitors enjoy a harmonious blend of humanity and nature: The most pristine of English countrysides decorated with time-passed villages, gracefully dilapidated homes of an impoverished nobility, tell-me-a-story stone fences, and "kissing gates" you wouldn't want to experience alone. Appreciated by hordes of 21st-century romantics, and in spite of local moaning about "the recession," the Cotswolds are enjoying new prosperity.

The area is provincial. Chatty locals, while ever so polite, commonly rescue themselves from a gossipy tangent by saying, "It's all very... ummm...yyya." Rich people open their gardens to support their favorite

It's hard to go wrong in the Cotswolds.

The Cotswolds

MAJOR ROAD
MINOR ROAD

TO STRATFORD

HIDCOTE MANOR

A·46

A·34

N

MICKLETON

TO EVESHAM & M-5

ILMING-TON

SHIPSTON

CHIPPING CAMPDEN

B·4035

BROADWAY→

A-44

B·4081

BROAD CAMPDEN

B·4429

STANTON

BLOCK-LEY

A·429

MORETON-IN-MARSH

COTSWOLD WAY FOOTPATH

SNOWSHILL

A·44

A·34

STANWAY

UPPER SWELL

A·424

A-44

WINCHE-COMBE

FORD

B·4077

TO OXFORD & BLENHEIM

LOWER SWELL→

A-436

STOW-ON-THE-WOLD

TO CHELTEN-HAM

GUITING POWER

B·4068

A·436

BOURTON-ON-THE-WATER

TO OXFORD

UPPER & LOWER SLAUGHTER

A·429

A·429

TO BURFORD & OXFORD

5 MILES

TO CIRENCESTER

DCH

charities, while the less couth enjoy "badger baiting" (a gambling cousin of cockfighting where a badger, with its teeth and claws taken out, is mangled by right-wing dogs).

The north Cotswolds are best. Two of the region's coziest towns, Chipping Camden and Stow-on-the-Wold, are eight and four miles respectively from Moreton, the only Cotswold town with a train station. Any of these—Chipping Camden, Stow, or Moreton—would make a fine home base for your exploration of the thatch-happiest of Cotswold villages and walks.

Chipping Campden is a working market town, home of some proudly thatched roofs and the richest Cotswold wool merchants. Both the great British historian Trevelyan and I call Chipping Campden's High Street the finest in England.

Walk the full length of High Street (like most market towns, wide enough for plenty of sheep business on market days). Near the south end you'll find the best thatched homes. Walking north on High Street, you'll pass the Market Hall (1627), the wavy roof of the first great wool mansion, a fine and free memorial garden, and, finally, the town's famous 15th-century Gothic "wool" church.

Stow-on-the-Wold has become a crowded tourist town, but most visitors are daytrippers, so even summer nights are lazy and quiet. The town has no real sights other than itself, some good pubs, cutesy shops, and art galleries draped seductively around a big town square. The tourist office sells a handy walking tour brochure called "Town Trail." A visit to Stow is not complete until you've locked your partner in the stocks on the green.

Moreton-in-Marsh, an easy home base for those without a car, is a Stow or Chipping Campden without the touristic sugar. Rather than gift and antique stores, you'll find streets lined with real shops. Ironmongers sell cottage nameplates, and carpet shops are strewn with the remarkable patterns that decorate B&B floors. A traditional market filling High Street with 260 stalls gets the whole town shin-kicking each Tuesday. There is an economy outside of tourism in the Cotswolds, and you'll feel it in Moreton.

Stanway, Stanton, and Snowshill, between Stow and Chipping Campden, are my nominations for the cutest Cotswold villages. Like marshmallows in hot chocolate, they nestle side by side—awaiting your arrival.

Stanway, while not much of a village, is notable for its manor house. Lord Neidpath, whose family tree charts relatives back to 1270, opens his melancholy home—Stanway House—to visitors ($5, August–September, Tuesday and Thursday from 2–5 p.m.).

While his bitchin' 14th-century Tithe Barn is no longer used to greet motley peasants with their feudal "rents," the lord still collects rents from his vast land holdings. But the place feels poor, his children live in London, and those invited to his parties don't even RSVP. His manor dogs have their own cutely painted "family tree," but Lord Neidpath admits that his current dog is "all character and no breeding."

Imprisoned by the charm of the Cotswolds

The manor house, with its likable Old World elegance, has a story to tell. And so do the docents (modern-day peasants who, even without family trees, probably have relatives going back just as far in this village) stationed in each room. Talk to these people. Probe. That's what they're there for. Learn what you can about this side of England.

Stanway and neighboring Stanton are separated by a great oak forest and grazing land with parallel waves actually echoing the furrows plowed by medieval farmers. Let someone else drive so you can pop out of the sunroof like a balloon—under an oak canopy, past stone walls and sheep—to Stanton.

In **Stanton,** flowers trumpet, door knockers shine, and slate shingles clap: A rooting section cheering visitors up the town's main street. The church, which dates back to the ninth century, betrays a pagan past. Stanton is at the intersection of two lines (called ley lines) connecting prehistoric sights. Churches such as Stanton's, built on a pagan holy ground, are dedicated to St. Michael. You'll see his well-worn figure above the door as you enter. Inside, above the capitals in the nave, find the pagan symbols for the moon and the sun. But it's Son worship that's long established, and the list of rectors goes back to 1269. Finger the back pew grooves, worn away by sheepdog leashes. A man's sheepdog accompanied him everywhere. The popular Mount Pub is just up the hill.

Snowshill, another nearly edible little bundle of cuteness, has a photogenic triangular square with a fine pub at its base. The Snowshill Manor is a dark and mysterious old palace filled with the lifetime collection of the long-gone Charles Paget Wade (who looks eerily like the tragic young Lord Neidpath of Stanway House). It's one big musty celebration of craftsmanship, from finely carved spinning wheels to frightening Samurai armor to tiny elaborate figurines carved by long-forgotten prisoners from the bones of meat served at dinner. Taking seriously his family motto, "Let Nothing Perish," he dedicated his life and fortune to preserving things finely crafted. The house (whose management made me promise not to promote it as an eccentric collector's pile of curiosities) really shows off Mr. Wade's ability to recognize and acquire fine examples of craftsmanship. It's all very...ummm...yyya.

The Cotswolds are walker country. The English love to walk the peaceful footpaths that shepherds walked back when "polyester" meant two girls. They vigorously defend their age-old right to free passage. Once a year the "Rambling Society" organizes a "Mass Trespass," when each of England's 50,000 miles of public footpaths is walked. By assuring each path is used at least once a year, they frustrate fence-happy landlords. Most of the land is privately owned and fenced in, but you're welcome (and legally entitled) to pass through, using the various sheep-stopping steps, gates, and turnstiles provided at each stone wall.

After a well-planned visit, you'll remember everything about the Cotswolds—the walks, churches, pubs, B&Bs, thatched roofs, gates, tourist offices, and even the sheep—as quaint.

For good-value accommodations in Chipping Campden, try Kettle House B&B (High Street, tel. 01386/840-328, fax 01386/841-740, www.kettlehouse .co.uk); in Stow-on-the-Wold, West Deyne B&B (Lower Swell Road, tel. 01451/831-011); and in Moreton-in-Marsh, Treetops B&B (London Road, tel. & fax 01608/651-036). For more hotels, visit www.ricksteves.com/update /intro.htm, and for all the travel specifics, see this year's edition of Rick Steves' Great Britain.

53. Mysterious Britain

Stonehenge, Holy Grail, Avalon, Loch Ness . . . there's a mysterious side of Britain steeped in lies, legends, and at least a little truth. Haunted ghost walks and Nessie the Monster stories are profitable tourist gimmicks. But the cultural soil that gives us Beowulf, Shakespeare, and "God Save the Queen" is fertilized with a murky story that goes back to 3000 B.C., pre-dating Egypt's first pyramids.

As today's sightseers zip from castle to pub, they pass countless stone circles, forgotten tombs, man-made hills, and figures carved into hillsides whose stories will never be fully understood. Certain traveling Druids skip the beefeater tours and zero right in on this side of Britain. But with a little background, even the skeptic can appreciate Britain's historic aura.

Britain is crisscrossed by lines connecting prehistoric Stonehenge-type sights. Apparently prehistoric tribes intentionally built sites along this huge network of lines, called ley lines, which some think may have functioned together as a cosmic relay or circuit.

Glastonbury, two hours west of London and located on England's most powerful ley line, gurgles with a thought-provoking mix of history and mystery. As you climb the Glastonbury Tor, notice the remains of the labyrinth that made the hill a challenge to climb 5,000 years ago.

In A.D. 37, Joseph of Arimathea—one of Jesus' wealthy disciples—brought vessels containing the blood and sweat of Jesus to Glastonbury and, with that, Christianity to England. While this is "proven" by fourth-century writings and accepted by the Church, the Holy Grail legend that sprang from this in the Middle Ages isn't.

In the 12th century, England needed a morale-boosting folk hero to

inspire its people during a war
with France. The ruins of a fifth-
century Celtic timber fort at Glastonbury were considered proof of
the greatness of that century's
obscure warlord, Arthur. Glastonbury became linked with King
Arthur and his knights after
Arthur's supposed remains were
found buried in the abbey.
Arthur's search for the Holy

Mysterious Britain

Grail, the chalice used at the Last Supper, could be mere legend. But many
people think the Grail trail ends at the bottom of the "Chalice Well," a
natural spring at the base of Glastonbury Tor.

In the 16th century, Henry VIII, on his church-destroying rampage,
wrecked the powerful Glastonbury Abbey. For emphasis he hung and
quartered the abbot, sending the parts of his body on four national
tours . . . at the same time. While that was it for the abbot, two centuries
later Glastonbury rebounded. In an 18th-century tourism campaign,
thousands signed affidavits stating that water from the Chalice Well
healed them, and once again Glastonbury was on the tourist map.

Today Glastonbury and its Tor are a center for searchers, too creepy
for the mainstream church but just right for those looking for a place to
recharge their crystals. Since the society that built the labyrinth wor-
shipped a mother goddess, the hill, or Tor, is seen by many today as a
Mother Goddess symbol.

After climbing the Tor (great view, easy parking, always open), visit
the Chalice Well at its base. Then tour the evocative ruins of the abbey,
with its informative visitors center and a model of the church before
Henry got to it. Don't leave without a browse through the town. The
Rainbow's End Café (2 minutes from the abbey on High Street) is a fine
place for salads and New Age people-watching. Read the notice board
for the latest on midwives and male bonding.

From Glastonbury, as you drive across southern England, you'll see
giant figures carved on hillsides. The white chalk cliffs of Dover stretch
across the south of England, and almost anywhere you dig you hit chalk.
While most of the giant figures are creations of 18th- and 19th-century
humanists reacting against the coldness of the industrial age, three Celtic
figures (the Long Man of Willmington, the White Horse of Uffington,
and the Cerne Abbas Giant) have, as far as history is concerned, always
been there.

Stonehenge is surrounded by barbed wire. This is as close as you'll get.

The Cerne Abbas Giant is armed with a big club and an erection. For centuries, people fighting infertility would sleep on Cerne Abbas. And, as my English friend explained, "maidens can still be seen leaping over his willy."

Stonehenge, England's most famous stone circle, is an hour's drive from Glastonbury. Built between 3100 and 1100 B.C. with huge stones brought all the way from Wales or Ireland, it still functions as a remarkably accurate celestial calendar. A recent study of more than 300 similar circles in Britain found that each was designed to calculate the movement of the sun, moon, and stars, and even to predict eclipses in order to help these early societies know when to plant, harvest, and party. Even today, as the summer solstice sun sets in just the right slot at Stonehenge, pagans boogie. Modern-day tourists and Druids are kept at a distance by a fence, but if you're driving, Stonehenge is just off the highway and worth a stop ($6). Even a free look from the road is impressive.

Why didn't the builders of Stonehenge use what seem like perfectly adequate stones nearby? There's no doubt that the particular "blue stones" used in parts of Stonehenge were found only in (and therefore brought from) Wales or Ireland. Think about the ley lines. Ponder the fact that many experts accept none of the explanations of how these giant stones were transported. Then imagine congregations gathering here 4,000 years ago, raising thought levels, creating a powerful life force transmitted along the ley lines. Maybe a particular kind of stone was essential for maximum energy transmission. Maybe the stones were levitated here. Maybe psychics really do create powerful vibes. Maybe not. It's as unbelievable as electricity used to be.

The nearby stone circle at **Avebury**, 16 times the size of Stonehenge, is one-sixteenth as touristy. You're free to wander among a hundred stones, ditches, mounds, and curious patterns from the past, as well as the village of Avebury, which grew up in the middle of this 1,400-foot-wide neolithic circle.

Spend some time at Avebury. Take the mile-long walk around the circle. Visit the fine little archaeology museum and pleasant Stones Café next to the National Trust store. The Red Lion Pub (also within the circle) has good, inexpensive pub grub. As you leave, notice the pyramid-shaped Silbury Hill. This man-made mound, nearly 5,000 years old, is a reminder that you've only scratched the surface of Britain's fascinating prehistoric and religious landscape.

A fine way to mix neolithic wonders and nature is to explore one of England's many turnstile-free moors. You can get lost in these stark and sparsely populated time-passed commons, which have changed over the centuries about as much as the longhaired sheep that seem to gnaw on moss in their sleep. Directions are difficult to keep. It's cold and gloomy, as nature rises like a slow tide against human constructions. A crumpled castle loses itself in lush overgrowth. A church grows shorter as tall weeds eat at the stone crosses and bent tombstones.

Dartmoor is the wildest moor—a wonderland of green and powerfully quiet rolling hills in the southwest near the tourist centers of Devon and Cornwall. Crossed by only two or three main roads, most of the area is either unused or shared by its 30,000 villagers as a common grazing land—a tradition since feudal days. Dartmoor is best toured by car, but it can be explored by bike, rental horse, thumb, or foot. Bus service is meager. Several national park centers provide maps and information. Settle into a small-town B&B or hostel. This is one of England's most remote corners—and it feels that way.

Dartmoor, with more Bronze Age stone circles and huts than any other chunk of England, is perfect for those who dream of enjoying their own private Stonehenge sans barbed wire, police officers, parking lots, tourists, and port-a-loos (English sani-cans). The local Ordnance Survey maps show the moor peppered with bits of England's mysterious past. Hator Down and Gidleigh are especially thought-provoking.

Word of the wonders lurking just a bit deeper into the moors tempted me away from my Gidleigh B&B. Venturing in, I sank into the powerful, mystical moorland. Climbing over a hill, surrounded by hateful but sleeping towers of ragged granite, I was swallowed up. Hills followed hills followed hills—green, growing gray in the murk.

Where was that 4,000-year-old circle of stone? I wandered in a world of greenery, eerie wind, white rocks, and birds singing but unseen. Then the stones appeared, frozen in a forever game of statue-maker. For endless centuries they had waited patiently, still and silent, for me to come. I sat on a fallen stone, holding the leash as my imagination ran wild, pondering the people who roamed England so long before written history documented their story. Grabbing the moment to write, I took out my journal. The moor, the distant town, the chill, this circle of stones. I dipped my pen into the cry of the birds and wrote.

For good-value accommodations in Dartmoor, try St. Johns West B&B (in Gidleigh, near Chagford, tel. 01647/432-468, e-mail: jwwest@ntlworld.com).

54. Dingle Peninsula: A Gaelic Bike Ride

Be forewarned, Ireland is seductive. In many areas, traditions are strong and stress is a foreign word. I fell in love with the friendliest land this side of Sicily. It all happened in a Gaeltacht.

Gaeltachts are national parks for culture, where the government protects the old Irish ways. Shaded green on many maps, these regions brighten the west coast of the Emerald Isle. "Gaeltacht" means a place where Gaelic (or Irish) is spoken. The Gaelic culture is more than just the old language. You'll find it tilling the rocky fields, singing in the pubs, and lingering in the pride of the small-town preschool that brags "all Irish."

Many signposts are in Gaelic only, with the old Irish lettering. If your map is in English . . . good luck. The old-timers are a proud bunch. Often, when the signposts are in both English and Gaelic, the English is spray-painted out. And Irish yuppies report that Gaelic is cool and on the rise.

Dingle Peninsula—green, rugged, and untouched—is my favorite Gaeltacht. While the big tour buses clog the neighboring Ring of Kerry before heading east to kiss the Blarney Stone, in Dingle it still feels like the fish and the farm actually matter. Fifty fishing boats sail from Dingle. And a nostalgic whiff of peat continues to fill its nighttime streets,

Ireland's top attraction—the friendliest people in Europe

offering visitors an escape into pure Ireland. For 15 years my Irish dreams have been set here, on this sparse but lush peninsula where locals are fond of saying, "The next parish is Boston." Of the peninsula's 10,000 residents, 1,300 live in Dingle town. Its few streets, lined with ramshackle but gaily painted shops and pubs, run up from a rain-stung harbor. During the day, kids—already working on ruddy beer-glow cheeks—roll kegs up the streets and into the pubs in preparation for another tin-whistle night.

Fishing once dominated Dingle, and the town's only visitors were students of old Irish ways. Then, in 1970, the movie *Ryan's Daughter* introduced the world to Dingle. The trickle of its fans has grown to a flood, as word has spread of its musical, historical, gastronomical, and scenic charms—not to mention the friendly dolphin that hangs out in the harbor.

THE DINGLE PENINSULA CIRCLE—BY BIKE OR CAR

The Dingle Peninsula is 10 miles wide and runs 40 miles from Tralee to Slea Head. The top of its mountainous spine is Mount Brandon—at 3,300 feet, the second tallest mountain in Ireland. While only tiny villages lie west of Dingle town, the peninsula is home to half a million sheep. The weather on this distant tip of Ireland is often misty, foggy, and rainy. But don't complain—as locals will explain, there is no bad weather . . . only inappropriate clothing. Good and bad weather blow by in a steady meteorological parade. With stops, the 30-mile circuit (go with the traffic—clockwise) takes five hours by bike or three hours by car.

Leaving Dingle town, it becomes clear that the peninsula is an open-air museum. It's littered with monuments reminding visitors that the town has been the choice of Bronze Age settlers, Dark Age monks, English landlords, and Hollywood directors. The Milestone B&B decorates its front yard not with a pink flamingo, but with a pillar stone—one of more than 2,000 stony pieces in the puzzle of prehistoric life here.

Across the bay, the manor house of Lord Ventry is surrounded by palms, magnolias, fuchsias, and fancy flora introduced to Dingle by the Englishman who once owned the peninsula. His legacy—thanks only to the mild Gulf Stream–protected weather—is the festival of fuchsias that lines the peninsula roads. And just down the street, locals point to the little blue house that kept Tom Cruise and Nicole Kidman cozy during the filming of *Far and Away*.

Near a yellow schoolhouse, a Gaelic street sign warns, "Taisteaal go Mall"—slow down. Near the playground students hide out in circular remains of a late Stone Age ring fort. In 500 B.C. it was a petty Celtic

Dingle Peninsula

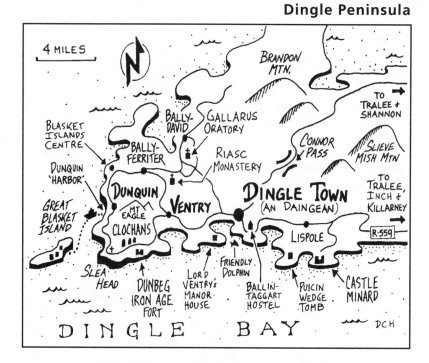

chieftain's headquarters, a stone-and-earth stockade filled with little stone houses. So many of these ring forts survived the centuries because of superstitious beliefs that they were "fairy forts."

In the little town of Ventry, talk with the chatty Irish you'll meet along the roadside. An elfish, black-clad Gaelic man might point out a landmark or sing you a song. When I asked if he was born here, he breathed deeply and said, "No, 'twas about six miles down the road." When I told him where I was from, a faraway smile filled his eyes as he looked out to sea and sighed, "Aye, the shores of Americay."

The wet sod of Dingle is soaked with medieval history. In the darkest depths of the Dark Ages, when literate life almost died in Europe, peace-loving, bookwormish monks fled the chaos of the Continent and its barbarian raids. They sailed to this drizzly fringe of the known world and lived their monastic lives in lonely stone igloos or "beehive huts," which you'll see dotting the landscape.

Several groups of these mysterious huts, called *clochans*, line the road. Built without mortar by seventh-century monks, these huts take you back. Climb into one. You're all alone, surrounded by dank mist and the realization that it was these monks who kept literacy alive in Europe. To give you an idea of their importance, Charlemagne, who ruled much of Europe in the year 800, imported Irish monks to be his scribes.

It was from this peninsula that Saint Brandon, the semimythical priest-explorer, is said to have set sail in the sixth century in search of a legendary western paradise. Some think he beat Columbus to North America . . . by nearly a thousand years!

Rounding Slea Head, the point in Europe closest to America, the rugged coastline offers smashing views of deadly black-rock cliffs and the distant Blasket Islands. The crashing surf "races in like white horses," while long-haired sheep—bored with the weather, distant boats, and the lush countryside—couldn't care less.

Just off the road you'll see the scant remains of the scant home that was burned by the movie-star equivalent of Lord Ventry as he evicted his potato-eating tenants in the movie *Far and Away*.

Even without Hollywood, this is a bleak and godforsaken place. Sand and seaweed heaped on the clay eventually became soil. The created land was marginal, just barely growing potatoes. Ragged patches of this reclaimed land climb the hillsides. Rocks were moved and piled into fences.

Stacks of history can be read into the stones. From the air, Ireland looks like alligator skin—a maze of stone fences. With unrivaled colonial finesse, the British required Irish families to divide their land among all heirs. This doomed even the largest estates to fragmentation, shrinking lots to sizes just large enough to starve a family. Ultimately, of course, the land ended up in the possession of British absentee landlords. The tiny rock-fenced lots that carve up the treeless landscape remind the farmers of the structural poverty that shaped their history. And weary farmers have never bothered with gates. Even today they take a hunk of wall down, let their sheep pass, and stack the rocks again.

Study the highest fields, untouched since the planting of 1845, when the potatoes never matured and rotted in the ground. The vertical ridges of the potato beds can still be seen—a reminder of that year's great famine, which, through starvation or emigration, nearly halved Ireland's population. Because its endearing people have endured so much, Ireland is called the Terrible Beauty.

Take your time at the Gallarus Oratory, circa A.D. 800, the sight-seeing highlight of your peninsula tour. One of Ireland's best-preserved early Christian churches, its shape is reminiscent of an upturned boat. Its watertight dry-stone walls have sheltered travelers and pilgrims for 1,200 years.

From the Oratory, continue up the rugged one-lane road to the crest of the hill, then coast back into Dingle—hungry, thirsty, and ready for...

DINGLE PUBS

With 50 pubs for its 1,300 people, Dingle is a pub crawl waiting to happen. Even if you're not into pubs, give these a whirl. The town is renowned among traditional musicians as a place to get work ("£30 a day, tax free, plus drink"). There's music every night ($2 beers and never a cover charge). The scene is a decent mix of locals, Americans, and Germans. While two pubs, the Small Bridge Bar and O'Flaherty's, are the most famous for their good beer and folk music, make a point to wander the town and follow your ear.

When you say "a beer, please" in an Irish pub, you'll get a pint of "the black beauty with a blonde head"—Guinness. If you want a small beer, ask for a half pint. Never rush your bartender when he's pouring a Guinness. It takes time—almost sacred time. If you don't like Guinness, try it in Ireland. It doesn't travel well and is better in its homeland. Murphy's is a very good Guinness-like stout, but a bit smoother and milder.

In an Irish pub, you're a guest on your first night; after that, you're a regular. Women traveling alone need not worry—you'll become part of the pub family in no time.

It's a tradition to buy your table a round, and then for each person to reciprocate. If an Irishman buys you a drink, thank him by saying, *"Guh rev mah a gut."* Offer him a toast in Irish—*"Slahn-chuh!"* A good excuse for a conversation is to ask to be taught a few words of Gaelic. You've got a room full of Gaelic speakers who will remind you that every year five languages go extinct. They'd love to teach you a few words of their favorite language.

Craic (crack) is the art of conversation—the sport that accompanies drinking in a pub. People are there to talk. Join in. Here's a goofy excuse for some *craic*: Ireland—small as it is—has many dialects. People from Cork (the big city of Ireland's south coast) are famous for talking very fast (and in a squeaky voice). So fast that some even talk in letters alone. "ABCD fish?" (Anybody see the fish?) "DRO fish." (There are no fish.) "DR fish." (There are fish.) "CDBD Is." (See the beady eyes?) "OIBJ DR fish." (Oh aye, be Jeeze, there are fish.) For a possibly more appropriate spin, replace "fish" with "bird" (girl). This is obscure, but your pub neighbor may understand and enjoy hearing it. If nothing else, you won't seem so intimidating to him anymore.

Also, you might ask if the people of one county are any smarter than the next. Kerry people are famous for being a bit out of it. It's said that when the stupidest man in county Cork moved to county Kerry, it raised the cumulative IQ in each area.

TRADITIONAL IRISH MUSIC

Traditional music is alive and popular in pubs throughout Ireland. "Sessions" (musical evenings) may be planned and advertised or impromptu. Traditionally, musicians just congregate and jam. There will generally be a fiddle, flute or tin whistle, guitar, *bodhran* (goat-skin drum), and maybe an accordion. Things usually get going around 9:30 or 10 p.m. "Last call" (last chance to order a drink before closing) is around "half eleven" (11:30 p.m.).

The *bodhran* is played with two hands: One wielding a small two-headed club and the other stretching the skin to change the tone and pitch. The wind and string instruments embellish melody lines with lots of improvised ornamentation. Occasionally the fast-paced music will stop, and one person will sing an a cappella lament. This is the one time when the entire pub will stop to listen, as sad lyrics fill the smoke-stained room. Stories—ranging from struggles against English rule to love songs—are always heartfelt. Spend a lament studying the faces in the crowd.

The music comes in sets of three songs. Whoever happens to be leading determines the next song, only as the song the group is playing is about to be finished. If he wants to pass on the decision, it's done with eye contact and a nod.

A session can be magic, or it may be lifeless. If the chemistry is right, it's one of the great Irish experiences. The music churns intensely while the group casually enjoys exploring each others' musical styles. The drummer dodges the fiddler's playful bow, with his cigarette sticking half-ash straight from the middle of his mouth. Sipping their pints, a faint but steady buzz is skillfully maintained. The floor on the musicians' platform is stomped paint-free, and barmaids scurry artfully through the commotion, gathering towers of empty cream-crusted glasses. With knees up and heads down, the music goes round and round. Make yourself perfectly at home, drumming the table or playing the 10-pence coins.

GREAT BLASKET

Great Blasket, a rugged, uninhabited island off the tip of Dingle Peninsula, seems particularly close to the soul of Ireland. Its population, once as many as 160 people, dwindled until the last handful of residents was moved by the government to the mainland in 1953. These people were the most traditional Irish community of the 20th century—the symbol of antique Gaelic culture. They had a special closeness to their island, combined with a knack for vivid storytelling. From this poor, primitive but proud fishing and farming community came three writers of international repute whose Gaelic work—basically tales of life on Great Blasket—is translated into

Ghost town on Blasket Island

many languages. In shops all over the peninsula you'll find *Peig* (by Peig Sayers), *Twenty Years a-Growing* (Maurice O'Sullivan), and *The Islander* (Thomas O'Crohan).

Today Great Blasket is a grassy three-mile poem, overrun with memories. With fat rabbits, ruffled sheep, abandoned stone homes, and a handful of seals, it's ideal for wind-blown but thoughtful walks.

An irregular ferry service shuttles visitors from a desperate wad of concrete known as "Dunquin Harbor" to Great Blasket. The schedule is dictated by demand and weather.

The state-of-the-art Blasket and Gaelic Heritage Center (on Dingle Peninsula facing the islands) creatively gives visitors the best possible look at the language, literature, life, and times of the Blasket Islanders. See the fine video, hear the sounds, read the poems, browse through old photos, and then gaze out the big windows at those rugged islands and imagine. Even if you never got past limericks, the poetry of these people—so pure and close to each other and nature—is an inspiration.

For good-value accommodations in Dingle, try Sraid Eoin B&B (John Street, tel. 066/915-1409, fax 066/915-2156) or Corner House B&B (simple, Dykegate Street, tel. 066/915-1516). For more hotels, visit www.ricksteves.com/update/intro .htm, and for all the travel specifics, see this year's edition of Rick Steves' Ireland.

55. Northern Ireland and Belfast

Ireland is a split island still struggling with questions left over from its stint as a British colony. While the island won its independence back in the 1920s, the predominantly Protestant northern section opted to stick with its pope-ophobic partners in London. While somewhere between a headache and a tragedy for locals, this adds up to some fascinating travel opportunities for you and me. And lately there are some good, solid reasons to be hopeful.

With so many people working so hard to bring Ireland together, a browse through Belfast will give you more faith in people than despair over headlines. There's a guarded optimism as creative grass-roots efforts to grow peace are taking hold.

Make your visit to Ireland complete by including Northern Ireland. This is a British-controlled six-county section of a nine-county area called Ulster. It offers the tourist a very different but still very Irish world. The British-ruled counties of Northern Ire-

With this Union Jack bulldog street mural, a Belfast Protestant neighborhood makes its Unionist feelings pitbull-clear.

land, long a secret enjoyed and toured mainly by its own inhabitants, are finally being recognized by international travelers.

Of course, people are being killed in Northern Ireland—but not as many as in New York City. Car accidents kill more Northern Irish than do bombs or guns. With common sense, travel in this area is safe. No American has ever been injured by "the Troubles," and travelers give Northern Ireland rave reviews.

Include Belfast in your Irish travel plans. Here's an itinerary that will introduce you to a capital city of 400,000 and Ireland's best open-air folk museum. At the same time, you'll meet some of the friendliest people on earth and learn firsthand about their struggle.

BELFAST

Seventeenth-century Belfast was only a village. With the influx, or "plantation," of Scottish and English settlers, Belfast boomed, spurred by the success of the local linen, rope-making, and shipbuilding industries. The Industrial Revolution took root with a vengeance. While the rest of Ireland remained rural, Belfast earned its nickname, "Old Smoke," when many of the brick buildings you'll see today were built. The year 1888 marked the birth of modern Belfast. After Queen Victoria granted city status to this town of 300,000, citizens built its centerpiece, City Hall.

Belfast is the birthplace of the Titanic (and many ships that didn't sink). The two huge mustard-colored cranes (the biggest in the world, nicknamed Samson and Goliath) rise like skyscrapers above the harbor, as if declaring this town's shipbuilding might. It feels like a new morning in Belfast. Security checks, once a tiresome daily routine, are now rare. What was the traffic-free security zone has shed its gray skin and

Belfast

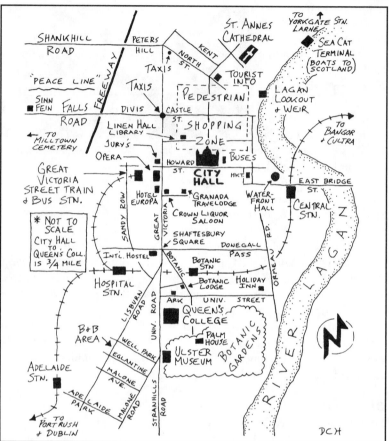

become a bright and bustling pedestrian zone. On my last visit, the children dancing in the street were both Catholic and Protestant—part of a community summer-camp program giving kids from both communities reason to live together rather than apart.

Still, it's a fragile peace and a tenuous hope. The pointedly Protestant billboards and the helicopter that still hovers over the Catholic end of town remain a reminder that the island is split, and about a million Protestants like it that way.

A visit to Belfast is actually easy from Dublin. Consider this plan for the most interesting Dublin daytrip: With the handy 90-minute Dublin–Belfast train ($46 "day-return" tickets), you can leave Dublin early and catch the Belfast City Hall tour at 10:30 a.m. After browsing through the pedestrian zone, ride a shared cab through the Falls Road neighborhood. At 2:30 p.m. head out to the Cultra Folk and Transport Museum. Picnic on the evening train back to Dublin. The well-organized daytripper will get a taste of both Belfast's Industrial Age glory and the present (and related) troubles. It will be a happy day

Wall murals reinforce political walls.

when the sectarian neighborhoods of Belfast have nothing to be sectarian about. For a look at what was one of the home bases for the Troubles, explore the working-class Catholic Falls Road neighborhood.

A few blocks from City Hall you'll find a square filled with old black cabs—and the only Gaelic-language signs in downtown Belfast. These shared black cabs efficiently shuttle residents from outlying neighborhoods up and down Falls Road and to the city center. All cabs go up Falls Road to Milltown Cemetery, passing lots of murals and Sinn Fein (the IRA's political wing) headquarters. Sit in front and talk to the cabbie. Easy-to-flag-down cabs run every minute or so in each direction on Falls Road. They do one-hour tours for about $25 (cheap for a small group of travelers).

At the Milltown Cemetery you'll be directed past all the Gaelic crosses down to the IRA "Roll of Honor"—set apart from the thousands of other graves by little green railings. They are treated like fallen soldiers. You'll see a memorial to Bobby Sands and the nine other hunger strikers that starved in support of a united Ireland in 1981.

The Sinn Fein headquarters is on Falls Road (look for the protective boulders on the sidewalk and the Irish Republic flag on the roof). The adjacent bookstore is worth a look. Page through books featuring color photos of the political murals that decorate the local buildings. Money raised here supports families of imprisoned IRA members.

A sad corrugated wall called the "Peace Line" runs a block or so north of Falls Road, separating the Catholics from the Protestants in the Shankill Road area.

While you can ride a shared black cab up Shankill Road, the easiest way to get a dose of the Unionist side is to walk Sandy Row—a working-class Protestant street behind the Hotel Europa (Europe's most-bombed hotel). You'll see a few murals filled with Unionist symbolism. The mural of William of Orange's victory over the Catholic King James II (Battle of the Boyne, 1690) stirs Unionist hearts.

Most of Ireland has grown disillusioned by the violence wrought by the Irish Republican Army (IRA) and the Protestants' Ulster Volunteer Force (UVF), which are now seen by many as rival groups of terrorists who actually work together in Mafia style to run free and wild in their established territories. Maybe the solution can be found in the mellowness of Ulster retirement homes, where old "Papishes" with their rosaries and old "Prods" with their prayer books sit side by side talking to the same heavenly father. But that kind of peace is elusive. An Ulster Protestant on holiday in England once told me with a weary sigh, "Tomorrow I go back to my tribe."

For a trip into a cozier age, take the eight-mile bus or train ride to the Ulster Folk and Transport Museum. The Folk Museum is an open-air collection of 30 reconstructed buildings from all over the nine counties of Ulster, designed to showcase the region's traditional lifestyles. After wandering through the old town site (church, print shop, schoolhouse, humble Belfast row home, and so on), you'll head into the country to nip into cottages, farmhouses, and mills. Each house is warmed by a peat fire and a friendly attendant. The museum can be dull or vibrant, depending upon your ability to chat with the people staffing each building.

The adjacent Transport Museum traces the evolution of transportation from its beginning 7,500 years ago, when someone first decided to load an ox, and continues to the present, with interesting exhibits on the local Gypsy (traveler) culture and the sinking of the Belfast-made Titanic. In the next two buildings, you roll through the history of bikes, cars, and trains. The car section goes from the first car in Ireland (an 1898 Benz), through the "Cortina Culture" of the 1960s, to the local adventures of John De Lorean with a 1981 model of his car.

Speeding on the train back to Dublin, gazing at the peaceful and lush Irish countryside while pondering De Lorean, the Titanic, and the Troubles, your delusions of a fairy-tale Europe have been muddled. Belfast is a bracing dose of reality.

For good-value accommodations in Belfast, try Ulster People's College Residential Centre (30 Adelaide Park, tel. 028/9066-5161, fax 028/9066-8111, e-mail: upc@cinni.org) or Malone Guest House (79 Malone Road, tel. 028/9066-9565, fax 028/9022-3020). For more hotels, visit www.ricksteves.com/update/intro.htm, and for all the travel specifics, see this year's edition of Rick Steves' Ireland.

SCANDINAVIA

56. Norway in a Nutshell: Oslo and the Fjords

Oslo is the smallest and least earthshaking of the Nordic capitals, but this brisk little city is a scenic smörgåsbord of history, sights, art, and Nordic fun. Add on a "Norway in a Nutshell" excursion over the mountains and to the fjords, and this is potentially one of Europe's best three-day packages of sightseeing thrills.

On May 17, Norway's national holiday, Oslo bursts with flags, bands, parades, and pride. Blond toddlers are dressed up in colorful ribbons, traditional pewter buckles, and ye old wool. But Oslo—surrounded by forests, near mountains, and on a fjord—has plenty to offer the visitor year-round.

In Oslo, sights of the Viking spirit tell an exciting story. From the city hall, hop the ferry for the 10-minute ride to Bygdøy. This cluster of sights reflects the Norwegian mastery of the sea. Some of Scandinavia's best-preserved Viking ships are on display here. Rape, pillage, and—ya sure you betcha—plunder were the rage 1,000 years ago in Norway. There was a time when much of a frightened Western Europe closed every prayer with, "And deliver us from the Vikings, amen." Gazing up at the prow of one of those sleek, time-stained vessels, you can almost hear the shrieks and smell the armpits of those redheads on the rampage.

Nearby, Thor Heyerdahl's balsa raft, *Kon-Tiki*, and the polar ship *Fram* illustrate Viking energy channeled in more productive directions. The *Fram*, serving both Nansen and Amundsen, ventured farther north and south than any other ship.

Just a harpoon toss away is Oslo's open-air folk museum. The Scandinavians were leaders in the development of these cultural parks that are now so popular around Europe. More than 150 historic log cabins and buildings

Oslo on parade—May 17th, Norway's Independence Day

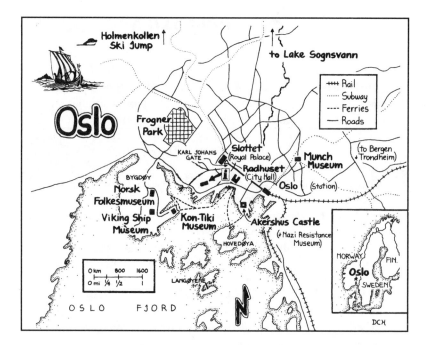

from every corner of the country are gathered together in this huge folk museum. Inside each house, a person in local dress is happy to answer questions about traditional life in that part of Norway. Don't miss the 1,000-year-old wooden stave church.

Linger at the folk museum for the Norwegian Evening, which includes a guided tour, refreshments, and folk dancing, presented by enthusiastic locals wearing traditional folk costumes. If folk dancing seems hokey, think of it as medieval flirting set to music, and ponder the complexities of village social life back then—and the experience will take you away (performances at 17:30 on Tuesday, Wednesday, Friday, and Saturday, July through mid-August).

Oslo's avant-garde city hall, built 40 years ago, was a communal effort of Norway's greatest artists and designers. Tour the interior. More than 2,000 square yards of bold, colorful murals are a journey through the collective mind of modern Norway. City halls rather than churches are the dominant buildings in the your-government-loves-you northern corner of Europe. The main hall of the city hall actually feels like a temple to good government—the altarlike mural celebrates "work, play, and civic administration." Each December the Nobel Peace Prize is awarded in this room.

Norway has given the world two outstanding modern artists: Edvard Munch and Gustav Vigeland. Oslo's Frogner Park features 150 bronze and granite sculptures representing 30 years of Vigeland creativity. The centerpiece is the 60-foottall totem pole of tangled bodies known as the *Monolith of Life*. This, along with the neighboring Vigeland Museum, is a must on any list of Oslo sights.

Norwegian art in Olso's Frogner Park

Oslo's Munch Museum is a joy. It's small, displaying an impressive collection of one man's work, rather than numbing you with art by countless artists from countless periods. You leave the Munch Museum with a smile, feeling like you've learned something about one artist, his culture, and his particular artistic "ism"—expressionism. Don't miss *The Scream*, which captures the exasperation many feel as our human "race" does just that.

You can also explore Oslo's 700-year-old Akershus Castle. Its Freedom Museum, a fascinating Nazi-resistance museum, shows how one country's spirit cannot be crushed, regardless of how thoroughly it's occupied by a foreign power. The castle itself is interesting only with a guided tour.

Language problems are few. The Norwegians speak better English than any people on the Continent. My cousin, who attends the University of Oslo, had to stipulate English or American in her language studies. She learned American—and can slang me under the table.

Oslo has been called Europe's most expensive city. I'll buy that. Without local relatives, life on a budget is possible only if you have a good guidebook and take advantage of money-saving options. Budget tricks like picnicking and sleeping in private homes offer the most exciting savings in this most expensive city.

ONE DAY FOR THE FJORDS?

If you go to Oslo and don't get out to the fjords, you should have your passport revoked. Norway's greatest claim to scenic fame is her deep and lush fjords. Sognefjord, Norway's longest (120 miles) and deepest (over a mile), is tops. Anything but Sognefjord is, at best, foreplay. This is it,

the ultimate natural thrill
Norway has to offer.
For the best one-day
look at fjords, do "Norway
in a Nutshell." This series
of well-organized train,
ferry, and bus connections
lays this most beautiful fjord
country spread-eagle on a
scenic platter.

Every morning, north-
ern Europe's most spectac-
ular train ride leaves Oslo at   *Norway's Sognefjord*
8:00 a.m. for Bergen. Cam-
eras smoke as this train roars over Norway's mountainous spine. The barren, windswept heaths, glaciers, deep forests, countless lakes, and a few
rugged ski resorts create a harsh beauty. The railroad is an amazing engi-
neering feat. Completed in 1909, it's 300 miles long and peaks at 4,266
feet—which, at this Alaskan latitude, is far above the tree line. You'll go
under 18 miles of snow sheds, over 300 bridges, and through 200 tunnels
in just under seven hours ($70, or free with railpass, reservations required;
in peak season—July to mid-August—book several weeks in advance).

At Myrdal, a 12-mile spur line ($10 supplement for railpass holders)
drops you 2,800 breathtaking feet in 50 minutes to the village of Flåm on
Sognefjord. This is a party train. The engineer even stops the train for
photographs at a particularly picturesque waterfall.

While most "Norway in a Nutshell" tourists zip immediately from
the train onto the scenic fjord boat in Flåm, those with time enjoy an
overnight stop on the fjord.

Flåm is a handy tourist depot with several simple hotels. Aurland, a
few miles north of Flåm, is more of a town. It's famous for producing
some of Norway's sweetest *geitost*—goat cheese. Aurland has as many
goats as people (1,900). Nearly every train arriving in Flåm connects with
a bus or boat to Aurland, also on Sognefjord. While nearby Bergen is
famous for its rain—more than six feet a year—Sognefjord is a relative
sun belt with only two feet a year.

The train from Myrdal to Flåm is quite scenic, but the ride doesn't
do the view justice. For the best single day's activity from Flåm, take the
train to Berekvam (halfway back up to Myrdal), then hike or bike (rentable
from the Flåm tourist office) the gravelly construction road back down
to Flåm. Bring a picnic and extra film.

Norway in a Nutshell

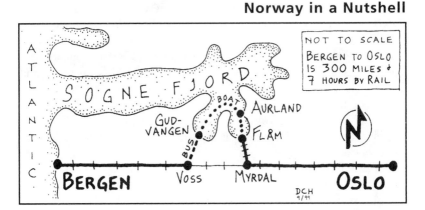

From Flåm, "Nutshellers" catch the most scenic of fjord cruises. Sightseeing boats leave throughout the day ($20, discounts with a student card or full-fare spouse). For 90 minutes, camera-clicking tourists scurry on the drool-stained deck like nervous roosters, scratching fitfully for a photo to catch the magic. Waterfalls turn the black-rock cliffs into a bridal fair. You can nearly reach out and touch the sheer, towering walls. The ride is one of those fine times, like being high on the tip of an Alp, when a warm camaraderie spontaneously combusts among the strangers who came together for the experience. The boat takes you up one narrow arm (Aurlandsfjord) and down the next (Nærøyfjord) to the nothing-to-stop-for town of Gudvangen, where waiting buses ($10) shuttle you back to the main train line at Voss. From Voss, return to Oslo or carry on into Bergen for the evening.

Bergen, Norway's second city and historic capital, is an entertaining place in which to finish the day (browse the touristy but fun wharf area, take a harbor ferry, zip up the funicular to the top of 1,000-foot-tall "Mount" Fløyen for city and fjord views) before catching the overnight train back to Oslo.

Back in Oslo's station, as you yawn and stretch and rummage around for a cup of morning coffee, it'll hit you: You were gone for 24 hours, spent very little money, experienced the fjord wonder of Europe, and saw Bergen to boot.

For good-value accommodations in Oslo, try Rainbow Hotel Astoria (Dronningensgate 21, tel. 22 42 00 10, fax 22 42 57 65) or City Hotel (Skippergata 19, tel. 22 41 36 10, fax 22 42 24 29). For more hotels, visit www.ricksteves.com/ update/intro.htm, and for all the travel specifics, see this year's edition of Rick Steves' Scandinavia.

57. Ærø: Denmark's Ship-in-a-Bottle Island

Few visitors to Scandinavia even notice Ærø, a sleepy, 6-by-22-mile island on the south edge of Denmark. Ærø has a salty charm. Its tombstones are carved with such sentiments as: "Here lies Christian Hansen at anchor with his wife. He'll not weigh until he stands before God." It's a peaceful and homey island, where baskets of new potatoes sit in front of farmhouses— for sale on the honor system.

Ærø's capital, Ærøskøbing, makes a fine home base. Temple Fielding said it's "one of five places in the world that you must see." Many Danes agree, washing up the cobbled main drag in waves with the landing of each ferry. In fact, this is the only town in Denmark that is entirely protected and preserved by law.

Ærøskøbing is a town-in-a-bottle kind of place. Wander down lanes right out of the 1680s, when the town was the wealthy home port to more than 100 windjammers. The post office dates to 1749, and cast-iron gaslights still shine each evening. Windjammers gone, the harbor now caters to German and Danish holiday yachts. On midnight low tides you can almost hear the crabs playing cards.

The Hammerich House, full of old junk, is a 1900s garage sale open daily in summer. The "Bottle Peter" museum on Smedegade is a fasci-nating house with a fleet of 750 dif-ferent bottled ships. Old Peter Jacobsen died in 1960 (probably buried in a glass bottle), leaving a lifetime of his tedious little creations for visitors to squint and marvel at.

Touring Ærø by car is like sam-pling chocolates with a snow shovel. Enjoy a breezy 18-mile tour of Ærø's subtle charms by bike. Borrow a bike from your hotel or rent one from the Esso station on the road behind the tourist office. On Ærø, there are no deposits and no locks. If you start in the morning, you'll be home in time for a hearty lunch.

Ready? Leave Ærøskøbing west on the road to Vra past many U-shaped farms, typical of this island. The three sides block the wind and are used for storing cows, hay, and

A warm and traditional welcome awaits you at an old-fashioned Danish country inn.

Denmark's Ærø Island Bike Ride

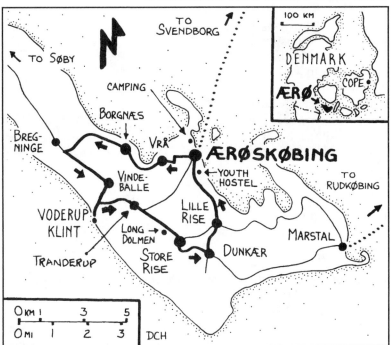

people. "Gaard" (meaning "farm") shows up in many local names. Bike along the coast in the protection of the dike, which turned the once-salty swampland to your left into farmable land. Pedal past a sleek modern windmill and Borgnæs, a pleasant cluster of mostly modern summer cottages. (At this point, bikers with one-speeds can shortcut directly to Vindeballe.)

After passing a secluded beach, climb uphill over the island's summit to Bregninge. Unless you're tired of thatched and half-timbered cottages, turn right and roll through Denmark's "second longest village" to the church. Peek inside. Then roll back through Bregninge, head a mile down the main road to Vindeballe, and take the Vodrup exit.

A straight road leads you to an ancient site on a rugged bluff called Vodrup Klint. If I were a pagan, I'd stop here to worship. Savor the sea, the wind, and the chilling view.

Pedal to Tranderup, past the old farm with the cows with the green hearing aids, a lovely pond, and a row of wind-bent stumps. At the old town of Olde, you'll hit the main road. Turn right toward Store Rise—marked by its church spire in the distance. Just behind the church is a

5,000-year-old neolithic burial place, the Langdysse (Long Dolmen) Tingstedet. Hunker down. Ærø had more than 100 of these. Few survive.

Inside the Store Rise church, notice the little boats hanging in the nave, the fine altar piece, and Martin Luther in the stern making sure everything's theologically shipshape.

Continue down the main road, with the hope-

Main Street, Ærøskøbing

ful forest of modern windmills whirring on your right, until you get to Dunkær.

For the homestretch, take the small road past the topless windmill. Except for "Lille Rise," it's all downhill as you coast home past great sea views to Ærøskøbing.

After a power tour of big-city Scandinavia, Ærø offers a perfect time-passed island on which to wind down, enjoy the seagulls, and pedal a bike into the essence of Denmark. After a break in this cobbled world you may understand the sailors who, after the invention of steam-driven boat propellers, decided that building ships in bottles was more their style.

For good-value accommodations in Ærø, try Pension Vestergade (Vestergade 44, tel. & fax 62 52 22 98) or Det Lille Hotel (Smedegade 33, tel. & fax 62 52 23 00, www.det-lille-hotel.dk). For more hotels, visit www.ricksteves.com/update /intro.htm, and for all the travel specifics—including a more thorough description of the bike ride, see this year's edition of Rick Steves' Scandinavia.

THROUGHOUT EUROPE

58. Dungeons and Dragons: Europe's Nine Most Medieval Castle Experiences

Castles excite Americans. Medieval fortresses are rotting away on hilltops from Ireland to Israel, from Sweden to Spain, lining the Loire and guarding harbors throughout the Mediterranean. From the west coast of Portugal to the crusader city of Rhodes, you'll find castle thrills lurking in every direction.

Most of Europe's castles have been discovered, but some are forgotten, unblemished by entrance fees, postcard racks, and coffee shops, and ignored by guidebooks. Since they're free, nobody promotes them. The aggressive traveler finds them by tapping local sources, such as the town tourist office and the friendly manager of your hotel or pension.

Here are nine medieval castles—some forgotten, some discovered—where the winds of the past really howl.

CARCASSONNE, FRANCE

Before me lies Carcassonne, the perfect medieval city. Like a fish that everyone thought was extinct, Europe's greatest Romanesque fortress-city somehow survives.

Medieval Carcassonne is a 13th-century world of towers, turrets, and cobblestone alleys. It's a walled city and Camelot's castle rolled into one, frosted with too many daytripping tourists. At 10 a.m. the salespeople stand at the doors of their main-street shops, their gauntlet of tacky temptations poised and ready for their daily ration of customers. But an empty Carcassonne rattles in the early morning or late-afternoon breeze. Enjoy the town early or late. Spend the night.

I was supposed to be gone yesterday, but it's sundown and here I sit—imprisoned by choice—curled in a cranny on top of the wall. The moat is one foot over and 100 feet down. Happy little weeds and moss upholster my throne. The wind blows away many of the sounds of today, and my imagination "medievals" me.

Carcassonne's gates now open wide.

Twelve hundred years ago, Charlemagne stood below with his troops—besieging the town for several years. As the legend goes, just as food was running out, a cunning townswoman had a great idea. She fed the town's last bits of grain to the last pig and tossed him over the wall. Splat. Charlemagne's restless forces, amazed that the town still had enough food to throw fat party pigs over the wall, decided they'd never succeed in starving the

Europe's Nine Best Castles

people out. They ended the siege, and the city was saved. Today the walls that stopped Charlemagne open wide for visitors.

WARWICK CASTLE, ENGLAND

From Land's End to John O'Groats, I searched for the best castle in Britain. I found it. With a lush, green, grassy moat and fairy-tale fortifications, Warwick Castle will entertain you from dungeon to lookout. Standing inside the castle gate, you can see the mound where the original Norman castle of 1068 stood. Under this mound (or motte), the wooden stockade (bailey) defined the courtyard as the castle walls do today. The castle is a 14th- and 15th-century fortified shell holding an 18th- and 19th-century royal residence surrounded by a dandy "Capability" Brown landscape job.

There's something for every taste—an educational armory, a terrible torture chamber, a knight in shining armor on a horse that rotates with a merry band of musical jesters, a Madame Tussaud re-creation of a royal weekend party with an 1898 game of statue-maker, a queenly garden, and a peacock-patrolled, picnic-

Warwick Castle—for kings and queens of any age

perfect park. The Great Hall and Staterooms are the sumptuous highlights. The "King Maker" exhibit (it's 1471 and the townfolk are getting ready for battle...) is highly promoted but not quite as good as a Disney ride. Be warned: The tower is a one-way, no-return, 250-step climb offering a view not worth a heart attack. Even with its crowds of modern-day barbarians and its robber-baron entry fee, Warwick's worthwhile.

ELTZ CASTLE, GERMANY

Germany's best medieval castle experience is the Eltz Castle. Eltz lurks in a mysterious forest above the Mosel River between Cochem and Koblenz. It's been left intact for 700 years and is elegantly furnished throughout as it was in the Middle Ages. Thanks to smart diplomacy and clever marriages, Burg Eltz was never destroyed. (It survived one five-year siege.) It's been in the Eltz family for 820 years. And each week, the countess still warms the castle's stony halls with fresh flowers.

Approaching the castle is part of the thrill. Hiking an hour up from the riverside ferry dock or the Moselkern train station, you'll venture through an eerie forest long enough to get you into a medieval mood, and then sud-

Eltz Castle, near Cochem on Germany's Mosel River

denly it appears, all alone—the past engulfed in nature—Burg Eltz.

Drivers can get within a 15-minute walk or quick shuttle-bus ride of the castle. Call and ask if there's a scheduled English tour that you can join (tel. 02672/950-500, www.burg-eltz.de). You'll learn that the lives of even the Middle Ages' rich and famous were "nasty, brutish, and short."

RHEINFELS CASTLE, GERMANY'S RHINELAND

Sitting like a dead pit bull above the medieval town of St. Goar, this mightiest of Rhine castles rumbles with ghosts from its hard-fought past. Burg Rheinfels (built in 1245) withstood a siege of 28,000 French troops in 1692. But in 1797 the French Revolutionary army destroyed it.

Today this hollow but interesting shell offers you the Rhine's best hands-on ruined castle. Start in the castle museum where a reconstruction shows how Rheinfels looked before the French flattened it.

Then step into the central courtyard and imagine the castle in its feisty glory. Five hundred years ago it was ready for a siege. Self-sufficient, it had a baker, pharmacy, herb garden, animals, brewery, well, and livestock. During peace time, 300 to 600 people lived here—during a siege as many as 4,500. The walls were plastered and painted white. Bits of the original 13th-century plaster survive.

Check out the classic dungeon with its ceiling-only access. The well (tour guides report) was dug by death row–type prisoners who were promised freedom if they hit water. They spent months toiling at the dark bottom of the hole. When they finally succeeded and were lifted, wet and happy, up into the daylight, they were immediately blinded by the bright sunlight. Ponder life in the Middle Ages as you enjoy a glorious Rhine view from the tallest turret.

Follow the path outside and around the walls, and look at the smartly placed crossbow arrow slit. Thoop...you're dead. While you're lying there, notice the stonework. The little round holes—used for scaffolds as the walls were built up—indicate this stonework is original. Take a look the chutes. Haaa! Boiling oil...now you're toast, too.

Continue along. Below, just outside the wall, is land where attackers would gather. Cleverly covered with thin slate roofs, tunnels filled with explosives ran under the land just outside the walls. Upon detonation, the force of the explosion blew upward, killing masses of attackers without damaging the actual castle. In 1626, a handful of underground Protestant Germans blew 300 Catholic Spaniards to—they figured—hell. You can explore these underground passages from the next courtyard. Bring a flashlight.

Germany's Rhine River is filled with castle-crowned hills. These can be enjoyed conveniently by train, car, or boat. The best 50-mile stretch is between Koblenz and Mainz. The best one-hour cruise is from St. Goar to Bacharach.

Shimmering Château Chillon

CHÂTEAU CHILLON, SWITZERLAND

Set romantically at the edge of Lake Geneva near Montreux, this wonderfully preserved 13th-century castle is worth a side trip from anywhere in southwest Switzerland. Follow the English brochure, which takes you on a self-guided tour from tingly perch-on-the-medieval-windowsill views through fascinatingly furnished rooms. The dank dungeon, mean weapons, and 700-year-old toilets will excite even the dullest travel partner. A handy but too-close-to-the-train-tracks youth hostel, Haut Lac, is a 10-minute stroll down the lakeside promenade toward Montreux (tel. 021-963-4934). Attack or escape the castle by ferry (free with your train pass).

REIFENSTEIN CASTLE, ITALY

For an incredibly medieval kick in the pants, get off the autobahn one hour south of Innsbruck at the Italian town of Vipiteno (called "Sterzing" by residents who prefer German). With her time-pocked sister just opposite, Reifenstein bottled up this strategic valley leading to the easiest way to cross the Alps.

Reifenstein offers castle connoisseurs the best-preserved original medieval castle interior I've ever seen. The lady who calls the castle home takes groups through in Italian, German, and *un poco di* English (4 tours daily except Monday—2 tours—and Friday—no tours, tel. 0472-647-196). You'll discover the mossy past as she explains how the cistern collected water, how drunken lords managed to get their keys into the keyholes, and how prisoners were left to rot in the dungeon (you'll look down the typical only-way-out hole in the ceiling). In the only surviving original knights' sleeping quarters (rough-hewn plank boxes lined with hay), you'll see how knights spent their nights. Lancelot would cry a lot.

The amazing little fortified town of Glurns hunkers down about an hour west of Reifenstein Castle (on the high road to Lake Como). Glurns still lives within its square wall on the Adige River, with a church bell tower that has a thing about ringing, and real farms, rather than boutiques, filling the town courtyards. You can sleep with the family Hofer near the church, just outside of town (tel. 0473-831-597).

MOORISH RUINS OF SINTRA, PORTUGAL

The desolate ruins of an 800-year-old Moorish castle overlook the sea and the town of Sintra, just west of Lisbon. Ignored by most of the tourists who

Run with the winds of the past in Europe's countless ruined castles. Here, with a little imagination, you're under attack a thousand years ago in Portugal.

flock to the glitzy Pena Palace (capping a neighboring hilltop), the ruins of Sintra offer a reminder of the centuries-long struggle between Moslem Moorish forces and European Christian forces for the control of Iberia. From 711 until 1492 major parts of Iberia (Spain and Portugal) were occupied by the Moors. Contrary to the significance that Americans place on the year 1492, a European remembers the date as the year the Moors were finally booted back into Africa. For most, these ruins are simply a medieval funtasia of scramble-up-and-down-the-ramparts delights and atmospheric picnic perches with vast Atlantic views in an enchanted forest. With a little imagination, it's 1,000 years ago, and you're under attack.

CASTLE DAY: NEUSCHWANSTEIN (BAVARIA) AND THE EHRENBERG RUINS (REUTTE IN TIROL)

Three of my favorite castles—two famous, one unknown—can be seen in one busy day. "Castle Day" takes you to Germany's Disneylike Neuschwanstein Castle, the more stately Hohenschwangau Castle at its foot, and the much older Ehrenberg Ruins across the Austrian border in Reutte.

Make the Austrian town of Reutte your home base. (It's just over the German border, three Alp-happy hours by train west of Innsbruck.) Its tourist office can find you a room in a private home "any day of the year" for $20 (tel. 05672/62336).

From Reutte, catch the early bus across the border to touristy Füssen, the German town nearest Neuschwanstein. (Planning ahead, note the times buses return to Reutte.) From Füssen, you can walk, pedal a rented bike, or ride a local bus a couple of miles to Neuschwanstein.

Neuschwanstein is the greatest of King Ludwig II's fairy-tale castles. His extravagance and romanticism earned this Bavarian king the title "Mad" King Ludwig (and an early death). His castle is one of Europe's most popular attractions.

Arrive by 8:30 a.m. to buy a ticket (about $14) and you'll likely be touring soon after. Your ticket lists appointed times for you to visit Ludwig's boyhood home, Hohenschwangau Castle, and then the neighboring

Some of Europe's most popular attractions, such as Mad Ludwig's castles, sell tickets with entry times. Arrive early to get tour appointments or risk not getting in at all.

Neuschwanstein on the hill. If you arrive late, you'll spend a couple of hours in the ticket line and may find all tours for the day booked. (Consider reserving a minimum of 48 hours in advance at www.ticket-center -hohenschwangau.de.) Hohenschwangau Castle, where Ludwig grew up, offers a good look at his life. Like its more famous neighbor, it takes about an hour to tour. Afterwards, head up the hill to Ludwig's castle in the air.

Neuschwanstein Castle, which is about as old as the Eiffel Tower, is a textbook example of 19th-

Highlights of Southern Bavaria and Tirol

century romanticism. After the Middle Ages ended, people disparagingly named that era "Gothic," or barbarian. Then all of a sudden in the 1800s, it was hip to be square, and neo-Gothic became the rage. Throughout Europe, old castles were restored and new ones built—wallpapered with chivalry. King Ludwig II put his medieval fantasy on the hilltop, not for defensive reasons, but simply because he liked the view.

The lavish interior, covered with damsels in distress, dragons, and knights in gleaming armor, is enchanting. (A little knowledge of Wagner's operas goes a long way in bringing these stories to life.) Ludwig had great taste—for a mad king. Read up on this political misfit—a poetic hippie king in the "realpolitik" age of Bismarck. After Bavarians complained about the money Ludwig spent on castles, he was found dead in a lake under suspicious circumstances, never to enjoy his medieval fantasy come true. After the tour, climb farther up the hill to Mary's Bridge for the best view of this crazy yet elegant castle.

This is a busy day. By lunchtime, catch the bus back to Reutte and get ready for a completely different castle experience.

Pack a picnic and your camera, and with the help of some local directions, walk 30 minutes out of town to the brooding Ehrenberg Ruins. You'll see a small hill crowned by a ruined castle.

The Kleine Schloss ("small castle") is really ruined but wonderfully free of anything from the 21st century—except for a fine view of Reutte sleeping peacefully in the valley below.

Standing like a conqueror on a broken piece of wall, imagine how proud Count Meinrad II of Tirol (who built the castle in 1290) would be to know that his *"Mad" King Ludwig's Neuschwanstein Castle* castle repelled 16,000 Swedish soldiers in the defense of Catholicism in 1632. When cloaked in a cloud shroud, you can peer into the spooky mist and almost see medieval knights in distress and damsels in shining armor. Grab a sword fern, shake your hair free, and unfetter that imagination.

Back in the 21st century, you'll find Ehrenberg's castle reconstructed on Reutte's restaurant walls. Ask at your hotel where you can find a folk evening full of slap-dancing and yodel foolery. A hot, hearty dinner and an evening of local Tirolean entertainment is a fitting way to raise the drawbridge on your memorable "Castle Day."

For good-value accommodations in Carcassonne, try Hôtel des Remparts (5 place de Grands-Puits, tel. 04 68 11 23 00, fax 04 68 25 06 60); in St. Goar, Hotel am Markt (Am Markt 1, tel. 06741/1689, fax 06741/1721, e-mail: hotel.am.markt@gmx.de); in Reutte, Moserhof Hotel (Planseestrasse 44, in nearby Breitenwang, tel. 05672/62020); and in Füssen, Altstadt-Hotel zum Hechten (Ritterstrasse 6, tel. 08362/91600, www.hotel-hechten.com). For more hotels, visit www.ricksteves.com/update/intro.htm, and for all the travel specifics, see this year's editions of the pertinent Rick Steves' country guides.

59. Sobering Sights of Nazi Europe

Fondue, nutcrackers, Monet, Big Ben ... gas chambers. A trip to once-upon-a-time Europe can be a fairy tale. It can also help tell the story of Europe's 20th-century fascist nightmare. While few travelers travel to Europe to dwell on the horrors of Nazism, most value visiting the memorials of fascism's reign of terror and honoring the wish of its survivors—"Forgive but never forget."

Of the countless concentration camps, **Dachau**, just outside of Munich, is most visited. While some visitors complain that it's too "prettied-up," it gives a powerful look at how these camps worked. Built in 1933, this first Nazi concentration camp offers a compelling voice from our recent, grisly past, warning and pleading "Never Again"—the memorial's theme. On arrival, pick up the mini-guide and check when the next documentary film in English will be shown. The

Nazi Sights

museum, the movie, the chilling camp-inspired art, the reconstructed barracks, the gas chambers, the cremation ovens, and the memorial shrines will chisel into you the hidden meaning of fascism. (Dachau is free, open Tuesday–Sunday 9 a.m.–5 p.m., and closed Monday.)

Auschwitz (or Oswiecim), near Krakow in Poland, and **Mauthausen**, near Linz on the Danube in Austria, are more powerful and less touristed. While many camps were slave-labor camps, Auschwitz, the dreaded destination of the Polish Jews such as those on Schindler's List, was built to exterminate. View the horrifying film shot by the Russians who liberated the camp in early 1945. In the museum, the simple yet emotionally powerful display of prisoners' shoes, hairbrushes, and suitcases puts lumps in even the most stoic throats. Allow plenty of time to wander and ponder.

A second Auschwitz camp, **Birkenau**, is two miles away. This bleak ghost camp, an orderly pile of abandoned barracks and watchtowers overlooking an ash-gray lake, is left as if no one after the war had the nerve to even enter the place. Today, pilgrims do. Auschwitz is just 90 minutes by train from the wonder of Krakow, Poland's best-preserved medieval city.

Mauthausen town sits cute and prim on the romantic Danube at the start of the very scenic trip downstream to Vienna. But nearby, atop a now-still quarry, linger the memories of a horrible slave-labor camp. Less tourist-oriented than Dachau, Mauthausen is a solemn place of meditation and continuous mourning. Fresh flowers adorn yellowed photos of lost loved ones. The home country of each victim has erected a gripping monument. You'll find yourself in an artistic gallery of grief, resting on a foundation of Never Forget. Mauthausen (open daily 8 a.m.–5 p.m.) offers

Memorial at the Dachau concentration camp

an English booklet, a free audioguide, an English movie, and a painful but necessary museum.

Paris commemorates the 200,000 French victims of Hitler's camps with the **Memorial de la Deportation.** A walk through this evocative park, on the tip of the Île de la Cité just behind Notre-Dame, is like entering a work of art. Walk down the claustrophobic stairs into a world of concrete, iron bars, water, and sky. Inside the structure, the eternal flame, triangular niches containing soil from various concentration camps, and powerful quotes will etch the message into your mind. Then gaze at the 200,000 crystals—one for each person who perished.

For some historical background, visit Paris' **Museum of Art and History of Judaism.** Located in a beautifully restored Marais mansion, it tells the story of Judaism in Europe, from the Roman destruction of Jerusalem to the Holocaust. Beautifully displayed state-of-the-art exhibits illustrate how this continually dispersed population has maintained its cultural unity.

In Amsterdam, **Anne Frank's House** gives the cold, mind-boggling statistics of fascism the all-important intimacy of a young girl who lived through it and died from it. Even bah-humbug types, who are dragged in because it's raining and their spouses read the diary, find themselves caught up in Anne's story.

Amsterdam's **Jewish History Museum**—four historic synagogues joined together by steel and glass to make one modern complex—tells the story and struggles of Judaism through the ages. The nearby Dutch Theater, which was used as an assembly hall for local Jews destined for Nazi concentration camps, is a powerful memorial. On the wall, 6,700 family names represent the 104,000 Jews deported and killed by the Nazis.

The small town of Haarlem, 20 minutes by train from Amsterdam, has its own Anne Frank–type story. Touring a cozy apartment above a clock shop just off the busy market square, you'll see **Corrie Ten Boom's** **"Hiding Place."** The sight was popularized by an inspirational book and movie about this woman and her family's experience hiding Jews from Nazis. Tipped off by an informant, Nazis raided their house but didn't find the Jews, who were hiding behind a wall in Corrie's bedroom. Because the Nazis found a suspiciously large number of ration coupons, they sent the Ten Boom family to a concentration camp. Only Corrie survived.

Each of these sights is committed to making the point that intolerance and fascism are still alive and strong. Their message: Fascism can emerge from its looney fringe if we get complacent and think the horrors of Hitler could never happen again.

While Hitler controlled Europe, each country had a courageous, if small, resistance movement. All over Europe you'll find streets and squares named after the martyrs of the resistance. Any history buff or champion of the underdog will be thrilled by the patriotism documented in Europe's Nazi resistance museums.

The **Oslo and Copenhagen resistance museums** are fascinating. But the most extensive of such museums is back in Amsterdam. In the **Dutch Resistance Museum** you'll see propaganda movie clips, study a forged ID card under a magnifying glass, and read of ingenious, daring efforts to hide local Jews from the Germans.

Since destruction and death are fascist fortes, only relatively insignificant bits and pieces of Hitler's Germany survive. Berlin, now that its Wall is history, is giving its Nazi chapter a little more attention. There are several new Nazi-related museums, memorials, and guided walks. You might visit Berlin's **Great Synagogue** (which was burned on Kristallnacht in 1938), the **Topography of Terror** exhibit (near what was Checkpoint Charlie, illustrating SS tactics), and the adjacent four small "mountains" made from the rubble of the bombed-out city. The gripping **Käthe Kollwitz Museum** is filled with art inspired by the horrors of Berlin's Nazi experience. The new **Jewish Museum Berlin** opened in the fall of 2001. Designed by the American architect Daniel Libeskind, the zigzag shape of the zinc-walled building is pierced by voids, symbolic of the irreplaceable cultural loss caused by the Holocaust.

In Nuremberg the ghosts of Hitler's showy propaganda rallies still rustle in the **Rally Grounds** (now Dutzendteich Park), down the Great Road, and through the New Congress Hall. The local tourist office has a helpful booklet entitled "Nuremberg 1933–1945."

The town of **Berchtesgaden**, near the Austrian border, is any

German's choice for a great mountain hideaway—including Hitler's. The remains of Hitler's Obersalzburg headquarters, with its extensive tunnel system, thrill some World War II buffs but are so scant that most visitors are impressed only by the view.

Knowing you can't take on the world without great freeways, Hitler started Germany's autobahn system. **Hitler's first autobahn rest stop** is on the lake called Herrenchiemsee, between Munich and Salzburg. Now a lakeside hotel for U.S. military personnel, it's still frescoed with *Deutschland über alles* themes. Take the Feldon exit and politely stroll around the hotel. The dining room has the best "love-your-Aryan-heritage-and-work-hard-for-the-state" art.

Your greatest opportunity to experience fascist architecture is in Rome, where you can wander through Mussolini's futuristic suburb called **E.U.R.** and the bold pink houses of fascist Italy's Olympic Village. South of Rome, on the coastal road to Naples, are several towns built in the Mussolini era (such as Latina, Sabaudia, Pontinia, and Aprilia), interesting for their stocky colonnades and the intentional sterility of their piazzas.

After completing his "final solution," Hitler had hoped to build a grand museum of the "decadent" Jewish culture in Prague. Today the museums and synagogues of Prague's Jewish Quarter, containing artifacts the Nazis assembled from that city's once-thriving Jewish community, stand together as a persistently unforgettable memorial (see Chapter 47, Prague).

Just outside of Prague is the **Terezin concentration camp.** This particularly insidious place was dolled up as a model camp for Red Cross inspection purposes. Inmates had their own newspaper, and the children put on cute plays. But after the camp passed its inspection, life returned to slave labor and death. Ponder the touching collection of Jewish children's art.

Possibly the most moving sight of all is the martyred village of **Oradour-sur-Glane**, in central France. This town, 15 miles northwest of Limoges, was machine-gunned and burned in 1944 by Nazi SS troops. Seeking revenge for the killing of one of their officers, they left 642 townspeople dead in a blackened crust of a town under a silent blanket of ashes. The poignant ruins of Oradour-sur-Glane—scorched sewing machines, pots, pans, bikes, and cars—have been preserved as an eternal reminder of the reality of war. When you visit, you'll see the simple sign that greets every pilgrim who enters: "*Souviens-toi* . . . remember."

EAST MEDITERRANEAN

60. Peloponnesian Highlights: Overlooked Greece

The Peloponnesian Peninsula stretches south from Athens. Studded with antiquities, this land of ancient Olympia, Corinth, and Sparta offers plenty of fun in the eternal Greek sun, with pleasant fishing villages, sandy beaches, bathtub-warm water, and none of the tourist crowds that plague the much-scrambled-after Greek Isles.

The Peloponnesian port town of Nafplion, two hours southwest of Athens by car or bus, is small, cozy, and strollable. It's a welcome relief after the black-hanky intensity of smoggy Athens. Not only is Nafplion itself fun, but it's a handy home base for exploring two of Greece's greatest ancient sights—Epidavros and Mycenae.

Nafplion's harbor is guarded by two castles, one on a small island and the other capping the hill above the town. Both are wonderfully floodlit at night. Just looking from the town up to its castle makes you need a tall iced tea.

But this old Venetian outpost, built in the days when Venice was the economic ruler of Europe, is the best-preserved castle of its kind in Greece and well worth the 999-step climb. From the highest ramparts you'll see several Aegean islands (great daytrips by boat from Nafplion) and look deep into the mountainous interior of the Peloponnesian Peninsula. Below you lies an enticing beach.

Nafplion has plenty of hotels, and its harbor is lined with restaurants specializing in fresh seafood. An octopus dinner cost me $8—succulent!

Epidavros' state-of-the-art acoustics

The infamous resin-flavored *retsina* wine is a drink you'll want to experience—once. Maybe with octopus. The first glass is like drinking wood. The third glass is dangerous: It starts to taste good. If you drink any more, you'll smell like it the entire next day.

On another night I left Nafplion's popular waterfront district and had a memorable meal in a hole-in-the-wall joint. There was no menu, just an entertaining local crowd and a nearsighted man who, in a relaxed frenzy, ran the whole show. He scurried about, greeting eaters, slicing, dicing, laughing, singing to himself, cooking, serving, and billing. Potato stew, meatballs, a plate of about 30 tiny fried fish with lime, and unlimited wine cost $20 for two—and could have fed four.

Epidavros, 18 miles northeast of Nafplion, is the best-preserved ancient Greek theater. It was built 2,500 years ago to seat 14,000. Today it's kept busy reviving the greatest plays of antiquity. You can catch performances of ancient Greek comedies and tragedies on weekends from mid-June through September. Try to see Epidavros either early or late in the day. The theater's marvelous acoustics are best enjoyed in near solitude. Sitting in the most distant seat as your partner stands on the stage, you can practically hear the *retsina* rumbling in her stomach.

Thirty minutes in the other direction from Nafplion are the ruins of Mycenae. This was the capital of the Mycenaeans, who won the Trojan War and dominated Greece 1,000 years before Socrates.

As you tour this fascinating fortified citadel, remember that these people were as awesome to the ancient Greeks of Socrates' day as those Greeks are to us. The classical Greeks marveled at the huge stones and workmanship of the Mycenaean ruins. They figured that only a race of giant Cyclops could build with such colossal rocks and called it "Cyclopean" architecture.

Visitors today can gape at the Lion's Gate, climb deep into a cool, ancient cistern, and explore the giant *tholos* tombs. The tombs, built in 1500 B.C., stand like huge stone igloos, with smooth subterranean domes 40 feet wide and 40 feet tall. The most important Mycenaean artifacts, like the golden "Mask of Agamemnon," are in the National Museum in Athens.

FINIKOUNDAS

The prize-winning Peloponnesian hideaway is the remote village of Finikoundas. Located on the southwest tip of the peninsula between the twin Venetian fortress towns of Koroni and Methoni (two hours by public bus from Kalamata), Finikoundas is big enough to have a good selection of restaurants, pensions, and a few shops, but it's small enough to escape the typical resort traffic, crowds, and noise. It's just right for a sleepy Greek sabbatical.

Finikoundas has plenty of private rooms, or *dhomatia*, for rent. Plan to spend $20 for a

You can be a guest of honor at a Greek wedding festival.

simple double a few steps from the beach. The little bay just east of the rock breakwater was the best beach I found, and the swimming was fine— even in October.

After a little Apollo worshipping, I wandered through town in search of Dionysus at just the right waterfront restaurant. The place I found couldn't have been more "waterfront." Since the fishing village had no dock, its Lilliputian fishing boats were actually anchored to the restaurant. I settled my chair comfortably into the sand and the salty atmosphere, as weak wavelets licked my table's legs. I dined amid rusty four-hooker anchors, honorably retired old ropes, and peely dinghies. A naked 20-watt bulb dangled from the straw roof, which rotted unnoticed by Greeks and a few perpetually off-season Germans who seemed to be regulars.

Cuisine in a village like this is predictable. I enjoyed fresh seafood, Greek salad, and local wine. After a few days in Greece you become a connoisseur of the salad, appreciating the wonderful tomatoes, rich feta cheese, and even the olive-oil drenching.

Almost within splashing distance of my table, young Greek men in swimsuits not much bigger than a rat's hammock gathered around a bucketful of just-caught octopi. They were tenderizing the poor things to death by whipping them like wet rags over and over on a big flat rock. They'd be featured momentarily on someone's dinner plate—someone else's.

Evening is a predictable but pleasant routine of strolling and socializing. Dice chatter on dozens of backgammon boards, entrepreneurial dogs and soccer goal–oriented children busy themselves as a tethered goat chews on something inedible in its low-profile corner. From the other end of town comes the happy music of a christening party. Dancing women fill the building, while their children mimic them in the street. Farther down, two elderly, black-clad women sit like tired dogs on the curb.

Succumbing to the lure of the pastry shop, I sat down for my day-end ritual, honey-soaked baklava. I told the cook I was American. "Oh," he said, shaking his head with sadness and pity. "You work too hard."

I answered, "Right. But not today."

For good-value accommodations in Finikoundas, try Korakakis Beach Hotel (tel. 0723/71221) or Dhomatia Anastasios Tomaras (private rooms, tel. 0723/71378). For more accommodations, visit www.ricksteves.com/update/intro.htm. While I don't write a regular Greece guidebook, we do produce and research a handy Greece guidebooklet for those who take our Turkey tours and wish to explore Greece afterwards (download at www.ricksteves.com/greecebook).

61. Crete's Gorge of Samaria

Swarms of tourists flock to the Greek island of Crete. Many leave, disappointed by the crowds. Try to avoid peak season and the crowded cities. Hike through the rugged interior instead and find a remote corner of the south coast. While ridiculously congested in the height of summer, the 10-mile hike through the Gorge of Samaria can be a Cretan highlight.

Don McCort

Your home base for this loop trip is Hania, a city on Crete's north coast serviced frequently by the overnight boat from Athens. Catch the earliest bus from Hania to Xyloskalo to beat the heat and midday crowds. After a scenic 25-mile bus ride, you'll be standing high above the wild Gorge of Samaria. Xyloskalo is a small lodge, the end of the road, and the beginning of the trail. The bus will be full of hikers; no one else would come here at this hour. The air is crisp, the fresh blue sky is cool, and most of the gorge has yet to see the sun. Before you lies a 10-mile downhill trek, dropping 5,000 feet through some of the most spectacular scenery anywhere in Greece to a black-sand beach on the south coast. (The hike takes 4 to 6 hours; the gorge is open from May through October and costs about $5 to enter.)

Pack light but bring a hearty picnic lunch, a water bottle, and extra film. Food can't be bought in this wonderfully wild gorge, and things get pretty dry and dusty in the summer. There are several springs, and you follow a pure mountain stream through much of the gorge. Wear light clothes but bring a jacket for the cool morning at the top. Come prepared to swim in one of the stream's many refreshing swimming holes.

Descend to the floor of the gorge down an hour of steep switchbacks, where you'll reach the stream, a great place for your picnic brunch. A leisurely meal here will bolster your energy, lighten your load, and bring you peace, as this break will let most of the other hikers get ahead of you. If the crowds just won't let up, find solitude by following a stream up a side gorge.

Between you and the Libyan Sea on Crete's southern shore are about eight miles of gently sloping downhill trails. Hiking along the cool creek, you'll pass an occasional deserted farmhouse, lazy goats, and a small ghost town with a well. In the middle of the hike, you'll come to the narrowest (and most photographed) point in the gorge, where only three yards separate the 1,000-foot-high cliffs. Keep your eyes peeled for the nimble, cliff-climbing *agrimi*, the wild Cretan mountain goats.

Finally, by midafternoon, signs of Greek civilization begin peeking through the bushes. An oleander chorus cheers you along the last leg of your hike to the coast. You'll find a tiny community with a small restaurant and a few cheap places to stay. The town, Agia Roumeli, is accessible only by foot or boat. Three to six times a day, a small boat picks up the hikers and ferries them to Chora Sfakion (last ride is usually around 6 p.m.). Before you begin your hike, confirm when the last boat leaves so you can pace yourself.

After you buy your ticket and while you're waiting for the boat, take a dip in the bathtub-warm, crystal-clear waters of the Libyan Sea. Africa is out there somewhere. The black-sand beach absorbs the heat, so wear your shoes right to the water's edge. A free shower is available on the beach.

The hour-long boat ride (or 8-hour hike) to Chora Sfakion passes some of Crete's best beaches and stops briefly at the pleasant fishing village of Loutro (with several pensions). Buses meet each boat at Chora Sfakion to return you to Hania. For another excursion, consider the great beach and village of Paleohora (west of Agia Roumeli), with a bus connection to Hania. In crossing the island of Crete, the bus goes through some dramatic scenery and several untouched villages inhabited by high-booted, long-mustachioed, espresso-drinking Cretans.

62. Turkey's Hot

Turkey is a proud new country. It was born in 1923, when Ataturk, the father of modern Turkey, rescued it from the buffet line of European colonialism. He divided church and state, liberated women (at least on paper), replaced the Arabic script with Europe's alphabet, and gave the battle-torn, corrupt, and demoralized remnants of the Ottoman Empire the foundation of a modern nation. Because of Ataturk, today's 60 million Turks have a flag—and reason to wave it. For a generation, many young Turkish women actually worried that they'd never be able to really love a man because of their love for the father of their country.

At the same time, Turkey is a musty archaeological attic, with dusty civilization stacked upon civilization. The more they dig, the more they learn that Turkey, not Mesopotamia, is the cradle of Western civilization.

I find Turkey even tastier, friendlier, cheaper, and richer in culture and history than Greece. But the average Turk looks like a character the average American mother would tell her child to run from. It's important that we see past our visual hang-ups and recognize Turks as the sincere and friendly people they are.

Those who haven't been to Turkey wonder why anyone would choose to go there. Those who've been dream of returning. Turkey is being discovered. Tourists are learning that the image of the terrible Turk is false, created to a great degree by its unfriendly neighbors. Turks are quick to remind visitors that, surrounded by Syria, Iraq, Iran, Armenia, Georgia, Bulgaria, and Greece, they're not living in Mr. Rogers' neighborhood.

Many Americans know Turkey only from the thrilling but unrealistic movie *Midnight Express.* The movie was paid for, produced, and performed by Armenians and Greeks (historically unfriendly neighbors). It says nothing about the Turks or Turkey today. Also, many visitors are put off by Turkey's "rifles on every corner" image. Turkey is not a police state. Its NATO commitment is to maintain nearly a million-man army. Except in the far east, where this million-man army is dealing with the Kurds and Iraq, these soldiers have little to do but "patrol" and "guard"—basically, loiter in uniform.

Today Turkey is on the move. It's looking West and getting there.

You can travel throughout the country on Turkey's great bus system. Telephones work. Hotels have fax machines. I had a forgotten plane ticket expressed across the country in 24 hours for $3. Fifty percent of Turkey's 42,000 villages had electricity in 1980. Now all do. Does all this modernization threaten the beautiful things that make Turkish culture so Turkish? An old village woman assured me, "We can survive TV and tourism because we have deep and strong cultural roots."

English is more widely spoken, and tourism is booming. Business everywhere seems brisk, but inflation is so bad that most hotels list their prices in euros or dollars. With thousands of Turkish liras to the dollar, shoppers carry calculators to count the zeros.

Travel in Turkey is cheap. Good, comfortable, double rooms with private showers cost $30. Vagabonds order high on menus. And buses, which offer none of the romantic chaos of earlier years, take travelers anywhere in the country nearly any time for about $2 an hour.

Turkey knows it's on the fence between the rising wealth and power of a soon-to-be-united Europe and a forever-fragile-and-messy Middle East. Turks know the threat of the rising tide of Islamic fundamentalism and, while the country is 98 percent Muslim, they want nothing of the Khomeni-style rule that steadily blows the dust of religious discontent over their border. But fundamentalists are making inroads. As they walk by, veiled women in tow, modern-minded Turks grumble—a bit nervously. On Ataturk Day, stadiums around the country are filled with students shouting in thunderous unison, "We are a secular nation."

Two months after the Gulf War, I enjoyed my ninth trip through Turkey, this time with 22 travel partners and a Turkish co-guide. We had a life-changing 15 days together, enjoyed a level-headed look at Islam, took a peek at a hardworking, developing country with its act impressively together, and learned how our mass media can wrongly shape America's assessment of faraway lands. No survey was necessary to know that we all brought home a better understanding of our world. But a survey did show that 14 people bought carpets (mostly under $1,000, one for $3,000), eight people had diarrhea (7 for less than two days, 1 for 6 days), and nine of us learned to play backgammon well enough to actually beat a Turk in a smoky teahouse. For $5 you can buy tea for 20 new friends, play backgammon until the smoke doesn't bother you, and rock to the pulse of Turkey. Oh, those tiny handmade dice . . . cockeyed dots in a land where time is not money.

Turkey reshuffles your cards. A beautiful girl is called a pistachio. A person with a beautiful heart but an ugly face is called a Maltese plum— the ugliest fruit you'll ever enjoy. Industrious boys break large chocolate bars into small pieces to sell for a profit. For $2, a Gypsy's bear will do a show called "your mother-in-law dancing in a Turkish bath."

Much of Turkey is scrambling into the modern Western world, but the Turkish way of life is painted onto this land with an indelible cultural ink. If you're able to put your guidebook aside and follow your wanderlust, you'll still find sleepy goats playing Bambi on rocks overlooking a nomad's black tent. High above on the hillside, the lone but happy song of the goatherd's flute plays golden oldies. The mother bakes bread and minds the children, knowing her man is near.

Riding the waves of Turkey is like abstract art, a riveting movie without a plot, a melody of people, culture, and landscape that you just can't seem to stop whistling.

GÜZELYURT—CAPPADOCIA WITHOUT TOURISTS

Cappadocia is rightly famous as the most bizarre and fascinating bit of central Turkey that accepts bank cards. The most exciting discovery I made on my last trip was a town on the edge of Cappadocia called Güzelyurt.

Güzelyurt means "beautiful land." It's best known in Turkey as the town where historic enemies—Greeks, Turks, Kurds, and Bulgarians—live in peace. The town is a harmony of cultures, history, architecture, and religions. Walk down streets that residents from 3,000 years ago might recognize, past homes carved into the rocks, enjoying friendly greetings of *merhaba*. Scowling sheepdogs, caged behind 10-foot-high troglodyte rockeries, give the scene just enough tension.

Walk to a viewpoint at the far side of town (above the Sivisli church), toward the snowy slopes of the Fuji-like volcano that rules the horizon. Before you is a lush and living gorge. The cliff rising from the gorge is stacked with building styles: Upon the 1,600-year-old church sit troglodyte caves, Selcuk arches, and Ottoman facades. And on the horizon gleams the tin dome of the 20th-century mosque, with its twin minarets giving you a constant visual call to prayer. The honey that holds this architectural baklava together is people.

Put your camera away, shut your mouth, and sit silently in the sounds of 1000 B.C. Children play, birds chirp, roosters crow, shepherds chase goats, and mothers cackle. (Ignore that distant motorbike.)

Below you, sleeping in the greens and wet browns of this tide pool of simple living, is the church of St. Gregorius. Built in 385, it's thought by Gregorian fans to be the birthplace of church music, specifically the Gregorian chant. Its single minaret indicates that it's preserved as a mosque today in a valley where people call god Allah.

Who needs three-star sights and tourist information offices? In

Güzelyurt, we dropped by
the city hall. The mayor
scampered across town to
arrange a lunch for us in his
home. He welcomed us
Christians, explaining, "We
believe in the four books"—
the local way of saying, "It
doesn't matter what you call
Him, as long as you call
Him." He showed us the
names of his Greek Christian friends, kept as safe and
sacred as good friends could
be in his most precious and
holy possession, the family
Koran bag.

Traditional lifestyles survive in Turkey.

The lady of the house made tea. Overlapping carpets gave the place
a cozy bug-in-a-rug feeling. As the lady cranked up the music, we all
began to dance like charmed snakes. It was very safe sex until our fingers
could snap no more. A small girl showed me a handful of almonds and
said, "Buy dem." *Badam* is Turkish for almond, and this was her gift to
me. Enjoying her munchies, I reciprocated with a handful of Pop Rocks.
As the tiny candies exploded in her mouth, her surprised eyes became
even more beautiful.

The town's name is spelled proudly across its volcanic backdrop. The
black bust of Ataturk seems to loom just as high over the small modern
market square. The streets are alive with the relaxed click of victorious *tavla*
(backgammon) pieces. The men of the town, who seem to be enjoying one
eternal cigarette break, proudly make a point not to stare at the stare-
worthy American visitors searching for postcards in a town with no tourism.

Güzelyurt, in central Turkey, is 35 miles from Nevsehir and a short
bus ride from Aksaray. It's near the Peristrema Valley, famous for its
seven-mile hike through a lush valley of poplar groves, eagles, vultures,
and early Christian churches.

Belisirma, a village near Güzelyurt, is even more remote. With a population of "100 homes," Belisirma zigzags down to its river, which rushes
through a poplar forest past the tiny Belisirma Walley Wellkome Camping (one bungalow). A group of bangled women in lush purple wash their
laundry in the river under the watchful eyes of men who seem to have
only a ceremonial function. Children on donkeys offer to show off the

troglodyte church carved into the hill just past the long, narrow farm plots. A lady, face framed in the dangling jewelry of her shawl, her net worth hanging in gold around her neck, points to my postcard, a picture of a little girl holding a baby sheep. The girl is her niece. They call the card "Two Lambs."

14 DAYS IN TURKEY

Turkey offers the most enjoyable culture shock within striking distance of Europe. But it's a rich brew, and, for most, two weeks is enough. Here's my recommendation for the best two-week look at Turkey.

Flying to Istanbul is about as tough as flying to Paris. For instance, if you fly SAS, both are about a two-hour flight from your Copenhagen hub. When planning your trip, remember that flying "open-jaw" into Istanbul and home from Athens is about $50 cheaper than flying in and out of Istanbul . . . and makes for a more diverse and efficient itinerary.

Spend your first two days in Istanbul. Take the taxi ($15) from the airport to the Hippodrome, near the Blue Mosque, where you'll find several decent small hotels and pensions.

For an easygoing first evening, walk over to the Blue Mosque and enjoy the free sound and light show in the park. Spend the next day doing the historic biggies: Topkapi Palace, Blue Mosque, and the Aya Sofya church. The latter was built in 537, when Istanbul was called Constantinople and was the leading city in Christendom. It was the largest domed building in Europe until Brunelleschi built Florence's great dome in the Renaissance, nearly a thousand years later.

Bone up on Anatolian folk life in the Islamic Arts Center (just off the old Roman racetrack called the Hippodrome), then taxi to the modern center of bustling Istanbul for dinner in the "Flower Passage," where Istanbul's beautiful people and tourists alike enjoy the funky elegance. If you like baklava, stroll the city's main drag, Istiklal Street, in search of a pastry shop. From the heartbeat of Istanbul, Taksim Square, catch a cab home. Less touristy dinner options include Kumkapi, a fishermen's wharf district teeming with seafood restaurants and happy locals (a pleasant walk from the Hippodrome), and the more romantic Ortakoy district (in the shadow of the Bosphorus bridge).

The next morning, browse the bizarre Grand Bazaar and Egyptian Spice Market. After lunch take an intercontinental cruise up the Bosphorus. If you disembark in Asian Istanbul, you can taxi quickly to the station to catch your overnight train to Ankara.

This, the only reliable train in Asian Turkey, gets you to the country's capital by 8 a.m. As you munch feta cheese, olives, tomatoes, and

14 Days in Turkey

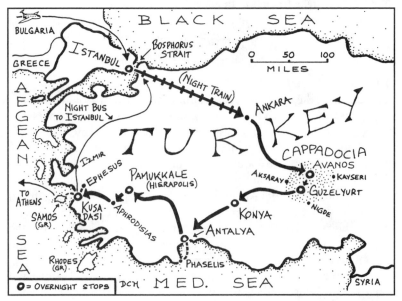

cucumbers for breakfast in the dining car, it dawns on you that you're far from home.

Ankara has two blockbuster sights. The Museum of Anatolian Civilizations is a prerequisite for meaningful explorations of the ancient ruins that litter the Turkish countryside. The Ataturk Mausoleum shines a light on the recent and dramatic birth of modern Turkey and gives you an appreciation of that country's love of its George Washington. For a happening scene, a great view, and a look at modern Turkey, ride to the top of the Ankara tower.

From Ankara, it's a four-hour bus ride to exotic and evocative Cappadocia, an eroded wonderland of cave dwellings that go back to the early Christian days, when the faithful fled persecution by hiding in Cappadocian caves. Cappadocia gives you a time-tunnel experience, with its horse carts, troglodytes, strangely eroded mini-Matterhorns called "fairy chimneys," traditional crafts, and labyrinthine underground cities. Don't miss the Back Door town of Güzelyurt (see above).

From mysterious Cappadocia, cross the Anatolian Plateau to Konya, the most conservative and orthodox Muslim city in Turkey, home of the Mevlana order and the Whirling Dervishes. The dance of the dervish connects a giving god with our world. One hand is gracefully raised, the

Exotic terrain, ornery transport... Cappadocia

other is a loving spout as he whirls faster and faster in a trance the modern American attention span would be hard-pressed to understand.

Then follow the steps of St. Paul over the Taurus Mountains to the Mediterranean resort of Antalya. You can hire a yacht to sail the Mediterranean coast to your choice of several beachside ruins. After a free day on the beach, travel inland to explore the ruins of Aphrodisias and its excellent museum.

Nearby is Pamukkale, a touristy village and Turkey's premier mineral spa. Soak among broken ancient columns in a mineral spring atop the white cliff, terraced with acres and acres of steamy mineral pools. Watch frisky sparrows hop through a kaleidoscope of white birdbaths.

For the final leg of your two-week swing through Turkey, head west to the coastal resort of Kusadasi. Nearby is my favorite ancient site, the ruins of Ephesus. For a relaxing finale, take a Turkish *hamam* (bath with massage) in Kusadasi before catching the daily boat to the entertaining island of Samos in Greece (see below). Boats and planes take travelers from Samos to other Greek islands and on to Athens.

SOME HINTS TO MAKE TURKEY EASIER

Good information is rare here, especially in the east. Bring a guidebook from home. Take advantage of Tom Brosnahan's guidebook to Turkey (Lonely Planet). Maps are easy to get in Turkey.

Eat carefully. Find a cafeteria-style restaurant and point. Choose your food personally by tasting and pointing to what you like. Joke around with the cooks. They'll love you for it. The bottled water, soft drinks, *chai* (tea), and coffee are cheap and generally safe. Watermelons are a

Islam in a Pistachio Shell

Five times a day, God enjoys a global wave as the call to prayer sweeps at the speed of the sun from the Philippines to Morocco. The muezzin chants, "There is only one God, and Mohammed is one of his prophets." Islam is the fastest-growing religion on earth. Unbiased listings place Mohammed above Jesus on rankings of all-time most influential people. For us to understand Islam by studying Khadafy and Hussein would be like a Turk understanding capitalism and Christianity by studying Hitler.

Your journeying may give you the opportunity to travel in, and therefore to better understand, Islam. Just as it helps to know about spires, feudalism, and the saints to comprehend your European sightseeing, a few basics on Islam help make your sightseeing in Muslim countries more meaningful. Here they are.

The Islamic equivalent of the Christian bell tower is a minaret, which the muezzin climbs to chant the call to prayer. In a kind of architectural Darwinism, the minarets have shrunken as calls to prayer have been electronically amplified; their height is no longer necessary or worth the expense. Many small modern mosques have one tin mini-minaret about as awesome as your little toe.

Worshipers pray toward Mecca, which, from Turkey, is about in the same direction as Jerusalem but not quite. In Istanbul, Aya Sofya was built 1,400 years ago as a church, its altar niche facing Jerusalem. Since it became an out-of-sync-with-Mecca mosque, the Muslim focus-of-prayers niche is to the side of what was the altar.

Ah, the smell of socks. A mosque is a shoes-off place. Westerners are welcome to drop in. The small stairway that seems to go nowhere is symbolic of the growth of Islam. Mohammed had to stand higher and higher to talk to his growing following. Today every mosque has one of these as a kind of pulpit. No priest ever stands on the top stair. That is symbolically reserved for Mohammed.

The "five pillars" of Islam are basic to an understanding of a religious force that is bound to fill our headlines for years to come. Followers of Islam should:

1. Say and believe, "There is only one God, and Mohammed is one of his prophets."
2. Visit Mecca. This is interpreted by some Muslims as a command to travel. Mohammed said, "Don't tell me how educated you are, tell me how much you've traveled."

Muslims in modern-day Turkey—a mix of east and west

3. Give to the poor (one-fortieth of your wealth, if you are
   not in debt).
4. Fast during daylight hours through the month of Ramadan.
   Fasting is a great social equalizer and helps everyone to feel
   the hunger of the poor.
5. Pray five times a day. Modern Muslims explain that it's
   important to wash, exercise, stretch, and think of God. The
   ritual of Muslim prayer works this into every day—five times.

You'll notice women worship in back of the mosque. For the same
reason I find it hard to concentrate on God at aerobics classes, Muslim
men decided prayer would go better without the enjoyable but prob-
lematic distraction of bent-over women between them and Mecca.

How Muslims can have more than one wife is a bigamistry to many.
While polygamy is illegal in Turkey, Islam does allow a man to have as
many wives (up to four) as he can love and care for equally. This originated as Mohammed's pragmatic answer to the problem of too many
unattached women caused by the deaths of so many men in the frequent wars of his day. Religious wars have been as common in Islam as
they have been in Christendom.

These basics are a simplistic but honest attempt by a non-
Muslim to help travelers from the Christian West understand a very
rich but often misunderstood culture worthy of our respect. And these
days, when those who profit from arms sales are so clever at riding
the bloody coattails of religious conflict, we need all the understanding we can muster.

great source of safe liquid. If you order a glass of tea, your waiter will be happy to "process" your melon, giving it to you peeled and in little chunks on a big plate.

Learn to play backgammon before you visit Turkey. Backgammon, the local pastime, is played by all the men in this part of the world. Join in. It's a great way to instantly become a contributing member of the local teahouse scene.

Really get away from it all. Catch a *dolmus* (shared taxi) into the middle of nowhere. Get off at a small village. If the bus driver thinks you must be mistaken or lost to be getting off there, you've found the right place. Explore the town, befriend the children, trade national dance lessons. Act like an old friend returning after a 10-year absence, and you'll be treated like one.

You'll be stared at all day long. Preserve your sanity with a sense of humor. Joke with the Turks. Talk to them, even if there's no hope of communication. One afternoon, in the town of Ercis, I was waiting for a bus and writing in my journal. A dozen people gathered around me, staring with intense curiosity. I felt that they needed entertainment. I sang the Hoagy Carmichael classic, "Huggin' and a-Chalkin'." When the bus came, my friend and I danced our way on board, waving good-bye to the cheering fans. From then on my singing entertained most of eastern Turkey.

Make invitations happen and accept them boldly. While exploring villages with no tourism, I loiter near the property of a large family. Very often the patriarch, proud to have a foreign visitor, will invite me to join him cross-legged on his large, bright carpet in the shade. The women of the household bring tea, then peer at us from around a distant corner. Shake hands, jabber away in English, play show and tell, pass around photos from home, take photos of the family, and get their addresses so you can mail them copies. They'll always remember your visit. And so will you.

THE BEST WAY FROM ATHENS TO TURKEY

The best thing about Athens is the boat to Turkey. Athens is a crowded, overrated, and polluted tourist trap. See what's important (Acropolis, Agora, Plaka, and National Museum) and leave! Catch a boat ($35 for deck class, $55 for cabin, 12 hours) or plane ($75, one hour) to Samos, Rhodes, or Kos. Each of these islands is connected daily by boat ($30, two hours) to Turkey. This short boat ride gives you more of a cultural change than the flight from the United States to Athens.

Leaving Greece via Samos offers a look at one of my favorite Greek islands and drops you in Kusadasi, a pleasant place to enter Turkey and a 20-minute drive from Ephesus.

Samos—green, mountainous, diverse, and friendly—has tourist crowds

but not as bad as other Greek islands. Bus transportation on the island is fine. And for $15 a day you can crisscross Samos on your own moped.

Pounding over potholes, dodging trucks, and stopping to dream across the sea at the hills of Turkey, spanked happily by the prickly wind and Greek sun, I count a moped ride around Samos as my annual jackhammer of youth.

The tourist map shows plenty of obscure sights on Samos. Gambling that the Spiliani monastery was worth the detour, I traded potholes for gravel and wound up the hill. The road ended at a tiny church overlooking the sunburnt island.

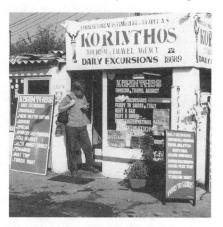

Greek and Turkish travel agencies are more helpful than they look.

Behind the church was the mouth of a cave, with whitewashed columns carved like teeth into the rock. I wandered into the drippy, dank darkness, cool and quiet as another world. Sitting still, I could almost hear the drip-by-drip growth of the stalagmites and the purr of my brain. The only motion was the slight flicker of slender candles. I was ready to venture out of Christendom and into Islam.

For good-value accommodations in Güzelyurt, try Hotel Karvalli (Karvalli Caddesi 4, tel. 382/451-2736, e-mail: khl-turizm@superonline.com). In Kusadasi, consider the Golden Bed Pansiyon (Ugurlu I. Cikmazi 4, tel. 256/614-8708) or Ozhan Pansiyon (Kibris Caddesi 5, tel. 256/614-2932). In Samos (Greece), try Hotel Samos (11 Th. Sofoulis, tel. 0273/28377, fax 0273/23771). For more accommodations, visit www.ricksteves.com/update/intro.htm.

63. Eastern Turkey

Istanbul and the western Turkish coast, while still fascinating, cheap, and eager to please, are moving toward European-style mainstream tourism. For the most cultural thrills, head east. Tour inland Anatolia with abandon, using Ankara as a springboard. From here, buses transport you to the region, culture, and era of your choice.

Find a town that has yet to master the business of tourism, like Kastamonu (5 hours northeast of Ankara). The business hotel where I stayed was cheap ($20 doubles) and comfortable but not slick. I handed a postcard to the boy at the desk, hoping he could mail it for me. He looked it over a couple of times on both sides, complimented me, and politely handed it back. As I left, he raised his right hand like a cigar-store Indian and said, "Hello." While changing money, I was spotted by the bank manager, who invited me into his office for tea. Since I was his first American customer, he wanted to celebrate.

Wandering in and out of small crafts shops, I met an 85-year-old, white-bearded wood-carver who bragged

Eastern Turkey

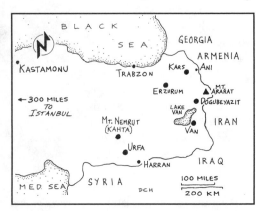

that his work decorated prayer niches in mosques all over Iran. As he sized up just the right chunk of wood, he held his chisel to the sky and said with a twinkle in his eye, "This... is the greatest factory in the world." A few minutes and a pile of wood shavings later, the man gave me a carved floral decoration with his signature in swirling Arabic. When I offered to pay, he refused. At his age, he explained, if I appreciated his art, that was pay enough.

In Turkey, you don't need museums—they're living in the streets.

Outside, a gaggle of men wearing grays, blacks, and browns were shuffling quietly down the street. A casket floated over them as each man jostled to the front to pay his respects by "giving it a shoulder."

Turkey is a land of ceremonies. Rather than relying on a list of festivals, travel with sharp eyes, flexibility, and some knowledge of the folk culture. Local life here is punctuated with colorful, meaningful events. As the dust from the funeral procession clears, you may see a proud eight-year-old boy dressed like a prince or a sultan. The boy is celebrating his circumcision, a rite of passage that some claim is an echo from the days of matriarchal Amazon rule, when entry into the priesthood required c-c-c-castration. This is a great day for the boy and his family. Turks call it the "happiest wedding"—because there are no in-laws.

Having an interpreter helps you explore and mingle with meaning, but it's not required. Many older Turks speak German. The friendliness of Turkey is legendary among those who have traveled beyond the cruise ports. While relatively few small-town Turks speak English, their eagerness to help makes the language barrier an often enjoyable headache.

Enjoy jabbering with the people you meet. If Turkish sounds tough to you, remember, it's the same in reverse. Certain sounds, like our "th," are tricky. My friend Ruth was entertained by the tortured attempts Turks made at pronouncing her name... woooott. Any English-speaking Turk can remember spending long hours looking into the mirror, slowly enunciating: "This and these are hard to say. I think about them every day. My mouth and my teeth, I think you see, help me say them easily."

Throughout Turkey, travelers cringe at the sight of ugly, unfinished construction that scars nearly every town with rusty tangles of steel rebar waiting to reinforce future concrete walls. But in Turkey, unfinished buildings are family savings accounts. Inflation here is ruinous. Any local in need of a hedge against inflation keeps a building under construction. Whenever there's a little extra cash, rather than watch it evaporate in the bank, Ahmed will invest in the next stage of construction. It's the goal of any Turkish parent to provide each child with a house or apartment with which to start adult life. A popular saying is, "Rebar holds the family together."

If you're looking for a rain forest in Turkey, go to the northeast, along the Black Sea coast, where it rains 320 days a year. This is the world's top hazelnut-producing region and home of the Laz people. A highlight of one tour (which I led through Eastern Turkey with 22 American travelers and a Turkish co-guide) was spending an evening and a night with a Laz family. Actually the families of three brothers; they all live in one large three-layered house provided to them by their now-elderly parents.

The people in our group were the first Americans that the 16 people who lived there had ever seen. We were treated to a feast. In Turkey it's next to impossible to turn down this kind of hospitality. As we praised the stuffed peppers, members of our group discreetly passed Pepto Bismol tablets around under the table. (The pouring tea didn't quite mask the sound of ripping cellophane.)

After dinner we paid our respects to the grandma. Looking like a veiled angel in white, she and her family knew she would soon succumb to her cancer. But for now she was overjoyed to see such a happy evening filling her family's home.

When we wondered about having an extended family under one roof, the sons said, "If a day goes by when we don't see each other, we are very sad." To assure harmony in the family, the three brothers married three sisters from another family. They also assured us that entertaining our group of 22 was no problem. If we weren't there, they'd have had as many of their neighbors in.

No Turkish gathering is complete without dancing, and anyone who can snap fingers and swing a Hula-Hoop can be comfortable on the living room dance floor of new Turkish friends. Two aunts, deaf and mute from meningitis, brought the house down with their shoulders fluttering like butterflies. We danced and talked with four generations until after midnight.

Stepping into the late-night breeze, I noticed what had seemed to be a forested hillside was now a spangled banner of lights shining through windows, each representing a "Third World" home filled with as many "family values" as the one we were a part of that night. So much for my stereotypical image of fanatical Muslim hordes. Before we left the next morning, our friends tossed a gunnysack of hazelnuts into our bus.

For decades this eastern end of Turkey's Black Sea coast was a dead end butting up against the closed border of Soviet Georgia. But today the for-

What century is it?

mer U.S.S.R. is ringed by sprawling "Russian markets" rather than foreboding guard posts.

From Finland to Turkey we found boxy Lada automobiles overloaded with the lowest class of garage-sale junk, careening toward the nearest border on a desperate mission to scrape together a little hard cash. In the Turkish coastal town of Trabzon, 300 yards of motley tarps and blankets displayed grandpa's tools, pink and yellow "champagnski" ($1.50 a bottle), Caspian caviar (the blue lid is best, $3), battered samovars, fur hats, and nightmarish Rube Goldbergian electrical gadgetry. A Georgian babushka lady with a linebacker build, caked-on makeup, and bleached blonde hair offered us a wide selection of Soviet pins, garish plastic flowers, and now-worthless ruble coins.

To satisfy my group's strange appetite for godforsaken border crossings, we drove out to the Georgian border. No one knew if we could cross or not. As far as the Turkish official was concerned, "No problem." We were escorted through the mud, past pushcarts bound for flea markets and huge trucks mired in red tape. In this strange economic no-man's-land, the relative prosperity of Muslim Turkey was clear. Just a prayer call away from Georgia, a sharp little Turkish mosque with an exclamation-point minaret seemed to holler, "You sorry losers, let us help you onto our boat." Young Georgian soldiers with hardly a button on their uniforms checked identity cards, as those who qualified squeezed past the barbed wire and through the barely open gate. A soldier told us we couldn't pass. In search of a second opinion, we fetched an officer who said, "Visa no, problem"—a negative that, for a second, I misinterpreted as a positive.

Driving inland from the Black Sea under 10,000-foot peaks, our bus crawled up onto the burnt, barren, 5,000-foot-high Anatolian plateau to

Erzurum, the main city of Eastern Turkey (24 hours by bus from Istanbul). Life is hard here. Blood feuds, a holdover from feudal justice under the Ottomans, are a leading cause of imprisonment. Winters are below-zero killers. Villages spread out onto the plateau like brown weeds, each with the same economy: ducks, dung, and hay.

But Allah has given this land some pleasant surprises. The parched plain hides lush valleys where rooftops sport colorful patches of sun-dried apricots, where shepherd children still play the eagle-bone flute, and where teenage boys prefer girls who dress modestly. And you can crack the sweet, thin-skinned hazelnuts with your teeth.

Entering a village, we passed under a banner announcing, "No love is better than the love for your land and your nation." Another hay, duck, and dung town, it took us warmly into its callused hands. Each house wore a tall hat of hay—food for the cattle and insulation for the winter. Mountains of cow pies were neatly stacked promises of warmth and cooking fuel for six months of snowed-in winter that was on its way. A man with a donkey cart wheeled us through town. Veiled mothers strained to look through our video camera's viewfinder to see their children's mugging faces. The town's annually elected policeman bragged that he keeps the place safe from terrorists. Children scampered around women beating raw wool with sticks—a rainbow of browns that would one day be woven into a carpet to soften a stone sofa, warm up a mud-brick wall, or serve as a daughter's dowry.

Driving east from Erzurum, we set our sights on 18,000-foot Mount Ararat. Villages growing between ancient rivers of lava expertly milk the land for a subsistence living. After a quick reread of the flood story in Genesis, I realized this powerful, sun-drenched, windswept land had changed little since Noah docked.

Turkey is in the middle of a small war in the east. Forty thousand Kurdish guerrillas ("terrorists" or "freedom fighters," depending on your politics) are "in the mountains," while 10 million Turkish Kurds, leading more normal lives, help provide their base of support. On a ridge high above our bus, I could make out the figure of a lone man silhouetted against a bright blue sky waving at us.

When I got up early the next morning to see the sunrise over Mount Ararat, I could make out a long convoy of Turkish army vehicles. It reminded me that these days it takes more than 40 days of rain to fix things. Our world is a complicated place in which the nightly news is just a shadow play of reality. To give it depth, you need to travel.

For the entire script of my Eastern Turkey PBS-TV program, check out www.ricksteves.com.

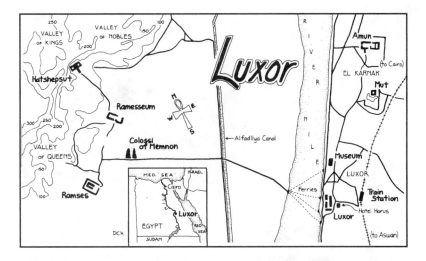

64. The Treasures of Luxor, Egypt

With my travel spirit flapping happily in the breeze, I pedal through
Luxor on my rented one-speed, catching the cool shade and leaving the
stifling heat with the pesky *baksheesh*-beggar kids in the dusty distance.

Choosing the "local ferry" over the "tourist ferry," I'm surrounded
by farmers rather than sightseers. As the sun rises, reddening the tomb-
filled mountains, I pedal south along the West Bank of the Nile. The
noisy crush of tourists is gone. The strip of riverbank hotels back in Luxor
is faint and silent. I'm alone in Egypt: A lush brown-and-green world of
reeds, sugarcane, date palms, mud huts, and a village world amazingly
apart from what the average tourist sees.

An irrigation ditch leads me into the village of Elbairat. Here, I am
truly big news on two wheels. People scurry, grabbing their families to
see the American who chose them over Tut. I'm sure, somewhere in the
Egyptian babble, were the words, "My house is your house." They would
have given me the Key to the Village, but there were no locks.

Elbairat is a poor village with a thriving but extremely simple farm
economy. A little girl balances a headful of grass—heading home with a
salad for the family water buffalo. A proud woman takes me on a tour of
her mud-brick home complete with a no-fly pantry filled with chicken
and pigeons.

This is the real Egypt...how the majority of Egypt's 60 million
people live. So close to all the tourists yet rarely seen.

Start your Egyptian experience in the urban jungle of Cairo. It has
a chaotic charm. With each visit, I stay at the Hotel Windsor. Stepping

into the ramshackle elevator most recently, I asked the boy who ran it if he spoke English. He said, "Up and down." I said, "Up." He babied the collapsing door to close it, turned the brass crank to send us up, and expertly stopped us within an inch of the well-worn second floor lobby where even people who don't write feel

One of the more interesting ways to see Egypt

like writers. I kept looking for the English Patient.

Across the street, the neighborhood gang sat in robes sucking lazy waterpipes called *sheeshaws* (a.k.a. hookas or hubbly-bubblies). With everyone wearing what looked like hospital robes, playing backgammon and dominoes with pipes stuck in their mouths like IVs, and clearly going nowhere in a hurry, it seemed like some strange outdoor hospital gameroom. For about 25 cents, the smoke boy brought me one of the big freestanding pipes and fired up some apple-flavored tobacco.

For a sensuous immersion in this cultural blast furnace, hire a taxi and cruise through the teeming poor neighborhood called "old Cairo." Roll down the windows, crank up the Egyptian pop on the radio, lean out, and give pedestrians high fives as you glide by.

Then head for Luxor. The overnight train ride from Cairo to Luxor is posh and scenic, a fun experience itself. A second-class, air-conditioned sleeping car provides comfortable two-bed compartments, fresh linen, a wash basin, dinner, and a wake-up service.

I spent more time in and around Luxor than in any European small town, and I could have stayed longer. On top of the "village-by-bike" thrills, there are tremendous ancient ruins. The East Bank offers two famous sites: Karnak (with the Temples of Amun, Mut, and Khonsu, one mile north of Luxor) and the Temple of Luxor, which dominates Luxor town.

To the ancient Egyptian, the world was a lush green ribbon cutting north and south through the desert. It was only logical to live on the East Bank, where the sun rises, and bury your dead on the West Bank, where the sun is buried each evening. Therefore, all the tombs, pyramids, and funerary art in Egypt are on the West Bank.

Directly across the Nile from Luxor is the Temple of Queen Hatshepsut, Deir el-Medina, Ramseseum, Colossi of Memnon, and the

Valleys of the Kings, Queens, and Nobles. Be selective. You'll become jaded sooner than you think.

Luxor town itself has plenty to offer. Explore the market. You can get an inexpensive custom-made caftan with your name sewn on in arty Arabic. I found the merchants who pester the tourists at the tombs across the Nile had the best prices on handicrafts and instant antiques. A trip out to the camel market is always fun—and you can pick up a camel for half the U.S. price. For me, five days in a small town is asking for boredom. But Luxor fills five days like no town its size.

FIVE DAYS IN LUXOR

Day 1. Your overnight train from Cairo arrives around 5 a.m. If it's too early to check in, leave your bags at a hotel, telling them you'll return later to inspect the room. Hop a horse carriage to be at the temples at Karnak when they open, while it's still cool. These comfortable early hours should never be wasted. Check into a hotel by midmorning. Explore Luxor town. Enjoy a *felucca* ride on the Nile at sunset.

Day 2. Cross the Nile and rent a taxi for the day. It's easy to gather other tourists and split the transportation costs. If you're selective and start early, you'll be able to see the best sites and finish by noon. That's a lot of work, and you'll enjoy a quiet afternoon back in Luxor.

Day 3. Through your hotel, arrange an all-day minibus trip to visit Aswan, the Aswan Dam, and the important temples (especially Edfu) south of Luxor. With six or eight tourists filling the minibus, this day should not cost more than $20 per person.

Day 4. Rent bikes and explore the time-passed villages on the west side of the Nile. Bring water, your camera, and a bold spirit of adventure. This was my best Egyptian day.

Day 5. Tour the excellent Luxor museum. Enjoy Luxor town and take advantage of the great shopping opportunities. Catch the quick flight or overnight train back to Cairo.

Egypt seems distant and, to many, frightening. The constant hustle ruins the experience for some softer tourists. But once you learn the local ropes, that's less of a problem, and there's a reasonable chance you'll survive and even enjoy your visit.

In the cool months (peak season), it's wise to make hotel reservations. Off-season, in the sweltering summer heat, plenty of rooms lie vacant. Air-conditioning is found in moderately priced hotels. Budget hotels with a private shower, fan, and balcony offer doubles for around $20. (Consider Hotel Horus, Karnak Temple Street, tel. 095/372-165.) A cot in the youth hostel costs $2. But Egypt is not a place where you should save money at the expense of comfort and health. For $100 you'll get a double room with a buffet breakfast in a First World resort-type hotel with an elitist pool and a pharoah's complement of servants. (Consider the riverside Sofitel Hotel Winter Palace; the new section is less atmospheric but half the price of the historic old palace, tel. 095/380-422, fax 095/371-192, e-mail: H1661@accor-hotels.com.)

Eat well and carefully. With the terrible heat, your body requires lots of liquid. Bottled water is cheap and plentiful, as are soft drinks. Watermelons are thirst quenching. Cool your melon in your hotel's refrigerator. Choose a clean restaurant. Hotels generally have restaurants comparable to their class and price range.

To survive the summer heat, limit your sightseeing day to 5 a.m. until noon. The summer heat, which they say can melt car tires to the asphalt, is unbearable and dangerous after noon. Those early hours are prime time: The temperature is comfortable, the light is crisp and fresh, and the Egyptian tourist hustlers are still sleeping. Spend afternoons in the shade. Carry water and wear a white hat (on sale there). An Egypt guidebook (I'd use one by Moon or Lonely Planet) is a shield proving to unwanted human guides that you need no help.

Stay on the budgetary defense. No tip will ever be enough. Tip what you believe is fair by local standards and ignore the inevitable plea for more. Unfortunately, if you ever leave them satisfied, you were ripped off. Consider carrying candies or little gifts for the myriad children constantly screaming *"Baksheesh!"* ("Give me a gift!") Hoard small change in a special pocket so you'll have tip money readily available. Getting change back from your large bill is tough.

Transportation in and around Luxor is a treat. The local taxis are horse-drawn carriages. These are a delight, but drive a hard bargain and settle on a price before departing. The locals' ferry crosses the Nile from dawn until late at night and costs only pennies.

Travel on the West Bank by donkey, bike, or automobile taxi. You can rent donkeys for the romantic approach to the tombs and temples of West Thebes. Sun melts the romance fast. Bikes work for the cheap and hardy. A taxi is the quickest and most comfortable way to explore. When split among four, a taxi for the "day" (6 a.m. until noon) is reasonable. Save money by assembling a tour group at your hotel. You'll enjoy the quick meet-you-at-the-ferry-landing service and adequately cover Luxor's West Bank sights.

Cruise on the Nile in a *felucca*, the traditional sailboat, for just a few dollars an hour. Lounging like Cleopatra in the cool beauty of a Nile sunset is a romantic way to end the day and start the night.

Send Me a Postcard—Drop Me a Line

If you enjoyed a successful trip with the help of this book and would like to share your discoveries, please drop me a line (Europe Through the Back Door, P.O. Box 2009, Edmonds, WA 98020) or e-mail me at rick@ricksteves.com. I personally read and value all feedback. Thanks in advance—it helps a lot—and I'll send you my Back Door quarterly newsletter free for one year. Anyone is welcome to request a free issue (tel. 425/771-8303).

For our latest travel information, tap into our Web site: www.ricksteves.com. For any updates to this book, check www.ricksteves.com/update.

Travel in Europe with Rick Steves

Throughout the U.S., 68 Rick Steves' travel shows are airing on public television, highlighting Rick's favorite places from the Nile to Norway. The first 52 programs are called *Travels in Europe with Rick Steves* (produced 1991–1998 by Small World Productions). The latest series is *Rick Steves' Europe* (16 episodes, self-produced). This new series includes a 90-minute travel-skills special—the essential tips from this book illustrated with examples filmed in Europe. An all-new season of shows—taking you from Amsterdam to Moscow—is being filmed now and will debut throughout the U.S. in September 2002. Call your local PBS station or the Travel Channel to ask when the series airs in your area. For more information or to order the home videos of either series, see www.ricksteves.com or call us at 425/771-8303.

A New Enlightenment through Travel

Thomas Jefferson said, "Travel makes you wiser but less happy." "Less happy" is a good thing. It's the growing pains of a broadening perspective. After viewing our culture from a coffeehouse in Vienna or a village in Tuscany, I've found truths that didn't match those I always assumed were "self-evident" and "God-given." And flying home gives me a healthy dose of culture shock in reverse. You know how I love Europe. But I haven't told you about my most prized souvenir—a new way of thinking.

The "land of the free" has a powerful religion—materialism. Its sophisticated priesthood (business, media, military, and political leaders) worships unsustainable growth. Contentment and simplicity are sins. Mellow is yellow. And evil is anything steering you away from being a good producer/consumer.

Yes, greater wealth could be wonderful. But for whom? The gap between rich and poor—both within our society and among humankind in general—is growing. Regulatory tax and spending policies in the United States since 1982 have caused the greatest trickle-up of wealth in our nation's history. And globally the richest 358 people now own as much as the poorest 45 percent of humanity put together. Designer fortifications protect the wealthy in much of the world. In the USA two kinds of communities are the rage: "gated communities" and prisons. The victims are the politically meek—those who don't or can't vote: the young, the poor, the environment, and the future. More and more Americans have lost hope. And when "freedom" grows at hope's expense, your children will ponder their blessings behind deadbolts.

Whoa! What happened to me? The young Republican traveled. I saw countries less wealthy than ours (but with bigger governments), where everyone had a home, enough food, and healthcare. And, like the early astronauts, I saw a planet with no boundaries—a single, tender organism painted with the faces of 6 billion equally precious people. I unpack my rucksack marveling at how some politically active American Christians can believe that we're all children of God—while fighting aid for the hungry and homeless.

A new Enlightenment is needed. Just as the French "Enlightenment" led us into the modern age of science and democracy, this new era will teach us the necessity of sustainable affluence, peaceful coexistence with other economic models, "controlling" nature by obeying her, and measuring prosperity by something more human than material consumption.

I hope your travels will give you a fun and relaxing vacation or adventure. I also hope they'll make you an active patriot of our planet and a voice for people who will never see their names on a plane ticket.

Appendix

Road Scholars' travel tips from

Rick Steves' Graffiti Wall

at www.ricksteves.com/graffiti

Rick's readers -- his Road Scholars -- have a wealth of travel information to share. For hundreds of great hot-out-of-the-rucksack tips on seventy different travel topics, visit www.ricksteves.com. Here are just a few travelers' tips from the packing, flying, and chocoholic sections.

Packing: Creative Extras

■ Xerox copies of mug-shot page of passport: For when a hotel or bank needs to have my Passport.

■ Extra pair of insoles: For when shoes get wet. Overnight, I pulled the insoles out of the pair I wore and let the shoes and insoles air out. Second pair of insoles much lighter than second pair of shoes.

■ Sarong. A large piece of lightweight material, quick dry, light, and tiny, it can be used as a towel, lightweight blanket, pillow, etc.

■ Disposable cameras: Once shot, break them apart, toss away all but the film, put the film in a Ziploc.

■ Inflatable hangers: Clothes dry faster ($5 at AAA, light and tiny)

■ The two most useful medicines: Tylenol is a general analgesic, and helps reduce fatigue. Benadryl is a great sedative and sleep aid.

■ Small suction cups with hooks: To hang toiletry bag from the mirror in small bathrooms and dangle money belt from the youth hostel shower wall.

■ Ladies--two words: Fem Wipes. Towelettes by Summer's Eve, individually wrapped like Handi-Wipes...great for freshening up and pigeon doo.

■ Half of a tennis ball – works as a stopper in any sink!

■ Earplugs – for the night the hostel gets rowdy!

■ Small Ziploc baggie: To save theater stubs, train tickets, subway tickets, and all kinds of other tiny souvenirs.

■ Dental floss or fishing line: Strong, versatile, waterproof, nearly weightless. Tied backpack together when it broke, doubled as a shoelace, etc.

■ "Freshette," a feminine standup urinary aide, made by Sani-Fem company, 1-800-542-5580.

■ Sleep machine/alarm clock: In noisy hotel rooms, the sleep machine (which emits various sounds, e.g., ocean, rain, forest sounds, white noise) is a true Godsend.

■ Local cassette tapes: We rented a car, and in each country we visited we bought cassette tapes of traditional music. We'd be driving down German side roads, passing May poles, and listening to tubas...up alpine roads and enjoying a yodel or two.

■ Comfy slippers: If your feet aren't happy, YOU aren't happy. Pamper them!

■ A combination alarm clock/flashlight/motion sensor alarm ($30 from Brookstone): Attach to the hotel door or window. If someone moves the door or window, my motion sensor emits a high-pitched sound similar to a fire alarm.

■ If you have a fancy camera, a little black electrician's tape across the brand name discourages thieves. What appears to be a generic camera is almost worthless to those who regularly "hunt" Canon, Leica, Nikon, and so on.

■ I "cinch tied" the opening of my backpack to make it less accessible for would-be thieves (punched holes in the band at the top of the bag and ran an extendable cable lock through the holes, pulled it tight and locked it).

■ Fake hair: My thin sweaty hair looks fabulous with Revlon's fake hair called Spare Hair (from $6.99 to $34.99). Of many styles, my favorite is the Twist,--a "scrunchie" of curled hair on an elastic band. I pull my hair back in a modified pony tail with some hair sticking up out of the elastic band like a bun, bobby pin the loose end of the pony tail around this and then use the Spare Hair scrunchie around the bun twice and it looks like I've spent hours curling my hair. It takes about 15 minutes to do. I can go days with only washing my bangs.

■ A headlight instead of a flashlight. Better for reading in bed. Frees your hands if needed.

■ Post-It notes to flag guidebooks.

■ Women, pack some yeast infection cream or Monistat 1-day suppositories--difficult to find in some countries.

■ Body Shop's "Refreshing Foot Spray" and "Peppermint Foot Lotion" in small, travel-size bottles: Sooth aching tired feet.

■ Tiny musical instrument: If you can play a harmonica, the spoons, the bones, or another tiny instrument – bring it. Unusual in certain areas. Playing them can break the ice, start friendships, and even earn you a free meal!

■ Pillowcase: To put your backpack/travel bag in while you sleep on it on an overnight train. Another obstacle for the thief to overcome. Also, set up the Coke can warning system on your compartment door (a few pennies in an empty can).

■ Put your extra camera lenses in a thick ankle sock. You can toss them in your day pack without worrying about damage and they take up less room than bulky lens cases.

■ Pack a picture of your home town and a small map to locate it.

■ Tie something distinctive, like a ribbon, to your luggage handle for quick spotting at airport carousels.

■ Mailing tubes: To collect prints and posters, also handy for small items and breakables. A very thin placemat from a favorite Paris restaurant made it home safely this way and is now framed and hanging in my home.

■ My Walkman for listening to the local radio stations.

■ Ziplocs: to store the second half of that huge café sandwich. Great snack later.

■ Digital tape recorder: Tiny, great way to catch the waves, traffic, sounds in the cafés and more. I send audio files to friends via the Internet, with digital photos.

■ Combo journal/scrapbook: Buy a fancy (lightweight) journal and take colored pens and glue stick. As you write each day, add creative touches by sketching in color, pasting arty museum tickets, or even cutting/pasting local brochures, etc.

■ Vitamin B6: Makes your blood undesirable to mosquitoes. You have to take it for a few days before it works. Also, a couple years ago I bought a neat little gadget at Babies-R-Us that keeps mosquitoes away. It's designed for babies (who are too young for bug-spray), but works for anyone! This magical red, plastic ladybug clips onto your clothing...or diapers.

Flying Smart

■ I went through www.cheaptickets .com. Their online site requires that you provide a Visa number, but their prices are the best.

■ I've saved hundreds of dollars booking flights on the Web, but always call the airline after you book to confirm that you actually have the reservation.

■ Can't get enough frequent flyer miles to take your whole family to Europe? Use your U.S. award to get your family to a busy airport such as Newark/New York, Washington D.C., or Miami where there are cheap departures. Using half the frequent flyer miles we'd need to get to Europe, we got free flights to Newark where our $300 round-trip tickets to London were less than half what we'd pay from Colorado. Extra bonus: We got a long layover on the east coast and spent a week with family there on the way to Europe.

■ With earplugs known as Earplanes, I overcame my problems with ear air-pressure equalization during flights.

■ For the flight over, take earplugs, ski socks, and a large bottle of Evian. Once the plane takes off, remove your shoes and put on the warm socks. Rather than constantly bug flight attendants for water, you'll have your own supply. For the kids, bring Benadryl, so they'll sleep (just don't tell Grandma).

■ For long flights with small kids: A small flashlight. This quiets a crying toddler.

Chocoholics Unite

■ Cadbury chocolate bars are awesome. The Dairy Milk, Crunchie, and Whispa bars are fantastic. Also, when in London, try the hot chocolate--tastes just like a liquid Dairy Milk bar.

■ After many years of Swiss chocolate adoration, I now bow to the Belgians. They are the masters.

■ The best chocolate is in Germany. I lived in Germany for twelve years and couldn't get enough of their chocolate. Milka and Ritter Sport are great! The Kinder Überaschung (Kid's Surprise) eggs are very popular. Also, during Christmas they come out with Advent calendars that have chocolate hidden behind the flip-open door for each day. Eating those made the wait bearable.

■ In London, visit Charbonnel et Walker, 28 Old Bond Street, near Kensington, for the best chocolates anywhere.

■ My favorite European chocolate: Ritter Sport. It's German but sold all over Europe. Ritter Sport is a square bar that comes in million varieties. My favorite is praline (dark blue wrapper).

■ Near Zurich, tour the Lindt factory in Kilchberg. Tours are free (Wednesday-Friday, S-1 or S-8 from Zurich Hauptbahnhof to Kilchberg, walk 3 minutes).

■ One word: Sprungli, Zurich, Bahnhofstrasse...O.K., that was three words, but when in Zurich go to the Sprungli shop on Bahnhofstrasse and enjoy...mmmm... makes my mouth water just thinking about it.

■ We did the equivalent of a pub-crawl in Bruges, sampling truffles at all the small chocolate shops. By noon we were on a major sugar buzz. The best was at Depla's, just over a canal.

■ Once I met a man on a plane who told me he was the chocolate taster for Hershey's and his job was to travel the world tasting chocolate. His favorite? Belgian.

■ A good friend from Brussels explained that "Mary's" had the best chocolate in Brussels (and thus the world). He noted that there are two stores of every type which are appointed by the King. One is a large, commercial, place (Godiva in this case) and one is a small place, where the King actually buys his goods. Mary's is that place.

■ If you are a chocoholic, then you must tour the Cadbury factory (train to Birmingham, then local train to Bournville, then a 10-minute walk). Upon entering, you're greeted with the most heavenly smell, a lively tour, and an entire chocolate bar! As you munch, you walk through the history of chocolate.

■ Try the hot chocolate in Paris to truly experience it the way it was meant to be. The best place is Angelina near the Louvre, across from the Tuileries on rue de Rivoli. Order the Africain, a pot of liquid pleasure. We loved Angelina so much that we named our cat after it.

■ After two trips to Paris, walking everywhere and tasting along the way, we've found our favorite chocolatier. It's Puyricard (on Avenue Rapp in the 7th).

■ The chocolate factory alone is reason enough to visit Cologne, Germany. They offer tours with a history of chocolate-making and a great look at all the machines in action. This was one of my favorite tours of my two months in Europe last summer.

Thanks to all our Road Scholars who take the time to share their travel intelligence. For piles more tips on everything from jet lag and tourist scams to ATM tricks and best beaches, visit our Graffiti Wall at ricksteves.com/graffiti. If you submit the best tip of the month, you'll get a $100 Europe Through the Back Door catalog gift certificate.

RICK STEVES' BACK DOOR GUIDE TO
European Railpasses

How to find the railpass that best fits your trip—and your budget.

When I started traveling in the 70s, the Eurailpass was king...cheap, simple, and the obvious best deal. My choices were kindergarten-simple: one month or two? Now, 26 years later, travelers have an exciting array of railpasses to choose from: Eurailpasses, Europasses, new Selectpasses, single-country passes, and even Rail & Drive passes. While most passes are available for purchase only outside of Europe, some can be bought only after you arrive in Europe. And, depending on your trip, it may be cheaper to buy tickets as you go.

The stakes are high and the choices are many. Travelers need to be more informed than ever in order to make the best choice. And no one explains your options better than my well-traveled "train-gang" staff does in this chapter.

First we will get you started on your trip, helping you learn how to make an informed choice. Then we'll describe this year's dizzying array of European railpass prices and features. Unlike any other source of information, we'll compare these passes to point-to-point tickets, and to passes sold only in Europe (a well-kept secret in the USA). Every few pages you'll find a money-saving analysis, matching the options to your travel dreams.

IMPORTANT NOTE: All pass prices and features in this guide are for **2001**. For a free copy of *Rick Steves' 2002 Guide to European Railpasses*, call (425) 771-8303, or visit **www.ricksteves.com** after 12/15/01.

HOW RAILPASSES WORK

COMPARING COSTS: RAILPASSES VS. TICKETS

You can ride the rails in Europe with a railpass, or with tickets you purchase at train stations as you travel. With this guide, you can figure out which is more economical for your trip.

Throughout this guide, you'll find maps that list the approximate prices for tickets (also called "point-to-point tickets"). Once you have a rough itinerary, use these maps to add up the cost of your journey. Compare the cost of tickets with the price of the railpass that best fits your trip. If the costs are close, it makes sense to buy the pass, unless you enjoy standing in lines at ticket windows.

CHOO-CHOOSING A RAILPASS

Consecutive-day or Flexi?

You'll generally have a choice between consecutive-day and flexipass versions of a pass. Major exceptions are the Europass and Selectpass, which come only in flexi versions.

Consecutive-day pass: If you plan to travel nearly daily and cover a lot of ground, a consecutive day pass is the right choice for you. You get unlimited train travel for the duration of the pass. If you have a 15-day pass, you can travel 15 consecutive days, hopping on and off trains many times each day. If you have a one-month pass, you can travel, for example, from April 26 through May 25. One-month passes last longer when started in a 31-day month.

Flexipass: If you like to linger for a few days at various places, a flexipass is the better choice. You have a certain number of travel days to use within a longer "window" of time (for example, any 10 days within a 2-month period). You can

sprinkle these travel days throughout your trip or use them all in a row. You can take as many separate trips as you like within each travel day. A travel day runs from midnight to midnight, but luckily, an overnight train or boat ride uses only one travel day. For details, see "Using Your Pass" later in this guide.

Saverpass: Designed to save money for groups of two to five travelers, a saverpass is a single coupon printed with all the names of a traveling group. Part of the group can use the pass while others stay in town or fly home, but those sharing a pass cannot split and go different directions by train. If you are a group of four, for no extra cost you can give yourselves more flexibility by ordering a separate pass for each couple.

First class, Second class, and Youth Passes

Wrestling with the choice between first and second class? Sometimes the choice is made for you...

If you're considering a Eurailpass, Europass or Selectpass: If you're age 26 or older, you must buy a first class railpass. Those under age 26 have the choice of buying either a second or a first class pass. For families traveling together, a first-class Saverpass for two costs the same as one first-class adult and one second-class youth.

If you're considering a country pass: Most single-country and regional passes are available in second class versions for travelers of any age.

If you're under 26: Some passes are discounted for youth traveling second class. To be eligible, you must be under 26 (according to your passport) the day you validate the pass in Europe. Generally, children from 4 to 11 get passes for half the cost of the adult first class pass (kids under 4 travel free). Ages vary a bit among different country passes.

If you're 60 or over: Even though some passes (Britrail, France) offer first-class-only senior discounts, you'll still save more by traveling in second class. Scandinavia and Holland have discounted senior passes for both classes.

Differences between first and second class: In train cars with compartments, first class is configured with six seats (three facing three) while second class sometimes has eight seats (four facing four). With open-style seating, first-class has three plush seats per row (two on one side and a single on the other) and second-class has four skinnier, basic seats.

Choosing first class: Remember that nearly every train has both first and second class cars, each going at precisely the same speed! If you have the extra money, riding first class is less crowded and more comfortable. First-class railpasses can be a good value, too. While individual first class tickets cost 50% more than second class, first class railpasses generally bump your price up only 25% to 40%.

Choosing second class: If you're on a tight budget, second class makes lots of sense. In most of Europe, the new second-class cars are as comfortable as the old first-class ones. And Back Door travelers know that the nuns and soldiers are partying in second class. First class is filled with Eurail and Europass travelers age 26+ who had no choice, and business travelers who paid 50% extra in hopes that they wouldn't have to sit with the likes of you and me.

Switching classes: Those with first-class passes may travel in second-class compartments (although the conductor may give you a puzzled look). Outside Britain, those with second-class passes can pay the 50% difference in ticket price to upgrade to first.

Rail & Drive Passes

Many passes come in "Rail & Drive" versions, offering a certain number of rail days and rental car days. For details, see Rick's complete *Guide to European Railpasses*. (Note: ETBD does not sell Rail & Drive passes. To order, call your travel agent, DER at 800/549-3737, or Rail Europe at 800/438-7245.)

Longer or Shorter Pass: Some Money-Saving Tips

Both consecutive-day and flexi railpasses offer a varying number of travel days. Once you've planned a route for your trip, you should try to figure out how many "travel days" you'll need to cover everything.

With some thoughtful juggling, a shorter consecutive-day pass can cover a longer trip. For example, you can take a one month trip with a 21-day Eurail-pass ($182 cheaper than a one month pass) by...

...starting and/or ending your trip in a city where you'd like to stay for several days or more. On, say, a Copenhagen-Rome trip, spend a few days in Copenhagen, validate your pass upon departure, and arrive in Rome as your pass expires.

...starting and/or ending your trip in a country not covered by your pass. For example, a Eurailpass does not cover Britain. On a trip that begins in London and ends in Amsterdam, start with a couple of days in London, take the Eurostar (not covered by any railpass) to Paris, sightsee in Paris for several days, then validate your consecutive-day pass when you leave Paris for wherever. Plan for your pass to expire in Amsterdam, where you can easily spend a few days making short, cheap day trips that don't merit the use of a railpass.

Depending on your itinerary, it can make sense to get a longer consecutive day pass to cover a shorter trip. One long train ride (for example, $210 first class from Florence to Paris) at the end of a 25-day trip can justify jumping from a 21-day consecutive-day railpass to a one-month pass. Similarly, if you plan to travel for five to seven weeks, consider buying a two-month Eurailpass for $1260 instead of a

Connecting the dots: *Approximate point-to-point one-way 2nd class rail fares in $US.*

one-month Eurailpass for $890. Priced at just $21 per day, you can afford to drop a few days at the end.

Stretch a flexipass by paying out of pocket for shorter trips. Use your flexipass only for those "travel days" that involve long hauls or several trips. To determine if a trip is a good use of a travel day, divide the cost of your pass by the number of travel days. For example, a 15-day Europass for $688 costs about $45 per travel day. If a particular trip costs significantly less than $45, pay out of pocket (and you'll have saved a flexi travel day for later in your trip).

Flexipasses are misnamed: they are cheaper, but cost you flexibility. Let's say you're planning a 21-day trip and choosing between a 21 consecutive-day Eurailpass ($718) and a cheaper 10-days-in-2-months Eurail Flexipass ($654). For $64 more, the consecutive day pass gives you the option to travel for 11 extra days, giving you the freedom to hop on any train without wondering if a particular trip justifies the use of a travel day. Of course, if you're sure you won't need any extra days, go with the cheaper flexipass.

More travel days on a pass = cheaper cost per day. Compared to shorter passes, longer railpasses are cheaper per travel day. For example, for a 15 consecutive-day Eurailpass at $554, you're paying $37 a day. With a three-month Eurailpass for $1558, you're paying only $17 a day. Most one-hour train rides cost more than that!

One pass is usually better than two. To cover a multiple-country trip, it's usually cheaper to buy one Europass, Selectpass or Eurailpass with lots of travel days than to buy several country passes with a few high-cost travel days per pass. If you decide to travel over a border (e.g., France to Italy) using separate France and Italy railpasses, then you will use up a day of *each* pass.

BUYING YOUR PASS

Most railpasses must be purchased in the USA and are not available in Europe. There are some exceptions: Eurailpasses are sold at some of Europe's major railway stations for about 10% more than the USA price. Some local passes (explained in each country's section of this guide) are available only in Europe.

Your neighborhood travel agent can sell you most of the passes listed in this guide; a $10 "handling fee" is common. Agents who don't do a lot of independent European travel may need your help to understand what's available. When you find a good travel agent, be loyal. If you don't have an agent, call someone who specializes in budget European travel (like us).

Save money by planning ahead. Since railpass prices usually go up every January, those traveling in the first half of 2002 will probably save 5% or so by buying in December 2001. After you buy a pass, you have six months to validate it in Europe.

BUYING POINT-TO-POINT TICKETS IN EUROPE

Probably ten percent of railpass travelers would have traveled smarter and cheaper by simply buying tickets as they went. While point-to-point tickets are sold by travel agents in the USA, you can keep your options open and save a little money by buying tickets in Europe as you need them. Tickets purchased in Europe are changeable and refundable; those purchased in the USA have change/refund restrictions.

Railpass shoppers can check out the local-ticket alternative by using the fare maps scattered throughout this guide to add up the cost of their journey, and then compare it with the cost of a railpass.

The "Time and Cost" map later in this rail guide shows the fares for international rides, while the country maps (listed in each country section) show the prices of domestic trips. These fares are listed in US dollars for one-way trips in second class (for first class, add 50%). For example, if you're taking the train from Amsterdam to Paris, it'll cost you about $95 in second class or $145 for first class. While travelers age 26 and older who choose Eurail must buy a first class pass, there are no age restrictions when buying individual second class tickets.

The point-to-point prices used in this rail guide are based on the "Eurail Tariff" fares which US travel agents charge for point-to-point tickets. After checking with station ticket offices in many European countries, I've concluded that these fares are generally accurate enough for the comparison purposes of this guide. Those willing to shop around in Europe and avoid the

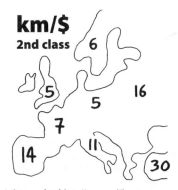

km/$
2nd class

Point-to-point tickets: How many kilometers you can cover by rail for $1 depends on where you are in Europe.

fast supplement-required trains will find some cheaper special point-to-point deals in Europe.

Local fares are always based on kilometers traveled. Each country has its own "schillings per kilometer" type of formula, although some (like France) charge more during peak-use times.

Rules vary from country to country, usually allowing anywhere from one day to two months to complete a journey with unlimited stop-overs along the route.

You'll find a list of Web sites with free 24-hour train route and schedule information (and some with fare information) on the next page. Or call Rail Europe's automated phone information service at 800/438-7245.

POINT-TO-POINT TICKET DEALS FOR SENIORS

Ask for details from each country's tourist office in the US, or locally in each country.

Country	Min. Age	Discount	Card Needed?
Austria	60 F, 65 M	50%	Vortek Senior Card (350 AS)
Belgium	65	Any local train 100 BEF roundtrip after 9 a.m. (Thalys not included)	No
Britain	60	33%	Senior Railcard (£18)
Denmark	65	20%	No
Finland	65	50%	No
France	60	25%	No, but Senior Card (285 F) gives more discounts
Germany	60	50%	Bahncard Senior (130 DM 2nd cl., 260 DM 1st cl)
Italy	60	20 – 30%	Carta d'Argento (L.40,000)
Norway	67	50%	No

Point-to-Point Ticket Deals for Youths

In Europe, travelers under 26 can buy discounted tickets (approx. 30% off) at over 6,000 travel agencies, or at any of Wasteels' 200 offices. *Let's Go* guidebooks list budget travel offices in each city, usually located in or near major train stations. These cheap tickets, often called "BIGE" or "BIJ," are good for about 90% of international departures, except for a few all-first-class and express trains. The tickets usually allow unlimited stopovers along the route within a 2-month window. Here are some sample one-way BIGE/BIJ fares: London-Rome, £110 ($176); London-Amsterdam, £44 ($70 via train-ferry-train, ferry included in price); and London-Paris, £57 ($90 via train-ferry-train, ferry included in price).

Point-to-Point Prices of International Boat Crossings

Some boat crossings are covered by railpasses, but if you're buying point-to-point tickets, it helps to get an idea of the costs. Price ranges are listed, because fees vary with the season and for who-knows-what-reason.

▼ **Brindisi, Ancona, or Bari, Italy to Patras, Greece:** 15-21 hrs, $25-$50, free deck passage with Eurailpass, except for a $3 reservation fee year round and a peak-season (July & August) surcharge of $20. Seats and berths cost extra ($20-$145).

▼ **Wales to Ireland:** 4 hrs, $35-$45 (free if you can talk your way into a car, which is allowed four free passengers).

▼ **Ireland to France:** 18 hrs, most days, crossing only costs $85-110 (half price with Eurailpass), add $50 and up for cabin. Sailings from Rosslare, Ireland and Cherbourg or Roscoff, France.

▼ **Newcastle, England to Bergen, Norway:** 26 hrs, $70-$300 (for specifics, visit www.fjordline.com).

▼ **Calais, France to Dover, England:** 1-2 hrs, daily, $30-$40.

▼ The sleek Eurostar "Chunnel" train makes the **London-Paris** trip in just over 3 hours. From downtown to downtown, the Eurostar train is actually faster than flying, and costs about the same ($75-$200 second class).

If Something Goes Wrong...

▼ **Insurance:** *Unless you have railpass insurance, lost or stolen passes are non-refundable.* If you decide to get pass insurance, which is offered by railpass retailers for $10-15 per pass, it must be purchased at the same time you buy your pass. This insurance does **not** replace your pass while in Europe, but allows you to make a claim at home for the unused portion of the pass that was lost or stolen. Personally, I keep my pass in my moneybelt and take my chances.

If you do not complete your trip, partially used passes are **not** refundable unless you have trip interruption/cancellation insurance (purchased separately from a travel agent for approx. 5% of the amount to be covered). This will cover financial losses if you must cancel your trip because you or a family member become ill. Ask a travel agent for details.

▼ **Exchanges:** Most unused, unvalidated passes can be exchanged for more expensive passes for a small fee. There is a penalty (15% or more) for downgrading from a longer pass to a shorter, cheaper pass.

▼ **Refunds:** Unused and unvalidated passes are refundable (minus a penalty of 15% or more) if returned to the place of purchase within six months (most country passes) or one year (Euro, Eurail, Select, Germany, France, Spain, Portugal, and Swiss passes). Most refunds take 6 to 8 weeks.

Weaving Around the Web

For detailed European rail and ferry schedules, check out these Web sites:

■ **Deutsche Bahn's Connection Search:** http://bahn.hafas.de/bin/query.exe/en

■ **Mercurio Railway Server:** http://mercurio.iet.unipi.it/misc/timetabl.html

■ **Dan Youra's Ferry Guide:** www.youra.com/ferry/intlferries.html

■ **Euraide** (sleeper prices, Rhine boat and Romantic Road Schedules, reservations): www.euraide.de/ricksteves

■ **Links to all of ETBD's favorite travel sites:** www.ricksteves.com/tips/links.htm

TRANSPORTATION OPTIONS FOR SEVEN GREAT THREE-WEEK TRIPS

Intimidated by all the data in this guide? Looking for a place to start? Here is a quick analysis of transportation options for my seven favorite three-week itineraries as described in my guidebook for that country or region (driving rates are roughly per person for 2 traveling together and include taxes, CDW, and some parking in big cities):

3 WEEKS IN EUROPE

Route: Amsterdam → Rhineland → Romantic Road → Tirol → Venice → Florence → Rome → Italian Riviera → Swiss Alps → Beaune → Paris. For this plan, let your dreams rather than the cost dictate your choice:

$550	Second class point-to-point tickets
$718	21 day 1st class Eurailpass
$654	10 days in 2 months Eurail flexipass
$628	10 days in 2 months Europass with Benelux, Austria add-ons.
$536	Cost per person for 2 traveling together, 10 days in 2 months Europass Saver with Benelux & Austria added.
$680	EurailDrive split by 2 ($339 ea.) + 5 extra rail days ($295 apiece) for 9 rail days and 2 car days + $45 per person for gas and CDW (good for two buddies with an interest in driving a little, in a small manual transmission car).
$700	Three weeks in a rented car (per person based on 2 traveling together incl. taxes, gas, CDW, tolls and parking)

3 WEEKS IN GREAT BRITAIN

Route: London → Bath → Cardiff → Cotswolds → North Wales → Windermere → Oban → Edinburgh → Durham → York → Cambridge → London.

$275	15 days in 30 flexi bus pass
$499	22 days 2nd class BritRail pass
$515	15 days in 2 months 2nd class BritRail flexipass
$510	Second class point-to-point tickets
$600	3 weeks in a leased car ($1200 split by 2)

3 WEEKS IN FRANCE

Route: Paris → Normandy → Brittany → Loire → Carcassonne → Provence → Alps → Burgundy → Alsace → Paris.

$360	9 days in 1 month 2nd class France Pass
$470	Second class point-to-point tickets
$454	France Rail & Drive Pass (9 second class rail days and 3 car days, two people), $409+$45 for gas/CDW.

3 WEEKS IN SCANDINAVIA

Route: Copenhagen → Kalmar → Stockholm → Helsinki → Stockholm → Oslo → Fjords → Bergen → Aarhus → Aero → Copenhagen.

$486	21 day first class ScanRail Pass
$310	Scanrail 10 days in 2 months 2nd class flexipass
$750	3 weeks in a rented car (split by 2) plus a round-trip boat to Finland
$700	2nd class point-to-point tickets

3 WEEKS IN ITALY

Route: Milan → Cinque Terre → Florence → Siena → Rome → Naples → Paestum → Venice → Dolomites → Como → Milan (2400 km).

$180	3,000 km first class Kilometric ticket purchased in Italy (or $110 second class, plus supplements)
$225	Second class point-to-point tickets
$429	12 days in a month first class Italy Rail Card
$286	12 days in a month 2nd class Italy Rail Card
$433	21 days first class Italy Rail Card
$289	21 days 2nd class Italy Rail Card
$700	3 weeks in a rented car (including Italian extras: theft insurance, extra-strength aspirin, city parking and autostrada tolls, split by 2)

3 WEEKS IN GERMANY, AUSTRIA & SWITZERLAND

Route: Frankfurt → Romantic Road → Reutte → Munich → Salzburg → Hallstatt → Vienna → Innsbruck → Appenzell → Interlaken → Bern → Lausanne → Baden Baden → Mosel → Rhine → Köln→ Frankfurt.

$576	10 days in 2 months Selectpass ($476) + $100 add'l. for 4 extra rail tickets
$650	Second class point-to-point tickets
$718	21 day 1st class Eurailpass
$748	15 days in 2 months Europass with Austria add-on
$598	German 4 rail days and 3 car days ($251), 3 days in 15 Austrian Flexipass $107, 6 days in a month Swiss Railpass ($240). (All 2nd class.)
$600	3 weeks in a rented car ($1200 split by 2).

3 WEEKS IN SPAIN & PORTUGAL

Route: Madrid → Salamanca → Coimbra → Lisbon → Algarve → Seville → Gibraltar → Nerja → Granada → Toledo → Madrid.

$200	Second class tickets as you go (best for tight budgets)
$500	3 weeks in a rented car split by two
$375	5 days in a month Spain 1st class flexipass ($270) and 4 days in 15 Portugal flexipass ($105)
$476	10 days in 2 months 1st class Selectpass for 3 countries
$475	9 days in a month 1st class Iberia pass
$400	Spain Rail & Drive split by 2 people with 3 rail days and 4 car days ($295) plus 4 days in 15 Portugal flexipass ($105).

MULTI-COUNTRY

Three multi-country railpass options make it easier than ever to find a pass that fits your trip. The "full-size" **Eurailpass** is valid for travel throughout 17 countries. The "mid-size" **Europass** (the most popular railpass) includes five countries in the core of Europe with the option to add up to two additional "zones." The new "compact-size" **Selectpass** lets you choose just 3 neighboring countries from the 17 Eurail participants. All the passes described on these two pages offer the same basic benefits and bonuses in the countries selected.

EURO

The "mid-size" Europass covers the most popular core of Europe: France, Germany, Switzerland, Italy, and Spain. For a little more money, you can add one or two of the available adjacent countries (called zones) at the time of purchase. Benelux counts as one zone, as does Austria/Hungary. But if you find you are adding lots of extra zones for your trip, a Eurailpass may be a better value.

Europass diagram key:

*Every **Europass** includes travel in the countries listed in the large box, above. Each smaller box represents one add-on zone, which costs extra.*
Note: You cannot add extra zones after you've purchased your pass!

EUROPASS

FIRST CLASS	5 standard countries	1 extra zone	2 extra zones
5 days in 2 months	$348	$408	$448
6 days in 2 months	388	448	488
8 days in 2 months	460	520	560
10 days in 2 months	528	588	628
15 days in 2 months	688	748	788

YOUTH EUROPASS

SECOND CLASS	5 standard countries	1 extra zone	2 extra zones
5 days in 2 months	$244	$286	$314
6 days in 2 months	272	314	342
8 days in 2 months	322	364	392
10 days in 2 months	370	412	440
15 days in 2 months	482	524	552

You must be under 26 on your first day of railpass travel.

Half-price Britrail for youths!

Travelers under 26 who buy a 2nd class Youth Eurailpass, Europass or Selectpass can also get a Youth BritRail Classic Pass or BritRail Flexipass for half price. See Great Britain section for details.

SAVER EUROPASS

FIRST CLASS	5 standard countries	1 extra zone	2 extra zones
5 days in 2 months	$296	$348	$382
6 days in 2 months	330	382	416
8 days in 2 months	392	444	478
10 days in 2 months	450	502	536
15 days in 2 months	586	638	672

Prices are per person, based on 2 or more traveling together. Kids 4-11 pay 1/2 adult 1st class or Saverpass fare. Under 4 travel free.

Saverpass = 15% off for groups!

Note that all the passes listed here offer First Class Saverpass options for 2 or more people traveling together. The prices listed include a 15% discount compared to individual First Class Eurailpasses, Europasses or Selectpasses. Members of each pair or group must order together.

RAILPASSES

EURAIL

The "full-size" 17-country Eurailpass allows you to travel freely through most of Western Europe, from Portugal to Finland to Greece (see diagram below). Of the passes on these two pages, only the Eurailpass offers consecutive-day versions, particularly useful for the whirlwind traveler who's riding the rails almost every day. It's also the only pass with a 3-month option, making it especially popular with student backpackers. Eurailpasses give the free-spirited traveler much more flexibility than Euro or Selectpasses, but at a higher price.

SELECT

For shorter, more focused trips, the "compact-size" Selectpass offers maximum customization. Choose three countries connected like a string of pearls by rail or ferry lines. You can travel outside the central core without the higher "Europass" cost of add-on zones (for instance, France-Italy-Greece or Benelux-Germany-Sweden). If you plan to visit more than three countries, or need more than 10 days of travel in 2 months, then a Europass or Eurailpass will be a better choice.

SELECTPASS

	1st Class Selectpass	1st Class Saverpass	2nd Class Youthpass
5 days in 2 months ...	$328	$280	$230
6 days in 2 months	360	306	252
8 days in 2 months	420	358	294
10 days in 2 months ...	476	406	334

Children 4–11 pay half of the adult First Class or Saver price, under 4 free. Saverpass prices are per person for two or more people traveling together. Youthpasses are for travelers under age 26 only. The Benelux area counts as one country. Austria and Hungary are each added separately.

EURAIL CONSECUTIVE DAY PASS

	1st Class Eurailpass	1st Class Saverpass	2nd Class Youthpass
15 consecutive days	554	470	388
21 consecutive days	718	610	499
1 month consec. days	890	756	623
2 months consec. days ...	1260	1072	882
3 months consec. days ...	1558	1324	1089

EURAIL FLEXIPASS

	1st Class Eurailpass	1st Class Saverpass	2nd Class Youthpass
10 days in 2 months flexi	$654	$556	$458
15 days in 2 months flexi .	862	732	599

Youthpasses are for travelers under age 26 only, no discounts for companions. Children 4-11 pay half, under 4 travel free. Saverpass prices are per person for 2 or more traveling together.

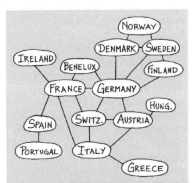

Eurailpass/Selectpass diagram key:

*Every **Eurailpass** includes travel in every country shown above. A **Selectpass** can be designed to connect a "chain" of any three countries in this diagram linked by direct lines. (Examples that qualify: Norway-Sweden-Germany; Spain-France-Italy; Austria-Italy-Greece.) "Benelux" is considered one country.*

See the next page for details on these passes, including restrictions.

Important Eurail-Euro-Select Pass Restrictions

▼ Be aware of your route. Passes are good for use only in the countries listed or selected. If your train passes through a country not on your pass, you must buy a separate ticket for that stretch in advance, or pay a fine for purchasing the ticket on board.

▼ Note that travel in Britain and most of Eastern Europe is not covered by these passes. See the pass and ticket prices for those areas later in this guide.

▼ Railpasses do not cover any seat or sleeper reservations, though they may be required. See "Reservations" and "Supplements" for details.

▼ Adding zones does not increase your number of rail days. Adding days does not increase your 2 month "window." Extra zones and days must be selected at the time of purchase and cannot be added in Europe.

The Thalys Problem

The privately-run Thalys high-speed train monopolizes direct service from Paris to Köln, Amsterdam, Brussels, and other Belgian cities. Railpass holders always need to pay extra to ride on the Thalys—but the amount can vary greatly. Here are the details:

Passholder fares on the Thalys are available *only* to those who have Euro, Eurail, or Select passes that include Benelux and every other country of travel on that train trip. While first-class Passholder Fares ($29) include a meal on weekdays (Mon–Fri), go second class ($14) if you're on a budget. Thalys limits the number of seats available to passholders, so you may need to reserve your seat a few days in advance.

France and Benelux passholders do *not* get any discounts on Thalys trains. Instead, you'll need to either buy a ticket for the entire Thalys trip (e.g., second-class fares from Paris to Brussels $65, Paris-

Amsterdam $100) or take a less direct route on cheaper trains and pay just for the segment not covered by your pass. For instance, on the popular Paris/Brussels/Amsterdam route, you have these options:

▼ From Paris (either the Gare du Nord or Charles de Gaulle Airport), take the TGV train to Lille, then transfer to another train (TGV or non-TGV) to Brussels, where you can transfer to an inexpensive train to Amsterdam. The reservation fees for two TGVs are about $8 total.

▼ From Paris' Charles de Gaulle Airport, take the international TGV direct to Brussels, where you can transfer to Amsterdam. The TGV reservation fee is about $11.

Bonuses with Railpass

The following European boat, bus and other non-rail rides are either free or discounted with any pass that covers the appropriate country (usually both countries for international trips). Free bonuses use a travel day of a flexipass; discounted bonuses do not, but travel must be within the validity period. The map that accompanies each pass explains these bonuses and their restrictions in detail.

Free Bonuses:

▼ International ferry crossings:
  • Brindisi, Ancona, or Bari, Italy to Patras, Greece
  • Sweden to Finland, Germany or Denmark
▼ German Rhine boats
▼ Swiss lake boats

Discounted Bonuses:

▼ International Ferry: Ireland - France 50% off
▼ German Romantic Road Bus 60% off
▼ German Castle Road Bus 60% off
▼ Swiss Jungfrau private railway 25% off
▼ Eurostar Chunnel train approx. 33-50% off

Adding Days to Any Pass

To determine if adding days is worth it, compute the per-day cost of the pass and compare that to the cost of buying individual point-to-point tickets. For example, if you are based in Paris, it doesn't make sense to add a day just to include the $10 side trip to Versailles, but it would pay off for a $100 round trip to the Loire Valley. Passes pay for themselves more quickly in the north where rail travel costs are higher. You may choose to buy several point-to-point tickets in Italy, where you can connect major cities for $20–25, and save your pass travel days for Germany.

These examples focus on the Saver version of each pass, but you can make the same comparison for individual or youth passes:

Flexi days in 2 months	SelectSaver per person includes 3 countries	EuroSaver per person includes 5 countries	EurailSaver per person includes 17 countries
5 days	$280 ($56/day)	$296 ($60/day)	N/A
10 days	$406 ($41/day)	$450 ($45/day)	$556 ($56/day)
15 days	N/A	$586 ($39/day)	$732 ($49/day)

▼ The per-day price difference between the 5-country Eurosaver and the 17-country EurailSaver averages only about $10 per day (less if Euro add-on zones are included). If you like to cover a lot of ground and keep your itinerary options open, you may be better off buying the full-blown Eurailpass.

▼ The per-day price difference between the 3-country Selectpass and the 5-country Europass averages only about $4 per day. The real value of the Selectpass is the opportunity to choose unique country combinations without paying for add-on zones.

▼ The more you travel with any pass, the more you save per day compared to buying tickets as you go.

Adding Europass Zones

The first zone you add to a Europass will cost $60, the second just $40 (slightly less for saver and youth passes). Remember to factor in extra travel days (about $35/day) if needed. Sometimes it's cheaper to simply buy tickets to supplement your pass. The chart below will help you to determine whether it's worth it to add a zone.

Add-on zone	Sample 2nd class tickets for trips in that zone
Austria/Hungary	Salzburg to Vienna, $40; north-south border, $25 (e.g., fare through Austria from Munich to Italy via Innsbruck); German border (near Salzburg) to Budapest, $75.
Benelux	Amsterdam to French border, $65; Amsterdam to German border, $25; Brussels to any border, $25. Important:Thalys trains from Brussels to Paris, Amsterdam, Koln, or Geneva accept passes only if they cover your entire ride on the train. Add this zone if you plan to use the Thalys.
Portugal	Lisbon to Algarve or Spanish border, $20.
Greece	Covers Italy boat crossing, worth $25 - $50 each way; may not run daily; Patras to Athens train, $15.

See the next page for a handy railpass selection worksheet.

See "International Hotel Trains" for costs and restrictions for railpass users on these particular trains.

RAILPASS WORKSHEET:

CONFUSED? With so many passes and prices to consider, choosing the right railpass can be downright intimidating. This worksheet shows you a step-by-step process our trip consultants use for finding the pass that best suits your trip.

Arriving at start of trip in (city) _____ on (date) _____

Departing at end of trip from (city) _____ on (date) _____

Where do you want to go? List the places you want to visit in order of importance:

1 _____   6 _____
2 _____   7 _____
3 _____   8 _____
4 _____   9 _____
5 _____   10 _____

What route will you follow? By plotting your destinations on the map to the right, you'll be able to connect the dots in a logical route (and see clearly which places may be too far out of the way). You'll find more detailed maps like this scattered throughout this guide, and you'll find some handy tips in "Transportation Options for Seven Great Three-Week Trips" and in the Itinerary Planning chapter.

How frequently will you be on the move? Count up your number of actual travel days (for example, staying 3 days in one city doesn't count as any travel days, but a day spent connecting cities does). This will help you determine how many "flexi" days you may need (or whether a consecutive day pass may be better for your trip).

Total days in Europe____   Actual travel days in Europe_____

How much will it all cost? Add up what your individual fares would cost using the following map (the individual country maps in this guide offer more detail), and compare your total to the price of the various passes. Europasses and Selectpasses are the best values for most rail travelers, so look at them first.

INDIVIDUAL FARES (from map on next page): _____   RAILPASS OPTION A:

_____ $ _____   _____ $ _____
_____ _____   _____ _____
_____ _____   _____ _____
_____ _____   Total _____ $ _____
_____ _____   RAILPASS OPTION B:
_____ _____   _____ $ _____
_____ _____   _____ _____
_____ _____   _____ _____
Total _____ $ _____   Total _____ $ _____

WHICH PASS IS BEST?

Connect the dots, add up the cost, and see if a railpass will save you money.

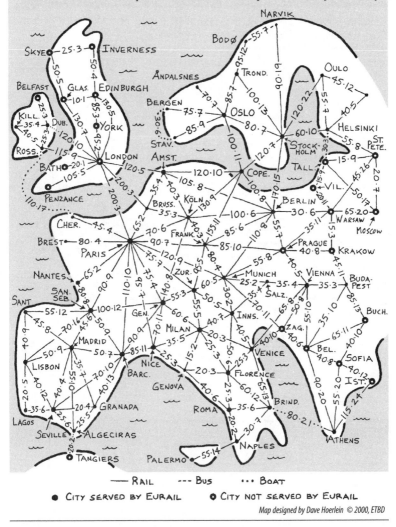

Map designed by Dave Hoerlein © 2000, ETBD

The **first number** between cities = **approximate cost** in $US for a 1-way, 2nd class ticket.

The **second number** = number of **hours** the trip takes.

Important: These fares and times are based on the Eurail Tariff Guide. Actual prices may vary due to currency fluctuations and local promotions. Local competition can cut the actual price of some boat crossings (from Italy to Greece, for example) by 50% or more. For approximate 1st class rail prices, multiply the prices shown by 1½. Travelers under age 26 can receive up to 1/3 off the 2nd class fares shown (buying at student travel agencies in Europe). Travel times are for express trains where applicable.

COUNTRY RAILPASSES

GREAT BRITAIN

The Britrail Pass gives you free run of the British train system in England, Scotland and Wales. (It does not cover Northern Ireland or the Republic of Ireland.) Since Britain is not included on the Eurailpass, and pay-as-you-go train fares are the highest in Europe, the Britrail pass is a big seller. Passes pay for themselves quickly if you travel at least from London to Scotland. Those on a budget will find that standard class (British for second class) is fine, and first-class passes are not worth the extra 50%. In fact, many "milk run" trains have only standard-class cars. If you're traveling with wee ones under 16, the Britrail Family Pass is a jolly good deal. Before buying a Britrail pass, consider the money-saving rail and bus deals available locally (see next two pages).

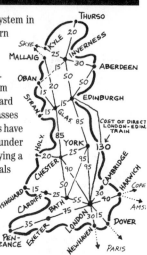

Half-price BritRail Youth Deal!

Travelers under 26 who buy a 2nd class Youth Eurailpass, Europass, or Selectpass can also get a BritRail Youth Classic Pass or Flexipass for half price. Both passes must be used by the same traveler, and both must be validated in Europe before your 26th birthday. One $10 Pass Protection fee gives coverage for both passes. Refunds (if necessary) will be adjusted for discount.

BRITRAIL CLASSIC PASS

	Adult first class	Adult standard	Senior (60+) first class	16-25 youth standard
8 consec. days	$399	$265	$339	$215
15 consec. days	599	399	509	279
22 consec. days	759	499	639	355
1 month	899	599	759	419

No senior 2nd class pass discount.

BRITRAIL FLEXIPASS

	Adult first class	Adult standard	Senior (60+) first class	16-25 youth standard
4 days in 2 months	$349	$235	$299	$185
8 days in 2 months	509	339	435	239
15 days in 2 months	769	515	655	359

Note: Overnight journeys begun on your Britrail pass or Flexipass's final night can be completed the day after your pass expires—only BritRail allows this trick. A bunk in a twin sleeper costs $40.

Britain map key:

Approximate point-to-point one-way 2nd class fares in $US by rail (solid line) and bus (dashed line). Add up fares for your itinerary to see whether a railpass will save you money.

Family pass:

For each adult pass you buy, one child (5-15) gets a pass of the same type free (specify when you order). Additional kids pay the normal half-adult rate. Kids under 5: free. The Family Pass is available with Britrail Classic, Flexi, Senior, Rail & Drive, and Plus Ireland passes.

Party pass:

While Britrail offers no "saver" version for traveling couples, lucky third and fourth members of traveling groups get 50% off on Classic and Flexi passes (1st class, "adult" or "senior" rates only, not possible to mix, members of party must travel together at all times).

Britrail Winter Special – 25% Off

Save 25% on Britrail Classic Passes and Britrail Flexipasses issued 11/1/01- 2/28/02 for travel completed by 2/28/02. To purchase these passes, multiply the normal price by .75 and round off to the nearest dollar. Indicate "Winter Special" when you order.

LONDON VISITOR TRAVELCARD

All Zones: 3 consec. days for $29; 4 consec. days for $39; 7 consec. days for $58.

These cover you on all 650 square miles of London's bus and subway (tube) system, including the tube (but not the "Airbus") trip from Heathrow airport and can be used any time during the day. Your travel agent will give you a voucher which you will exchange for your pass at any major underground or transport office, including Heathrow airport. Children 5 to 15 pay $13, $16, and $25.

Central Zone: 3 consec. days for $20; 4 consec. days for $25; 7 consec. days for $30. Not valid from Heathrow Airport. Children 5 to 15 pay $9, $10, and $13.

BRITRAIL SOUTHEAST PASS

	First class	Standard class
3 out of 8 days	$106	$73
4 out of 8 days	142	106
7 out of 15 days	189	142

Covers trips from London to much of S.E. England including Oxford, Cambridge, Salisbury, and Exeter. Not valid for Bath, service via Reading, Great Western trains, Heathrow Express, or Chunnel. Kids 5-15 pay $31 (1st cl) or $21 (2nd cl) flat fare per pass.

FREEDOM OF WALES FLEXIPASS

Any 4 rail days within 8 consecutive bus days $85
Any 8 rail days within 15 consecutive bus days $159
Standard class on rail and major bus es. Kids 5-15 half fare.

FREEDOM OF SCOTLAND TRAVELPASS

4 days out of 8 flexi $134
8 days out of 15 flexi 168
12 days out of 20 flexi 219

Good on all trains, standard class only, and covers Caledonian MacBrayne and Strathclyde ferry service to Scotland's most popular islands, some Citylink busses & more. Children 5-15 half fare. Children under 5 free.

BUY-IN-LONDON ALTERNATIVES TO THE VISITOR TRAVELCARD

Many travelers save money by buying cheaper alternatives to Travelcards once they are in London. Remember that most sightseeing occurs within or near the Central Zone (also known as Zones 1 & 2). Weekend passes offer 2 days at a 25% discount. Families also get a discount. Passes are easy to buy at any major London tube station (Info: 011-44-20-72-22-12-34), and include (with rough dollar costs):

▼ One day Zones 1 and 2, good for most of downtown, everything within and including the Circle Line, all day, but not before 9:30 a.m. on work days: £3.90 ($6).

▼ Same pass, but for all zones, includes Heathrow airport: £4.70 ($7).

▼ One Day LT Card covers tube and bus travel in zones 1 and 2, no time restrictions: £5 ($8).

▼ 7 Day Central Zone Pass with no 9:30 a.m. limit: £18 ($29) and a photo.

BRITISH RAIL DEALS NOT SOLD IN THE USA

In Britain, round-trip "same-day-return" tickets can cost as little as 10% more than the one-way fares. Britain also offers **Super Advance Return** tickets at a savings of a few pounds—purchase before 6 p.m. the day before your trip. For bigger savings, consider **Apex** fares (buy at least 1 week in advance for trips of 100+ miles) or **Bargain Return** fares (buy at least 1 week in advance for trips of 250+ miles). Apex deals get snapped up fast in summer, can be booked up to 8 weeks ahead, have limited seat availability and refund restrictions, and can be ordered from the USA by credit card (call to Britain 011-44-8457-484-950 for 24-hour information; they'll give you another number to purchase tickets). For a London-Edinburgh round-trip, the regular fare known as "Saver," is £77 ($110); the "Super Advance," bought by 6:00 p.m. on the day before, is £63 ($90); the "Apex," bought 7 days ahead, is £49 ($70); the "Bargain Return," bought 7 days ahead, is £36 ($52). Visit www.thetrainline.com. *Continued on next page*

For £18 ($26), the **Young Person's Railcard** (for ages 16 – 25, or full-time students 26+ with ISIC) or the **Senior Railcard** (for age 60+) gets you a third off most point-to-point tickets for a year. The **Family Railcard** for £20 ($29) allows adults to travel 20 – 33% cheaper while their kids aged 5 – 15 pay just £2 apiece for most trips. Not valid on the Heathrow Express, Eurostar, or some busy weekday morning commuter trains.

BRITRAIL OR BRITBUS...

While many small towns and rural areas of Britain are not served by trains, travelers can go anywhere just about any time by coach. ("Coach" is British for any long distance bus. "Bus" means city bus.) Coach travel is the cheap way to explore Britain. While some argue you get a closer look at Great Britain through a bus rather than a train window, I'd bus Britain only to save money and to fill gaps in the train system.

Many buses are ideal for daytrips from London. People over 49 or under 26 can buy a £7 ($13) discount card in Great Britain for up to 30% off on all National Express coaches.

There are a couple of super cheap hop-on-and-hop-off bus circuits that take mostly hostelers around the country cheap and easy. For instance, **Stray Travel** does a 1,600-km circle connecting London, Bath, Stratford, the Lakes, Edinburgh, York, Cambridge, and London hostels (open-ended pass £129, tel. 020/7373-7737, www.straytravel.com). See student guidebooks for similar bus deals covering Scotland and Wales.

BRITISH TOURIST TRAIL FLEXI BUS PASS

2 days in 3 flexi	£49 ($70)
5 days in 30 flexi	£85 ($122)
8 days in 30 flexi	£135 ($195)
15 days in 30 flexi	£190 ($274)
15 days in 60 flexi	£205 ($295)

Allows unlimited bus travel in England, Scotland and Wales on the extensive National Express bus service. (The prices in parentheses are the approx. $ cost to buy the passes in Great Britain; prices are much higher if purchased in the U.S.) Special youth and senior passes save about 30% for those over 49 or under 26.

COMPARING TRAIN AND COACH TRAVEL IN BRITAIN

From London to:	miles	by train	by coach
Bath	107	25 per day / 1.25 hr / $55	10 per day / 3 hr / $20
Cambridge	56	31 per day / 1 hr / $30	20 per day / 1.75 hr / $15
Cardiff, Wales	145	21 per day / 1.75 hr/ $70	10 per day / 3.25 hr / $25
Edinburgh	390	17 per day / 4 hr / $130	3 per day / 9 hr / $35
Oxford	60	35 per day / 1 hr / $25	50 per day / 1.75 hr / $15
Stratford	110	4 per day / 2 hr / $45	3 per day / 3hr / $20
York	188	27 per day / 2 hr / $95	4 per day/ 4.25 hr / $30

BY SEA FROM BRITAIN TO THE CONTINENT:

The old-fashioned way of crossing the Channel is twice as romantic (when Channel waters are calm), but twice as complicated and time-consuming, and just a little less expensive. You'll get better prices in London than from the USA (get latest fares there). Round-trips are a bargain. By train/boat, London to Paris: £40 one-way, £50 round-trip within 5 days, 7 hours. By train/boat, London to Calais: £22 one-way, £32 round-trip, 4 hours. Same-day round trips on the boats are as cheap as £5 or £10 but no luggage is allowed. For Dover-Calais, Folkestone-Boulogne, Newhaven-Dieppe, or Dover-Ostende routes, contact Hoverspeed (tel. 08705/240-241; www.hoverspeed.co.uk). For Harwich-Hoek van Holland (2/day, $75, 4-5 hrs), contact Stena Line (tel. 08705/707-070). Dan Youra's Ferry Guide (www.youra.com) is another great resource.

ENGLISH CHANNEL BY EUROSTAR

The fastest and most convenient way to get from Big Ben to the Eiffel Tower is by rail. **Eurostar** zips you from downtown London to downtown Paris (15/day, 3 hrs) or Brussels (10/day, 3 hrs) faster and easier than flying. The actual tunnel crossing is a 20-minute, black, silent, 100 mph non-event. First class prices include a classy meal. Easy TGV connections in Lille take you to Disneyland Paris, Charles de Gaulle Airport, or southern France without ever stopping in Paris (on some days there is even a direct London-Disneyland train).

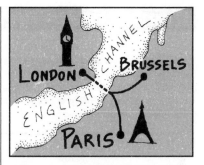

You can book Chunnel tickets at any major European train station. If you're ready to commit to a travel date and time, you can purchase in advance at US or Eu-

ropean prices. Cheaper fares have more restrictions and sell out early. For updates and specials, go to www.eurostar.com and select the country of purchase. If booking online, be sure to read all terms and conditions. (French online booking is a hassle since tickets must be picked up in France within a few days.)

EUROSTAR "CHUNNEL" FARES

Between London and Paris or Brussels (one way fares)

US Fares: Available through Rail Europe (800/438-7245), DER (800/549-3737) or your travel agent (*not* from ETBD). Tickets will be delivered to you in the US, prices don't include "handling."

Fare type	1st class	2nd class
Full fare	$279	$199
Leisure (refund restrictions)	$219	$139
Senior (60+)	$189	NA
Leisure Round-trip* (2-night stay, nonrefundable)	$124*	$79*
Youth (under 26, 2nd cl)	$165	$79
Eurail, Euro, Select, Britrail, France or Benelux Passholder	$155	$75
Child rate varies with fare type.		

British Fares: These are a sample of the wide price range and are subject to change. It's often cheaper to pay for a round-trip special even if you're only traveling one-way. Book online at www.eurostar.co.uk or call 011-44-1233-61-75-75 from the US or 08705-186-186 within Britain. Tickets will be held at Waterloo station. £1 = about $1.60.

Fare type	1st class	2nd class
Full fare	£200	£165
Weekender (travel Sat, Sun, or holiday)	NA	£100
Youth (under 26, nonrefundable)	NA	£45
Leisure Apex 14 Return* (14-day advance, Sat. night stay, nonrefundable)	£60*	£35*
Weekend Day Return* (travel Sat, Sun, or holiday; nonrefundable)	£55*	£35*
Eurail, Euro, Select, Britrail, France or Benelux Passholder	£100	£50
Child (4 – 11)	£45	£29

*Multiply by 2 for required roundtrip purchase price. Passholder fare does *not* take a day off a flexi railpass, but to qualify for the Passholder discount your trip must take place during your pass' validity period. Under 4 free.

REPUBLIC OF IRELAND

Ireland's trains fan out from Dublin but neglect much of the countryside. The bus system is far better and cheaper (e.g., $15 Dublin-Galway, $20 Dublin-Cork). Any of the various bus+rail combo passes offer a better value than the pricey Britrail plus Ireland Pass. The Emerald Card is your best all-inclusive north+south bus+rail value.

BRITRAIL PLUS IRELAND PASS

	1st class	Standard
5 days out of 1 month	$529	$399
10 days out of 1 month	749	569

This pass covers the entire British Isles (England, Wales, Scotland, Northern Ireland and the Republic of Ireland) including a round-trip Stena Line ferry crossing between Wales or Scotland and the Emerald Isle during the pass's validity (okay to leave via one port and return via another). Reserve boat crossings a day or so in advance—sooner for holidays. One child (5-15) travels along free with each pass. Extra kiddies pay half fare; under 5 free.

DEALS ONCE YOU GET TO IRELAND:

These local specials are sold at major train stations in Ireland. Irish £1 = about $1.40.

Ireland map key:

Approximate point-to-point one-way 2nd class fares in $US by rail (solid line), bus (dashed line), and ferry (dotted line). Add up fares for your itinerary to see whether a rail and/or bus pass will save you money. Note: The only Northern Ireland destinations listed on this map are Derry and Belfast.

Pass Name	Version	Area	Duration	Price
Emerald Card	Rail & Bus	Republic & North	Any 8 days in 15	£115
			Any 15 days in 30	£200
Irish Explorer	Rail & Bus	Republic only	Any 8 days in 15	£100
Irish Rover	Rail only	Republic & North	Any 5 days in 15	£83
Irish Explorer	Rail only	Republic only	Any 5 days in 15	£67
Irish Rover	Bus only	Republic & North	Any 3 days in 8	£40
			Any 8 days in 15	£90
			Any 15 days in 30	£140
Irish Rambler	Bus only	Republic only	Any 3 days in 8	£30
(Schedules available at www.busireann.ie)			Any 8 days in 15	£70
			Any 15 days in 30	£100

Student travel: Students can use their ISIC (student card) to get discounts on rail tickets (up to 50%), but only if they first purchase a **Travel Save Stamp** (for about £15) at any major railway station in Ireland.

SEALINK FERRIES AND CATAMARANS CONNECTING BRITAIN AND IRELAND

British port to...	Irish port	crossings daily	ferry/cat. hrs	ferry/cat. cost
Holyhead	Dun Laoghaire [1]	8	3.5 / 1.5	$30 / $40
Fishguard	Rosslare	6	3.5 / 1.5	$30 / $40
Stranraer	Larne	9	2.25 / 1.5	$35 / $40
London (RR + boat) [2]	Dublin	2	10 / 7	$85 / $90

Call 800/677-8585 in the US for information on European ferry connections or visit our Web site at: www.ricksteves.com/tips/links.htm. You'll find ferry links under "Transportation." [1] Dun Laoghaire is a 30-minute bus or train ride from Dublin. [2] Travelers from London to Dublin may find it worthwhile to catch a quick $80 shuttle flight (see www.cheapflights.com). National Express (Britain's Greyhound) offers great London-Dublin bus+ferry tickets for as low as £19 ($30), restrictions apply.

SPAIN/PORTUGAL

The best public transportation strategy in Iberia is to mix it up. Buses, taxis, and even flights are cheap and efficient for short hops and where train service can be sparse. Railpasses are relatively expensive compared to cheap point-to-point ticket prices and are best used only for your longest travel days and nights. A 5-day 3-country Selectpass is a better value than a 5-day 2-country Iberic Flexipass.

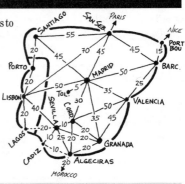

IBERIC FLEXIPASS

1st class: Any 3 days in 2 months $205

Covers Spain and Portugal. Extra rail days (7 max.): $45.
Kids 4-11 half fare, under 4 free.

Iberia map key:
Approximate point-to-point one-way 2nd class rail fares in $US. Add up fares for your itinerary to see whether a railpass will save you money.

SPAIN FLEXIPASS

	1st class	2nd class
Any 3 days in 2 months	$200	$155
Extra rail days (max. 7)	35	30

Kids 4-11 half fare, under 4 free.

PORTUGUESE FLEXIPASS

1st class: Any 4 days out of 15 .... $105.

Kids 4-11 half fare, under 4 free.

COMPARING TRAIN AND BUS TRAVEL IN IBERIA

	By train		By bus
Barcelona – Madrid	6/day, 7–9 hrs, $50		12/day, 8 hrs, $25
Madrid – Segovia	9/day, 2 hrs, $7		2/hour, 1.25 hrs, $4
Sevilla – Lisbon	AVE to Madrid + night train, $40		2/day, 10 hrs, $25
Sevilla – Algeciras	3/day, 5 hrs w/change, $25		10/day, 4 hrs direct, $12
Malaga - Gibraltar	3/day, 4 hrs w/change, $17		11/day, 3 hrs direct, $8

INTERNATIONAL HOTEL TRAINS

Spain's fancy overnight Hotel Trains (known collectively as Talgo Night) all have fancy names: Lusitania (Madrid-Lisbon), Francisco de Goya (Madrid-Paris), Joan Miro (Barcelona-Paris), Pau Casals (Barcelona-Zurich), and Salvador Dali (Barcelona-Milan). These trains are not covered by railpasses, but Eurail, Euro, Select, Spain, Iberic, France, and consecutive-day Swiss Passholders can get discounted fares on routes within their pass boundaries (give up a flexi day and pay about half the full fare, which results in a range from an $85 second class quad couchette to a posh $235 Gran Class single compartment). Fast and direct, the trains make just a few stops. First-class fares (for singles or doubles) include breakfast and your own toilet and washbasin. Gran Class adds dinner and a shower in your compartment.

To avoid this expensive luxury, change trains at the Spanish border (at Irun on Paris runs, at Cerbere on the eastern side, too many changes toward Lisbon). You'll connect to a normal night train with $20 couchettes on one leg of the trip. This plan takes more time, and may use two days of a flexipass. Ask for details at the station, or consult one of these extensive schedules: http://bahn.hafas.de/bin/query.exe/en or the *Thomas Cook European Timetable*.

GERMANY

Since it costs $50 to $100 to travel between most German cities, the flexi German Railpass is a good value for an all-Germany trip. Salzburg, France and Basel, Switzerland are covered if approached from Germany. Couples can save 25% with a Twinpass.

GERMAN RAILPASS

	1st class	1st twin	2nd class	2nd twin	2nd Youth
4 days in a month	$252	$189	$174	$130.50	$138
Extra rail days (max. 6)	$32	$24	$22	$16.50	*$6 -18

Covers KD Line boats on the Rhine and Mosel, 60% off Romantic Road and Castle bus ride. "Twin" price is per person for two traveling together. Youth passes are available for those under 26. *Youth pass extra rail days: add $18 for the 1st extra day, $6 for the 2nd extra day, and $12 for each additional extra day (max.6). Kids 5 and under free. Kids 6-11 half of full fare.

SOLD ONLY IN GERMANY...

The 260DM **BahnCard** gives a 50% discount on 2nd class tickets for a year. Those 60 or older, under 23, students under 27, and spouses (traveling with someone with the 260 DM card) get the same card for 130 DM (children under 18, 65 DM). The **Guten Abend** ticket lets night owls go anywhere in Germany second class between 7 p.m. (2 p.m. Saturdays) and 2 a.m. the next day for about 60 DM; 75 DM on Fridays and Sundays. The wild **Schönes Wochenende** ticket for 40DM gives a group of up to five people unlimited travel on nonexpress trains for one whole day – either Saturday or Sunday. Buy these local specials at a German train station. 2DM = about $1.

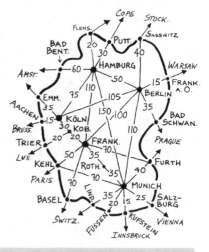

Germany map key:
Approximate point-to-point 1-way 2nd class rail fares in $US. Add up fares for your itinerary to see whether a railpass will save you money.

AUSTRIA

AUSTRIAN FLEXIPASS

	1st cl	2nd cl
Any 3 days out of 15 days	$158	$107
Add-on days (max 5):	20	15

Children 6-11 half price. Bonuses include 50% off some Danube boats, 10% off Lake Constance boats.

Austria map key:
Point-to-point one-way 2nd class rail fares in $US. Add up fares to see whether a railpass will save you money.

When considering the 3 days in 15 Austrian Flexipass for $158, remember there is a first class "European East Pass" which gives you any 5 days in a month for $210 and covers Austria with the Czech Republic, Slovakia, Hungary and Poland to boot. If you're going to Prague or Budapest, this may actually beat the Austrian pass.

SWITZERLAND

We don't usually recommend railpasses for small countries, but Switzerland is a small *expensive* country where a railpass can save you money. For a few days in Switzerland, your Europass or Eurailpass is fine. It can get you discounts on some lifts and mountain trains (ask at local stations) and free boat trips on Swiss lakes. But if you plan to take lots of trains, lifts, and boats, Swiss railpasses are usually a better value. You may purchase a second class pass regardless of age. "Saver" passes save 15% for two or more traveling together.

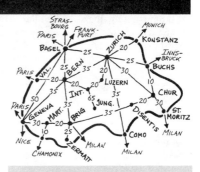

Switzerland map key:

Approximate point-to-point one-way 2nd class rail fares in $US. Add up fares for your itinerary to see if a railpass will save you money.

SWISS PASS AND SWISS FLEXIPASS

	1st class	1st cl Saver	2nd class	2nd cl Saver
4 consec. days	$245	$208	$160	$136
8 consec. days	330	281	220	187
15 consec. days	400	340	265	225
21 consec. days	458	390	305	260
1 month	525	445	345	294
3 days in 1 month flexi	234	198	156	132
Add'l flexi days (first 3, per day)	42	36	28	24
Add'l flexi days (next 3, per day)	32	27	21	18

Covers all trains, boats and buses with 25% off on the high mountain rides. Saverpass prices are for 2 or more people traveling together at all times. All Swiss passes are also available in major train stations.

SWISS CARD

Sold in America, the **Swiss Card** gives you a round-trip train ride (each direction completed in one day) from any Swiss airport or border point to any point in Switzerland, plus 50% discounts on all Swiss railways, lake steamers, postal buses and most mountain lifts for a month ($145 first class or $110 second class).

Continued on next page

SWISS FAMILY CARD

The Swiss Family Card allows children under 16 to travel free with their parents. Based on the validity of the parent's ticket or pass, this works even on the high mountain routes. The Swiss Family Card is available for 20 SF at major Swiss train stations, but you can request a free Swiss Family Card when you order an adult Swiss Pass, Swiss Card, or Swiss Transfer Ticket in the USA. Kids 6-15 not accompanied by parent are half price, under 6 free.

A Swiss Card is basically a one-month Half-Fare Travel Card (see below) with a round-trip train fare into and out of the country. Kids under 16 travel free with a parent using a Swiss Family Card, other kids 6-15 half fare, under 6 free. **Swiss Transfer Ticket:** One round trip (as above) $114 first class; $76 second class; Swiss Family Card and kids discounts apply.

DEALS AVAILABLE ONCE YOU GET TO SWITZERLAND

Sold at Swiss train stations, the **Half-Fare Travel Card** gives you 50% off on all national and private trains, postal buses, lifts, and steamers for 90 SF a month. This can save you money if your Swiss travel adds up to at least $120 in point-to-point tickets.

The **Berner Oberland Pass**, giving you a combination of free and discounted use of virtually all the trains, boats, and lifts in the Bern-Interlaken-Luzern area, is the most useful of Switzerland's regional passes. You can choose any 5 days of free travel plus 10 days of 50% discounts in a 15-day period for 205 SF second class (approx. $145) or any 3 free days plus 4 days of 50% discount in 7 days for 165 SF (approx. $115). The highest mountain lifts are 25%-50% off during the validity of the pass (e.g., Kleine Scheidegg to the Jungfraujoch, or Murren to the Schilthorn, are 50% off). Both versions of the pass are available in 1st class for 25% more; if you have a Swiss Pass or Swiss Card all prices are 20% less. To see a map of discounted rides, go to www.bls.ch/english/sites/a_c_d_1regiopasse.html

SWISS TRAINS AND LIFTS COVERED—AND NOT COVERED— BY EURAIL-EURO-SELECT PASSES

Here are the best scenic rides that *are* covered by Eurail-Euro-Select passes *and* Swiss passes:

▼ Geneva to Brig.

▼ Montreux to Spiez "Golden Pass" (a locally-made reservation is required).

▼ Interlaken to Luzern (Lucerne).

▼ Chur, Switzerland to Tirano, Italy "Bernina Express" (reservation required, through Rail Europe in USA, or locally; Italy portion is $24 extra with Swiss passes).

The following private trains are *not* covered by Eurail-Euro-Selectpasses, but they *are* covered by Swiss railpasses. The most important are (prices are approximate):

▼ Many trains in the Jungfrau region south of Interlaken ($7 from Inter-laken to Grindelwald; $10 to Gimmel-wald; $130 round-trip to Jungfraujoch, or $60 even with a Swiss Pass). Note: If you have a validated Eurail/Europass you can get a 25% discount on most Jungfrau area trains and lifts, without using up a pass day. Ask at local ticket offices for specifics, or call the U.S. Swiss Tourist Office at 212/757-5944.

▼ All but the $30 Brig-Disentis segment of the "Glacier Express" that scenically crosses Alp-filled southern Switzerland from Martigny to Chur.

▼ The private train to see the Matterhorn (Brig-Zermatt 37SF, $25).

ITALY

Traveling with point-to-point tickets in Italy is cheap, rewarding those who make an effort to communicate with local ticket agents. The Italy Rail Card loses some of its convenience if you need reservations—you'll either stop for them before each trip or reduce your flexibility by making reservations all at once. The high-speed *TAV* trains run frequently between main cities and require reservations (up to $15 extra with Rail Card or Kilometric Ticket). During the summer, first class is worthwhile for its smaller crowds and better air conditioning. Many train station chores (reservations or tickets) can be handled quickly, cheaply and easily at major travel agencies in town centers. Italy Rail Cards are sold in a few major train stations.

ITALY RAIL CARD

.... 1st class .... 2nd class
8 consec. days .... $299 .... $199
15 consec. days 373 249
21 consec. days 433 289
30 consec. days 522 348
Any 4 days in 1 month flexi 239 159
Any 8 days in 1 month flexi 334 223
Any 12 days in 1 month flexi 429 286
Kids 4-11: half price, under 4: free.

DEALS AVAILABLE ONLY IN ITALY

See **www.fs-on-line.com** for more information on these local offers:

▼ The **Tariffa Mini-Group** is a 20% discount on point-to-point tickets for 3 - 5 people traveling together (except in July, August, and holiday seasons). You must ask each time you buy.

> **Italy map key :**
>
> *Approximate point-to-point one-way 2nd class rail fares in $US (first #) and number of **kilometers** (second #) between the cities shown above. Add up fares for your itinerary to see whether a railpass will save you money.*

▼ The **Carta d'Argento** (for age 60+) and the **Carta Verde** (under age 26) each cost $20 (L45,000) and give you 20% off 2nd class or 20-30% off 1st class tickets for 6 months.

▼ The flexible-but-complex **Italian Kilometric Ticket** (Biglietto Chilometrico) allows 1 to 5 people to split up to 3,000 kilometers of travel within 2 months for about $110 (L.226,000) second class or $180 (L.350,000) first class. Buy it at a major train station or travel agency (may not be available at airport or border stations). The "ticket" is a book of 20 coupons, each good for a one-way journey (same-day stops allowed) for any or all of the listed travelers. You need to validate each trip at a local train station or travel agency before departing. The ticket agent will subtract kilometers for each person. (Kids 4 to 11 "cost" your pass only half as many kilometers as an adult.) Supplements of a few dollars per segment will be charged for high-speed trains such as IC and EC, or up to a maximum of $15 for TAV trains. Despite the supplements, this pass saves money if you use up the kilometers (use our map to add up distances).

FRANCE

The France Flexipass is a good deal, paying for itself easily with one Paris-Avignon round trip. High-speed TGV reservations cost 20F ($4) in addition to your pass.

France passes are not valid on the privately-run Thalys (see The Thalys Problem earlier in this guide), which monopolizes direct service linking Paris with Köln, Amsterdam, Brussels, and other Belgian cities. (Thalys can sometimes be avoided with a night train or less direct routing.) Pass-holders can get a discounted rate on the Eurostar "Chunnel" train (see Eurostar Chunnel" Fares).

Unlike most countries, point-to-point French ticket prices are discounted in non-peak times (our map reflects peak time fares). If you don't mind being flexible with your schedule, you can save a few francs.

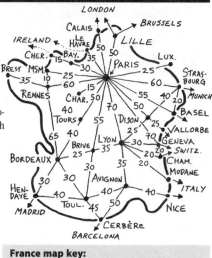

France map key:

Approximate point-to-point one-way 2nd class rail fares in $US. Add up fares for your itinerary to see whether a railpass will save you money.

FRANCE FLEXIPASS

	Adult 1st class	Adult 2nd class	Senior 1st class	Youth 1st class	Youth 2nd class
Any 3 days in 1 month	$210	$180	$199	$150	$130
Extra rail days (max 6)	34	30	30	24	20

Seniors 60+, Youth under 26. Kids 4 – 11 half adult fare.

FRANCE FLEXI SAVERPASS

	Adult 1st cl	Adult 2nd cl	Senior 1st cl
Any 3 days in 1 month	$171	$146	$159
Extra rail days (max 6)	30	30	27

Prices are per person for two or more traveling together. OK to mix kids and adults (kids 4–11 half adult fare) but senior rates (age 60+) cannot be mixed with adults or kids on the same pass.

FRANCE 4-DAY WEEKENDER PASS

	1st class	2nd class
4 consecutive days	$139	$119

Four-day period must include a Saturday and Sunday. Travel dates must be selected at time of purchase and commence within 3 months of issue. Kids 4–11 half fare. Purchase by February 28, 2001. (This pass may be reintroduced as a "winter special" in late 2001.) Nonrefundable and non-exchangeable.

The French have a knack for making things complicated, all in the name of offering more choices. If you'll be in France for awhile, and have the flexibility in your travel schedule to play the game, the French offer quite a few money-saving ticket deals for off-peak times, travelers under 26, seniors, couples—you name it. Begin your journey by visiting the French Rail Web site at www.sncf.com. Click on "English Version," Passenger's Guide," then "Available Fares."

BENELUX COUNTRIES

Most visits to Belgium, Luxembourg or the Netherlands don't cover enough miles to justify a railpass. This region has more than its share of money-saving local deals. For example, the Amsterdam station offers many same-day round-trip fares for only 25% over the regular one-way fare. For day-tripping sightseers there are some discounted train/museum deals; ask about *Rail Idée*. Benelux passes are **not** valid on the privately run Thalys (see The Thalys Problem earlier in this guide), which monopolizes direct service to Paris, Amsterdam, and Köln from Brussels and other Belgian cities. (Thalys can sometimes be avoided with a night train or less direct routing.) TGV service between Brussels and Lille is not covered by any railpass.

Benelux countries map key:
Approximate point-to-point one-way 2nd class rail fares in $US. Add up fares for your itinerary to see whether a railpass will save you money.

BENELUX TOURRAIL PASS

	1ˢᵗ class	2ⁿᵈ class	Jr 4-25 2ⁿᵈ class
5 days in 1 month flexi	$217	$155	$104
Twinpass	$163	$116.50	N/A

Covers trains in Belgium, Luxembourg and the Netherlands. You can buy this pass in Belgium for $10 to $20 less. Pass holders get discounts on Eurostar "Chunnel" train. Kids under 4 free. Twinpass prices are per person for two traveling together.

FOR SALE IN BELGIUM ONLY

Belgian train stations offer several discount cards and formulas for travel within Belgium, though many are restricted to Monday - Friday after 9 a.m., and are not valid on international trains such as EC and Thalys. **Kids** under 12 travel free with an adult and **seniors** 65+ travel anywhere for 100 BF ($2) roundtrip in 2ⁿᵈ class. The **Go Pass** gives youths under 26 any ten 2ⁿᵈ class trips for 1490 BF ($32). The **Golden Railpass** gives seniors 60+ any six rides for 1320 BF ($28) 2ⁿᵈ class or 2030 BF ($43) 1ˢᵗ class. **Pass 9+** gives you ten trips in six months for 220 BF ($47) in 2ⁿᵈ class or 3390 BF ($72) in 1ˢᵗ class. Visit www.b-rail/E/index.html for details on these and other discounts.

HOLLAND RAILPASS

	1ˢᵗ cl Adult	2ⁿᵈ cl Adult	1ˢᵗ cl Senior (60+)	2ⁿᵈ cl Senior (60+)	2ⁿᵈ cl Junior (12 – 26)
Any 3 days in a month	$98	$65	$78	$52	$52
Any 5 days in a month	147	98	119	79	79
Twinpasses:					
Any 3 days in a month	$73.50	$49	$58.50	$39	$39
Any 5 days in a month	110.50	73.50	89.50	59.50	59.50

Twinpass prices are per person, based on 2 people traveling together. Kids 4 – 11 pay *approximately* half of either adult or adult twinpass rate. Passes can be purchased in the USA, or for the equivalent price in guilders at Dutch train stations (including Schiphol airport).

SCANDINAVIA

SCANRAIL PASS	1st cl adult	1st cl 60+	1st cl under 26	2nd cl adult	2nd cl 60+	2nd cl under 26
Any 5 days out of 2 months	$276	$246	$207	$204	$182	$153
Any 10 days out of 2 months	420	374	315	310	276	233
21 consecutive days	486	432	365	360	321	270

Covers Denmark, Norway, Sweden and Finland. Trolls 4-11 half price. Kids under 4 free. Five and 21 day passes are available in Scandinavia at lower prices, 10 day pass available only in the U.S.

Train travel is expensive in Scandinavia, making the ScanRail Pass worth serious consideration. First-class passes are a good value when compared to first-class point-to-point tickets. Although second class is plenty comfortable, for $4 to $14 a day extra, you might consider first class. Here are some Scandinavian country specifics (~8 kroner = dollar):

Norway: All express trains require a 25NOK ($3) reservation. Sleeping cars generally have 3 berths and cost 110NOK ($14), about the same as a 6-bed couchette elsewhere in Europe. Those wanting more privacy will pay 275NOK ($34) for a 2 berth room, 550NOK ($69) for a single. The scenic Myrdal to Flam trip now costs 50NOK, even for railpass holders. Norway offers point-to-point ticket discounts for certain "green departures" at off-peak times. Special "green departure mini-price tickets" take travelers from Oslo to any major Norwegian city for about 400NOK ($50). These are sold at any station, but must be purchased at least 7 days in advance. Youth and student discounts let you fly in Norway for about the price of a train ticket.

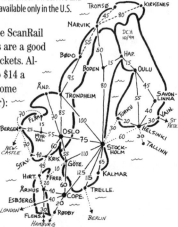

Scandinavia map key:

Approximate point-to-point one-way 2nd class rail fares in $US. Add up fares for your itinerary to see whether a railpass will save you money.

Sweden: SAS airlines offers a standby fare to those under 26 for about 400 kr ($57) per flight. High-speed X200 train reservations cost about $7.

International ferry connections: The Silja Line ferry from Stockholm to Finland is free with Eurail and about half price with Scanrail. Other ferry rides are discounted anywhere from 20-100%. When the train actually goes on the ferry (e.g., Denmark to Germany, Norway or Sweden), the crossing is usually free if you have a railpass that covers both countries. Point-to-point ferry prices can be more reasonable than train fares (for example, Oslo to Copenhagen for as low as $70). Check with ferry companies or travel agents for specifics once you're in Scandinavia or check online at www.youra.com.

NORWAY RAILPASS	1st cl	2nd cl	60 + 1st cl	60 + 2nd cl
3 days in a month	$181	$139	$144	$111
4 days in a month	224	172	179	139
5 days in a month	250	192	200	154

Few Norwegian trains offer 1st class, so save money and go with a 2nd class pass. Kids 4-15 half price, under 4 free.

SWEDEN RAILPASS

	1st class	2nd class
4 days within a month	$215	$159
5 days within a month	244	181
6 days within a month	273	202

Two kids under age 15 can ride along for free.

FINNRAIL PASS

	1st class	2nd class
3 days in a month	$162	$108
5 days in a month	216	144
10 days in a month	291	194

Children 6-16 half price, under 6 free.

EASTERN EUROPE

Point-to-point tickets are very cheap throughout eastern Europe and the Balkans. The only reason to buy a country railpass is to avoid the need to change money and the hassle of buying tickets as you go. It's so easy to buy tickets in any German/Austrian train station to cover the Czech part of a Prague trip that there is little reason to buy a Prague Excursion Pass. The European East Pass pays for itself with a Vienna-Prague-Warsaw-Budapest-Vienna loop.

EUROPEAN EAST PASS

Any 5 days in 1 month (first class) $210

Covers Austria, Czech Republic, Slovakia, Hungary and Poland. Add up to 5 extra days for $24/day. Kids 4-11 pay half fare.

PRAGUE EXCURSION PASS

	1st class	2nd class
Adult	$55	$35
Youth (12 - 25)	45	30
Child (4 - 11)	28	18

Good for two train rides within a 7 day period: from any Czech border into Prague, and then from Prague to any border crossing (stops on the way are allowed). This pass is also available at Euraide offices in Berlin and Munich.

CZECH FLEXIPASS

Any 5 days in 15 (first class) $72

HUNGARY PASS

Any 5 days out of 15 (first class) $67
Any 10 days in a month (first class) 84

Kids 5-14 half fare, Huns go free.

Eastern Europe map key:
Approximate point-to-point one-way 2nd class rail fares in US. Add up fares for your itinerary to see if a railpass will save you money.

BULGARIAN FLEXIPASS

Any 3 days in 1 month (first class) $70

Kids 4 - 11 half fare.

ROMANIAN FLEXIPASS

Any 3 days in 15 days (first class) $72

Kids 4 - 11 half fare.

BALKAN FLEXIPASS

Includes Bulgaria, Greece, Macedonia, Romania, Turkey, and Yugoslavia. Kids 4-11 half fare. Think twice before buying this pass. You're better off on the bus.

	Adult	Youth
Any 5 days in 1 month	$152	$90
Any 10 days in 1 month	264	156
Any 15 days in 1 month	317	190

European Weather

Here is a climate chart. This can be helpful in planning your itinerary, but I have never found European weather to be particularly predictable. The first line shows the average daily low, the second line is the average daily high, and the third line shows the average number of days without rain.

	J	F	M	A	M	J	J	A	S	O	N	D
AUSTRIA • Vienna												
	25°	28°	30°	42°	50°	56°	60°	59°	53°	44°	37°	30°
	34°	38°	47°	58°	67°	73°	76°	75°	68°	56°	45°	37°
	16	17	18	17	18	16	18	18	20	18	16	16
BELGIUM • Brussels												
	30°	32°	36°	41°	46°	52°	54°	54°	51°	45°	38°	32°
	40°	44°	51°	58°	65°	72°	73°	72°	69°	60°	48°	42°
	10	11	14	12	15	15	14	13	17	14	10	12
CZECH REPUBLIC • Prague												
	23°	24°	30°	38°	46°	52°	55°	55°	49°	41°	33°	27°
	31°	34°	44°	54°	64°	70°	73°	72°	65°	53°	42°	34°
	18	17	21	19	18	18	18	19	20	18	18	18
DENMARK • Copenhagen												
	29°	28°	31°	37°	45°	51°	56°	56°	51°	44°	38°	33°
	37°	37°	42°	51°	60°	66°	70°	69°	64°	55°	46°	41°
	14	15	19	18	20	18	17	16	14	14	11	12
EGYPT • Cairo												
	47°	48°	52°	57°	63°	68°	70°	71°	68°	65°	58°	50°
	65°	69°	75°	83°	91°	95°	96°	95°	90°	86°	78°	68
	30	27	30	30	31	30	31	31	30	31	29	30
FINLAND • Helsinki												
	17°	15°	20°	30°	40°	49°	55°	53°	46°	37°	30°	23°
	26°	25°	32°	44°	56°	66°	71°	68°	59°	47°	37°	31°
	11	10	17	17	19	17	17	16	16	13	11	11
FRANCE • Paris												
	34°	34°	39°	43°	49°	55°	58°	58°	53°	46°	40°	36°
	43°	45°	54°	60°	68°	73°	76°	75°	70°	60°	50°	44°
	14	14	19	17	19	18	19	18	17	18	15	15
FRANCE • Nice												
	35°	36°	41°	46°	52°	58°	63°	63°	58°	51°	43°	37°
	50°	53°	59°	64°	71°	79°	84°	83°	77°	68°	58°	52°
	23	22	24	23	23	26	29	26	24	23	21	21
GERMANY • Munich												
	23°	23°	30°	38°	45°	51°	55°	54°	48°	40°	33°	26°
	35°	38°	48°	56°	64°	70°	74°	73°	67°	56°	44°	36°
	15	12	18	15	16	13	15	15	17	18	15	16
GREAT BRITAIN • London												
	36°	36°	38°	42°	47°	53°	56°	56°	52°	46°	42°	38°
	43°	44°	50°	56°	62°	69°	71°	71°	65°	58°	50°	45°
	16	15	20	18	19	19	19	20	17	18	15	16
GREECE • Athens												
	44°	44°	46°	52°	61°	68°	73°	73°	67°	60°	53°	47°
	55°	57°	60°	68°	77°	86°	92°	92°	84°	75°	66°	58°
	15	17	20	21	23	26	29	28	26	23	18	16

	J	F	M	A	M	J	J	A	S	O	N	D
IRELAND • Dublin												
	34°	35°	37°	39°	43°	48°	52°	51°	48°	43°	39°	37°
	46°	47°	51°	55°	60°	65°	67°	67°	63°	57°	51°	47°
	18	18	21	19	21	19	18	19	18	20	18	17
ITALY • Rome												
	40°	42°	45°	50°	56°	63°	67°	67°	62°	55°	49°	44°
	52°	55°	59°	66°	74°	82°	87°	86°	79°	71°	61°	55°
	13	19	23	24	26	26	30	29	25	23	19	21
ITALY • Palermo, Sicily												
	46°	47°	48°	52°	58°	64°	69°	70°	66°	60°	54°	49°
	60°	62°	63°	68°	74°	81°	85°	86°	83°	77°	71°	64°
	19	20	23	24	28	28	31	29	26	23	22	21
MOROCCO • Marrakesh												
	40°	43°	48°	52°	57°	62°	67°	68°	63°	57°	49°	42°
	65°	68°	74°	79°	84°	92°	101°	100°	92°	83°	73°	66
	24	23	25	24	29	29	30	30	27	27	27	24
NETHERLANDS • Amsterdam												
	31°	31°	34°	40°	46°	51°	55°	55°	50°	44°	38°	33°
	40°	42°	49°	56°	64°	70°	72°	71°	67°	57°	48°	42°
	9	9	15	17	16	14	13	11	11	9	10	
NORWAY • Oslo												
	19°	19°	25°	34°	43°	50°	55°	53°	46°	38°	31°	25°
	28°	30°	39°	50°	61°	68°	72°	70°	60°	48°	38°	32°
	16	16	22	19	21	17	16	17	16	17	14	14
PORTUGAL • Lisbon												
	46°	47°	50°	53°	55°	60°	63°	63°	62°	58°	52°	47°
	57°	59°	63°	67°	71°	77°	81°	82°	79°	72°	63°	58°
	16	16	17	20	21	25	29	29	24	22	17	16
PORTUGAL • Faro (Algarve)												
	48°	49°	52°	55°	58°	64°	67°	68°	65°	60°	55°	50°
	60°	61°	64°	67°	71°	77°	83°	83°	78°	72°	66°	61°
	22	21	21	24	27	29	31	31	29	25	22	22
SPAIN • Madrid												
	35°	36°	41°	45°	50°	58°	63°	63°	57°	49°	42°	36°
	47°	52°	59°	65°	70°	80°	87°	85°	77°	65°	55°	48°
	23	21	21	21	21	25	29	28	24	23	21	21
SPAIN • Almeria (Costa del Sol)												
	46°	47°	51°	55°	59°	65°	70°	71°	68°	60°	54°	49°
	60°	61°	64°	68°	72°	78°	83°	84°	81°	73°	67°	62°
	25	24	26	25	28	29	31	30	27	26	26	26
SWEDEN • Stockholm												
	26°	25°	29°	37°	45°	53°	57°	56°	50°	43°	37°	32°
	30°	30°	37°	47°	58°	67°	71°	68°	60°	49°	40°	35°
	15	14	21	19	20	17	18	17	16	16	14	14
SWITZERLAND • Geneva												
	29°	30°	36°	42°	49°	55°	58°	58°	53°	44°	37°	31°
	38°	42°	51°	59°	66°	73°	77°	76°	69°	58°	47°	40°
	20	19	22	21	20	19	22	20	20	21	19	21
TURKEY • Istanbul												
	37°	36°	38°	45°	53°	60°	65°	66°	61°	55°	48°	41°
	46°	47°	51°	60°	69°	77°	82°	82°	76°	68°	59°	51°
	13	14	17	21	23	24	27	27	23	20	16	13

Metric Conversion Table

1 inch	=	25 millimeters		1 ounce	=	28 grams
1 foot	=	0.3 meter		1 pound	=	0.45 kilogram
1 yard	=	0.9 meter		temp. (°F)	=	9/5 °C + 32
1 mile	=	1.6 kilometers		1 kilogram	=	2.2 pounds
1 sq. yd.	=	0.8 square meter		1 kilometer	=	0.62 mile
1 acre	=	0.4 hectare		1 centimeter	=	0.4 inch
1 quart	=	0.95 liter		1 meter	=	39.4 inches

Index

FREE-SPIRITED TOURS FROM

Rick Steves

Great Guides

Big Buses

Small Groups

No Grumps

Best of Europe ■ **Village Europe** ■ **Eastern Europe** ■ **Turkey** ■ **Italy** ■ **Britain**
Spain/Portugal ■ **Ireland** ■ **Heart of France** ■ **South of France** ■ **Village France**
Scandinavia ■ **Germany/Austria/Switzerland** ■ **London** ■ **Paris** ■ **Rome**

Looking for a one, two, or three-week tour that's run in the Rick Steves style? Check out Rick Steves' educational, experiential tours of Europe.

Rick's tours include much more in the "sticker price" than mainstream tours. Here's what you'll get with a Europe or regional Rick Steves tour...

■ **Group size:** Your tour group will be no larger than 26.

■ **Guides:** You'll have two guides traveling and dining with you on your fully guided Rick Steves tour.

■ **Bus:** You'll travel in a full-size 48-to-52-seat bus, with plenty of empty seats for you to spread out and read, snooze, enjoy the passing scenery, get away from your spouse, or whatever.

■ **Sightseeing:** Your tour price includes all group sightseeing. There are no hidden extra charges.

■ **Hotels:** You'll stay in Rick's favorite small, characteristic, locally-run hotels in the center of each city, within walking distance of the sights you came to see.

■ **Price and insurance:** Your tour price is guaranteed for 2002. Single travelers do *not* pay an extra supplement (we have them room with other singles). ETBD includes prorated tour cancellation/interruption protection coverage at no extra cost.

■ **Tips and kickbacks:** All guide and driver tips are included in your tour price. Because your driver and guides are paid salaries by ETBD, they can focus on giving you the best European travel experience possible.

Interested? Call (425) 771-8303 or visit www.ricksteves.com for a free copy of Rick Steves' 2002 Tours booklet!

Rick Steves' Europe Through the Back Door

130 Fourth Avenue North, PO Box 2009, Edmonds, WA 98020 USA
Phone: (425) 771-8303 ■ Fax: (425) 771-0833 ■ www.ricksteves.com

Free, fresh travel tips,
all year long.

Call (425) 771-8303 to get Rick's free
64-page newsletter, or visit
www.ricksteves.com for even more.